CURRICULUM
IN CONTEXT

74

Companion Volumes

The companion volumes in this series are: *Learning and Knowledge* edited by Robert McCormick and Carrie Paechter, *Learners, Learning and Assessment* edited by Patricia Murphy and *Learners and Pedagogy* edited by Jenny Leach and Bob Moon.

All of these Readers are part of a course, Learning, Curriculum and Assessment, that is itself part of the Open University MA programme.

The Open University MA in Education

The Open University MA in Education is now firmly established as the most popular postgraduate degree for education professionals in Europe, with over 3,500 students registering each year. The MA in Education is designed particularly for those with experience of teaching, the advisory service, educational administration or allied fields.

Structure of the MA

The MA is a modular degree, and students are therefore free to select from a range of options the programme which best fits in with their interests and professional goals. Specialist lines in management and primary education are also available. Study in the Open University's Advanced Diploma and Certificate programmes can also be counted towards the MA, and successful study in the MA programme entitles students to apply for entry into the Open University Doctorate in Education programme.

COURSES CURRENTLY AVAILABLE:
- Management
- Child Development
- Primary Education
- Learning Curriculum and Assessment
- Inclusive Education
- Language and Literacy
- Mentoring
- Education, Training and Employment
- Gender in Education
- Educational Research
- Science Education
- Adult Learners
- Maths Education

OU supported open learning

The MA in Education programme provides great flexibility. Students study at their own pace, in their own time, anywhere in the European Union. They receive specially prepared study materials, supported by tutorials, thus offering the chance to work with other students.

The Doctorate in Education

The Doctorate in Education is a new part-time doctoral degree, combining taught courses, research methods and a dissertation designed to meet the needs of professionals in education and related areas who are seeking to extend and deepen their knowledge and understanding of contemporary educational issues. It should help them to:

- develop appropriate skills in educational research and enquiry

- carry out research in order to contribute to professional knowledge and practice.

The Doctorate in Education builds upon successful study within the Open University MA in Education programme.

How to apply

If you would like to register for this programme, or simply to find out more information, please write for the *Professional Development in Education* prospectus to the Course Reservations Centre, PO Box 724, The Open University, Walton Hall, Milton Keynes, MK7 6ZS, UK (Telephone 0[044] 1908 653231).

CURRICULUM IN CONTEXT

edited by
Bob Moon and Patricia Murphy
at the Open University

Paul Chapman
Publishing Ltd

Paul Chapman Publishing

in association with

The Open
University

The Open University

Compilation, original and editorial material
© Copyright 1999, The Open University
First published in 1999

 Paul Chapman Publishing Ltd
A SAGE Publications Company
6 Bonhill Street
London EC2A 4PU

SAGE Publications Inc.
2455 Teller Road
Thousand Oaks, California 91320

SAGE Publications India Pvt Ltd
32, M-Block Market
Greater Kailash - I
New Delhi 110 048

British Cataloguing in Publication Data
A catalogue record for this book is available from the British Library

ISBN 1 85396 422 0
ISBN 1 85396 423 9 (pbk)

Library of Congress catalog card number available

Typeset by Dorwyn Ltd, Rowlands Castle
Printed in Great Britain

A   B   C   D   E   F   G   H   4   3   1   0   9

Contents

Section 3 Change Perspectives

Series Introduction

Learning, curriculum and assessment are at the core of the educational process. In the politically charged and value laden context of curriculum reform, an understanding of well grounded evidence about learning theories, knowledge and teaching and assessment practice is essential. Policy development and educational practice in a number of countries is being built around new understandings about the nature of mind, an acknowledgement that knowledge has long outgrown the traditional discipline categorisations of schools and universities and a realisation that learning and assessment is an essentially social process.

This book is one of a series of four readers that gather together recent research and writing around a number of key issues and themes in curriculum. The books, therefore, act as sources from which a number of narratives can be deduced. The broader contexts of curriculum are considered in the first volume of the series, the remaining three books focus us on learning and assessment, knowledge and pedagogy. The selection is a resource for anyone seeking a deeper understanding of the way any curriculum, formal and informal, is constructed, enacted and experienced. The accompanying Open University course (E836 *Learning, Curriculum and Assessment*) sets out to show one interpretation of the relevance of these ideas to practice in schools, colleges and other educational settings.

Jenny Leach
Robert McCormick
Bob Moon
Patricia Murphy
The Open University, Milton Keynes

Acknowledgements

The editors and publishers wish to thank the following for permission to use copyright material:

Carfax Publishing Ltd for material from R. Aedo Richmond and M. Richmond (1996) 'Recent Curriculum in Post-Pinochet Chile', *Compare*, 26:2, pp. 197–232; and Martin Woodhead (1998) "Quality" in early childhood programmes – a contextually appropriate approach', *International Journal of Early Years Education*, 6:1, pp. 5–17;

The Curriculum Journal for material from T. Taylor (1995) 'Movers and Shakers: high politics and the origins of the [English] National Curriculum', *The Curriculum Journal*, 6:2, pp. 161–84; and P. Bourdieu (1990) 'Principles for Reflecting on the Curriculum [in France]', *The Curriculum Journal*, 1:3, pp. 307–14;

Curriculum Studies for material from Crain Soudain (1996) 'Race, Culture and Curriculum Development in the USA: a study of the process of introducing a multicultural dimension into the curriculum', *Curriculum Studies*, 4:1, pp. 43–64;

Harvard Educational Review for material from Richard F. Elmore (1996) 'Getting to Scale with Good Educational Practice', *Harvard Educational Review*, 66:1, pp. 1–26. Copyright © 1996 by the President and Fellows of Harvard College;

Harvard University Press for material from Jerome Bruner (1996) *The Culture of Education*, pp. 1–42. Copyright (©) 1996 by the President and Fellows of Harvard College;

Journal of Information Technology for Teacher Education for material from Robert McCormick (1992) 'Curriculum Development and New Information Technology', *Journal of Information Technology for Teacher Education*, 1:1, pp. 24–41;

Open University Press for material from P. Broadfoot (1996) *Education, Assessment and Society: a sociological analysis*, pp. 102–24;

Taylor & Francis for material from H. M. Kliebard (1996) 'Constructing the concept of curriculum on the Wisconsin Frontier: how school restructuring sustained a pedagogical revolution', *History of Education*, 25:2, pp. 123–39; and A. Green (1995) 'Technical Education and state formation in nineteenth century England and France', *History of Education*, 24:2, pp. 123–39;

John Wiley & Sons, Inc for material from T. Lewis (1993) 'Valid knowledge and the problem of practical arts curriculum', *Curriculum Inquiry*, 23:2, pp. 175–202.

Every effort has been made to trace the copyright holders but if any have been inadvertently overlooked the publishers will be pleased to make the necessary arrangement at the first opportunity.

1

Perspectives on the Context of Curriculum

Bob Moon and Patricia Murphy

Curriculum is inextricably linked to social context. Broad historical, cultural, economic and political forces inter-relate to form and shape teaching and learning. This process is ongoing and accounts for the contested nature of curriculum change.

Over the last few decades, as the field of curriculum inquiry has deepened and diversified, a more analytical understanding of the socially situated nature of curriculum has developed.

The book brings together a number of recent chapters that illustrate the breadth and diversity of work in the field. These are grouped under three headings of historical, cultural and change perspectives on curriculum. The aim is to provide a source book for those exploring the origins and contemporary structures of curriculum. This introduction provides a brief resumé of each chapter and points to a number of general issues addressed by the collection as a whole.

Section 1 begins with two contrasting historical perspectives on curriculum development in the USA and Britain. Herbert Kliebard has written extensively on the historical origins of the American curriculum (Kliebard, 1986). In this chapter he demonstrates how the structure and organization of the curriculum in the frontier schools of Wisconsin changed to meet the needs and requirements of the bureaucracies associated with newly developed, large-scale education systems. The rituals of the school day, the structure of the school year and most significantly the organization of students into grades or years are now taken for granted. Kliebard shows how, once the now bureaucratic structure began to take hold, it generated its own dynamic and with that development far-reaching pedagogical practices consistent with the new organizational structure were reinforced and extended.

Tony Taylor looks at the more recent history made in the setting up of a national curriculum in England and Wales at the end of the 1980s. An education system which was often quoted as a prime example of a decentralized, schools-based model of curriculum organization became in 1988, almost literally overnight, one of the most centralized in the world. There are a few myths around this transformation. Moon (1990), for example, has shown that the English had a centrally prescribed curriculum for the first half of the century and that the loss of government control only occurred in the post-Second World War period. The curriculum legislation, however, of 1988 was undoubtedly significant in combining the continental European tradition and a highly prescriptive approach to national syllabuses with the testing system that has been more commonly associated with North America.

Taylor's chapter, however, is interesting from a number of points of view. He depicts the people and the personal politics behind the change process. How power is brokered and the interplay of different interest groups make fascinating reading. But he also illustrates how the people are messengers for different conceptions and perceptions of what the purposes of a curriculum are. He identifies three contested views: that held by Her Majesty's Inspectors (HMI) (for a broadly based approach representing areas of experience rather than subjects); the view of Margaret Thatcher and her advisers (for a free market approach but with a tested core of key subjects); and the Kenneth Baker perspective (a uniform establishment curriculum formed around ten subjects). Sharply more radical models of curriculum existed at the time but, given the nature of political control, these were of little importance. The HMI model, itself subject to considerable criticism, was the torch-bearer for the more holistic, student-centred ideas that some had been advising.

All three perspectives reflect what can be termed the 'specified' curriculum. In the political infighting of late 1980s England there was little thought as to how this might be 'enacted' (as Taylor's final paragraph makes clear) and still less a concern as to how such a formulation might be 'received' by learners in primary and secondary schools.

The English have always been ambivalent towards vocational education. Andy Green's description of the way in which the technical curriculum developed in contrasting ways in France and England picks up some of the same threads that Taylor explores. Andy Green reveals how very different models of technical and vocational education emerged in France and England, in part because of political infighting, but also more significantly, because of the different cultural constraints in which these battles came to be fought. The revolution in France created an educational impulse that embraced technical education. This did not happen in England and through the nineteenth and twentieth centuries structures and attitudes began to evolve in different ways. And so in England, says Green:

> Growing up as an extension of the apprenticeship system and reliant on employer initiatives, it developed in a fragmented and improvised manner: perennially low in status, conservatively rooted in workshop practice, and hostile to theoretical knowledge, publicly funded technical education became normatively part time and institutionally marooned between the workplace and mainstream education. A century later we have still not overcome the deep divisions between theory and practice and between academic and vocational learning which were first entrenched in these nineteenth-century institutional structures.

The final chapter in Section 1 analyses the way assessment systems have evolved in a variety of industralized countries. Patricia Broadfoot explores some of the issues that Herbert Kliebard uncovered when he delved into the schools of Wisconsin. She is particularly concerned with the extent to which policy and practice are influenced by the way in which a system is organized. Her analysis suggests that different forms of control (central or local, for example) have important consequences for curriculum and assessment. Broadfoot's chapter is an interesting summary of a number of sociological perspectives on the way assessment systems have emerged in contemporary societies. She points to the constant contradiction between the need to differentiate pupils on the basis of an order of merit, which ultimately serves to legitimate differential chances in the labour market, and the need to involve pupils, parents and teachers in a way which enables the school to be seen as serving commonly conceived purposes. It was not always so, she suggests, quoting Durkheim (1947, p. 159):

> We are so accustomed to believing that emulation is the essential motivating force in academic life, that we cannot easily imagine how a school could exist which did not have a carefully worked out system of graduated awards in order to keep the enthusiasm of pupils perpetually alive. Good marks, solemn statements of satisfactory performance, distinctions, competition essays, prizegivings; all these seem to us in differing degrees, the necessary accompaniment to any sound education system. The system that operated in France and indeed Europe, until the sixteenth century, was characterised by the surprising fact that there were no rewards at all from success in examinations. What is more, any candidate who had assiduously and conscientiously followed the course of studies was certain of success.

She identifies a number of analytic themes (individualism, rational authority, contradiction and legitimation) which are characteristic of modern societies and which give rise to the necessity for a set of procedures which we now recognize as assessment. The fundamental role of assessment procedures in advanced, postindustrial societies is seen as a constant but the institutional expression of that role will vary according to the social context and over time.

Section 2 provides sharply contrasting perspectives on the social and cultural context of curriculum. Joanna Le Métais examines the way in which values and aims are expressed in the curriculum and assessment policies of countries across the world. In an ideal world, she suggests, values, clearly understood and shared by all, would form a coherent thread through all education systems. In looking at different national systems, however, she observes that values may be neither national nor discrete and she considers a number of factors that contribute to the ambiguity inherent in value statements. Like Patricia Broadfoot she sees the centralized or decentralized organization of systems as important with models of assessment as a possible touchstone through which to explore the underlying aims and purposes of different national systems.

Martin Woodhead's examination of early childhood programmes ranges, as did Le Métais's, across a wide selection of national contexts. Woodhead argues that the, well intentioned, attempts to establish standards for good practice in early childhood programmes can create an orthodoxy that gives scant respect to local conditions. And he continues that, given the dominance of western practice in the literature and in the work of international organizations, the apparently universal standard too often reflects a particular cultural perspective on child development. In Woodhead's view, early childhood programmes are

> human systems involving numerous individuals and interest groups. There are many different potential criteria of quality, which are closely linked to beliefs about the goals and functions of programmes. These beliefs are in turn shaped by different perspectives on childhood and child development, different cultural patterns and personal values.

Judgements about standards or quality, therefore, must take account of context. The problem for most formal systems of education, however, is just how relative such judgements can be. In his conclusion Woodhead argues that quality is relative but, importantly, is not arbitrary. He sees an adequacy boundary or limit to any early childhood environment but within such boundaries he suggests are numerous pathways to quality. The challenge comes in defining the limits or boundaries of adequacy.

The threads of earlier analyses about the historical and cultural influences on curriculum are picked up in Theodore Lewis's exploration of why some forms of knowledge came to be more valued than others in curriculum formation. Lewis argues that the meagre existence of practical arts subjects in the curriculum comes about as a result of the persistence of the Platonic ideal of what constitutes valued knowledge. He pursues the same theme as Andy Green in noting the uncertain relationship of formal education to industrial culture despite the impact of industrial revolutions on the expansion of human knowledge. Lewis traces back some recent contemporary debates in the USA and the UK to ancient conceptions of what knowledge is seen to be of most significance. He argues for giving the practical arts an equal status to other areas of the curriculum.

Finally, in Section 2, Jerome Bruner looks at the way ideas about culture, mind and education have evolved over the last century. He shows how the theories that teachers hold about learning help determine what is included in the curriculum and how it is taught and assessed. These views he sees as culturally, socially and historically bound. Bruner gives a sweeping overview of the evolution in theories about mind over the last half of the twentieth century. He describes how in the 1950s the cognitive revolution was a challenge to establish 'meaning' as the central concept of psychology. His view of the cognitive revolution was not as a transformation of existing theories that were widespread in education, but as a more profound reconceptualization of learning.

Bruner argues that the model of mind to which one adheres shapes the pedagogy of practice. His chapter sets out two broad perspectives on mind, the computational and the cultural, but these he suggests are not so linked to particular models of mind as to be shackled in particular pedagogies. In his view their differences are of quite a different kind and not necessarily contradictory.

Bruner's interest, however, is in a culturally orientated psychology which neither dismisses what people say about their mental states; nor treats their statements only as if they were predictive indices of overt behaviour. What he takes as central, is that the relationship between action and saying (or experiencing) is in the ordinary conduct of life, interpretable.

Section 3 of the reader looks at the experience of curriculum change in a variety of situations. The impact of social and cultural context on the change process is clearly evident in Ken Harley and Volker Wedekind's account of the way headteachers are responding to curriculum change in postapartheid South Africa. The case illustrates the complex range of forces that come to bear on educational reform. School principals, the authors argue, symbolize in their views the historical antecedents that impinge so directly on reform efforts.

Their ideas, however, about education and change in the new South Africa appear to remain essentially conservative with a vivid disjuncture emerging between progressive political and educational rhetoric and the language of contemporary economic thinking about efficiency and resourcing. Harley and Wedekind trace the lack of any transformatory curriculum model back to the role of the school in the apartheid era as a place for resistance to an oppressive state. At best, they suggest, schools had served as sites for political mobilization, and unlike their counterparts in Mozambique or Cuba had never been seen as sites for educational progressivism.

Similar processes are at work in post-Pinochet Chile as Ruth Aedo-Richmond and Mark Richmond's account reveals. In Chile the response to the period of authoritarian rule between 1973 and 1990 has been to introduce a significant phase of decentralized reform. Curriculum reform, however, as with South Africa, began with a national blueprint around which a significant level of consultation was built.

Gaining the support of teachers, and sustaining a consensus around the unknown concept of local and school-based curriculum development, were crucial elements in the reform process. The historically deep-rooted attitudes towards statism and central control were important potential barriers to change. The pursuit of consensus, the authors argue, was a new departure for Chile, where educational policy traditionally was 'governmental' or 'party political' rather than 'national' in character.

The next two chapters by Crain Soudien and Robert McCormick look at specific aspects of the curriculum change process. Both demonstrate the influence of a complex range of factors on experimentation and reform.

Crain Soudien, echoing some of the argument in the South African case study above, agrees that change in the context of the USA is emblematic of the contested nature of representation. Key questions arise. How are the images and symbols purporting to stand for different groups constructed and who controls the construction of such images? In focusing on process in curriculum development, rather than the broader context, the paper indicates how dominant conceptions of multiculturalism leave mainstream knowledge unproblematicized.

Robert McCormick also argues that the view of curriculum change employed by many policy-makers is inadequate. He advocates a focus on the school as central to any systematic change; a policy, as we have seen above, that is intended to characterize the 1990s phase of reform in Chile. The chapter looks at curriculum change exemplified through introduction of information technologies into schooling and curriculum. McCormick argues that teachers' professional development needs to occur on a number of fronts with, for him, the institution as the prime focus. But he also demonstrates how the negotiations for status, resources and territory at the institutional level (however large or small) feed off the interpretations of external policies and programmes.

Pierre Bourdieu, a leading sociological analyst of the relationship between education and broader social and economic forces, was asked at the end of the 1980s to advise a newly elected French Socialist government on the process of curriculum reform. He chaired a committee that formulated seven principles to inform the process of curriculum reconstruction. It is interesting to analyse the principles in terms of the extent to which they are located in the postindustrial character of late 1980 France. The ideas around teacher collaboration and team teaching demonstrate progressive influences. But the attempts to address the issue of curriculum overload, the relationship of 'compulsoriness and transmittability', and the wish to reconcile the universalism and relativism are all contemporary themes in any process of curriculum reform.

Richard Elmore has written extensively on the process of educational change. He is writing in the context of the USA. He proposes four main strategies for scaling up successful reform to systems-wide acceptance.

- *Developing strong external normative structures.* Here he advocates the development of good role exemplifications, not merely from central agencies but also through all the informal channels that legitimate educational practice.
- *Developing organizational structures that intensify and focus the challenge on conventional practice.* In this, studying the need to work within smaller units of reform which can interact with each other to create the momentum of change is proposed: smaller units and smaller subunits of institutions appearing will, he suggests, be more likely to provide the foundation for successful reform – scaling down in order to scale up!
- *Creating international processes for the reproduction of success.* Much reform is naive, he suggests, in the assumptions it makes about the dissemination of success: this has to be thought about in explicit terms and a number of ways of going about this are suggested. Finally:
- *Structures need creating that promote learning of new practices, and incentive systems need to support that.* The very structure of reform, he suggests, must in this analysis take account of what we know about learning and incentives, in all the myriad of forms available.

To conclude, therefore, the aim of this volume is to provide a range of sources from the vast literature available. The choices inevitably reflect some personal knowledge and interests but the selection is planned to allow readers, and those developing programmes in the field of curriculum inquiry, to construct a range of contrasting, even competing, narratives.

References

Kliebard, H. (1986) *The Struggle for the American Curriculum, 1893–1958*, London and New York, Routledge & Kegan Paul.

Moon, B. (1990) The National Curriculum: origins and context, in Brighouse, T. and Moon, B. (eds.) *Managing the National Curriculum: Some Critical Perspectives*, Harlow, Longman.

SECTION 1
HISTORICAL PERSPECTIVES

2

Constructing the Concept of Curriculum on the Wisconsin Frontier: How School Restructuring Sustained a Pedagogical Revolution

Herbert M. Kliebard

By 1901, John Dewey was already troubled about the failure of many educational reforms. With astonishing regularity, promising pedagogical innovations had made their appearance enjoyed a brief day in the sun, and then quietly vanished. In attempting to account for this phenomenon, Dewey called attention to what he believed to be at least one source of this failure – an incompatibility between the organization and management of schools and many pedagogical reforms:

> It is easy to fall into the habit of regarding the mechanics of school organization and administration as something comparatively external and indifferent to educational purposes and ideals. We think of the grouping of children in classes, the arrangement of grades, the machinery by which the course of study is made out and laid down, the method by which it is carried into effect, the system of selecting teachers and assigning them to their work, of paying and promoting them, as, in a way, matters of mere practical convenience and expediency. We forget that it is precisely such things as these that really control the whole system, even on its distinctively educational side. No matter what is the accepted precept and theory, no matter what the legislation of the school board or the mandate of the school superintendent, the reality of education is found in the personal and face-to-face contact of teacher and child. The conditions that underlie and regulate this contact dominate the educational situation.[1]

This pivotal connection between school organization and management on one hand and what Dewey called 'the face-to-face contact of teacher and child' on the other even today is under-appreciated. On the surface at least, such matters as the structure of the school year and the organization of pupils into groups of like achievement and expectations seem to be matters 'of mere practical convenience and expediency'; but these structural features of schooling, it appears, are in fact intimately bound to the very core of the educational process. If Dewey's hypothesis is correct, then pedagogical changes, even dramatic ones, may be sustained or undermined depending on whether the organization and management of schools are compatible with those changes.

What follows is an attempt to trace the relationship between organizational restructuring and the emergence of two revolutionary pedagogical changes derived largely from data relating to a single country school in Columbia County, Wisconsin in the latter half of the nineteenth century. The evidence suggests that these closely interrelated pedagogical changes, (1) the appearance of a concept of curriculum that was above and beyond what was dictated by the textbook and (2) what is called here *ensemble teaching* (as distinct from teaching as monitoring individual recitations), are intimately connected with a major reconstruction of the management and organization of schooling across the state of Wisconsin and in the United States generally. That organizational change, age stratification, it would appear, prompted fundamental revisions both in terms of how the curriculum was conceptualized and in how teachers taught. Although it was surely not the first instance either of age stratification or of the emergence of a modern conception of curriculum nor was it the first time that teachers reached beyond the common practice of hearing individual recitations as the predominant form of teaching, it does mark one early and vivid illustration of how structural changes undergirded a major reconstruction of prevailing conceptions of curriculum and teaching.

Curriculum and Teaching in Country Schools on the Middle Border

At its most fundamental level, what we call the curriculum embodies what is to be taught, and what we call teaching refers to those actions that a teacher undertakes in order to implement the curriculum. When seen in such broad terms, there was certainly such a thing as a curriculum in country schools of the period just after the Civil War in the American Midwest, and there were obviously actions undertaken by the teacher that could reasonably be called teaching; but the forms they assumed were considerably different in character from our modern and more elaborated understanding of those concepts.

In the case of curriculum, there were of course subjects, and it is subjects that were (and remain today) the basic building blocks from which a curriculum is constructed. What was called a subject then, however, was so intimately tied to the textbook used to convey that subject that the line between subject and textbook was virtually indistinguishable. This correspondence between subject and text goes back at least to the colonial period in America. In fact, during the seventeenth and eighteenth centuries, the names of the subjects and the names of the textbooks were often one and the same.

The subject of reading could be represented as the *New England Primer*, the subject of arithmetic as James Hodder's *Hodder's arithmetick, or that necessary art made most easy*, and the subject of Latin as Cheever's *Accidence* or the *Colloquies of Corderius*. When a school undertook to publish its curriculum, it was often recorded as the names of textbooks.[2]

For most of the nineteenth century, the curriculum as the object of professional concern in the United States consisted largely of discussion of the benefits presumably derived from the study of the subjects, including, here and there, some disagreement as to the respective value of the subjects to be taught. To a large extent, the actual content of these subjects as subjects was ill-defined. When the *Wisconsin Journal of Education* was launched in 1856, for example, its inaugural issue included the first of a series of four articles devoted to the course of study. The author, identified as J. L. P. (actually J. L. Pickard of Platteville, Wisconsin), waxed poetic over certain subjects of study. Reading was described as 'the mouth of the mind, through which must be received all its nourishment'.[3] With respect to the subject of penmanship, Pickard declared, 'Words written are but the clothing of ideas'; whereas in the case of arithmetic, 'No other study has so wide a range of influence or exerts such a power in the formation of character . . .'.[4] Beyond the idea that these subjects have such salubrious properties, there was little to guide the teacher in actually teaching those subjects. By implication at least, what the teacher actually taught in their name was set forth in the textbook.

If the curriculum was defined by the textbooks that children brought with them to school, then teaching in country schools consisted largely of hearing children recite from those textbooks. What is more, the lack of uniformity in textbooks even within a single school made the process of teaching difficult to manage. Not only were textbooks not supplied by country schools in the early part of the nineteenth century, they were different from one child to the next. Even children of the same age and school experience would recite individually from the textbooks that they happened to bring with them to school in the various subjects.[5] As Barbara Finkelstein observes, 'In the one-room schools of the countryside . . . where students of varying ages, backgrounds and levels of achievement brought their own texts to class, the teachers treated each pupil as unique – making individual assignments, hearing individual recitations and rendering individual appraisals'. She cites, for example, the recollections of an Indiana farmer who recalls of his country schooling in the 1840s,

> There was no program to be followed, no order of exercises, no system. When a scholar felt that he had studied his lesson well and was prepared to recite, he would take his book in hand, and go forward to the master's desk . . .[6]

In short, there was no course of study in the contemporary sense. Teaching as well was considerably different from modern practice. By and large, when country teachers taught, it took the form of making assignments in a textbook for each student and then listening to the student recite that lesson as time permitted. To be sure, a teacher might engage his or her class in a group activity every now and then, such as group singing or a spelling bee, but teaching was essentially a process of monitoring individual recitations from a bewildering array of different textbooks.

While the ingenious or daring teacher could depart from this pattern, for the most part, learning a lesson meant committing some portion of a textbook to memory. As Mary Bradford was to recall of her schooling in the 1860s, 'To recite meant to repeat the words of a book: to study meant to commit to memory words for such a recitation. The one who possessed the best word-memory was the most satisfactory pupil.'[7] Although group recitation undoubtedly played some role, a typical day of teaching consisted of children marching one by one to the teacher's desk to recite their lessons. Keeping order rather than teaching was seen as the teacher's main duty. In one joint district school in Columbia County, Wisconsin, for example, where visitors to the school in the 1870s were asked to record their reactions, the comments centred almost exclusively on issues of order and management rather than teaching *per se*. Over the course of about a decade, the only visitor's comment related to teaching as opposed to discipline or order was 'Recitations good'.[8]

For a time, this practice of teaching essentially as hearing individual recitations seemed immutable. To a large extent, that pattern of teaching was perpetuated by the fact that the teachers themselves had been taught through textbook recitation, and, lacking formal training for the most part, they taught in the only way they knew how. The practice of recitation was also reinforced by the reigning pedagogical theory of the day, mental discipline. Since the object of education according to that theory was to strengthen certain innate faculties of the mind, what could be more efficacious in that regard than to set up rigorous muscle-building exercises for the children to recite? Fundamental changes in curriculum and teaching awaited a constituent alteration in the management and organization of schooling.

Summer and Winter Terms at the Otsego Village School, 1867–80

Many of our management and organizational practices with regard to schooling are now so well established that it is difficult not to take them for granted. Take, for example, the modern practice of organizing instruction within the context of a school year. The school year not only serves as the calendar unit during which school services are available; it also represents the unit of time for which teacher contracts are offered. It is the organizational framework for what Dewey called 'the system of selecting teachers and assigning them to their work'. In the period just after the Civil War on the Wisconsin frontier, however, the school year was anything but an established fact. Rather, country schools on the Middle Border were organized around two distinct and separate periods of schooling, the winter term and the summer term. When interested citizens in School District No. 3 of Otsego, Wisconsin, for example, gathered for their first annual meeting, one of the main items of business was to set the beginning and ending dates of each of the two terms. Accordingly, on 2 September 1867, those citizens of Otsego School District No. 3 in attendance voted to raise $285 in taxes for the ensuing year, $160 of which would cover teacher wages and $125 for the contingent fund. They then set the starting dates of the two terms as 1 November and 1 April with each term running for four months.[9] In ensuing years, however, the summer term was often shorter than the winter term, sometimes only two and a half months in duration.

Until 1880, each term and hence each teacher contract was subject to the time spans set at each annual meeting. In Otsego's one-room school, the summer term was usually set to begin after the spring planting of the potato crop, and the winter term would begin after harvest. Generally, as David Angus, Jeffrey Mirel and Maris Vinovskis put it, 'Going to school in the country was a seasonal activity contingent on the need for agricultural labor at home'.[10] In fact, the older farm boys would often attend school only in the winter term. Since these boys were reputed to be obstreperous, winter terms were regarded as more difficult to teach and, from time to time, Otsego residents as well as citizens guiding country schools elsewhere voted specifically to hire a male teacher for the winter term and a female teacher for the summer term. In School District No. 5 in the nearby town of Scott, for example, specifying male teachers for the winter term and female teachers for the summer term was the rule rather than the exception.[11]

Table 2.1 indicates the variation in the beginning dates of the school term in the Otsego School over a fourteen-year span. Derived from actual school contracts and minutes of meetings, the data also convey the considerable variation in salaries of teachers and teacher hiring practices, especially with respect to the discontinuity from one term to the next.[12]

What is especially striking about this picture compared with modern school organization is the discreteness of each term. Although city schools began awarding school-year contracts earlier, the concept of a school year as we know it today seems not to have existed in Otsego prior to 1880. Otsego was unexceptional in this regard. In rural schools generally, teacher contracts were typically drawn up individually for each of the two terms of three to four months each. Although this appears to be a rather trivial detail relating to the vagaries of school management rather than to pedagogical demands, it is tied in rather profound ways to how children were taught. Because different teachers were usually hired for each of the terms, children would experience almost no coherence with respect to their studies from one term to the next. One small-town newspaper editor recalling his school experiences in the 1860s in Berks County, Pennsylvania, for example, reported that in his seven terms of public schooling he had had seven teachers.[13] Under such circumstances, since there was no curriculum

Table 2.1   *Otsega School details, 1867–79*

Term	Beginning date	Teacher's name	Salary
Winter 1867	5 November	Susan Waters	$40
Summer 1868	Not recorded	Susie Waters	$40
Winter 1868	9 November	Jennie Mitchell	$35
Summer 1869	27 April	Jennie Mitchell	$40
Winter 1869	15 November	Cyrus R. Heuton*	$40
Summer 1870	No data	No data	No data
Winter 1870	No data	No data	No data
Summer 1871	I May	Jennie Grout	$27
Winter 1871	13 November	A. W. Grout*	$40
Summer 1872	29 April	Nora Waters	$30
Winter 1872	18 November	John Grout	$45
Summer 1873	5 May	Viola Nicholson	$25
Winter 1873	17 November	Daniel W. Hall*	$40
Summer 1874	27 April	Cora A. Downs*	$25
Winter 1874	23 November	John E. Grant	$20 for 17 weeks
Summer 1875	3 May	Celia S. Pulver*	$17 for 16 weeks
Winter 1875	15 November	Celia S. Pulver	$12 for 17 weeks
Summer 1876	1 May	Evelyn Todd	$20
Winter 1876	13 November	Frances Palmer*	$25
Summer 1877	30 April	Mary A. James	$18
Winter 1877	20 November	William E. Ritter	$30
Summer 1878	22 April	N. G. Dunning*	$18
Winter 1878	18 November	J. B. Meridth	$38
Summer 1879	13 April	Celia P. Randalls*	$18
Winter 1879	8 September	Nellie Gabrielson[1]	$20
Winter l879	1 December	J. B. Meridth*[2]	$33
Winter 1879	28 December	Charles Williams*[3]	$30

1. Nellie Gabrielson's contract was for only the first two months of the 1879 winter term.
2. J. B. Meridth's contract called for his services only in the month of December.
3. Charles Williams taught the remaining two and a half months of the 1979 winter term.

to guide the teacher, what little continuity there was came from the textbooks that the pupils brought with them to school.

Of the 25 different teachers serving in the one-room Otsego Village School between 1867 and 1880, only Susan Waters, Jennie Mitchell, Celia Pulver and J. B. Meridth served as many as two terms and, even then, each of their contracts was awarded for just one term at a time. 'Susie' Waters and later Celia Pulver were the only teachers ever to serve two consecutive terms. Over the 13-year period prior to 1880, no teacher was hired for as many as three terms. In general, then, children in the Otsego School District No. 3 were almost certain to confront a new teacher with each new term. This changed abruptly on 30 August 1880. At their annual meeting, the assembled citizens took the unprecedented step of passing a motion 'that the board hire a female teacher for the whole year'. It was not, then, until Hannah Slattery obtained the contract covering both terms at once did that situation change, and the modern concept of a school year begin to emerge in Otsego School District No. 3. In the following year, for example, a similar motion was passed to hire a teacher for the full year, this time specifically authorizing the board to hire either a male or a female teacher.[14]

This departure from a longstanding practice may have been signalled a year earlier when the opening date for the winter term in 1879 was set at 8 September. As the table indicates, this was approximately four to seven weeks earlier than the customary starting date at Otsego. Following the new pattern, Hannah Slattery's first day on her unprecedented two-term contract was 6 September 1880, a date not unlike the start of the school year in contemporary US schools. In the 1880s, going to school was beginning to take precedence over the need for the help of children during the potato harvest, but there is no reason to believe that this change was dictated by a dramatically new appreciation of the value of education on the Wisconsin frontier. Rather, this early example of an emerging continuity within the school year was probably a by-product of new strictures emanating from the state level. On the surface, these regulations addressed the organization and management of schools in the state of Wisconsin, but, as Dewey was to observe two decades later, such arrangements can profoundly affect the very heart of the educational process.

Impact of Grading on Curriculum and Teaching

It appears that a simultaneous trend to what was called *grading* strongly influenced the way in which the school year was conceived. Although the term *grading* was sometimes used to convey different meanings, it referred principally to the practice of assigning pupils to grade levels according to some estimate of achievement. Age classification in city schools had been practised since at least the 1850s, but it was much less feasible in one-room country schools like Otsego's.

Increasingly, however, this new organization of schooling was being recommended whether or not pupils of different ages and levels of achievement were taught in the same room. The idea of grade levels carried with it ramifications involving what expectations were appropriate for each grade and what programme of studies was likely to fulfil those expectations. For a child to progress through the grades rather than to make one's way individually through a textbook, in other words, implied not just regular attendance but continuity and coherence in what he or she studied from one term to the next. The commonly held notions of promotion and retention at the end of a school year or school term, for example, would not be conceivable without reasonably uniform expectations as to satisfactory progress over a defined period of time. Under a system based primarily on individual recitations, on the other hand, it would be perfectly plausible for a scholar simply to resume schooling in a new reader or in the next chapter of a geography textbook whenever that child returned to school and with whoever happened to be the teacher that term.

Beginning around the 1860s, calls for the grading of pupils in country schools in Wisconsin became common. In 1863, for example, the first of a series of short promotional articles began to appear on the subject of grading by an author identified as A. P. (actually Aaron Pickett of Horicon, Wisconsin). As proposed by Pickett, grading involved 'not only a system of uniform gradation, but also of uniform instruction and studies for each grade'. The classification of pupils into groups called grades and the development of a defined programme of studies for each of those groups, therefore, were intimately connected. When Pickett undertook to spell out his scheme of classification, for example, he did so by setting forth what we now think of as curricular objectives for each of the grades. Part of the problem he sought to address was the inexperience of country teachers. To a considerable extent, they were deemed incapable of devising a course of study. As Pickett put it, 'For a long time to come the most of our country schools must be taught by those who are comparatively young and inexperienced, and consequently in this cause of so great moment [creation of a course of instruction] and embracing so much difficulty and complication, we cannot expect success without system, nor without making that system so plain that a teacher though a mere youth cannot err therein'.[15] In short, he was recommending that teachers be given a curriculum to follow as a corrective for youth, inexperience or lack of resourcefulness on the part of teachers.

Thus, in first-grade arithmetic, Pickett stipulated among other objectives, 'To count the number forward or backward' and 'To add one to, or subtract it from any number, from one to fifty',[16] and, in geography, 'the class should . . . learn the meaning of a linear inch, a square inch, a linear foot, linear rod, square rod, of the acre, quarter section, section and town'. These learning expectations amounted to a curriculum independent of a textbook. Of equal importance was the fact that these objectives were obviously meant to apply to categories of students – grade levels – not to individuals. Pickett specified, for example, that in teaching geography, the teacher should draw a map of the town on the blackboard indicating such features as principal streams and bodies of water, valleys. swamps, schoolhouses, churches and roads.[17] Clearly, A. P.'s conception of curriculum was dramatically different from that of his colleague, J. L. P., as expressed only a few years before. Subjects were no longer just generalized purveyors of desirable qualities of mind or character: they were the repositories of specific things that had to be learned in a kind of regular progression.

Agitation for grading in Wisconsin was consummated in 1879 in State Superintendent William C. Whitford's widely distributed plan for grading (classifying) the pupils in Wisconsin schools. As was the case with earlier proposals, grading, as interpreted by Whitford, presupposed not just periodic examinations but a *course of study*, that is, a suitable set of learning activities associated with a particular grade level. Specific standards of achievement in the common branches of study were to be tied to each of the three proposed levels: the primary form, the middle form, and the upper form.[18] In presenting his justification for the new plan, Whitman specified, as one advantage, that a 'definite end can be presented for the pupils to attain in pursuing their studies, and a fixed course of action covering several years to which they must conform in reaching this end'. Moreover, movement from one grade to the next would 'be accurately determined as the result of an efficient system of examinations'.[19] In short, grading (classification of students) implied anticipated levels of achievement for each grade or form; anticipated levels of achievement implied examinations to determine the appropriate grade and appropriate progress: and, all together, this implied a curriculum above and beyond what amounted to a place marker in a textbook. The concept of grading, in other words, required a new way of thinking about the curriculum.

It could hardly be a coincidence that new state regulations requiring grading of pupils were first promulgated only a year before Otsego School District No. 3 undertook to award Hannah Slattery their first full school-year contract. Whether teachers are hired for just one term or for a whole year seems to be of less than earth-shaking significance, but grading of pupils as a managerial change carried with it the seeds of how we conceive of the very process of education. It provided both the structural framework and the impetus by which continuity in the curriculum could be maintained from one term to the next. The awarding of Hannah Slattery's contract for the 1880 school year was a signal not only that major organizational changes were being instituted but that significant pedagogical changes were afoot on the Wisconsin frontier and in the USA generally. Whether the organizational changes actually provided the impetus for the pedagogical change or vice versa is difficult to establish. It is clear, nevertheless, that the pedagogical and organizational changes are critically interdependent.

Once learning expectations were set by grade level rather than by individual textbook, the very activity of teaching had to change. With pupils organized into groups of like expectations, the teacher was obliged to teach them as a group rather than hearing individuals recite. Thus, ensemble teaching had to replace, at least in part, the predominant practice of teaching as listening to recitations from the textbooks children happened to bring with them. In fact, the trend in the direction of group instruction is marked by the growing trend toward using uniform textbooks for each grade in country schools. In Otsego School District No. 3, for example, the first recorded instance of textbooks formally adopted by the board of education occurred on 18 November 1878.[20] It seems likely, then, that three almost simultaneous organizational changes, Otsego's first uniform textbook adoption in 1878, Superintendent Whitford's edict requiring grading in the state of Wisconsin's schools in 1879 and Otsego's decision to award their first two-term teacher contract in 1880 are related phenomena. They are all consistent with the trend toward greater continuity in the curriculum and therefore toward uniformity in instruction.

Significantly, the practice of grading even in one-room schools was not by any means restricted to country schools in Wisconsin. In an address

delivered before the Kansas State Teachers' Association in 1878, Henry
Clay Speer, then superintendent of schools in Atchinson, Kansas and later
to become the state superintendent, made a similar call for a clear classification of pupils in country schools. Speer was unambiguous as to the
implications of grading for the curriculum. 'What is arithmetic?' he asked;
his answer was that 'it is time these questions were defined somewhere else
than in text books . . .'. The 'somewhere else' clearly was the centralized
state bureaucracy. Moreover, Speer was obviously referring not simply to
designating the subjects to be studied; he had in mind the actual curriculum, much as the term is used today.

    One thing that made Speer's address so striking was his blunt justification
for advocating this course of action. He simply had no faith that teachers had
either the training or the ingenuity to devise their own courses of study. This
had to be done for them by true professionals like himself. 'It is utterly
senseless', he declared, 'to put teachers in the work of artists.' Designing the
school curriculum, in other words, was the province neither of teachers nor
of textbooks but of a handful of professionally trained specialists. Teaching
was one thing and devising what to teach was another. Teachers, Speer
asserted, are 'master workmen . . . not architects . . . There is no genius
wanted. Good intelligent, discreet teachers are needed.'[21] Here, then, is an
early indication of what was to become a major feature of American schooling in the twentieth century: the virtual isolation of the design of the formal
curriculum from its execution in the classroom.

    By 1887, grading had already gained national acceptance. In an address
before the Department of Superintendence in Washington, DC, the state
superintendent of public instruction in Indiana, J. W. Holcome, treated
upgraded country schools as a thing of the past, and with that change, in his
view, there emerged such a thing as a systematically organized curriculum.
He cited, for example, a communication from a county superintendent as
stating, 'A few years ago, what a boy studied was determined by his own
caprice or by family tradition and custom. The teacher, confronted by forty
or fifty pupils, found as many different courses of study, and was compelled
to pass day after day in giving individual lessons to individual pupils. In
such a school much time and energy were wasted, the greatest amount of
labor being required to produce the smallest result.' To Holcome, Indiana's
state superintendent, the issue was no longer one of policy but of implementation. In his mind, grading in country schools was similar to grading in
city schools requiring only certain adjustments. Taking his own state as
typical of the country, he reported that 82% of the teachers were employed
in country schools, and 72% of the children were educated there rather
than in cities.[22] With the extension of grading to rural America, it was now
clearly becoming the standard practice nationally.

    In the discussion that followed the Indiana superintendent's speech, the
superintendent of schools in Columbia, South Carolina concurred. 'In most
of the States, if not all,' he said, 'there is already a system of gradation in
the schools from the lowest primary into the colleges, constituting a ladder

upon the rounds of which the city boy may mount from the gutter of degradation to the pinnacles of usefulness and honor.' He deplored the fact that children in country schools had in the past been asked to go over the same lessons in their textbooks for five consecutive years with five different teachers.[23] Superintendent Speer from Kansas, arriving too late to hear the main address in its entirety, reiterated his pessimism regarding the ability of the country teacher to create a course of study under the new grading system. 'The average teacher of the country schools', he asserted, 'is not a man or woman upon whom you can depend for the development of the course of study. That is why I say it belongs to the State superintendent.'[24] While it would be an obvious exaggeration to claim that the new class of education professionals was actually created by the system of grading, it is fair to say that an emerging class of professionals, consciously or unconsciously, saw in grading a splendid opportunity to centralize the control of public schooling and thereby to enhance their own status.

By 1898, when the first book on grading was published, the classification of students into grades in both city and country schools had proceeded to such an extent that the author felt obliged to propose ways of achieving a measure of flexibility within the classification structure. The author, William J. Shearer, a former country school teacher and at the time superintendent of schools in Elizabeth, New Jersey, attributed the origin of the idea in the United States to John Philbrick who initiated the first graded school in 1847. By 1860, Shearer claimed, most cities and large towns had already adopted the practice. Writing in the 1890s, Shearer, acknowledging that grading was now common in country schools as well, reported that 'thoughtful educators are studying this problem as never before, and are planning to strangle the demon of uniformity . . .'.[25] In general, he recommended a shorter class interval (one term) rather than the more common practice of classification by a whole year and was highly critical of the tendency in country schools to limit classification to only three forms. Whatever the particular scheme of classification, however, it is clear that the spread of grading first to cities and then to country schools over the course of half a century had been nothing short of spectacular. Obviously, such a phenomenon was closely related to the rise in the student population at both the elementary and secondary levels. In fact, the emergence of mass popular education helps explain why age stratification arose first in cities and only later in rural schools such as Otsego's.

The Transformation of the Otsego School

Whatever may have been the motivation of the new class of education professionals for insisting on age grading in the schools of Wisconsin and for simultaneously creating the concept of a curriculum that went beyond textbook recitation, the effects were revolutionary. Records for the one-room school for Otsego School District No. 3 in the first few years of the twentieth century paint a far different picture of what school was like for the inhabitants of country schools from what it was before 1880.

The most obvious difference was the greater continuity in studies from one term to the next. This was made possible by the fact that, to a much larger extent than earlier, the same teacher returned each semester. Unfortunately, the records of Otsego School District No. 3 are not as complete after 1880 as in the years before, but they do indicate that Hannah Slattery was still drawing her teacher's wages as late as 1882. A three-year tenure for a teacher at the Otsego school was absolutely unheard of only a few years earlier. In general, the period from 1880 to 1905 seems to have been a transitional one at Otsego, with teachers sometimes staying on for as many as three years followed by a reversion to individual term hiring. During the mid- to late 1880s and the early 1890s, for example, there appears to have been a temporary reversion to term-to-term hiring of teachers. Christina Crossman, however, began teaching at the school in 1893 and, although a male teacher was hired for the 1894 winter term, she is still recorded as drawing her teacher's wages as late as 1896. In 1905, Jessie M. Ellis was hired and remained until 1908, and her replacement, Della Curtis, stayed on for two years. Country school teaching was anything but a long-term career for most teachers until well into the twentieth century, but it was no longer a strictly interim occupation of only a few months' duration. But beyond the length of the teachers' tenure at the Otsego Village School, there was an evident transformation in the nature of their work. Beginning in 1905 in Otsego, *Harvey's District School Register* was used to record not only student data such as age, grade classification and attendance but also notations as to what the various classes or forms (Primary, Middle and Upper) had been doing in the various subjects of study. While Jessie Ellis's notations are somewhat sketchy, they do provide some idea as to how the work of teaching had been transformed over the previous quarter century.

To be sure, the textbook continued to play a large part in the instruction as it does today, and there are frequent references to where groups of children stand with respect to a particular textbook; but there is also clear evidence that Miss Ellis ventured beyond recitation from the textbook despite the fact that she was obliged to teach 45 students in the three forms during the 1905 school year. In the upper form, for example, eight students were recorded as having given 'exercises on foods, healthy habits of cleanliness and the effects of narcotics on the system'. There are indications of 'work from charts and black board' in arithmetic for seven students, and another group of seven is recorded as having studied 'Current events. Important Federal officers . . . and the names of these'. Moreover, there were 'original practical problems' given as well as practice in 'Commercial forms' to a group of four. Despite the obvious logistical problems in handling so large a class, it is clear that individual recitation had given way to some extent to ensemble teaching that did not always reflect direct instruction from a textbook.

By 1908, Miss Ellis included in her records supplementary reading from library books, map-drawing and letter writing, and there are persistent references to reading words and sentences from the blackboard and cards. Eight students in 1908 planted seeds and made observations as they sprouted. The students participating in each of these activities were recorded by number as they appear in the class roster at the beginning of the register. From the tenor of the notations, it is evident that a major purpose of the records was to ensure that there would be continuity for these groups of students from one year to the next. With group instruction and a curriculum independent of the textbook in place, it was no longer possible to rely on the page number in the textbook as the only indicator of where each pupil stood academically.[26] In short, major pedagogical changes had taken place in the way children were being taught at Otsego over the space of a few years, and the direction of these changes is reflective of the now widespread practice of age stratification.

Summary and Conclusions

With so many things happening at the same time, it is difficult to establish a strict chronological rendering of these remarkable changes in country schools, but the logical connections seem clear:

1. An organizational change, grading (age stratification), requires children to be grouped according to like achievement and expectations.
2. Grading cannot really function effectively without a curriculum that expresses common achievement expectations for clusters of students. In this way, the grip of textbook as curriculum is loosened.
3. Under these circumstances, ensemble teaching is supported with a corresponding decline in teaching as monitoring individual recitations from textbooks.
4. The new conception of the teacher's role requires another organizational change, longer term contracts for teachers, so that continuity in the curriculum can be fostered from one term to the next. Teachers are also obliged to keep records of student progress in the event of a change of teachers.

This intimate interrelationship between management and organization on one hand and pedagogical change on the other is exactly what Dewey was talking about in 1901. In fact, as Dewey saw it, it is, if anything, organizational factors (in this case the new state regulation requiring grading of pupils) that 'really control' the pedagogical side. In a sense, then, the Otsego, Wisconsin case and related data may be seen as offering empirical evidence in support of Dewey's contention.

What happened on the Wisconsin frontier, however, was by no means an isolated phenomenon. Grading, and with it a new conception of curriculum, was sweeping the USA in the latter part of the nineteenth century. By the time of the National Education Association's Committee of Ten report on secondary school studies in 1893 and the Committee of Fifteen's report on elementary schools studies in 1895, the association of a distinct curriculum with various grade levels is simply taken for granted. David Hamilton has also identified the emergence of the concept of 'class' with the term 'curriculum' in a European context. ' "Class" ', Hamilton says, 'emerged not as a substitute for school, but, strictly speaking, to identify subdivisions within "schools".'[27] What Hamilton calls class and what in Wisconsin was called grading, therefore, amount to the same thing – what Dewey called 'the grouping of children in classes'. The two terms specify a cluster of pupils within the same school defined according to common expectations as to standards of achievement. Necessarily, there had to be a curriculum that embodied those common expectations.

Grading, in other words, created the structural framework for a curriculum in the modern sense to emerge. At a minimum, grading implied that there exist learning expectations above and beyond the textbooks for groups of students to master at a more or less uniform rate as A. P. was beginning to articulate in 1863. While a curriculum could still be text-dependent in a particular school, especially one with a uniform textbook policy, a curriculum independent of the textbook was necessary to guide instruction across schools and school districts, since textbooks would most likely be different in different schools in any given state. Since the creation of a curriculum is tied to the notion of school *systems*, it began, naturally enough, in urban school districts and spread only later to country schools. Even in urban centres, then, it seems likely that what we think of today as a curriculum is a phenomenon of the latter part of the nineteenth century and one directly associated with the grouping of students into grades.

Ensemble teaching or what Hamilton refers to as 'simultaneous recitation' was an equally revolutionary innovation.[28] By virtue of having several students grouped according to like characteristics as to academic achievement, it became plausible to offer the same instruction to a group of pupils. In ensemble teaching, the teacher could still rely on the textbook of course, but he or she needed to interact with a cluster of pupils – not simply with individual pupils serially. While the practice of hearing individual recitations unquestionably continued, the nature of teaching gradually began to assume a significant new dimension.

Conceiving of curriculum and teaching in new ways, in turn, required further organizational change. Neither the new concept of curriculum nor ensemble teaching makes sense without assuming regular attendance on the part of pupils over a sustained and reasonably uniform period of instruction. The new expectation was that the group stay together. For all intents and purposes, they were semi-permanent units, and their creation by state mandate in 1879 marked the beginning of the end of single-term contracts as the basis of teacher employment. Hannah Slattery's unprecedented academic-year contract in Otsego in 1880 is but one visible manifestation of that organizational change. As long as children on the Wisconsin frontier could return to school after a six- or seven-month hiatus and simply resume their recitations with the next lesson in the textbook, no concept of school year was necessary: but a pupil grouped with others needed the continuity of a school year and sustained instruction in order to progress with that group. Single-term contracts re-emerged here and there after the introduction of grading in Otsego and elsewhere, but that practice was doomed in the end.

The issue, however, goes well beyond whether teachers were given contracts for only one term or for longer periods. In district schools, the very notion of what it meant to be a teacher began to undergo transformation around 1880 in conjunction with the growing acceptance of changing conceptions of both curriculum and teaching. Longer periods of continuous service for teachers and the idea of a school year rather than a two-, three- or four-month term as the basic span of instructional time were just outward signs of that larger transformation. With the growing acceptance of the notion that curriculum design was a critical part of the pedagogical process, influential administrators and policy-makers began to appropriate that crucial responsibility for themselves. Curriculum making was being seen as an activity requiring a technical skill or perhaps a level of intelligence beyond that of the ordinary teacher, as Superintendent Speer and other administrators continually maintained. Thus, teachers were, on one hand, being asked to engage in the more difficult task of ensemble teaching, and, on the other, they were being asked to implement a curriculum dictated not strictly by a textbook but, ironically, by another external authority. This transfer of the important curriculum-making function carried with it significant implications with regard to the status of the largely female teaching force *vis-à-vis* the predominantly male administrators.

The question then arises as to why the idea of a curriculum beyond the textbook should emerge at this time. No single-factor explanation is entirely persuasive, but one thing is certain: a curriculum is a useful device for creating and maintaining bureaucratic control. The modern idea of a curriculum emerged at a time when popular education in country schools and in cities as well was burgeoning. How long could a system of popular education be managed efficiently when teachers popped helter-skelter in and out of the system, and pupils, more or less, did likewise? Furthermore, the fact that the curriculum was determined primarily by the textbooks that the children happened to bring with them to school stood in the way of centralized management.

In the interest of efficient regulation, education policy-making also had to be rescued from the vagaries of district control, then in the hands of what Wayne Fuller calls 'educators in overalls' and vested in a central authority represented by an emerging professional class.[29] This could be accomplished in part by transferring the power to certify teachers from hundreds of local town superintendents to relatively few county superintendents as was done by the Wisconsin legislature in 1861; but it was also abetted by creating such powerful new concepts as grouping (class) and curriculum. As Hamilton observes in relation to the effect of the introduction of those concepts in Europe, 'teaching and learning became, for good or ill, more open to external scrutiny and control'.[30]

Whether or not political control of schooling was indeed the motivating force behind the new grading regulation is actually of less significance than the effect. What is crucially important is that the locus of control in country schools, like urban schools before them, was in fact being shifted from independent citizens and becoming embedded in an emerging bureaucratic framework run, for the most part, by a new breed of professional educators. Once this new bureaucratic structure began to take hold, it generated its own dynamic, and with that development, far-reaching pedagogical practices consistent with the new organizational structure were reinforced and extended. It is in this sense that the grouping of pupils in a school into subdivisions called grades, forms or classes, the appearance of an expanded, more complex concept of curriculum, the practice of ensemble teaching and the introduction of a school year for pupils as well as the awarding of long-term contracts to teachers were all of one piece.

Notes

1.   John Dewey, 'The situation as regards the course of study', *Journal of the Proceedings and Addresses of the Fortieth Annual Meeting of the National Education Association* (1901), 337–8.

2.   Colyer Meriwether, *Our Colonial Currriculum*, 1607–1776 (Washington, 1907).

3.   J. L. P., 'Course of instruction for our schools: Number One', *Wisconsin Journal of Education*, 1 (March 1856), 13.

4.   J. L. P., 'Course of instruction for our schools: Number Two', *Wisconsin Journal of Education*, 1 (April 1856), 49.

5.   Wayne E. Fuller, *The Old Country School: The Story of Rural Education in the Middle West* (Chicago, 1982), 93.

6.   Robert Dudley (James Baldwin), *In My Youth* (Indianapolis: Bobbs-Merrill, 335). Quoted in Barbara Finkelstein, *Governing the Young: Teacher Behavior in Popular Primary Schools in Nineteenth-century United States* (New York, Falmer), 42.

7.   Mary D. Bradford, *Memoirs of Mary D. Bradford* (Evansville, WI, 1932), 100.

8.   *Teachers' Daily Register*, Joint District No. 2, Scott and Marcellon, n.p., Columbia County Historical Society, Pardeeville, Wisconsin.

9.   *Proceedings of School District No. 3 of the Town of Otsego, Wisconsin*, 2 September 1867, n.p.

10.   David L. Angus, Jeffrey E. Mirel and Maris A. Vinovskis, 'Historical development of age stratification in schooling', *Teachers College Record*, 90 (Winter 1988), 213.

11.   *Proceedings of School District No 3 of the Town of Scott, Wisconsin*, Columbia County Historical Society. Pardeeville, Wisconsin, *passim*.

12.   This table is reproduced from Kliebard, 'The feminization of teaching'. The asterisks next to the names of certain teachers indicate that they were residents of Otsego when hired.

13.   Lewis S. Schimmell, 'Reminiscences of a former Hereford schoolboy'. *Pennsylvania-German*, 8/2 (November 1907), 11–15. Reprinted in Finkelstein.

14.   *Proceedings*, Otsego School District No. 3, 1867–1880. n.p.

15.   A. P., 'Gradation and course of instruction for common schools', *Wisconsin Journal of Education*, 8 (December 1863), 183.

16.   A. P., 'Gradation and course of instruction for common schools', *Wisconsin Journal of Education*, 8 (January 1864), 213.

17.   A. P., 'Gradation and course of instruction for common schools', *Wisconsin Journal of Education*, 8 (June 1864), 382–3.

18.   William C. Whitford, 'The grading system for the country schools', *Wisconsin Journal of Education*, 10 (November 1880), 455–71: 10 (December 1880), 509–24.

19.   Whitford. 'The grading system', 468–9.

20.   *Proceedings*, Otsego School District No. 3, 9.

21.   Henry Clay Speer. 'A course of study for common schools'. *Programme and Proceedings of the State Teachers' Association of Kansas, and the Papers Read at the Session of the Association* (Topeka, 1878), 22–3.

22.   J. W. Holcome, 'A system of grading for country schools', in National Education Association, *Proceedings of the Department of Superintendence*, Bureau of Information Circular of Information No. 3 (1887), 138–40.

23.   H. O. Johnson, 'Discussion', in National Education Association, *Proceedings of the Department of Superintendence*, Bureau of Information Circular of Information No. 3 (1887), 145–6.

24.   H. C. Speer, 'Discussion', in National Education Association, *Proceedings of the Department of Superintendence*, Bureau of Information Circular of Information No. 3 (1887), 148.

25.   William J. Shearer, *The Grading of Schools* (New York: H. P. Smith, 1898), 31.

26.   Otsego, *School Register, passim.*

27.   David Hamilton, *Towards a Theory of Schooling* (London, 1989), 42.

28.   Ibid., 21.

29.   Fuller, *The Old Country School*, 79–112.

30.   Hamilton, *Towards a Theory of Schooling*, 49.

3

Movers and Shakers: High Politics and the Origins of the National Curriculum

Tony Taylor

> Once you put out an approved curriculum, if they have got it wrong, the situation is worse afterwards than it was before. (Margaret Thatcher, April 1990)

Prologue

During the 1970s and early 1980s, a broad consensus began to grow among politicians and education professionals in the United Kingdom that a major reform of school curriculum was both inevitable and desirable. At that time the atomistic nature of school management in the United Kingdom, where local education authorities (LEAs) managed individual 'state' schools for the Department of Education and Science (DES), had virtually allowed each school to devise its own curriculum, since there were merely two statutory constraints on the development of school-specific curricula: first, that each local authority school had to provide a daily act of collective worship; and second, that an agreed form of non-compulsory religious education be provided for all pupils. By the early 1970s, however, even these 'core' activities had, in some schools at least, begun to fall into disuse.

This mosaic of unsupervised curriculum development had been further complicated by a burgeoning school-based curriculum movement in the mid-1970s. Moreover, educational debate of the 1960s and 1970s tended to focus on subsidiary issues such as the status of comprehensive education, the success or failure of numeracy and literacy teaching, the value of mixed ability classes and the raising of the school-leaving age to 16. All of these discussions dealt with parts of the mosaic, but there was no apparent debate about the whole.

By the mid-1970s, then, with the practice of educational innovation operating in either a local, sectional (e.g. middle school) or a subject-specific context, the schools themselves appeared to be entrenched as the major arbiters of curriculum policy. Although this was a situation which left some senior figures in both major political parties uneasy, it was the right wing in

---

This chapter has been edited.

politics who were the most vociferous critics, arguing that the 'educational establishment', an informal coalition of school leaders, teacher unions, local education authorities, educational journalists and university departments of education, were allies engaged in fostering a culture of mediocrity. The famous/notorious *Black Papers*[1] raised issues of competence, consistency and ideology, a conservative pamphleteering approach which began to attract headlines in both the broadsheet and tabloid press, while the political rhetoric of curriculum debate was further polarized by a bitter conflict between the back-to-basics supporters of the *Black Papers* and supporters of the liberal–progressive–permissive camp, a struggle which caused much professional and popular disquiet.

It was in this context that a change in public and political perception occurred when that *cause célèbre*, the William Tyndale case, resulted in a much-publicized inquiry into the affairs of an Inner London Education Authority primary school. Under an allegedly permissive headmaster this Islington school, to many Conservatives at least, seemed to be out of control; but to the progressives in the debate the school's activities appeared to be a scapegoat for right-wing fantasies. The William Tyndale *débâcle*, a hardy perennial in the press headlines from 1975 until its final resolution in 1978, helped to create a new climate of popular opinion. These events must have had some influence on the Labour government of the time for it was James Callaghan, then Labour Prime Minister, who gave voice to this popular anxiety when, in October 1976, he gave his famous Ruskin College speech in which he called for a 'Great Debate' on the subject of schooling.

Callaghan's motivation for this initiative stemmed from his own conservative, working-class vision that schooling should be both rigorous and relevant.[2]

> I have always been a convinced believer in the importance of education, as throughout my life I had seen how many doors it could unlock for working-class children . . . I was also aware of growing concerns among parents about the direction some schools were taking and I was anxious to probe this.
>
> Many schools had developed experimental methods of learning . . . I raised four areas of concern with the Secretary for Education. Was he satisfied with the basic teaching of the three Rs; was the curriculum sufficiently relevant and penetrating for older children in comprehensive schools, especially the teaching of science and mathematics; how did the examination shape up as a test of achievement; and what was available for the further education of sixteen- to nineteen-year-olds?

Because of this speech, with its attendant publicity and activity, Callaghan's place as the prime mover of a centralist national curriculum movement is firmly established, a phenomenon made all the more remarkable since it came from a Labour politician and not from a Conservative leader. Traditionally, Labour had always supported the notion of a devolved 'progressive' schooling, precisely the curricular climate which Callaghan now viewed with suspicion. But if Callaghan started the debate, it was that figurehead of aggressive Toryism, Margaret Thatcher, who in 1988 turned discussion into action when she sponsored her government's

Education Reform Act, the starting point for the implementation of a highly prescriptive, highly contentious National Curriculum.

Elected to government in 1979, Thatcher had initially placed the DES under the leadership of the placid and amiable Mark Carlisle, a situation which was not to last long (1979–81) for Carlisle was replaced by Thatcher's ideological mentor and court favourite, Keith Joseph. The Joseph era at the DES (1981–6) was marked by conflict between a driven but agonized Secretary of State on the one hand and a demoralized and furious teaching profession on the other, a struggle which resulted in many battles and some educational reforms of consequence, but which left the issue of national curriculum ownership unresolved. In May 1986, following Joseph's resignation, Thatcher appointed Kenneth Baker as the new Secretary of State, the opening round in a move to gain total, centralized control of what was now referred to as the National Curriculum. This new initiative, soon to be criticized by many educationists for its doctrinaire and prescriptive approach, was based on a strategy which deliberately eschewed any form of consultation with the loathed 'educational establishment', a development which quickly gave rise to an anti-government and anti-Baker myth that the National Curriculum had been devised by a cabal of right-wing economists working to Thatcher's formula of a basic 'core' curriculum for twentieth-century helots.[3]

> There was a determined effort not to consult the DES or the civil servants or chief education officers or local politicians. Under the discreet eye of Professor Brian Griffiths . . . the outline of a radical reform was set down in bold lines from which there was no going back.

This chapter will argue, however, that Margaret Thatcher's plans, which did indeed propose a narrow, hard-right, core curriculum, were thwarted by her own Secretary of State, Kenneth Baker, who, in the face of Thatcher's hostility, pushed through his own scheme. Working with the assistance of HMI and two very able and senior DES officials, Baker eventually succeeded in creating a personal, ministerial vision of a National Curriculum. The outcome, Baker's Education Reform Act of 1988, was certainly not dominated by Thatcher's vision, nor was it the creation of a DSPU [Downing Street Policy Unit] agenda. In order to understand just how this unusual and surprising turn of events came about, this chapter will examine the views of those who were directly involved in the creation of a 'National Curriculum' and it is the published and unpublished reminiscences of these main players which form the major source for this chapter.

The Origins of the National Curriculum

Most educational analysts have nominated as a turning point in the current debate James Callaghan's Ruskin College speech of 1976, but those directly involved vary in their perceptions of the start of the recent drive for a National Curriculum. There is, however, a consensus that the term 'National Curriculum' was virtually unknown before 1985, only creeping into public awareness during the period 1986–7 with the crucial decision to legislate arriving early in 1987.

Jack Cantwell* (CEO), represents a common position among most interviewees.

> I'd come across the phrase 'An Entitled Curriculum'. I'd come across a 'Framework for Curriculum'. I certainly never came across the notion that there would be a legislated National Curriculum much before . . . '86 or '87. (Cantwell* CEO)

Arthur Best* (HMI), at that time closer to the inner workings of government, is prepared to go back much further in his search for the origins of a national curriculum and refers to the tentative activities of a former colleague whose work had allegedly been blocked by teacher unions.

> A Staff Inspector named Jack Hatter (?) in the 1960s I think or the early 1970s formed a little group to look at the curriculum – to start to think about the curriculum, and it became publicly known that that was done and there was an outcry from the teachers' associations, that this was a sinister development. (Best* HMI)

Best's* own involvement came later and quite clearly indicates that HMI took up the running in getting the DES to deal with national curriculum issues:

> I really think the first time (the idea of the national curriculum was broached) was starting with the work of the Inspectorate. It happened to me personally when we did the big national surveys of the 1970s, which, I suppose, was the first big look at secondary and primary school systems for a good number of years. There was 10 per cent sampling and immense variations emerged that couldn't be justified because of rich diversity or anything else and I think that then they (HMI) started to be certain that the idea that there be a national governmental involvement, that the voice that had been missing in a way, the legitimate, interested voice, had not been playing its part. (Best* HMI)

By the late 1970s, HMI had become increasingly anxious about lack of control over a patchwork of schools which worked to no centrally directed or monitored curriculum policy:

> The primary school curriculum, with the disappearance of 11+ selection, was unrecognizable. The secondary school curriculum was a matter of concern. The comprehensive schools – what on earth was happening (in them)? The grammar schools having come and gone (and) hardly being documented at all. The technical schools never having really got started and secondary moderns being generally regarded as a disappointment – and so the Inspectors said 'Well, what had the curriculums to be . . .'? (Best* HMI)

And Callaghan's Labour government began to move, however slowly, into the business of owning the curriculum:

> The actual move of the government into this issue is really Callaghan's Ruskin speech. By the time Prime Ministers make speeches, they are well on the way to doing what the speech is going to be about. They were moving (towards) a national voice on the curriculum and Shirley Williams produced the first Circu-

lars asking authorities, somewhat tongue-in-cheek, who was responsible for the curriculum. What came out of that exercise was that we have a system here where nobody was taking an overview. Already the shift had started and for the first part of the Thatcher regime, I think Carlisle simply picked up (that) baton, took it further but not in any radical (way). He took up the baton in the government's interest in what was actually taught. (Best* HMI)

Jack Cantwell* (CEO), not a natural ally of HMI, agrees with Best's* view:

They (HMI) had authored a broad bounds curriculum. They prepared the way for a national broad bounds curriculum. (Cantwell* CEO)

Best* clearly implies that HMI's role was changing during the early 1980s:

After Sheila Browne's period (as Senior Chief Inspector 1974–83) we were back in full inspection, a lot of inspection. Government was involved again. (Keith Joseph) began to actually read my reports, so he publicly described them as the most important change agents in the system and therefore they all ought to be published – which he pushed through. (Best* HMI)

But Joseph's administration of the DES was marked by political indecision as, on the one hand, the apostle of the free market was, in 1983, forced to accept that market forces did not necessarily apply to schools and schooling.

Keith Joseph is a very intelligent man. He had no illusions that he could simply make a case for the free open market in education – it was a limitation on the market notion. He went to the Conservative Party Conference and (said) 'I've got to tell you it won't work'. (Best* HMI)

In addition, it became apparent to HMI that, because of the unwieldy nature of the collaborative/consultative model of educational administration, coercion was needed in the form of complete legislation. But Joseph was not a legislator.

When Joseph started he was not a narrow 'core' man. (He said) the first thing we needed was a common playing field which is broad, balanced and relevant and we need to have a framework of assessment that allows us to know how we are doing (but) he would not legislate, he was not a *more* government man. He could not bring himself to legislate but by then he had been in (the DES) for four-and-three-quarter years or so, a long time. He was getting very tired. (Best* HMI)

Margaret Thatcher's patience with her senior colleague and mentor was sorely tested and by 1985 Downing Street had given up on Joseph as an initiator of change. Chris Charlton* explains:

Keith Joseph fell in 1986 partly because it became apparent to a lot of people at roughly the same time – around the Brecon and Radnor by-election (1985) which the Conservatives lost – that education was a big issue. For the first time in many years, votes were going to turn (on educational issues). People came back from the Brecon by-election for a meeting at Chequers which, coincidentally, was to talk about public expenditure and all they talked about was education. Keith Joseph got hammered by large numbers of politicians in a huge discussion about education. He didn't survive that very well. (Charlton* DES)

Joseph asked to leave the DES in 1986, taking advantage of a government reshuffle to make his exit and leaving behind a controversial legacy but having nevertheless gained a reputation as a genuinely committed (if ideologically motivated) educationalist.

> His civil servants had always had a very high opinion of him (Joseph) and I can remember when he resigned, and of course there was fair notice of that resignation, there was a party at the DES, I was told, at which many of the civil servants were in tears. They had a deep affection, particularly the people in his private office. (Watkins NCC)

The Political Background

Joseph was replaced by Kenneth Baker who, according to Thatcher, 'had won hands-down the propaganda battle against the Left in the local authorities'. Thatcher, simultaneously horrified and gratified by the activities of Labour's 'loony left' chose Baker because 'I felt I needed a first class communicator', appointing him to act as front man for her own educational crusade which she hoped to operate via her own Downing Street Policy Unit (DSPU) rather than through the DES.

It is a political commonplace that Margaret Thatcher's ideas drove Conservative policy during the 1980s and much has been made of the demise of Cabinet government during her administration, a consequence of her personalized and autocratic management style which used the DSPU as a policy formulation group, often at the expense of Whitehall.

This strategy, of cabalistic DSPU policy formulation, in this case in education, seems to have been caused by two factors. The first was Thatcher's contempt for the DES which, combined with her distrust of HMI, meant that she needed to extricate policy-making from the grasp of the civil servants. Second, if the news escaped that the Prime Minister and her private policy unit were personally driving education policy, the political consequences, with a General Election due in 1987, could be counter-productive, especially in a year (1986) which had seen Thatcher's popularity damaged by her involvement in the Westland scandal and by her allegedly slavish support for Ronald Reagan's bombing attack on Libya.

The decision to introduce educational reform, however, had to be a political decision and had to be taken at the highest level, if only because educational change is a complex issue fraught with political danger – but there was indeed much more to Thatcher's commitment to educational change than the mere need for Prime Ministerial authority. As a one-time novice Minister for Education Thatcher had, it was said, suffered at first hand the kind of obfuscation for which Whitehall was famous, an experience which left her an embittered enemy of the DES:[4]

> The DES never enjoyed much esteem in her eyes. Much later (than her term of office as Secretary of State for Education 1970–4) she did come to value a few members of the species civil servant. The high-class officials who surrounded her in Downing Street became her closest advisers, most admired associates, most

intimate colleagues, closer to her, many observers noted, than all but a handful of politicians. At the DES none entered that category.

But if the DES was to be discounted by Downing Street in the political struggle for control of the curriculum, the same could not be said of its Secretary of State, Kenneth Baker. Although agreeing with Thatcher that the educational establishment (particularly the teacher unions) should be ignored when formulating education policy, he refused to play the role of the interested observer whose job it would be to sell a Thatcher agenda:

> Baker was very active because that was what he wanted to be seen as – the mover and shaker of events, enjoying a bit of mischief, throwing things up in the air and shaking them about – but a fast mover, a man who didn't think things through as agonizingly and as long-term as Keith Joseph. (Best* HMI)

The new Minister's own analysis of his approach to education policy indicates that he felt confident and experienced in educational matters because of his previous membership of H Committee, a Cabinet Committee which had already discussed in detail several of Keith Joseph's reform proposals. Not all Thatcher's Cabinet colleagues, however, greeted Baker's appointment with approval. Chancellor Nigel Lawson, who had just finished reading Corelli Barnett's depressing condemnation of British education in *The Audit of War* was one (silent) critic:[5]

> Kenneth is a most civilized man with an agreeably sunny disposition, but not even his greatest friends would describe him as either a profoundly political thinker or a man with a mastery of detail. His instinctive answer to any problem is to throw glossy PR and large quantities of money at it and his favoured brand of politics is the instant response to the cry of the moment.

It seems quite clear, too, from Thatcher's own words, that she shared Lawson's misgivings and yet she quite deliberately appointed Baker to take charge of a Ministry where, as she knew from her own experience, grasp of detail was crucial to the success of a Secretary of State. It could be argued that the Prime Minister's appointment of Baker was a cosmetic exercise designed to disguise the real instigator of curriculum reform, Margaret Thatcher herself, but there are two points that need to be borne in mind here. First, during that period of summer 1986 through to spring 1987, Thatcher was distracted by foreign affairs and an upcoming election and, to a large extent, handed over responsibility for education initiatives to her parliamentary and official advisers on the one hand (Baker and the DES) and to her political advisers on the other (Griffiths and the DSPU). The second point to take into account is that Kenneth Baker soon proved to be no pushover:

> Baker was not prepared to let things be hijacked by the ideological right. He wanted it to be something that could last and be enduring. (Stiles* DES)

If Baker, then, had been put in place to front a Thatcher/DSPU initiative, that, as it turned out, was not how events transpired.

The Decision to Legislate

In late 1986 Baker's first task was to tidy up after Joseph's administration, the former Secretary of State having very efficiently left his successor a written list of tasks that needed completion, but this activity was in the lower realms of policy, mere 'brushfires' to use Baker's own terminology. The real policy issue of what to do about the National Curriculum was not dealt with straightaway by the new Minister, as Chris Charlton* reports. Charlton,* who was promoted shortly after Baker's appointment, noticed that the DES (including HMI) had become despondent about the future of a national curriculum:

> Keith Joseph's idea (of a consensus curriculum) survived until Baker arrived and I think initially I'd say he (Baker) accepted it but sometime during the course of that autumn (1986) leading up to the North of England Conference speech (January 1987) people began to say 'Well, that is not going to work. We will never get there. It will be the turn of the century. It will be decades.' It was partly politicians (who said that), partly civil servants. (Charlton* DES)

Thatcher quickly established a Cabinet subcommittee on Educational Reform (E(EP)) in the autumn of 1986 which was chaired by the Prime Minister and which included Lawson and Baker. This subcommittee dealt not only with the issue of how to implement curriculum reform but also examined what kinds of broader, political proposals the government needed to put forward in education. Lawson explains how the subcommittee worked:[6]

> The . . . committee proceeded in a way unlike any other on which I have served. The process would start by Margaret putting forward various ideas – in addition to the Anson (Treasury official) paper she had the Number 10 Policy Group heavily involved in the subject, and its then head Brian Griffiths, was engaged in little else at this time – and there would then be a general discussion . . . At the end of it Margaret would sum up and give Kenneth his marching orders. He would then return to the next meeting with a worked out proposal which bore little resemblance to what everyone else recalled as having been agreed . . . and owed rather more to his officials at the DES.

> After receiving a metaphorical handbagging for his pains, he would then come back with something that corresponded more closely to her ideas, but often as not without any attempt by his Department to work them out properly.

> Baker, caught in the middle, was operating under pressure from HMI and from the right wing, shall we say, to – not so much legislate, I mean that was a fairly late decision – but to do things on the curriculum, on the sort of back to basics map – 'Let's hope for pen and paper tests of a very simplistic variety and let's get them doing grammar and spelling. Let's get them doing tables. Let us get our political hands on the curriculum.' (Stiles* DES)

During that autumn of 1986, Baker, anxious to get on with curriculum reform, initially relied on his Department, particularly Eric Bolton, the Senior Chief Inspector, for advice but Thatcher, running a parallel policy game, turned to her political adviser Brian Griffiths (DSPU) for directions.

Griffiths who, according to Lawson, 'was inclined to tell her only what she wanted to hear' was the Prime Minister's gofer and details man. Baker, who in characteristically charitable fashion describes Griffiths as 'a distinguished academic . . . (who) had a particular interest in education. We (worked) very closely together over the coming years',[7] seems initially to have deferred to the DSPU's closeness to Thatcher and to Griffiths's knowledge of educational detail, but that initial co-operative approach was soon to change.

The new Education Minister's concern at that stage was a subject-based anxiety about the whole school curriculum and it was out of these autumn discussions on the nature of the new curriculum that the idea of legislating for a National Curriculum came. Its original source was HMI who had already recommended legislation, but for a broad curriculum (according to Best*). The DSPU, however, wanted a core curriculum of three subjects and no legislation, advocating a Thatcherite policy of decentralization which would allow the local authorities to handle the details, with the DES possibly using the long-established approach of administration through regulation:

> The idea of legislation was not part of the original scenario. There was a very strong push for the core curriculum and to make local authorities do it but the idea of legislation was not I think there originally . . . and we actually had to fight in Cabinet to get legislation agreed – the simple idea of legislation as opposed to content. (Stiles* DES)

Baker, doubtful that permissive legislation or even regulation would be enough, accepted HMI advice:

> His (Baker's) question was 'Will they (the LEAs) do what Keith has asked?' (about the curriculum) and the answer had to be 'No'. He decided to legislate. (Best* HMI)

The Minister then attempted to pre-empt further DSPU influence in December 1986 when he appeared on a major television programme (*Weekend World*) to push his notion of a statutory or legislated 'National Curriculum'. Even Thatcher admired his gall:[8]

> It was a gamble, but when I saw Margaret shortly afterwards she rather approved of this calculated bounce, a leaf out of her own book. 'Kenneth,' she said, 'never underestimate the effectiveness of simply just announcing something.'

Not that everybody can have been paying attention on that wintry Sunday afternoon since Charlton* dates the beginning of the new public phase as January rather than December:

> (at) the North of England Conference in early January, which . . . was at Rotherham, he hinted at a statutory curriculum. (Charlton* DES)

Baker's decision to legislate had firmed up after Christmas and he now began a determined public relations campaign to push for a bill with another speech at the Society of Education Officers conference early in 1987, probably part of a conscious attempt to block Griffiths's preferred policy. In public, Baker was apparently in harmony with his Prime Minister, but in private Baker was unequivocally hostile to the Griffiths approach, an attitude which was soon to become a focus for political and media gossip:

> Baker as an educator has to be set against Margaret Thatcher and the core curriculum. What Baker did was to in effect say 'There is a head of steam which would enable us to legislate for a national curriculum. I do not like what Brian Griffiths and his mob – and indeed the Prime Minister are proposing – it stinks – I want a much more holistic approach. I do want certain things which I, Baker, value, like a proper approach to history – kings and queens of England and English history – an intense nationalistic patriotic (view). I want poetry, I want literature, I want kids to enjoy learning English.' He was totally convinced that the curriculum should lead assessment whereas Griffiths and co. were coming up with something which was very much assessment led. (Stiles* DES)

But while Baker, the DES, HMI and the Cabinet subcommittee E(EP) were working on educational change *qua* educational change, Thatcher, exercised by a forthcoming General Election campaign, was simultaneously approaching the topic of educational reform from a purely political viewpoint. On 1 February 1987, an *ad hoc* inner Cabinet of Nigel Lawson, Norman Tebbit and Nicholas Ridley met at Chequers to discuss, with the Prime Minister, the forthcoming election and the framework of the manifesto. Thatcher, still lacking faith in Baker's grasp of detail, had relied on Griffiths to put the education package together and she placed the finished product before her Cabinet colleagues:[9]

> Education would, we all agreed, be one of the crucial areas for new proposals in the manifesto. Largely as a result of the work of Brian Griffiths, I was already clear what these should be. There must be a core curriculum . . . graded tests . . . greater financial autonomy . . . new per capita funding . . . open enrolments . . . more powers for head teachers . . . . direct grant status.

The problem that faced the Cabinet, however, was that the more Thatcher and Griffiths attempted to do in education, the clearer it became that legislation (rather than regulation) was necessary, and even an anti-collectivist like Thatcher, increasingly suspicious that the DES would not enforce the DSPU policy, was forced to move towards coercion:[10]

> The fact that since 1944 the only compulsory subject in the curriculum had been religious education (sic) reflected a healthy distrust of the state using central control of the syllabus (sic) as a means of propaganda. But that was hardly the risk now: the propaganda was coming from left-wing local authorities, teachers and pressure groups, not us.

In Cabinet, using Thatcher's reluctant support for legislation, Baker pushed for a big bill which would deal with both curriculum and political issues (such as the abolition of the Inner London Education Authority – a Tory *bête noire*):

> (The Cabinet) had decided that they would go for something in the area of local management of schools and grant maintained was beginning to be thought about – in other words there was a fuzzy edge to the legislation, that something could be worked up on 'opting out' and also giving parents choices to which local authorities area they wished to send their child. These were the components that were being talked about along with city technology colleges. It was already 'big

bill–big bang' from the outset – nobody standing against it and, I gather from Baker, that normally when he went along to Cabinet on any of these issues, the discussion was almost solely between himself and Margaret Thatcher – if you could call it discussion – and that all the rest of them sat there and coughed quietly from time to time. (Stiles* DES)

On 7 April Baker, having softened up the parents and the professionals with his public appearances earlier in the year, and having argued his way in through Cabinet, took the decision to Westminster for the first time when he broke his news to a Parliamentary Select Committee in Easter 1987:

> I'll never forget this. Parliament had pretty much gone down and the only oppor-
> tunity he'd got (to make the announcement) was a routine appearance in front of
> the Parliamentary Select Committee. So he decided to announce it (legislating
> for the national curriculum) there. He went in. I was sitting next to him. He
> started to read this out to them (chuckles). They realized. They knew exactly
> what was happening. He gave (them) probably the most important educational
> announcement. They were having the privilege of being told it first (chuckles).
> (Best* HMI)

By Easter 1987, then, the hints of the previous autumn had turned into promises, with Baker and the Conservative Manifesto promising substantial educational reform; but if Baker had won the battle to legislate, the next campaign was for the shape of the curriculum.

Defining the Curriculum

There were three contesting views in the fight for the shape of the curriculum. First, the long-standing HMI view was that a major curriculum reform should be broad based and have equal applicability to primary and secondary schools. Beyond that the DES itself, as distinct from HMI, had no special brief on the content of the curriculum for its main concerns were with the administration and finance of whatever was decided. Second, Thatcher's view, and that of her political advisers, was that there should be clearly constructed syllabuses in core areas of English, mathematics and science, syllabuses which should have a strong factual base and be rigorously tested. This narrow, functional view of the curriculum was criticized by liberal opponents because of its basis in economic expediency. Finally, Baker's view was that the curriculum should be reformed across the whole school, but on a ten-subject basis, a predominantly secondary (public) school view. He wanted all pupils to have access to all ten subjects and he wanted the assessment for all subjects to be part of a uniform evaluation procedure. Baker had already discussed this with Thatcher in June 1986 when he had put to the Prime Minister that:[11]

> We would have to be quite specific about the range and content of subjects so
> that pupils, teachers and parents would know the progress which could be ex-
> pected in schools from the ages of five to sixteen.

Baker refused to allow only three subjects to dominate the whole school curriculum, but he was also reluctant to allow the HMI view of the broad curriculum, with its suspiciously progressive ideas about child-centred teaching, problem-solving, integrated studies and skills-building. He, a traditionalist like Thatcher but with a broader view of the school curriculum, went for what he considered to be the middle way, his ten-subject curriculum.

To assist him with his deliberations Baker recruited Jenny Bacon from the Manpower Services Commission. Bacon, a tough, no-nonsense, high-level operator provided Baker with both the committee muscle and the educational background which would allow her to shore up her Minister's subject-based curriculum against what was perceived as the right-wing lunacy of the DSPU on the one hand and the wimpishly liberal HMI brief on the other. Baker who, it was quite clear, had already made up his own mind and was heading down a particular path, was then brought up short by a DES official:

> I said to Kenneth Baker 'There we are – all these things are on your manifesto. These are the things you are going to do. You're going to have great difficulty with legislation. Are you going to consult anybody before you introduce the legislation?' 'Oh,' he said, 'I never thought.' So between June and August we wrote seven (consultation documents), I think. (Charlton* DES)

And Bacon, who together with DES official Nick Stuart, was a key player during this crucial period, began to make her mark:

> HMI were telling me at the time that they had been totally ignored in this, that the consultation paper on the National Curriculum had been produced literally overnight by a senior civil servant, I think her name was Bacon . . . most people at the time knew that it was Bacon. (Moon OU)

Others began to notice a change in style in DES publications:

> You only have to read the language of HMI during the 1970s and early 1980s and then read it now and notice the change . . . It reflects the difference from 'bottom up' to 'top down'. They (HMI) must have been as taken aback as we were by a Policy Practice document . . . probably written by a Civil Servant. (Cantwell* CEO)

But if a formidable team had been established, with Bacon and Baker shaping the subject-based nature of the curriculum and Nick Stuart managing the overall shape of the Bill, there still remained battles to be fought with the DSPU, who continued to wrestle with the DES over the nature of the curriculum:

> The one (document) that took all the time and was most keenly fought over, particularly by the (Downing Street) Policy Unit was that red document (*The National Curriculum 5–16*, DES, 1987), a consultancy document which defined then very carefully what the National Curriculum was . . . In other words there was quite a battle over the nature of the ten subject National Curriculum whether it should be ten subjects. (Charlton* DES)

Best* denies that there was conflict between HMI and the Minister:

> HMI's advice really was the National Curriculum should be a broad curriculum. Of course what emerges was not what HMI would have put in place. There was the experience which we developed over a period of time in co-operation and collaboration with others and it got knocked. Now one of the things that got

about was that (we) were defeated by other advisers to the government and they went for a subject oriented National Curriculum (but) the (broad) model was never a curriculum. It's a form of planning (but of) the notion I had, that you needed to think of the whole curriculum, there was not much notice taken I think by (DES) officials. They began to move on quickly to parts and bits of the curriculum. (Best* HMI)

Chris Charlton,* while admitting that there had been a fight, denies that HMI lost:

It was a kind of draw really . . . (but) to the extent that Kenneth Baker kept his ten subject National Curriculum – he won. (Charlton* DES)

But if it was neither the Minister nor HMI who had lost the first round, it had certainly been Griffiths and Thatcher who had been defeated, trounced by a stubborn resistance:

I was pretty appalled at the kind of stuff that Brian Griffiths and the Policy Unit and Sheila Browne were putting forward . . . patent nonsense and Baker thought so too . . . he could see that he had to do something about it and it looked to be thoroughly politically driven, some of it from overseas, picking up the worst kind of fundamentalist approach from the States. It had nothing to do with any of the education research . . . it was based on prejudice . . . some of it was religious. (Stiles* DES)

The Battle for Supremacy

In the continuing struggle for command of the curriculum, Baker's position seemed quite clear. Although he had initially consulted the Prime Minister and the DSPU about how to proceed, the direction of the legislation he claimed for himself and the details he left to Jenny Bacon and Nick Stuart. For a brief but crucial period Baker's political position in 1986–7 had been particularly strong, since Thatcher, distracted by the forthcoming election and by her overseas visits, gave way, in an uncharacteristic fashion, to Baker who at that time was being touted by commentators as a potential successor to the Prime Minister:

He (Baker) wasn't a softy when he fought in Cabinet. He was the one person that shouted Margaret Thatcher down on the (curriculum). (Stiles* DES)

Griffiths, handicapped by not having direct access to either the Cabinet subcommittee or to Cabinet, was effectively sidelined over the curriculum issue at a time when Thatcher really needed detailed backing. Moreover she was faced with a Minister whose ambitions went beyond the DES, on his way to the top, but who wanted his name to go down in the annals of educational reform:

He was a man, and is a man, who, I think, is very proud to be the proponent of a big piece of legislation and, on a personal level, that's where Ministers make their name, by getting big legislation through . . . So on a rather cynical level . . . as an ambitious politician . . . here was a big piece of legislation that would go down on the record books. (Best* HMI)

He was also prepared to fight Thatcher for his beliefs:[12]

> After the Election (May 1987), I secured the approval of Number 10 and my colleagues to a consultation paper on the Curriculum which was published on 24th July. But that was not the end of the matter . . . I argued at length with Margaret and colleagues so that they would understand that if we did not have a full prescribed curriculum we would achieve very little improvement in the overall standards of education.

Despite being faced with a persistent advocacy by Baker of his ten-subject curriculum, Thatcher developed her own misgivings. Her main concern was the seeming complexity of Baker's scheme. Reluctant to blame her Minister outright and blinkered by remembrances of her own years as Education Minister, she blamed the DES:[13]

> by mid-July (1987) the papers I was receiving from the DES were proposing a national curriculum of ten subjects which would account for 80–90 per cent of school time . . . the original simplicity (sic) of the scheme had been lost and the influence of HMI and the teacher's unions was manifest (sic).

And to some extent her qualms were justified since the DES, using a new concept, came up with a structure based on three core foundation subjects and seven (mere) foundation subjects, a solution which temporarily mollified the suspicious Prime Minister but which, in the light of subsequent events, was to produce a more evenly balanced emphasis on all ten subjects than Thatcher wanted:

> It was at that time that we began to firm up upon the core curriculum Maths, English and Science and to leave Art, Music and PE as a kind of penumbra at the end . . . where they were going to be subject to attainment targets and programmes of study but in somehow a much looser and less involved way. (Charlton* DES)

The struggle intensified in July when Baker proposed setting up a Task Group on Assessment and Testing (TGAT), a suggestion which Thatcher and her advisers considered to be over-complex and suspiciously educational. She opposed TGAT:

> Baker was convinced by the TGAT approach. He saw its advantages, he saw its political advantages in selling it to the education sector and so he went in and had a fight with Maggie and Brian Griffiths and he came back very sort of long-faced and said 'I don't think I am necessarily winning.' At the same time we had (Professor) Higginson reporting on A and AS levels and Higginson wanted to go for something which was much more like the IB (International Baccalaureate) . . . carrying on through the National Curriculum approach into A levels which was very much what a lot of us wanted to see but we knew we'd had difficulty because A levels were the jewel in the crown . . . so anyway the political tradeoff was Higginson got ditched and our A levels remained the jewel in the crown, the gold standard and we got TGAT. In retrospect it may have been the wrong tradeoff. (Stiles* DES)

In front of Thatcher's eyes, the DES had played a conjuring trick. In order to meet Thatcher's demands, Stuart and Bacon had come up with a modified ten-subject curriculum which had been divided into two parts ('core foundation' and 'foundation'), but as soon as both parts were subjected to a TGAT review, the implication had to be that all subjects would have to be treated equally, an outcome which might have been obvious to the DES officials in July 1987 but which did not occur to the Prime Minister until later that year.

And it was later that year that Thatcher persisted in attempting to undermine Baker's concept. Reinvigorated after her successful General Election campaign in the summer of 1987, Thatcher tried to regain lost ground in the autumn. For Baker, the issue reached crisis point in October when the minutes of the E(EP) meeting were altered (Baker's interpretation) to drop art and music from the ten-subject curriculum, reducing the main curriculum to 70 per cent of total school time. Baker was furious at Thatcher's attempt to wrestle back the initiative:

> I took the most unusual step of challenging these minutes in a personal minute to the Prime Minister. This is almost unknown in Whitehall, and it goes to the very heart of the Cabinet system because I was challenging the accuracy of what was recorded as having been agreed. I was asked by the Prime Minister to withdraw my minute, but I refused to do so and saw her privately. I said, 'If you want me to continue as Education Secretary then we will have to stick to the curriculum . . . This was a tough meeting but I was not prepared to give in to last minute rearguard action . . . The broad-based (sic) curriculum was saved – for the time being.[14]

The struggle continued in December when Paul Black brought out his TGAT Report:

> We have this group on assessment and testing under Paul Black and basically he came up with a system which was complex, as had been shown subsequently, but he did evolve a pretty good balance between teacher assessment in school – not based on doing tests – and a supportive framework of testing which would enable you to crosscheck on what the teachers had been doing . . . I myself think that it was pretty good and intellectually satisfying . . . Needless to say Brian Griffiths thought it was abominable and that . . . Donald Naismith was meanwhile doing things down in Wandsworth (which) were supposed to be much more what we should have come up with. (Stiles* DES)

Thatcher, realizing that Baker and the DES had sidestepped her, was furious:[15]

> Ken Baker warmly welcomed the report. Whether he had read it properly I do not know: if he had it says much for his stamina. Certainly I had no opportunity to do so before agreeing to its publication . . . That it was then welcomed by the Labour Party, the National Union of Teachers and the *Times Educational Supplement* was enough to confirm for me that it was suspect. It proposed an elaborate and complex system of assessment – teacher dominated and uncosted.

Thatcher covered up her loss to Baker by rewriting history:[16]

> I minuted out my concerns to Ken Baker but by now, of course, it had been published and was already the subject of consultation

but despite the Prime Minister's attempts to cover her own tactical loss to a Minister she held in low regard and to a Department of which she was contemptuous, there is no escaping the conclusion that Baker had won. His ten-subject curriculum was saved and TGAT formed the basis of the assessment procedure for the National Curriculum, something of a pyrrhic victory as it turned out.

The bill, increasingly burdened with other Conservative agenda items such as the grant-maintained option for local authority schools who wanted to opt out, the abolition of the ILEA and the reform of higher education, was published in November, reaching its Second Reading early in December. The measure next went to a wordy and extended Committee stage in the Commons early in 1988. It then encountered some stiff opposition in the House of Lords from Lord Joseph (among others) before being proclaimed in August 1988: Kenneth Baker's GERBIL or Great Education Reform Bill had finally become law.

Conclusion: Demolishing the Myth

It is a curious coincidence that the architects of the three great education measures of the twentieth century – Balfour (1902), Butler (1944) and Baker (1988) – should all be alliteratively titled and Tories, but it is no mere accident that Kenneth Baker placed himself in that small pantheon of Conservative educationists. From the beginning, Baker was keen to acquire a reputation as a major figure in educational reform:

> Baker was a man who grew up in a hurry. I don't think he saw himself as being with the Department (DES) for (long) though at that time he saw himself as Baker the Great Education Reformer. It was going to be Balfour–Butler–Baker . . . he saw himself in those terms. My own view of him was that he was a shallow man but at the same time he was a man who genuinely cared he really did care. (Watkins NCC)

But it was precisely because Baker was so personally ambitious and at the same time so personally involved in education issues that he was able to exhibit such tenacity in the face of the Prime Minister's hostility to his schemes. Baker, like so many politicians who are heavily involved in educational reform, had a very strong private vision of the value of schooling which was partly based on his own experiences as a pupil at St Paul's, Hammersmith. With James Callaghan, whose educational background could scarcely have been more different, Baker shared a belief in the importance of structure and rigour but, unlike Margaret Thatcher, he believed that this broad approach should apply across as wide a range of school *subjects* as possible: for Baker, education transcended mere vocationalism and that is why he fought so hard.

His struggle was unusually successful. Normally, with Thatcher firmly in control of all Cabinet Committees and unassailable in Cabinet itself, Baker might have expected to give way to Prime Ministerial authority, but during the period when the details of legislation were being hammered out, an ebullient Baker was placed in the adventitious position of facing Thatcher at a low point in her political life, just when Baker had reached what eventually proved to be the zenith of his own career.

Other circumstances, too, were favourable to Baker in 1986–7. HMI, gratified that at last the DES had acquired a dynamic political chief in Baker and led by a determined Eric Bolton, had provided the official impetus for a National Curriculum and, in the world of schools at large, an apparent professional consensus created an initially sympathetic arena for debate. Finally, when the details of the bill were to be negotiated in committee, two very able DES officials in Stuart and Bacon provided precisely the kind of detailed support that Baker needed to outmanoeuvre, both tactically and strategically, the Griffiths camp.

It was in these circumstances that the Secretary of State faced a distracted Thatcher whose only inspiration turned out to be tired and jejune clichés from her own childhood on the one hand and a politically weak Brian Griffiths on the other. Her colourless DSPU adviser, excluded from Cabinet discussions, and a man who was anyway regarded with disdain even by the driest Tory ministers, was no match for a well-briefed Baker in full flood.

As for Cabinet, Thatcher's other Ministers offered her no support and by remaining outwardly neutral allowed Baker to seize the curriculum initiative. All this came, too, at a time when, National Curriculum notwithstanding, Thatcher and Griffiths were inclined to focus on what they considered to be the more urgently political aspects of educational change such as grant-maintained status and the abolition of the ILEA. In doing so, to use a sporting analogy, they took their eyes off the ball and, when they returned to the game, the other side had already scored.

Nevertheless, despite Baker's apparent victory, the popular myth that a hard-right Thatcherite clique forced through Baker's bill in an effort to gain central control of the curriculum was still current as late as October 1993. A more realistic final interpretation has got to be, as far as the National Curriculum is concerned, that Secretary of State Baker stood in the way of that right-wing cabal and, in 1988 at least, Baker won. A modified HMI curriculum, adapted by Baker with the assistance of the DES, was pushed hard by the Secretary of State in the face of Thatcher's and Griffiths's opposition and, in adopting his ten-subject model, Baker saved English schools from a naive and simplistic hard-right response to the Great Debate.

In doing so, however, Baker had created the framework for an over-complex and virtually unmanageable curriculum which, by the spring of 1993, had produced a torrent of noisy opposition from an unprecedented alliance of parent groups, school governors, LEA chief executives, teacher unions and head-teachers. In fighting Thatcher in 1986–8, Baker had created a model which eventually, after five years of confusion, recrimination and retribution, had to be changed by a reluctant Conservative government. But Baker's Act, flawed as it was, had at least temporarily rescued the schools of England from the narrow philistinism of DSPU, a vision which saw pupils as mere economic units in an educational marketplace.

Epilogue

But if Thatcher and Griffiths had lost the struggle over the shape of the curriculum in 1988, there were still battles to be fought, first over subject content and second over assessment:

> Sheila Browne, Griffiths and 'that lot' felt that they had lost on the 1988 legislation. It did not concentrate on the things that they wanted. The curriculum was far too broad . . . TGAT was not wanted . . . the 'right-wing' camp, if you like, were trying to recover ground and as soon as they saw the chinks opening up, they went in . . . that was their instrument for grabbing back the National Curriculum in the way that Brian Griffiths and others had originally intended. (Stiles* DES)

But that, as they say, is another story.

Notes

The author interviewed a range of individuals who were either closely associated with the origins of the Education Reform Act or who were prominent commentators. Several of these subjects preferred to remain anonymous because of the terms of their employment and so have been accorded pseudonyms (indicated thus*) by the author. Interviewees quoted and referred to include:

Arthur Best* – former senior HMI.
Jack Cantwell* – Chief Executive Officer of a major LEA and former academic.
Chris Charlton* – former senior official at the DES.
Professor Bob Moon – Open University (OU).
Robin Stiles* – former senior official at the DES.
Peter Watkins – former Deputy Chief Executive, National Curriculum Council (NCC).
Kenneth Baker and Lord Joseph were approached by the author but both declined to be interviewed. Kenneth Baker said he was too busy and Lord Joseph was recovering from an illness.

I should like to thank the Australian Research Council for sponsoring this research project and Monash University for allowing me fieldwork leave to conduct interviews.

1. *The Black Papers*, a series of radical conservative political booklets edited by C. B. Cox and A. E. Dyson first appeared in March 1969.
2. J. Callagan, *Time and Chance* (London, 1987) 409.
3. Stuart Maclure, *Education Reformed* (London, 1992 edn), 178–9.
4. Hugo Young, *One of Us* (London, 1989), 73.
5. Nigel Lawson, *The View from No. 11* (London, 1993), 606.
6. Lawson, *The View*, 609–10.
7. Kenneth Baker, *The Turbulent Years* (London, 1993), 169.
8. Baker, *Turbulent Years*, 191–2.
9. Margaret Thatcher, *The Downing Street Years* (London, 1993), 570.
10. Thatcher, *Downing Street*, 590–1.
11. Baker, *Turbulent Years*, 190.
12. Baker, *Turbulent Years*, 196.
13. Thatcher, *Downing Street*, 594.
14. Baker, *Turbulent Years*, 196–7.
15. Thatcher, *Downing Street*, 595.
16. Thatcher, *Downing Street*, 595.

4

Technical Education and State Formation in Nineteenth-Century England and France

Andy Green

Introduction

Modern economists generally see human skills as *the* key factor in economic competitiveness.[1] Vocational education has consequently been a high priority for policy makers, particularly in Britain where provision is seen to lag behind that of other competitor nations.[2] This situation has given rise to intense public debate about the causes of underachievement amongst young people in post-compulsory education and training. Current discussions focus on the narrow and over-specialized nature of academic study, the relative unpopularity and low status of alternative vocational tracks, and on the fragmented and incoherent nature of the post-compulsory system as a whole.[3] In addition to multiple institutional distinctions in the sector, and the fragmented and dispersed nature of control over these institutions and over the qualifications system, there is a deep and damaging divide between 'academic' and 'vocational' learning. This is often believed to impede access and achievement amongst students and to perpetuate the low status of the vocational routes which the government wishes to enhance.[4]

Although the current intensity of the debate over these issues is unparalleled in this century, there were similar debates in the nineteenth century. This was particularly the case during the period from 1870 when, as now, the country was undergoing an economic recession and also experiencing the first bitter taste of the relative economic decline which has dominated subsequent British history.[5] Contemporary policy making has much to learn from revisiting these historic debates to understand better the nature of this problem and the specific national causes which underlie it. A comparative analysis of the development of technical education in France and England can assist this process.

This chapter has been edited.

The Underdevelopment of Scientific and Technical Education in Nineteenth-Century England

With the exception of pure science, which developed largely independently of formal educational institutions, England was, throughout the nineteenth century, notably backward in most areas of scientific and technical education by comparison with other major states in northern Europe. This judgement, shared by many late nineteenth-century commentators and the vast majority of subsequent economic and educational historians, applied not only to the state of science teaching, or the lack of it, in schools and universities, but also to post-school vocational education, whether in institutes, colleges or universities.[6]

For working-class boys and girls, elementary education was too sparse and narrow to provide a proper foundation for technical and scientific study and facilities for full-time post-elementary education were largely absent. State organized trade schools for artisans and skilled workers, which were common in continental Europe, had not developed in England where received opinion regarded the workshop as the only fit place for learning a trade.[7] There was also a virtual absence of those intermediate vocational schools, like the *Écoles des Arts et Métiers* and the *Écoles Primaires Supérieurs* in France, which trained students from the upper ranks of the working class and from the lower rungs of the middle class for supervisory and lower managerial positions in commerce and industry. Whilst in France and Prussia there was a plethora of such institutions by the 1840s, England had to wait until the 1880s for the development of the higher grade schools, and the first technical colleges, which would perform a similar function.[8]

Provision for the middle class was equally deficient in this area. Public and grammar schools remained frozen in the classical mould, and, until the last quarter of the century at least, universities contributed virtually nothing towards scientific and technical needs.[9] Engineering did not become an examination subject in Cambridge until 1894 and Oxford had no Chair in Engineering until 1908.[10] This again was in striking contrast to major continental states where not only was secondary and university education somewhat more scientific,[11] but where also a layer of higher technological institutions has emerged in the form of the *Polytechnique*, the French *Grandes Écoles* and the German *Technische Hochschule* (technical high school). Equivalent polytechnics and civic universities did not begin to emerge in England until the 1880s and then remained chronically underfunded until the beginning of the next century.[12] By 1910 Germany had 25,000 university students of science and technology compared with some 3000 in England.[13]

Until the last quarter of the nineteenth century England had thus not even begun to develop a system of full-time state technical schools, at either elementary, intermediate or higher levels, such as existed in many continental states and this was the true measure of its backwardness in vocational education. What it had instead was an apprenticeship system which was the sole means of training for most trades and for many of the new professions, and a profusion of adult evening classes, first in the form of the popular Mechanics Institutes and later supplemented by the classes funded by the Department of Science and Art. However, the apprentice-ship was often of dubious efficacy and rarely sought to train beyond the level of basic practical skills and the evening class provision was geograph-ically uneven and often ineffective as training; hampered as it was by the lack of prior learning amongst students and the often desultory and un-systematic nature of the teaching.[14]

During the first half of the century, whilst Britain was still basking in the sunshine of its first successful industrial revolution and its still unchallenged economic supremacy, this state of affairs caused relatively little alarm. However, from the mid-century onwards it was increasingly apparent that continental countries were fast developing economically and this raised con-siderable concern about the state of Britain's education and training. This was fuelled by the reports of German and French technical achievements displayed at the various international Exhibitions and by the writings of educational lobbyists, such as Playfair, Huxley, Samuelson, Arnold, Thompson and Russell, who came back from their investigative travels on the Continent with dire warnings about the superiority of continental educa-tion and training and the dangers this posed for Britain's economic position.

These writers offered substantially different accounts of the problems inherent in English education and training. Some, like Huxley and Playfair, were strong supporters of workshop training and somewhat suspicious of the theoretical nature of continental trade schools;[15] others, like Sylvanus Thompson, the first Principal of Finsbury technical college, and John Scott Russell,[16] civil engineer and fellow of the Royal Society of London, were keen to adopt the school-based training model. However, they were unani-mously agreed on two points: that English technical training was deficient and that this was endangering the economic health of the country. As Thompson put it in his book, *Apprentice Schools in France* (1879):

> The lack of technical education is costing us dearly – has cost us terribly dear – in spite of the oft-repeated warnings of those who saw the efforts which continental nations were making to surpass us, as they could only surpass a nation possessing vast natural advantages, by organizing the technical education of their artisans, and by giving to the sons of the wealthier commercial classes and employers of labour that sound scientific training which alone would qualify them to use to the highest advantage the technical training given to the artisans.[17]

These warnings about the deficiencies in English technical education began with individual lobbyists and their beliefs were certainly not shared by all commentators or indeed, as far as we can tell, the majority of manufacturers at the time. However, in time they gained increasing credibility, reinforced by the verdict of successive Royal Commissions which noted the backward-ness not only of technical training but of English education in general. The Schools Inquiry Commission reported in graphic terms to this effect in 1868:

... our evidence appears to show that our industrial classes have not even the basis of sound general education on which alone technical education can rest ... In fact our deficiency is not merely in technical education, but ... in general intelligence, and unless we remedy this want we shall gradually but surely find that our undeniable superiority in wealth and perhaps in energy will not save us from decline.[18]

The Royal Commission on Technical Instruction (1884), chaired by Bernhardt Samuelson, later reinforced the judgement about England's comparative disadvantage with a wealth of data on continental schooling. It found that the 'dense ignorance so common among English workmen' was unknown in Germany[19] and that the advance of continental manufactures could not have been achieved had it not been:

... for the system of high technical instruction in their schools, for the facilities for carrying on original scientific investigation, and for the general appreciation of the value of that instruction and of original research, which is felt in these countries.[20]

Explanations of English Underdevelopment

The most popular explanation of English backwardness in scientific and technical education is the so-called 'cultural critique' which focuses on the supposedly anti-industrial and anti-utilitarian culture of the Victorian political élite and the landed class from which they mostly came. Versions of this thesis have emerged both from the right and the left and can be found in the works of a series of eminent historians and social commentators – most notably: G. C. Allen, Perry Anderson, Correlli Barnett, Anthony Sampson, Martin Wiener and, most recently, Michael Sanderson.[21] The argument, broadly summarized, is that Britain, the first successful industrialized nation, never experienced a full bourgeois revolution and thus never fully displaced the landowner class from its dominant political and ideological position. The culture of the landed class, and of the old professions and sections of the bourgeoisie who became assimilated to it, was predominantly rural and conservative, suspicious and sometimes contemptuous of industry and commerce, and disinterested in science and technology and anything that smacked of base utilitarianism. Since this class continued to dominate the British establishment it fostered a style of political leadership which was more amateur than expert and policies which were hostile to modernization and economic development. The dominance of this 'anti-industrial' culture is said to have determined the resistance of the Anglican-controlled universities and secondary schools towards science and technology and the failure of governments to modernize the educational system.

The problem with the argument is that whilst these traits were predominant amongst the landed classes, and some of the older professional groups allied to them, they by no means constituted the dominant or hegemonic

ideology of Victorian England.[22] Certainly there were aspects of the traditional landed ideology that remained distinctly influential in some areas,
particularly in the Anglican Church, in the rural areas and in certain
branches of the state, like the Army, the Home Office and the Foreign
Office. There was also a powerful current of thought amongst sections of
the intelligentsia which was overtly antagonistic to the dominant bourgeois
ethos of the time. The romantic conservative tradition, which extended
down from Coleridge to Carlyle, Ruskin and even Dickens in his later
years, was deeply opposed to the narrow materialism and harsh self-
interest of the liberal creed and at times appeared both unsympathetic to
the urban world and hostile to industrialism itself. As both Wiener and
Anderson rightly insist, these influences, combined with the lure of the
gentlemanly, pastoral lifestyle, proved uniquely attractive to sections of the
bourgeoisie and the old professional class.

However, the wide resonance and compelling attraction of this view of the
world owed precisely to the very dominance of liberal and materialist values
in this the most urbanized and industrial country in the world. It was an
inevitable reaction and had important consequences, particularly in the later
period, but it hardly dislodged the mainstream bourgeois values from their
hegemonic position. The overwhelmingly dominant values of the Victorian
era were those of individualism, enterprise and *laissez-faire* liberalism, at
once both tempered and sharpened by religion, Whatever their antecedents,
these were nothing now if not the values of a confident and predominantly
bourgeois capitalism, and the heart of the metropolitan culture which held
sway in the politics of the industrial cities. The Liberal governments of the
middle decades of the century may have been dominated by landowners, but
many of these had been won over to the values of the middle classes and
where it mattered most succumbed to their wishes. For the most part, as
Marx well observed, the 'aristocratic state' served as representative of the
bourgeois interest.[23] This bourgeois interest, though perhaps dominated
more by finance and commerce than manufacture, was nevertheless, as
Rubinstein has recently argued, triumphantly pro-business.[24]

Thus whilst it is certainly true that the anti-modern attitudes of the old
élites still fashioned the character of the Anglican public schools and the
grammar schools, and contributed towards their characteristic elevation of
character over intellect and classics over science, it can hardly be said that
the wholesale failure of the state to create other, more modern, institutions
derived from this cause. After all, the old landed classes still maintained
immense influence in most continental states during the nineteenth century, as Arno Mayer has demonstrated, but this did not prevent the
development of technical education.[25] The remnants of the *ancien régime*
in France, the *Junkers* and old bureaucracy in Germany, and the landowners and *Samurai* in Japan, all retained residual cultural traces of the old
conservative values and were sometimes overtly hostile to modernization.
All over Europe, the traditional humanist education, dominated by the
study of classics, continued to retain the high status it had enjoyed since

Aristotle first designated it as the only civilized education proper for the leisured classes, and it continued to be defined in opposition to utilitarian learning.[26] The German concept of *Bildung*, as defined by Von Humboldt, and the French concept of *culture générale*, as lauded by the likes of Victor Cousin, no less than Cardinal Newman's notion of learning for its own sake, were all anti-utilitarian and were used by the educational establishment in secondary schools and universities in all countries to resist the encroachments of professional or vocational education.[27] Where England differed from France and Germany was in the failure of the rising middle classes to secure reforms to these recalcitrant institutions or to ensure the development of alternative institutions. On the continent, and in *Meiji* Restoration Japan, these reforms were generally achieved through the action of a modernizing state. In England decisive state action was slower to occur, thus prolonging the retarding influence on education of the old cultural conservatism.

The underlying causes of the peculiarly delayed development of scientific and technical education in England should be sought, therefore, not so much in the culture of the old establishment but rather in the responses of the new industrial and bourgeois classes to it. The most striking aspect of this whole story is the failure of the bourgeoisie to secure adequate reforms in technical education despite the fact that they were clearly in favour of industrial development and in other respects quite capable of fighting for and winning those conditions which would secure it. The paradoxical fact is that the majority of this pioneer class was neither generally aware of the singular importance of scientific and technical education to economic advance nor willing, when they became aware of it, to argue for the state to take the necessary remedies. Underlying this were two historical causes, which more than anything else constituted the peculiarities of the English situation: the first of these was the fact and consequences of having the first Industrial Revolution and the second was the nature of the liberal state and the individualist creed that underpinned it.[28]

In continental Europe industrialization occurred under the tutelage of the state and began its accelerated development later when techniques were already becoming more scientific; technical and scientific education had been vigorously promoted from the centre as an essential adjunct of economic growth and one that was recognized to be indispensable for countries which wished to close on Britain's industrial lead. By contrast, Britain's early industrialization had occurred without direct state intervention and developed successfully, at least in its early stages, within a *laissez-faire* framework. This meretricious industrial start had two consequences for technical education. First, state intervention was thought unnecessary for developing technical skills, where the initial requirements were slight and adequately met by traditional means. The customary empirical approach of the apprenticeship seemed adequate and eminently practical. In fact, Political Economy suggested that state intervention might be positively injurious. Not only would it offend against liberal principles and

create an unwanted additional tax burden, but it would interfere in the
market, undermine the manufacturers' own training provision and endanger trade secrets. Second, the very success of Britain's early industrial
expansion encouraged a complacency about the importance of scientific
skills and theoretical knowledge which became a liability in a later period
when empirical knowledge, inventiveness and rule-of-thumb methods were
no longer adequate.

The first cause of England's failure to develop scientific and technical
education was thus a deeply entrenched complacency which derived from
its uniquely fortunate position. As John Scott Russell put it in 1869:

> We have been enjoying the fruits of the inventions of a few men of genius who
> had created the whole system of modern manufacturing industry, and providence
> had also endowed [us] with the accumulated wealth of countless centuries shored
> up in the bowels of the earth in the shape of iron and coal.[29]

Such complacent confidence lasted well into mid-century and goes some
way to explaining the lack of urgency felt in matters of technical education
until this time. However, there was also another cause for inaction which
outlasted the first for a further twenty years and this was the resistance to
state involvement in education of any sort, whether elementary, secondary
or technical.

The doctrine of *laissez-faire* and the minimal state, as first advocated by
Adam Smith in the eighteenth century, became the fundamental tenet of
nineteenth-century liberalism, permeating the culture and values not only
of Dissent and the middle class but of all sections of society. When applied
to education it provided powerful arguments against state involvement and
led to the failure of countless reform initiatives during the first half of the
century.[30] Although various liberal ideologists, such as Jeremy Bentham
and John Stuart Mill, recognized that there must be exceptions to the rule
of non-intervention, and particularly in the case of public goods like education, the predominant view of Political Economy during the first sixty years
of the nineteenth century was that the state should let alone wherever
possible, including in the field of education. State education was frequently
condemned as a 'Prussian' heresy – as alien to the English national character and tradition.[31] As well as costing the taxpayers money, it was often
claimed to be prejudicial to voluntary effort, detrimental to the family and
enfeebling for the individual. Above all it was considered to be fundamentally illiberal and conducive towards state tyranny over the minds of individuals. Despite the small encroachments made by the state into education
since the 1830s, this view was still widely held in the 1850s, as evidenced by
the considerable popularity of Herbert Spencer's *State Education Self Defeating* and Samuel Smiles's *Self Help*, both of which eulogized the individualist creed and berated state involvement in education.[32]

When, in the decades following the Franco-Prussian war, *laissez-faire*
ideas came to be increasingly questioned, and state intervention seen more
favourably, there emerged a body of opinion which was frankly sceptical of
voluntarism in education. By the 1870s both John Stuart Mill and Matthew

Arnold had acknowledged that opposition to state intervention was a major cause of English educational backwardness. Although he saw good cause for not allowing the state a monopoly of education, Mill recognized in his later years that 'jealousy of government interference' and opposition to 'centralization' could be a mere prejudice and one to which the middle class was particularly prone.[33] Matthew Arnold, like his father a long-time advocate of state intervention, roundly condemned the English middle class for their opposition to state secondary education which he believed to be the only way to achieve schools for the middle class comparable in excellence to the *lycées* of France and the German *Gymnasien*. Writing on *Higher Schools and Universities in Germany* in 1892, he quite accurately linked this opposition to state action to the characteristic British hostility to expertise and science:

> . . . our dislike of authority and our disbelief in science have combined to make us leave our school system . . . to take care of itself as best it could. Under such auspices, our school system has very naturally fallen into confusion; it has done nothing to counteract the indisposition to science which is our great intellectual fault.[34]

From a later vantage point Michael Sadler, who was certainly no supporter of unfettered state control, summed up the particular problem of English educational development by a series of contrasts with Germany:

> The crucial difference between the history of German education and that of English during the nineteenth century lay in the different use which the two countries made of the power of the state. In Germany that power was exercised unflinchingly, with great foresight and clearness of purpose and without any serious resistance from public opinion. In England it was used reluctantly, with deliberate rejection of any comprehensive plan of national reorganization and in the teeth of opposition which had to be conciliated at every turn. As a result, Germany has constructed an educational system which works with fairly simple machinery: England has a complicated machinery, but no well-defined system of national education.[35]

By the 1900s even the Board of Education could acknowledge, in retrospect, that voluntarism had failed, arguing, in its 1905/6 Report, that reforms had been held up by 'the formidable inertia of the nation reinforced by intense jealousy of state interference and dislike of public control'.[36]

English technical education, like elementary and secondary schooling, was a major casualty of voluntarism and *laissez-faire*, and by the 1870s there were increasing numbers who were prepared to acknowledge this. Few of its advocates were as sanguine about state intervention as Arnold in respect of secondary schools, and indeed it would not have been politic to be so given the importance of the industrial lobby in the cause. However, there were some, such as J. Scott Russell, whose analysis of the problems in technical education closely mirrored those of Arnold and Sadler. Russell identified the same popular impediment to reform as Arnold:

> . . . we dislike System, organization, and methodical control . . . We despise the paternal governments of foreign nations, and spurn interference, control or direction from the executive for our own government.[37]

The result of this aversion to systematic organization in English education, Russell argued, was all pervasive, affecting every branch of the system, including technical education. Most specifically, it had prevented the development of an organized system of full-time technical institutions, such as had developed in many continental states since early in the century.

The Development of French Technical Education

We can see more clearly the particularities of English technical educational development by comparing it with France. In France the development of vocational schools predated both the Revolution and industrialization by over a century. Technical education developed under the tutelage of the absolutist state from the time of Louis XIV onwards. It was an important part of the process of early state formation underscored by the mercantilist doctrines which argued for the enhancement of national wealth and prestige through the exercise of state power. The *ancien régime* established schools of art and design and also a number of higher vocational schools such as the *École des Ponts et Chaussees* (1747), the *École du Corps Royale du Génie* (1749), the *École Royale Militaire* (1753), the *École de Marine* (1773), and the *École des Mines* (1783). The Revolution which, as de Tocqueville argued,[38] perpetuated many of the centralizing tendencies of the *ancien régime*, destroyed many of the religious schools, but had positive results for vocational schooling. The Thermidorean regime set up the *Écoles Centrales*, which were arguably the pioneers of a modern model of secondary schooling; the Directory (1795–9) created the *École Polytechnique*, soon to become the foremost science faculty in Europe, and numerous *Écoles d'application.* The latter provided training for a diverse range of occupations including sailors, agriculturists, pharmacists, veterinarians, and midwives.[39]

After the Revolution, the centralized, *étatist* policies first promulgated by the absolutist monarchs, and later consolidated by the revolutionary regimes, continued to support the development of technical education. Napoleon, although the architect of the *Université*, the heart of the burgeoning French national education system, was notably conservative in his beliefs on education, abandoning the revolutionary principles of the *Écoles centrales* for a quasi-meritocratic but still traditionalist classicism in the new state *lycées* which he founded.[40] More concerned with the creation of loyal and disciplined officers and expert public administrators than with the needs of industry and commerce, he gave little attention to technical education for civil occupations. However, he did give his support to the *École des Arts et Métiers*, which had originally been founded by the Duc de la Rochefoucauld on his estate at Liancourt for training war orphans in skilled trades. He also had two similar institutions set up at Chalons (1806) and Angers (1811) and, according to Frederick Artz, the Chalons school quickly gained the reputation for being the best elementary trade school in Europe.[41] Later in the century these schools, which combined practical training with theoretical instruction in applied science, became a key source of engineering skills. Their graduates, known as *Gadzarts*, often came to occupy key positions as managers and production engineers in small and medium-sized companies concerned with the design, construction, installation and maintenance of heavy machinery and power plants.[42]

After the ravages of the Napoleonic Wars France was far behind England in the development of industry and manufacturing. However, the Restoration brought a revival of economic activity which increased the demand for skills which would no longer be available from Britain which had banned the emigration of artisans to France. Initially, the Bourbon regime did little to promote technical education and the *Université* remained wedded to the ideas of classical education. However, there was increasing pressure from industrial and business leaders to provide more technical education and this received growing support from Liberals, such as the economist J. B. Say, and from technologically minded Saint-Simonians; the desire to see France catch up with English industrial development gave impetus to this movement. During the 1820s the main initiatives came from private individuals with encouragement from the state. In 1820 a group of Parisian capitalists, including Laffite, Casimir and Périer, set up the *École Supérieure de Commerce de Paris*. Initially encouraged by government officials such as Chaptal, this finally received government funding in 1839. Likewise the *École Centrale des Arts et Manufactures* was originally founded in 1829 by a group of private individuals including the Saint-Simonian Eugéne Péclet and scientists Olivier, Binet and Lavallée. The school was designed to train civil engineers for the private sector, originally recruiting from amongst unsuccessful but able candidates for the *École Polytechnique.* With a supremely talented scientific faculty the school was dedicated to promoting the new field of applied science *(la science industrielle)* as a holistic discipline. Its motto – 'industrial science is one, and every *industrielle* must know it in its totality or suffer the penalty of remaining inferior to this task' – well symbolized its novel and demanding aspiration to unite the theory of pure science and the practice of engineering and in so doing helped reinforce the high status already acquired by the engineering profession through its association with the state and public works.[43] In time it became one of the chief sources for highly trained civil engineers in France, becoming a state institution in 1857.

During the July Monarchy the state played a more active role in promoting vocational and technical education. The 1833 *Loi Guizot* did much to improve primary education and also required the creation in every commune of over 6000 people of an *École Primaire Supérieure*. These taught a modern curriculum with some commercial subjects. Whilst seen as inferior to the *collèges* by many, they grew in strength to 352 by 1841.[44] Although out of favour during the Second Empire they were revived during the Third Republic. By 1887 there were 700 of these institutions (about two hundred of which were for girls) providing children from petit-bourgeois families with a vocationally orientated education to fit them for work as small manufacturers, artisans and white-collar employees.[45] During the July Monarchy the state, both local and central, also created a wide range of elementary vocational schools. By the mid-century there were some 50 trade schools, 35 agricultural schools as well as numerous naval, mining and design schools.[46] Although some of these were private establishments the majority existed by virtue of state support.

The Second Empire took relatively few initiatives in vocational education but substantial progress did occur in the development of a more modern secondary education. Louis Napoleon instructed his minister Fortoul to create a modern scientific stream in the *collèges* but his bifurcation policy was fiercely resisted by the *Université* and the scheme was finally scrapped by Duruy. However, there was clearly a strong demand for a more modern secondary curriculum and local initiative saw to it that this was at least partly met. A survey by Gustav Rouland found that a sixth of all *lycéens* and 50% of those in municipal *collèges* were already involved in vocational courses during the 1850s.[47] In 1865 Victor Duruy's law on *l'enseignement secondaire spéciale* was finally successful in creating a viable modern programme in the *collèges*. This scheme flourished and in 1880 its status as a full secondary course was acknowledged by the creation of a *baccalauréat* for special education. By this time some 33% of children were following the special modern programmes which involved systematic science education.[48]

The Third Republic was most noted for its achievement in primary and secondary education, but there were also important new initiatives in vocational and technical education. Jules Ferry battled successfully against the traditionalists in the *Université* to create a new range of applied science faculties which could recruit students from the technical schools. Although their degrees did not at first have parity with the state diplomas, the faculties were popular and developed good links with industry. There were also important developments at the lower levels of technical education. During this period a strong lobby for technical education grew up around the Ministry of Industry and Commerce's *Conseil Supérieur de l'Enseignement Technique* and a tussle ensued between this ministry and the Ministry of Public Instruction for control over vocational education. The two ministries between them created a new network of vocational schools. From the 1880s onwards they instigated numerous *Écoles Manuelles d'Apprentissage* which later became known as *Écoles Pratiques de Commerce et l'Industrie*. These recruited the sons and daughters of workers and petit-bourgeois families from primary schools and trained them to be skilled workers and office employees. By 1913 there were some 14,766 students in such schools, one quarter of whom were girls.[49] The Government also set up four regional boarding schools, known as *Écoles Nationales Professionnelles*, for the training of foremen and supervisors as well as reviving the higher primary schools. Day estimates that these, together with the intermediate technical schools, were by 1914 enrolling at least 150,000 students.

Despite opposition from the *Université* and some of the old élites, the French state, in collaboration with progressive private individuals, had created a system of technical education probably only rivalled in Europe by that in Germany.[50]

The Development of Technical Education in England

In contrast with the state-led development of technical education in France. England relied for the greater part of the century on individual private initiative for the development of its skills training. [. . .] For the greater part of the nineteenth century English training was based on the apprenticeship and this remained the paradigmatic form of all future technical education. Privately organized by employers and independent craftsmen, the apprenticeship system received no public funds and embodied a characteristically practical approach based on on-the-job experience rather than theoretical study. The same principle was adopted in training for professional engineering. Whilst vocational education for doctors and lawyers was widespread, particularly with the numerous medical schools, a scientific and technical education for engineers and manufacturers was hard to find, reflecting the bias against science and the new professions in much middle-class education. This contrasted strongly with the typical practice in continental states. The 1968 Report of the Institute of civil engineers noted:

> The education of foreign engineers is strongly contrasted with that in England in every particular. Practical training by apprenticeship is unknown; the education begins at the other end, namely, by the acquirement of a high degree of theoretical knowledge, under the direction, and generally at the expense of government.[51]

Where government intervention later supplemented this system it was in an ancillary role that left its fundamental features intact. State-assisted technical education was predominantly part time, practically orientated and in administration largely marginalized from mainstream educational provision. When anxieties about the superiority of French design in silk manufactures prompted the government to create a school of design and later to fund other such schools in industrial areas (of which there were seventeen by 1852), the council which administered them was characteristically located within the Board of Trade, insulated from contact with educational administration. The schools were bedevilled by bureaucratic and factional conflicts and represented a very inauspicious beginning for state intervention in technical education. They were intended as a stimulus to technical education, but never as an alternative form to the apprenticeship.[52]

By the 1850s the limitations of this approach were becoming increasingly evident. Industrial development was entering into a new phase which made different demands on education. As Eric Hobsbawm has written:

The major technical advances of the second half of the 19th century were essentially scientific, that is to say they required at the very least some knowledge of recent development in pure science for original invention, a far more consistent process of scientific experiment and testing for their development and an increasingly close and continuous link between industrialists, technologists, professional scientists and scientific institutions.[53]

What was absent in England was precisely this link between pure science and its application, such as had been pioneered in the *École Centrale* and the *Écoles des Arts et Métiers*. In short, technical education. The limitations of this were becoming increasingly obvious with the development of new technologies – the electric telegraph, the synthesis of aniline dyes, artificial fertilizers, and so on – which were highly dependent on scientific knowledge, particularly on chemistry, and in which Britain was at some disadvantage.

[. . .]

Thus by mid-century there was increasing anxiety about the state of technical education. The Great Exhibition of 1851 had alerted more far-sighted observers to the potential industrial challenge from the Continent. Lyon Playfair, a leading chemist and champion of scientific education, returned from a tour of the Continent to warn of the superiority of their technical schools. In a much publicized lecture entitled *Industrial Instruction on the Continent* (1852), he argued that as improved transport lessened the competitive advantage to be gained from an abundance of raw materials, so science and technical skills would become increasingly important. However, it was in this area of technology that:

> . . . we English are weak. Philosophy we have in abundance. Manual skills we possess abundantly. But we have failed to bridge the interval between the two. On the contrary, there is a dead wall separating our men of theory from our men of practice.[54]

Changing economic circumstances and the agitation of men such as Playfair and Henry Cole, the recently appointed Secretary of the School of Design, prompted government intervention and in 1853 the Department of Science and Art was created under the Board of Trade. The aim was to create a more effective central body to stimulate and co-ordinate efforts in technical education, including existing schools and sundry public institutions such as the Government School of Mines and the Division of Practical Geology. However, the system it supported would remain 'local and voluntary . . . [and] in the main self-supporting'.[55] The department had mixed fortunes. Under Cole's energetic supervision the existing design schools were revived and by 1858 there were 56 flourishing schools of art with 35,000 students.[56] The science division was less successful, initially; most of the new science schools failed and by 1859 only 450 students attended courses. Aid to science classes from the department between 1853 and 1859 amounted to a mere £898. However, in the following decade, with Henry Cole as sole secretary of the department and Captain Donelly as Inspector of Science, a more energetic regime evolved and pupils in Science Schools and evening classes increased to 10,230.[57] Payment by results was instituted throughout the schools and classes receiving funds, and outside examiners were brought in to assess the school results.

However, this limited government action still left scientific and technical education in an inadequate state. The department's schools, like the Mechanics Institute classes, with which they partially merged, were part time, and their effectiveness was undermined by the paucity of elementary education amongst their students and the desultory nature of the classes. Michael Sadler's later reflection on this tradition of evening schools was characteristically perceptive:

> Thus alike in their excellence and their effects, the evening classes have borne the characteristic features of the English educational organization. Free in their development, vigorous in some of their achievements, and often well-adapted to the requirements of the persevering and strong, they were unsystematic in arrangement, weakened by deficits in the early training of their pupils, and from a national point of view, insufficiently adjusted to the needs of the rank and file.[58]

Criticism of existing provision continued and intensified, as burgeoning economic realities kept this issue alive in public debate. The Paris Exhibition of 1867 had a chastening effect since the failings of Britain's industrial performance were now evident. In all of the ninety classes of manufacturers, Britain was pre-eminent in only ten. Lyon Playfair, who was one of the jurors, reported back on the exhibition with some foreboding and, in a much quoted open letter to Lord Taunton, warned that Britain was losing its industrial lead owing to the fact that continental countries 'possess good systems of industrial education and that England possesses none'.[59]

Growing anxiety about the scientific ignorance of foremen, industrial managers and proprietors and the deleterious effects of this on the economy prompted a series of public enquiries into the state of technical education. In the year following the Exhibition, the Select Committee on Scientific Instruction reported; this was followed by eight reports from the Devonshire Royal Commission on Scientific Instruction and the Advancement of Science (1872–5) and then in 1884 with reports from the Samuelson Royal Commission on Technical Instruction. Each report praised the achievement of continental education and noted the industrial advances that could not have occurred without it. While all reports defended the notion of workshop training, they each found many defects in English provision.

[. . .]

As to the apprenticeship system, opinions expressed in the reports varied. The Samuelson Report acknowledged the benefits of continental trade schools, concluding that 'secondary instruction of a superior kind is placed within the reach of children of parents of limited means to an extent [of] which we have no conception in this country'.[60] However, a number of witnesses criticized the overly theoretical nature of these schools and maintained the superiority of the workshop as a means of imparting practical skills. Some of the most perceptive comments were offered in evidence given by Flemming Jenkins, a Professor of Civil Engineering at University

College. Explaining that in his experience apprentice supervision was often very lax, he maintained that whilst the best apprentices learnt a good deal, the idle ones learnt nothing at all. Comparing the apprenticeship system with the continental trade schools Jenkins argued that, in terms of practical ability and commonsense, the English apprentice was a match for anyone, and even for the products of the Polytechnic. However, he continued:

> When in after life, the two men came to fill the higher stations, the English engineer would begin to feel the want of elementary training very severely, and he is at a disadvantage compared with the man abroad, in the judging of new problems which come under his eye.[61]

Other contemporary commentators, such as John Scott Russell and Silvanus Thompson, were less generous to the apprenticeship system, claiming that in all respects it was inferior to the continental trade school. Thompson, in his book, *The Apprentice Schools in France*, argued that the English apprentice spent six years in repetitive drudgery that failed 'to make anything but a bad, unintelligent machine'. By contrast the French trade school, with its combination of theoretical and practical training, had demonstrably better results with its students:

> They are more methodical and intelligent in their work, steadier in general conduct, have a far better grasp of the whole subject, and are pronounced to be more competent than the average workman at executing repairs, since they have learned the principles and have not been kept doing the same thing . . . all through the years of their apprenticeship.[62]

The reports made various recommendations for the improvement of science teaching in elementary and secondary schools and the better training of science teachers. Most significant was probably the recommendation of both the Devonshire and Samuelson Commissions that means should be found to integrate the work of the Department of Science and Art and the Education Department. Samuelson found much to criticize in the confusion and overlapping between the two departments and suggested that scientific and technical education was best advanced in the context of a broad and integrated secondary provision. Unable to go beyond the technical brief the report recommended the creation of a central authority for all matters relating to scientific and technical education.

Despite widespread acceptance of the findings of the Commissions, their more wide-ranging proposals were not adopted immediately. During the next ten years technical education expanded within its existing structures. The Department of Science and Art, which had become linked to the Education Department in 1856 but still remained essentially separate, expanded its support and supervision of Science and Art schools and classes. However, these remained unintegrated with elementary and secondary education and the dual administration of these sectors became increasingly fractious, wasteful and inefficient.[63] With the instigation in 1880 of the independent City and Guilds of London Institute for the Advancement of Technical Education and with the creation of the new polytechnics in the

1880s, this *ad hoc* proliferation of technical provision was becoming increasingly muddled and chaotic.

The last decade of the century did finally bring some important advances in technical education. The 1889 Technical Instruction Act allowed the new local councils to set up technical instruction committees which could be financed by a one penny rate. As often happened with such permissive legislation the take-up of this was very uneven at local level with only twelve amongst 108 councils using this provision by 1894.[64] However, the 1890 Local Taxation (Whiskey Money) Act also provided public funds which could be spent on technical education and this was more widely used. Together the measures contributed to considerable growth in technical education and encouraged many towns to build their first technical colleges.

This was the golden age of the English technical education movement. The changes it brought were made possible through reform in the structures of the state. There were two aspects to this. First, there was the reform of local government. Prior to 1888 England, unlike France and Germany, had no local state apparatus as such and this had been an enormous handicap in setting up a nation-wide education system. After the 1888 Local Government Act, this situation was rectified creating the basis for systematic development through local state initiative. Second, there was a general change in attitude towards the role of the state which occurred during the last quarter of the century.

The nature of this change has been much debated. Some contemporaries such as Dicey regarded the Liberal reforms of the late nineteenth century as a manifestation of the wholesale abandonment of *laissez-faire* for a new anti-individualist collectivism.[65] Later historians, such as Polanyi, have tended to see these changes merely as pragmatic responses by the state to the recognition of overwhelming social needs which could not be met by the market.[66] The truth is probably somewhere in between. There were strong immediate problems, both economic and social, whose solution seemed to require new responses. The economic challenge of Germany and the USA after 1870, along with the depression of that period, suggested the need for more vigorous state action to maintain Britain's economic supremacy, not least in the field of education. Likewise, the social problems, brought graphically to light by the investigations of Booth, Mearns and Rowntree, imposed themselves on the social conscience of the middle class which, given the political implications of the extended franchise and the rise of mass democracy, increasingly felt the need for decisive action. All these factors suggested the necessity for more government intervention.

At the same time new ideologies were emerging in the closing decades of the century which embodied new conceptions of the role of the state. Chamberlain's radical followers broke with orthodox liberalism to develop a new philosophy of 'social Imperialism'. This yoked together ideas of imperial strength abroad with national efficiency and social reform at home in a new reactionary collectivism under the sign of the strong state. The new Fabian Society, created in 1884, combined the Benthamite tradition of

expert administration with notions of national efficiency in a top-down
programme of gradualist social reform and municipal socialism. In the
same year the Social Democratic Federation was formed which marked the
rise of a more revolutionary socialist tradition. These political movements
all, in different ways, echoed the emergence of new and more intervention-
ist conceptions of the role of the state in academic disciplines from philosophy (T. H. Greene) to economics (Jevons and Marshall). Together they
marked the beginning of what Harold Perkin has termed the 'rise of professional society'.[67]

The beginning of concerted government action, now made possible in a
climate less hostile to state intervention, drove the reforms in technical
education in this period, and their relative success only highlighted the
limitations of the former voluntarist creed. However, despite this late out-
break of good sense, the long record of neglect left an enduring legacy.
Technical education had been cast in a mould that subsequent legislation
would find hard to break. Growing up as an extension of the apprenticeship
system and reliant on employer initiatives, it developed in a fragmented
and improvised manner: perennially low in status, conservatively rooted in
workshop practice, and hostile to theoretical knowledge, publicly funded
technical education became normatively part time and institutionally mar-
ooned between the workplace and mainstream education. A century later
we have still not overcome the deep divisions between theory and practice
and between academic and vocational learning which were first entrenched
in these nineteenth-century institutional structures. Nor, it would seem,
have we quite outgrown the voluntarist reflex which gave rise to them.

Notes

1. M. Porter, *The Competitive Advantage of Nations* (New York, 1990).
2. A. Green and H. Steedman, *Educational Provision, Educational Attainment
and the Needs of Industry: A Review of Research for Germany, France, Japan, the
USA and Britain.* Report Series Number 5, National Institute of Economic and
Social Research (London, 1993).
3. For a summary of these debates, see National Commission on Education,
Learning to Succeed (London, 1993).
4. C. Ball, *Learning Pays*, Royal Society of Arts (London, 1991); D. Finegold,
E. Keep, D. Miliband, D. Raffe, K. Spook and M. Young, *A British Baccalauréat*
(Institute for Public Policy Research, London).
5. A. Gamble, *Britain in Decline* (London, 1981).
6. For economic historians, see, for example, E. J. Hobsbawm, *Industry and
Empire* (Harmondsworth, 1968) and D. Landes, *The Unbound Prometheus* (London, 1969). For education historians, see, for example, E. Ashby, 'Technology and
the academies. An essay on universities and the scientific revolution', in A. H.
Halsey *et al.*, *Education, Economy and Society* (London, 1961); S. Cotgrove, *Technical Education and Social Change* (1958); A. Green, *Education and State Formation*
(London, 1990); G. Roderick and M. Stephens, *Education and Industry in the
Nineteenth Century* (London, 1978); H. Silver and J. Brennan, *A Liberal Vocationalism* (London, 1988); and M. Sanderson, *The Missing Stratum: Technical School*

Education in England, 1900–1990s (Athlone, 1994). A rare recent dissenter from this view is W. D. Rubinstein in *Capitalism, Culture and Decline in Britain, 1750–1990* (London, 1993).

7. T. Huxley, 'Technical education', in C. Bibby, ed., *T. H. Huxley on Education* (Cambridge, 1971).

8. G. Roderick and M. Stephens, op. cit.

9. E. Ashby, op. cit.

10 G. Roderick and M. Stephens, op. cit.

11. F. Ringer, *Education and Society in Modern Europe* (Bloomington, 1979); R. D. Anderson, *Education in France, 1848–1870* (Oxford, 1985).

12. G. Roderick and M. Stephens, op. cit; J. H. Weiss, *The Making of Technological Man: The Social Origins of French Engineering Education* (Cambridge, MA, 1982).

13. G. Roderick and M. Stephens, op. cit., 107.

14. S. P. Thompson, *Apprentice Schools in France, 1879*; M. Sadler, *Selections from Sadler: Studies in World Citizenship,* compiled by J. Higginson (Liverpool, 1979).

15. T. Huxley, 'Technical education', in C. Bibby, ed., *T. H. Huxley on Education* (Cambridge, 1971); L. Playfair, *The Industrial Education on the Continent,* lecture at the Government School of Mines, Science and Applied Arts, London, 1852.

16. J. Scott Russell, *Systematic Technical Education for the English People* (London, 1869); S. P. Thompson, op. cit.

17. S. P. Thompson, op. cit., 4.

18. Quoted in Roderick and Stephens, op. cit., 205.

19. Quoted in C. Barnett, 'Technology, education and industrial and economic strength', in A. Finch, and P. Scrimshaw, eds, *Standards, Schooling and Education* (London, 1980), 67.

20. Royal Commission on Technical Instruction, *Second Report* (1984), 508.

21. G. C. Allen, *The British Disease* (Hobart Paper, London, 1967): P. Anderson, 'The origins of the present crisis', *New Left Review*, 23 (1964); *idem,* 'Figures of descent', *New Left Review*, 161 (1987); C. Barnett, *The Audit of War: The Illusion and Reality of Britain as a Great Nation* (London, 1986); A. Sampson, *The Changing Anatomy of Britain* (London, 1983); M. Sanderson, op. cit.; M. J. Wiener, *English Culture and the Decline of the Industrial Spirit, 1850–1980* (Harmondsworth, 1981).

22. A. Green, *Education and State Formation,* op. cit.; H. Perkins, *Origins of Modern English Society* (1985).

23. Marx's Review of Guizot, in J. Fernbach, ed., *Surveys from Exile* (London, 1993).

24. W. D. Rubinstein, in *Capitalism, Culture and Decline in Britain, 1750–1990* (London, 1993).

25. A. Mayer, *The Persistence of the Old Regime* (New York, 1981).

26. H. Silver and S. Brennan, op. cit.

27. J. Albisetti, *Secondary School Reform in Imperial Germany* (Princeton, 1983): R. D. Anderson, *Education in France, 1848–1870* (Oxford, 1985).

28. A. Green, *Education and State Formation,* op. cit.

29. J. Scott Russell, op. cit., 80.

30. B. Simon, *The Two Nations and the Educational Structure, 1780–1870* (London, 1969).

31. The classic statement of this case can be found in the polemical open letters written by Edward Baines Junior, the leading Dissenter and editor of the Leeds Mercury, to Lord John Russell: Letters to the Right Honourable John Russell, *On State Education* (London, 1946).

32. S. Smiles, *Self Help* (London, 1859); H. Spencer, *State Education Self Defeating* (London, 1851).

33. J. S. Mill, *Autobiography,* J. Stillinger, ed. (London, 1971).

34. M. Arnold, *Higher Schools and Universities in Germany* (1892), quoted in Roderick and Stephens, op. cit., 6.

35. M. Sadler, op. cit., 93.

36. Quoted in Roderick and Stephens, op. cit., 30.

37. J. Scott Russell, op. cit., 3.

38. A. de Tocqueville, *The Old Regime and the French Revolution,* trans. Stuart Gilbert (New York, 1955).

39. F. D. Artz, *The Development of Technical Education in France, 1500–1850* (Cambridge, MA, 1966).

40. R. D. Anderson, *Education in France, 1848–1870* (Oxford, 1985).

41. Ibid.

42. C. R. Day, *Education and the Industrial World: The École d'Arts et Métiers and the Rise of French Industrial Engineering* (Cambridge, MA, 1987).

43. J. H. Weiss, op. cit.

44. F. D. Artz, op. cit.

45. R. Grew and P. Harrigan, *Schools, State and Society: The Growth of Elementary Schooling in the Nineteenth Century* (Ann Arbor, 1991).

46. F. D. Artz, op. cit.

47. C. Day, op. cit.

48. C. Day, op. cit.

49. C. Day, 43.

50. Ibid.

51. Quoted in G. Roderick and M. Stephens, op. cit., 132.

52. A. S. Bishop, *The Rise of a Central Authority in English Education* (Cambridge, 1971).

53. E. J. Hobsbawm, op. cit., 173.

54. L. Playfair, op. cit.

55. A. S. Bishop, op. cit., 161.

56. Ibid., 159.

57. Ibid., 167.

58. Quoted in G. Roderick and M. Stephens, op. cit., 21.

59. Quoted in A. S. Bishop, op. cit., 174.

60. Royal Commission on Technical Instruction, *Second Report,* vol. 1, part 1, 23.

61. Select Committee, *On the Provision for Giving Instruction in Theoretical and Applied Science to the Industrial Class (1867–8),* 130.

62. S. Thompson, op cit., 8, 44.

63. A. S. Bishop, op cit.

64. G. Roderick and M. Stephens, op. cit.

65. A. V. Dicey, *Lectures on Law and Opinion* (1905).

66. K. Polanyi, *The Great Transformation* (London, 1957).

67. H. Perkin, *The Rise of Professional Society: England since 1880* (London, 1989).

5

Assessment and the Emergence of Modern Society

Patricia Broadfoot

Introduction

[. . .]

The complex and wide-ranging analysis that follows is directed at an understanding of some of the deepest societal characteristics that underpin the now widespread use of educational assessment procedures in all societies with mass education systems. An attempt is made to understand the role of educational assessment in representing the demands of the instrumental order and of the prevailing ideological basis for social control, and to understand the source of its dual role in opening up avenues for personal liberation and occupational mobility while at the same time playing a key role in social reproduction. The intention is to draw, eclectically, on the common and relevant insights of often contradictory perspectives in addressing a specific question, rather than to undertake the inevitably vain project of seeking to reconcile fundamental divisions in sociological perspective or, equally undesirably, to ignore many valuable insights in seeking to maintain the coherence of a unitary perspective. In particular the analysis focuses on the work of four leading sociological theorists – Weber, Durkheim, Bernstein and Foucault – whose work is taken to be most centrally relevant to the issues in question.

Despite what are often profoundly conflicting perspectives, a number of central issues emerge from the various theoretical perspectives reviewed as the basis for an understanding of the growth of educational assessment. These may be summarized as follows.

1. *Individualism:* instrumental and expressive social functions are now organized on the basis of the individual. Thus both instrumental and expressive legitimating ideologies, the whole basis for social integration and control, are now defined in terms of the individual.
2. *Rational authority:* traditional, coercive authority, is replaced by a rational and impersonal (scientific) basis for hierarchical control. This authority increasingly takes the form of hierarchical observation and normalizing judgement (i.e. evaluation), which, with the growing dominance of a technological rationality, the individual is increasingly powerless to resist.

This chapter has been edited.

3. *Contradiction and legitimation:* despite the carefully concealed power relations underlying the institutions of rational authority, the fundamental irreconcilability between the need to provide for social integration (by 'buying' commitment, through economic growth, by 'moral socialization', by the arguments of scientific rationality or by disciplinary mechanisms) and the need to maintain inequality leads to a continuing tension, not to say crisis within capitalist society.

It is because educational assessment is central to all three of these characteristics of capitalist societies that it has become so central to contemporary social organization. In education, as in other areas of social life, the advent of 'normalizing judgement' makes possible the idea of fixed definitions of competence. This normalizing judgement combines with the idea of 'hierarchical observation' to provide the 'rational authority' for competition and selection. It will be argued that this Benthamite notion of 'panoptic' surveillance, in which individuals learn to judge themselves as if some external eye was constantly monitoring their performance, encourages the internalization of the evaluative criteria of those in power, and hence provides a new basis for social control. Competence, competition and control will be traced as the characteristic themes of the new disciplinary power that education provides in industrial societies. At the same time, the possibility of individuals and institutions using these same assessment mechanisms to empower creative social action through a more conscious awareness of their own strengths and weaknesses will also be traced as a reflection of the equally profound potential for liberation embodied in the change to a more individualistic society

The Characteristics of Industrial Society

Assessment has become integrally connected with teaching and learning as we know it in contemporary educational practice simply, yet fundamentally, because in its broadest sense of evaluation – to make reference to a standard – assessment is one of the most central features of the rationality that underpins advanced industrial society itself. Assessment procedures are the vehicle whereby the dominant rationality of the corporate capitalist societies typical of the contemporary Western world is translated into the structures and processes of schooling. As Cherkaoui (1977: 162) suggests, the system of assessment that emerged with mass education systems must be understood as 'organically connected with a specific mode of socialisation' – a mode of socialization in which preparation for a division of labour, bureaucracy and surveillance were dominant characteristics.

Sociologists have been much concerned to conceptualize the difference between 'traditional', 'pre-modern' and 'industrial' societies. Although varying widely in their perspective on central issues such as the basis for social order, social divisions or the scope for creative social interaction, sociologists spanning the whole range of order versus control and system versus action perspectives (Dawe 1970; Bernstein 1977; Banks 1978) find substantial areas of common ground in their discussion in general terms of the changes in the basis for social institutions which characterized the transition from 'traditional' to 'industrial' societies. Such changes included a number of different social institutions, notably the legal, the religious, the economic, the political and the familial. But, while it is relatively easy to identify associations between the changes that took place in these different social institutions, the attribution of causation is necessarily a good deal more problematic since the emerging nature of industrial society was reflexively related – as both cause and effect of the changing nature of social life.

The changes made necessary by the changing economic order of the industrial revolution were both 'practical' and 'ideological'. Under 'practical' would be included the necessity for a mobile workforce in which individuals – not the family or the community – would take responsibility for a particular unit or stage of production, the whole process of which they might not even be able to conceptualize. This was in marked contrast to the hitherto prevailing work organization, in which one individual was typically responsible for the whole task. Given the cost of any long-term use of 'power-coercive' control strategies (Chin and Benne 1978), it was a 'practical' imperative that these new workers should come to accept as quickly as possible the legitimacy of a system in which they were paid a money wage which was only a proportional return for their contribution to a system they were powerless to control.

These changes in the nature of work – its increasing fragmentation and alienation for some, expanding entrepreneurial activities for others – offered and required a degree of geographical and social mobility which brought about associated changes in the family's economic and educational role (Coleman 1968). This increase in flexibility and mobility was also increasingly apparent in the ascendancy of Protestantism over Catholicism in many industrializing countries, and in legal innovations based on the right of the individual before an impersonal law which came to replace the old feudal system of reciprocal obligation. Associated with legal developments of this kind were political movements which also had at their centre the idea of liberal democracy: the right of individuals to self-determination (Smith 1980).

These changes reached their apotheosis in the major scientific, religious and political movements which marked the end of the Middle Ages: the Enlightenment, the Reformation and the French Revolution respectively. Herein lies the link between associated changes in social forms, between the economic base and the social and ideological superstructure. Although the profound changes that took place in every aspect of life at this time were legitimized and reinforced by the challenge and, later, the hegemonic domination of a new entrepreneurial class, the most central theme in the changes taking place went far beyond class relations in both its origins and its implications and, for this reason, cannot be neatly categorized as either cause or effect. This was the theme of individualization.

The change from a predominantly communalist basis for social integration to a more individualist orientation is of crucial importance since it was this new orientation that made possible changes in the whole range of social institutions and legitimating ideologies in the newly industrializing societies. The key to these changes was the growth of a particular kind of rationality. This is the rationality of science, of logic, of efficiency and of individual rights and responsibilities.

The nature and significance of these changes is a central theme in sociology and particularly in the work of Weber, Durkheim and Marx, whose very different approaches to the study of post-feudal society are characteristic of the range and significance of attempts to understand these changes within sociology. Clearly there is a monumental volume of writing now available on this subject and of necessity the discussion of it here is confined to those aspects of the work available which bear centrally upon the question being explored here – the origins of educational assessment.

Weber and the Rise of Rationality

Weber's analysis of the transformation from feudalism to capitalism is dominated by a preoccupation with the rationality that informed the scientific-technical progress of the age, together with the associated bureaucratic and institutional structures which also developed at this time. Durkheim's very different social system perspective nevertheless emphasizes the same ideas of the rational, individual, hierarchical and specific allocation of roles in his fundamental distinction between mechanical and organic solidarity. Building on this Durkheimian tradition, Parsons (1951) conceptualized the distinction in terms of 'pattern variables' with 'affective neutrality', 'universalism', 'achievement' and 'specificity' replacing the 'affectivity', 'particularism', 'ascription' and 'diffuseness' of 'traditional' or 'simple' societies. These distinctions enunciate very clearly some of the key characteristics of the modes of social organization which emerged. Actors were increasingly required to perform specific, defined roles in a whole range of social institutions, notably the division of labour. They were increasingly chosen on the basis of their demonstrated competence as measured by some rational criterion. In this process – assessment – in one form or another – would henceforth be central.

The Protestant ethic

To offer such a brief description of the changes in the social order which accompanied the rise of capitalism is very much simpler than any attempt to explain the source of these developments. An over-simplistic reading of the Weberian perspective suggests that capitalism was brought about by the associated rise of Protestantism despite the fact that specific instances can be found where both capitalism and Protestantism have flourished independently of the other.

In fact, Weber's analysis suggests a more limited attribution of causality. Weber is careful to be historically specific, linking particular stages and types of capitalism with other specific social formations. Thus his account of the transition from feudalism to capitalism in Europe refers to the significance or the traditional European distinction within the peasant household of the functions of ownership, production and consumption – a relationship further specified in, for example, England by the existence of the market which was at least partly owing to the nature of state institutions and the rational legal system imposed by the Norman conquest (Marshall 1982). Even the notion of rationality itself is not used as a blanket term but as an historical specific.

Although it would be inappropriate to go into the details of Weber's wide-ranging analyses here, the general thrust of his argument is central: that there is an important, empirically documentable, relationship between a particular world view and a particular form of economic relations, between superstructure and substructure, but that the direction of causality between economic, political, legal and religious factors is not generalizable [. . .].

Weber's refusal to descend to determinism in this respect is a product of his sociological perspective: his respect for empirical reality and for detailed historical study and his lack of sympathy with deductive approaches which refer to the concrete merely to substantiate general theories. Weber's distrust of abstract theorizing is based on his ideas of social action. For Weber, ideas can exert an independent influence on social conduct; understanding of the world can change independent actors' views of their material situation.

> I would like to protest the statement . . . that some one factor be it technology or economy, can be the 'ultimate' or 'true' cause or another. If we look at the causal lines, we see them run, at one time, from technical to economic and political matters, at another from political to religious and economic ones, etc. There is no resting point. In my opinion, the view of historical materialism, frequently espoused, that the economic is in some sense the ultimate point in the chain of causes is completely finished as a scientific proposition.
>
> (Weber 1923: 456, quoted by Marshall 1982: 151)

Thus, as Marshall (1982) suggests, Weber avoids any attempt to formalize his implicit theory of the relation between substructure and superstructure because he denied all forms of necessary determinism in the social sphere. 'Empirical research alone can establish, in each instance, whether ideas exert a direct and independent influence on social action' (Marshall 1982: 155).

Marshall argues that Weber was insistent that ideas became significant in history and are causally effective in shaping social conduct because, at certain points, a class or status group with specific material or ideal interests takes up, sustains and develops these ideas, and is influenced by them. Weber, he suggests, was insistent that ideas are shaped by and in turn help to shape interests and action, though accepting too, as a general principle, that the 'inner logic' of their development does not proceed independently of all other spheres of social reality.

Thus Weber's analysis is important because it emphasizes general themes in the development of capitalism while in no way denying the significance of specific social forms in mediating the precise effect of such movements. It therefore points the way to the kind of approach being adopted here, which seeks to understand how educational assessment procedures relate in general terms to education under capitalism by a study of the specific *and different* forms it takes in individual systems. Weber's emphasis on the independent contribution of interest groups in the process of 'structuration' (Dallmayr 1982; after Giddens 1976) justifies the detailed attention given to national educational politics [. . .] both in theoretical terms [. . .] and in empirical terms [. . .].

This balance between 'the general' and 'the specific' is similarly reflected in Weber's analysis of the characteristics of Protestant mentality as expressed in the dominant social form of bureaucracy – 'the institutional prototype of the emerging rationalised society' (Wilson 1977, quoted by Salaman 1981: 188). While the institution of bureaucratic organization is common to all industrial societies in some degree, there is also clearly a good deal of variation between societies in the extent to which this mode of organization is predominant. In the provision of mass education, for example, elements of Weber's 'ideal type' of bureaucracy are necessarily manifest in every national education system, but there are equally significant variations in bureaucratic style, so that notions of hierarchy, general rules, continuous and impersonal offices and the separation between official and private life must be interrelated with historically specific social situations (Gouldner 1952).

Thus there are different styles of bureaucratic provision just as there are significant differences in all the other social institutions in countries which nevertheless share a common history of capitalist and industrial revolution.

Bureaucracy

It is this emphasis on bureaucracy which forms one of the major distinctive features of the Weberian perspective. Although Weber shares with other sociological theorists, and Marx in particular, an emphasis on the economic interests arising out of the ownership of property as the key to social conflict and change, the Weberian perspective includes other important sources of social power. These other sources include the control of organizational resources especially in state and private bureaucracies and control of cultural resources, notably religious ones initially, but increasingly in secular terms through, for example, the education system. Thus from a Weberian perspective, interest groups and their associated struggles reflect the whole range of economic, cultural and political divisions in society, divisions institutionalized in terms of Weber's well-known distinction between status and party. Collins (1979) argues that the education system embodies all three of these struggles in its economic concern with the production of appropriately skilled workers, its cultural concern with social integration and the maintenance of prestige and its political concern with the legitimation of control through certain formal organizations. Collins (1979: 252) argues, following Weber, that

> education, which has arisen as part of the process of bureaucratisation, has been shaped by the efforts of elites to establish impersonal methods of control; the content of education here is irrelevant but the structure of grades, ranks, degrees and other formal credentials is of central importance as a means of discipline through hierarchy and specialisation.

It is this Weberian emphasis on the form or mode of control, as well as its purpose, that is crucial to the attempt to understand the origins of educational evaluation. The Weberian emphasis on social action, on multiple sites for struggle, on bureaucratic organization and on scientific rationality are themes which dominate the emergence of mass schooling while allowing for all its variety. In particular, it provides a specific rationale for the developing significance of formal evaluation and qualifications as a logical and integral part of this process – a theme which is taken up in similar vein, if in much more detail, in more recent post-structuralist work, notably that of Foucault.

Although there are many similarities here with Marxist perspectives on the capitalist state, there is clearly a fundamental distinction to be made as to whether primacy is given to economic determinants. Marxism locates forms of struggle other than the economic in the determined superstructure in which the battle to legitimate the power relations of the economic and social status quo is waged through the ideological domination of various forms of false consciousness. It would seem, however, that most Marxists, as well as many non-Marxists, would want to concede 'some measure of genuine interaction between the spheres of production and other spheres of social life . . . and, at the level of individual actors a "dialectical" relationship between class interest and ideological representation' (Marshall 1982: 145). For the purpose in hand, it is less necessary to adjudicate between these fundamental distinctions than to recognize their common identification of the importance of the new forms of essentially ideological control in the changing basis of social organization which characterized industrial society.

Thus the characteristics of the social order associated with the emergence of capitalism as the dominant economic system were neither simply causes of, nor caused by, this economic development. Rather they must be regarded as mutually dependent and reinforcing developments, the lack of either of which would have inhibited the development of both. It is certainly true that the central themes of this chapter – rationality and individualism – are deeply integrated with both the economic and the social order, finding their origin and their expression in both arenas.

In the Western world individualism has emerged as both the necessary practical basis for the rational allocation of roles and the necessary source of legitimation. As the dominant ideology it allows classes to be reduced to individual persons who are then reorganized into various imaginary and non-antagonistic unities such as the 'nation' and the 'community' (Poulantzas 1973). Taking up this point, Larson (1981) argues that this allows the principle of equality between atomized individuals to be the cornerstone of the new inequality which appears to be based only on the rational criteria of will, competence, drive and, more recently, choice. In particular the existence of state education systems which apparently provide for meritocratic competition on the basis of equality of opportunity and, increasingly, the discipline of the market deflect the criticism of professional elites and allow them to legitimate their own position.

If some conflict theorists like Poulantzas and Larson emphasize the strategic importance for the maintenance of social order of the ideology of individualism as a major way of fragmenting and thus deflecting self-conscious class action, others have taken a more pessimistic view of it. From this dependence on individualism it is possible to identify a profound contradiction between the instrumental and the expressive order, between public and private life, between general and particular interests. This contradiction is particularly evident in education, since this plays a crucial role in the process of allocation to social and occupational roles and in that of social integration.

> There is a fundamental contradiction within the heart of education: while embodying and reproducing a system of domination based on hierarchical control, the *form* of the discourse – and hence content – in education is that of the liberal discourse of the state, according to which rights are vested equally in all members of the community. This contradictory position of education explains its dual progressive/reproductive role promoting equality, democracy, toleration, rationality, inalienable rights on the one hand, while legitimising inequality, authoritarianism, fragmentation, prejudice and submission on the other.
>
> (Gintis 1980: 20)

This contradiction is not new; it is, as Habermas (1976) suggests, the perennial 'legitimation crisis' arising out of the fundamental contradiction of capital – the necessity for wealth to be socially produced while being privately appropriated. 'Because the reproduction of class societies is based on the privileged appropriation of socially produced wealth, all such societies must resolve the problem of distributing the surplus product inequitably and yet legitimately' (Habermas 1976: 96).

Thus the education system embodies a constant contradiction between the need to *differentiate* pupils on the basis of an order of merit which ultimately serves to legitimate differential chances in the labour market and the contradictory need to *integrate* pupils, parents and teachers in a way which enables the school to be seen as serving commonly conceived purposes. While the need for the former is conceived by teachers in terms of a relatively fixed distribution of basic 'abilities' which pupils, as individuals, may be identified as possessing, the need for the latter is a social imperative which has to be worked for in terms of desirable *general* social attributes based on principles that may be accepted as legitimate.

This fundamental contradiction between the need to divide and yet unite, to create inequality and, at the same time, to promote social cohesion is a problem that goes well beyond a Marxist interpretation framed specifically in terms of class struggle, to the heart of the division of labour itself and the problems of social order.

As suggested earlier, the contradiction is essentially between the 'instrumental' function of education – the training of people for jobs in terms of the requisite skills and knowledge and through anticipatory socialization, in terms of appropriate personal expectations and behaviour – and the 'expressive' function of education, aimed at fostering at least a minimal level of social integration despite the inevitable and disintegrative effects of the prevailing individualist 'instrumental ideology' and the potentially even more divisive tendencies of the associated inequality. Although class-based inequality is central here, it is the form of social organization and legitimation characterizing the current basis for inequality – namely individualism – which gives rise to this distinctive problem. Unlike other more explicitly coercive forms of economic exploitation – as found under feudalism or tribalism, for example – capitalist society is a manifestation of the change in the nature of social bonds which has at its heart rationality and individualism. This latter point is clearly made by Durkheim, for whom 'capitalism' is essentially an 'abnormal form' (O'Connor 1980) and for whom the issue of individualism and the consequent problems of social integration were fundamental.

Durkheim and the Problem of Social Control

The theme of Durkheim's *The Division of Labour in Society* (1947) is the source of social solidarity and social order. He argues that the increasing occupational specialization which characterizes a division of labour replaces the 'mechanical' solidarity of pre-market societies based on homogeneous social and occupational roles. With occupational specialization comes 'organic' solidarity based on people's mutual interdependence. The political and social upheavals of nineteenth-century France eventually forced Durkheim to modify his earlier analysis to argue in *Moral Education* (1961) that new forms of social solidarity do not occur spontaneously but require new social institutions to be set up. He envisaged that these institutions would be a sort of occupational 'guild' which would bind individuals into special interest organizations and hence to the state. Durkheim saw a key role for schools in this – preparing and socializing individuals for their place in the division of labour and, at the same time, providing the basis for communalism and true organic solidarity.

Durkheim's distinction between social divisions arising from anomie and social divisions arising from egoism is also useful here since the former refers to a lack of 'system integration' – the weak integration of social functions – and the latter to the integration of people themselves into such social functions. From this distinction, Durkheim's work offers an implicit critique of the ideology of egalitarianism, as expressed in strategies for income redistribution and equality of opportunity, for, although such strategies may militate against egoistic social division, far from ending anomie, where self-interest becomes a defining social principle, anomie is increased. The recent rise of New Right ideologies in many Western countries provides a contemporary graphic illustration of Durkheim's analysis. What would be required to counteract it, in Durkheim's view, would be 'moral' regeneration and a fundamental change in the nature of social relationships.

Clearly there are important parallels here with the emphasis in Marxist theory on the necessity for a change in consciousness, as well as economic relations, as the precursor of a genuinely socialist society. Durkheim is not specifically concerned with class struggle and his work provides important general insights into the basis for social order and particularly the contribution schooling has to make in this respect.

In the search to understand the associated question of the origins and significance of assessment as a social and educational characteristic, this Durkheimian emphasis is likewise valuable. [. . . It has been] suggested that the institution of formal evaluation procedures within education was directly instrumental in rationalizing educational provision into a system and, in particular, emphasized three themes which became dominant in the provision of schooling, namely the attestation of competence (including the rationalization of syllabus content), the regulation of competition and provision for individual and systemic control. The first two themes may readily be associated with the *instrumental* role of education in providing and selecting individuals for specific slots in the division of labour. The third, control, is associated with the *expressive* order. This control may be mediated through one or more of the following: the apparently objective testing of individual potential (intelligence tests), assessing individual performance (e.g. continuous assessment, guidance and examinations), the evaluation of teaching or school performance (inspection and accountability) and the evaluation of the system and performance as a whole (national monitoring).

The operation of these forms of control depends upon the dominance and consequent legitimacy of an individualist rationality of personal talent, personal responsibility, personal endeavour and personal reward. It is the unquestioned acceptance of the individualist ethos (Mills 1979) that permits social integration and control to be mediated in this way, since such judgements and their more or less pleasant consequences are seen to be a legitimate, rational basis for the inequalities associated with a division of labour. Thus assessment plays a central role in making the education system responsive to larger social pressures, and it plays an equally important role in helping to minimize the effects of the contradiction between the instrumental and expressive functions of education by providing for the legitimation of the necessary inequalities.

This contradiction is that between the training and allocation of people for different jobs (both in terms of the requisite skills and knowledge and in terms of appropriate personal expectations and behaviour) and the need for social integration to be maintained despite a hierarchical division of labour and diverse pressures towards individualism (Durkheim 1947). Both these aspects of school functioning – the 'instrumental' and the 'expressive' – are informed by the dominant individualist rationality.

To explain how this change came about, Durkheim goes back to the major historical transformations which immediately preceded industrialization. To begin with, Durkheim (1947) protests that:

> Even the most cursory historical survey is enough to make us realise that degrees and examinations are of relatively recent origin; there was nothing equivalent in classical antiquity . . . the word and the thing only appear in the Middle Ages with the university.
>
> (p.126)

The explanation Durkheim offers for this invention is that the system of degrees and examinations derives from the corporate organization of educational provision. He suggests that the existing feudal model of the series of initiations or stages which must be gone through before penetrating to the heart of any organization – such as page, squire and bachelor before becoming a fully armed knight – was a natural model for educational 'stages' to be introduced once the teachers, 'instead of teaching separately, formed themselves into a corporation with a sense of its own identity and governed by communal laws' (Durkheim 1947: 130). That is to say, the advent of certification depended on the institutionalization of education in the form of schools and colleges. From this it was but a short step to the institution of some organized course of study or curriculum (see Hamilton 1981).

At this stage the function of assessment was almost entirely ritualistic: a *rite de passage* [. . .] modelled on traditional concepts of initiation, which served the purpose of demarcating those who had reached a level of scholarship and commitment that justified their entry to the next level. The assessment itself was in practice a legitimation device – a public relations exercise which confirmed a selection that had already been undertaken, informally, by the teacher. But although the French universities Durkheim was describing have kept this manifestation of their corporate existence almost entirely unchanged in its essential structure until the present day, one element that did change fundamentally was the use of assessment for motivating and controlling students.

Durkheim describes the situation of the young arts student in the Middle Ages, who at between 13 and 15 years of age was accorded almost complete freedom from supervision or exhortation:

> We are so accustomed to believing that emulation is the essential motivating force in academic life, that we cannot easily imagine how a school could exist which did not have a carefully worked out system of graduated awards in order to keep the enthusiasm of pupils perpetually alive. Good marks, solemn statements of satisfactory performance, distinctions, competition essays, prizegivings; all these seem to us in differing degrees, the necessary accompaniment to any sound education system. The system that operated in France and indeed Europe, until the sixteenth century, was characterised by the surprising fact that there were no rewards at all from success in examinations. What is more, any candidate who had assiduously and conscientiously followed the course of studies was certain of success.
>
> (Durkheim 1947:159)

Until the end of the fifteenth century, pupils were treated like autonomous adults. Then, in France at least, the status of pupils gradually changed. They became minors, shut off from the world in educational institutions in which they were powerless to resist the authority of those put in to teach and regulate them. Although the timing of this process was particular to the educational history of France, the link between the advent of institutionalized education, organized around substantial, monastic-style disciplinary powers, and the advent of educational assessment is a more general one (Broadfoot 1991). 'Academic discipline implies a system of rewards no less than a system of punishment' (Durkheim 1947: 159).

Nowhere was this more clearly seen than in the education practices of the Jesuits from the mid-sixteenth century. The Jesuits placed equal emphasis on the power of competition.

> Not only were they the first to organise the competitive system in the colleges but they also developed it to a point of greater intensity than it has ever subsequently known . . .
>
> Academic work involved a kind of perpetual hand-to-hand combat. Camp challenged camp, group struggled with group, supervised one another, corrected one another and took one another to task. It was thanks to this division of labour between the teacher and the pupils, that one teacher was able without much difficulty to run classes which sometimes numbered as many as 200–300 pupils. In addition to such methods of chronically recurring competition there were intermittent competitions too numerous to enumerate . . . Thus an infinite wealth of devices maintained the self-esteem of pupils in a constant state of extreme excitation.
>
> (Durkheim 1947: 261)

One effect of this policy, Durkheim suggests, was that the genuinely intensive activity which it fostered was flawed by being expended on the superficial rather than the profound, still a major criticism of the effect of exam-motivated learning.

The reason for this sudden shift from the extreme of no assessment to that of extreme competition, Durkheim suggests, was the advent of individual self-consciousness that characterized the Renaissance. Thus education too had to become individualized, no longer a uniform and homogeneous activity: the teacher must get to know pupils and be able to provide differentially according to their diverse needs. In the same way, 'the individual cannot be motivated or trained to act in the same way, as an amorphous crowd, he must be convinced and moved by considerations which are specifically appropriate to him' (Durkheim 1947: 264) – notably, competition.

Not only did the institution of formal assessment procedures encourage the growth of individual competitiveness in education, it also helped to change the quality of the teacher–pupil relations to one which emphasized a more personal, 'formative-evaluation' in teaching in place of the older, more impersonal style.

Durkheim's analysis evokes an important general question in relation to assessment, concerning the currently widespread view that a more individualistic emphasis in assessment is desirable, as found, for example, in the Records of Achievement initiative and the corresponding fear among other people that such approaches also have the potential to lead towards new, more intrusive modes of 'surveillance' and hence social control (Broadfoot 1992). Certainly it can be argued that it is the political dimension to such assessment, and the way in which such procedures covertly delineate a particular set of values, which is likely to be of critical importance. However, in a very real sense, the desirability of identifying individual characteristics has always been an informing principle of educational assessment, a *sine qua non* that attracts unquestioning commitment from scholars and practitioners.

Durkheim's analysis is applicable more generally than to French history alone. It is possible to argue that the various ideologies of schooling that have developed – the developmental, the child-centred, the moral and the meritocratic (Hargreaves 1979) – are all options within an individualist rationality which emphasized personal needs, personal responsibility, personal reward and even personal fulfilment. Furthermore, all of them are predicated on both the concept and the practice of educational assessment. It is therefore necessary to draw on some more recent sociological theory – notably that of Bernstein, whose work is strongly influenced by Durkheim – to consider the more contemporary manifestations of these concepts within formal educational provision.

Bernstein and the Significance of Educational Codes

Bernstein is one of the very few sociologists of education to have attempted to conceptualize the relationship between the constant requirements of education systems in capitalist societies and the particular variations in the way in which those requirements are fulfilled in particular national systems. In a now well-known quotation, Bernstein asserts:

> How a society selects, classifies, distributes, transmits and evaluates the educational knowledge it considers to be public, reflects both the distribution of power and the principles of social control. From this point of view, differences within and change in the organisation, transmission and evaluation of educational knowledge should be a major area of sociological interest.
>
> (Bernstein 1977: 55)

The Durkheimian echo in this quotation is not accidental. Bernstein is preoccupied with questions of social order, social control and social reproduction. He sees the education system as a major determinant of both the strength and the nature of that order in that it regulates (a) the kind of worker produced (with all that that implies for economic efficiency and industrial relations), (b) the kind of social integration upon which social order will be based and (c) which individuals will accede to positions of power and privilege (i.e. control). Implicit in his theories is the need for the circle of control to be made complete, in that society must possess the means of determining and controlling the education system because it is to a great extent determined and controlled by it. However, Bernstein does not take 'control' in a Durkheimian, structural-functionist sense, despite the fact that Durkheim's categories of social order are used; rather the education system is seen as working in the interests of particular, dominant class groups. It accomplishes this by being slow to change from traditional modes of enshrining privilege (e.g. the collection code), but at the same time incorporating new control techniques which allow the education system to respond to new social and economic conditions or to establish its legitimacy (public confidence) if inequalities or inefficiencies inherent in it seem likely to become too glaring.

Thus, [. . .] the pressure of population, the values of traditional humanism, the requirements of democratic equality and the needs of a sophisticated industrial economy are among many powerful social and economic trends which during recent decades have led to international pressure for educational change. Particularly notable initially was a trend towards the structural reorganization of schools, the abolition of internal school divisions, the institution of a common curriculum and the democratization of assessment procedures (Neave 1980). All these dimensions of change involve a breaking down of educational barriers in favour of a more flexible, open and democratic basis for educational competition. More recently, the emphasis has become more explicitly a reflection of the prevailing economic imperatives resulting from intensifying international competition and the new skills sought as a result of changing working practices (Organization for Economic Co-operation and Development 1989). Assessment is central to such changes, for the shift in the basis of social order that Bernstein identifies as being reflected in such policy development is integrally bound up with the way in which educational assessment procedures represent the changing characteristics and requirements of the social context within the provision and process of schooling.

Employing Durkheim's categories of social order, Bernstein identifies a tendency in contemporary society for there to be a transition from a social and economic order based on overt mechanical solidarity and covert organic solidarity to one of overt organic solidarity and covert mechanical solidarity. One outward sign of this change in education systems is a trend towards invisible pedagogies and integrated codes represented by more student-centred teaching and cross-curricular approaches. The latter are presented by Bernstein as a movement towards weak classification and weak framing, in which subject boundaries are broken down and teachers enjoy considerable freedom over what and how to teach. The reason for this trend, Bernstein argues, is developments in technology which have given rise to the need for a more flexible, inner-directed labour force (which may be envisaged as the likely outcome of an education system that develops pupil, rather than teacher, control of learning and seeks to inhibit the development of specific subject identities). Although there is by no means a consistent development in this respect in any society, since any such change comes up against a whole range of powerful sources of resistance which are rooted in traditionalist ideologies and vested interest (as in the current backlash against 'progressive' educational ideas in the United States and the United Kingdom), international evidence concerning the changing shape of educational qualifications and thus courses would nevertheless appear to demonstrate a continuing trend (Broadfoot 1992).

Such a development, Bernstein argues, may challenge *society*'s basic classifications and frames (for example, assumptions about job identities, authority structures and status) and *therefore* its structures of power and principles of social control (which of course include social reproduction). He suggests that if the integrated code is successful – if in producing its less specialized outputs it is successful in perpetrating effectively and implicitly an ideology which is explicit, elaborated and closed – then order based on mechanical solidarity will follow. This is exactly the same situation as that facing a team of teachers seeking to implement an integrated course in a school in which the traditional standards and controls provided by individual subjects have disappeared and hence the curriculum can only be successful to the extent that the mechanical solidarity of a common ideology and situation is adhered to by the teachers concerned. If integrated codes are not 'successful', Bernstein suggests, social order, in all its forms, is immediately made problematic.

Little of Bernstein's work is directly concerned with evaluation. Nevertheless, his emphasis on the *interrelationship* of curriculum and pedagogy – classification and frame – is highly relevant to an understanding of assessment practice. Although Bernstein has not produced a concept equivalent to classification and frame for his third message system – 'evaluation' – he makes many references to changes in such procedures associated with the shift from visible to invisible pedagogies and from collection to integrated codes. Fundamentally, Bernstein argues, there has, in recent years, been a change of emphasis from overt to covert assessment and from specific to

diffuse evaluation criteria. In visible pedagogy, the 'objective grid' for evaluation is based on clear criteria, delicate measurement and standardization,
which can allow comparison between schools so that pupil, parent and
teacher can all make an apparently objective assessment of a child's progress. This very objectivity, this recourse to scientific rationality, lends to
the assessment a legitimacy which makes it hard to refute. (Outstanding in
this respect are, of course, intelligence tests and public examinations.)

In invisible pedagogies, evaluation procedures are multiple, diffuse and
not easily subject to apparently precise measurement, so that it is difficult
to compare pupils or schools. The tendency of invisible pedagogy to be
associated with weak classification and framing means that there are few
traditional criteria for evaluation, and there is little standardization of
curriculum content or pedagogy between teachers and schools. Thus assessment comes to be part of the pervasive and private personal relationship between teacher and taught. Bernstein suggests that in visible
pedagogies, assessment will be in terms of those dispositions of a child
which become candidates for labelling by a teacher and, given that in such
visible pedagogies the attention of the child is focused on the teacher, the
teacher will tend to compare children in terms of motivation and interest,
attentiveness, cooperation, persistence and carefulness. The judgements
will usually be short, stereotyped, unexplicated and public. By contrast,
the invisible pedagogy is likely to be associated with a dossier covering a
wide variety of the child's internal processes and outer acts and the
teacher's explanation of the relationship between the two. Recent research into the impact of National Assessment requirements in English
primary schools bears out Bernstein's more theoretical analysis. It documents teachers' preference for intuitive, idiosyncratic assessment strategies rather than the more 'categoric' assessment requirements of the
National Curriculum, which they see as producing only 'dead data' for
reporting purposes (Pollard *et al.* 1994; Broadfoot *et al.* 1993). Teachers'
preferred assessment mode of a private 'diagnostic discourse' concerning
individual children is arguably more likely to provide educational experiences which are of maximum benefit to the learner. Alternatively, they
can be argued to allow a much more subtle and pervasive discrimination
and control, because they make assessment harder to challenge and
hence raise the teacher's power. The current emphasis on 'student-
centred assessment' and 'person-centred schools' (Munby 1989; Broadfoot 1991) in some of the more radical literature concerned with assessment certainly seems to support this latter argument.

This part of Bernstein's analysis was made before the current fashion for
the concept of accountability and this is evident in his writing, since he does
not draw out here the implications that his analysis of invisible pedagogy
and its accompanying informal assessment are likely to have for maintaining confidence in the education system as a form of control and legitimation. It is clear from English and American experience that trends in the
1950s and 1960s towards invisible pedagogies in basic schooling together

with the decline or abolition of the external control exerted by public assessment procedures has been a direct source of worry about standards and thus of associated calls for more 'categoric' measures of accountability (control). In England at least, such measures have helped to restore the legitimacy of more traditional educational transmissions, in Bernstein's terms: strong classification, strong framing, visible pedagogy and formal, 'categoric', overt assessment.

In his more recent work, Bernstein (1982) has revised his theory to associate weak classification and weak framing with economic expansion, strong classification and strong framing with economic contraction. This suggests that Bernstein's analysis is now more in line with current 'crisis' theory in associating educational codes with changes in the legitimating context rather than in the mode of production itself. Equally, his more recent work gives a more explicit role to evaluation as part of the 'pedagogic device' which is 'the condition for the production, reproduction and transformation of culture and which, in turn, provides the intrinsic grammar of pedagogic discourse through distributive rules, recontextualising rules and rules of evaluation' (p. 21). Bernstein further suggests that the realization of the pedagogic device, the conceptualization of which he traces back to Durkheim, carries the contradictions, cleavages and dilemmas that are generated by the power relations underpinning such realizations (p. 64). Bernstein thus stresses the need to conceptualize 'evaluation' as a separate, albeit determined, variable of pedagogic practice. However, it could be argued from contemporary evidence that because assessment procedures are so closely bound up with the legitimation of particular educational practices, because they are the overt means of communication from schools to society and, to a greater or lesser extent in different societies, the covert means of that society's response in the form of control, assessment may be the *most* important of the three message systems. Assessment procedures may well be the system that determines curriculum and pedagogy and, hence, social reproduction.

As Bernstein (1982: 98) further suggests, 'The public examination system is based upon a visible pedagogy as it is realised through strong classification and strong frames.' As such it must be regarded as the mediator of 'symbolic property' – educational goods exchangeable in the educational market. 'Knowledge under collection is private property with its own power structure and market situation' (p. 97): the traditional order of capitalism which still retains ideological legitimacy.

[. . .] The current trend away from narrow, academic, externally imposed certification procedures towards broader, more continuous, teacher-based certification procedures (Nisbet 1993) means that the criteria of successful performance are increasingly being left to teachers to decide. Even where the criteria for such assessment are externally agreed, the breadth of such assessments can make any effective moderation of the *application* of the criteria almost impossible (GNVQ 1994) leaving teachers very significant power in determining life chances.

More recently, many of the countries which veered towards more school-based assessment in recent decades have tended to encounter a reassertion of externally imposed assessment criteria as, at best, the credibility of school-based assessment has diminished in the face of pessimistic views about educational standards and pupil achievement, and, at worst, there has been widespread abuse and cheating, as in, for example, Sri Lanka. Tests are perceived as symbols of order and control in the midst of diversity, chaos, competition for dwindling school resources, and the need for external verification of educational standards (Airasian 1988: 307). Thus Airasian echoes Bernstein's emphasis on *symbolic control* as increasingly the central problematic and one in relation to which testing and assessment has grown rapidly to become of critical importance. School-based assessment continues as a powerful grassroots movement in many countries, however, leading to an interesting dualism in assessment paradigms [. . .].

But although changes in the power of different parts of the education system are of considerable significance in themselves, the power relations involved in the definition of such criteria are very complex and go considerably beyond any simple dualism involving central government and teachers. Bernstein himself has recognized both the significance of the issue and its extreme complexity in an analysis in which he tries to provide a model for the highly complex and reflexive articulation between central government rhetoric, actual and perceived constraints and professional ideology in the formulation of educational 'modalities'. Bernstein (1982: 351) has attempted to conceptualize what he terms the 'discourse of education' in terms of the 'primary' context, 'where specialised discourses are developed, modified or changed', and the 'secondary' context, where various types of educational agencies engage in the 'selective reproduction of educational discourse'. Such discourse, he argues, relates the context for primary contextualizing – that is, the 'positions, relations and practices arising out of production' itself – with the recontextualizing involved in the generation of 'pedagogic theory, research and practice'.

Assessment procedures which provide the language of accountability are a vital element in this reflexive process, since the assumptions and the priorities they ensure may be regarded as the code which is translated into the appropriate forms of discourse at each stage of the recontextualization. How this process actually works in practice is a highly complex, empirical question which resurrects the theme of this [chapter], namely that the fundamental role of assessment procedures in advanced and, indeed, post-industrial societies is a constant but that the institutional expression of that role will vary according to the social context and over time.

The extent to which such variations are essentially determined – the different institutional mediations of a common economic order – and the extent to which such variations represent real differences in the actual content of educational messages is again an empirical question. That is to say, are the apparent differences in the organization and provision of education systems of different capitalist societies simply reflections of different *instrumental* legitimating ideologies or are they at least to some extent reflections of differences at the level of the expressive order itself – of the fundamental value systems of each society?

Part of the answer to this question is embodied in the rationale for the move towards more 'invisible' evaluation – the increasing difficulty of identifying educational objectives and, hence, criteria of achievement which will command support from all sections of the community. The conflict of aims which has always been implicit in educational provision between the 'old humanists', 'new industrialists', 'public educators' and 'state bureaucrats' (Salter and Tapper 1981) has recently been greatly exacerbated by economic recession, youth unemployment, technological change and other, equally fundamental, changes in the social order.

Following Habermas and Marcuse, among others, it may be argued that the potential 'crisis' that this diversity of educational aims produces is largely kept in check by the elevation of the pursuit of rationality – always a characteristic of industrial society – from being merely the *means* of providing for efficient social organization (the instrumental ideology) to being the *end* itself (the expressive ideology). There is considerable disagreement among sociologists as to whether this trend is but one element in the hegemonic domination of a particular class and is thus still part of the instrumental order or whether the growth of scientism and technical rationality has been such as to render increasingly anachronistic traditional definitions of class struggle. The changes currently taking place in assessment procedures strongly support this latter argument [. . .]. Before we proceed to such a substantive analysis, however, it is necessary to clarify the general issues involved in identifying one final theme in this review of educational assessment in industrial society, that of technological rationality.

Rationality and Legitimation

This emphasis on the form of social life and its significance for social control is dealt with at length in the writing of the German philosopher Jürgen Habermas. Although some kind of distinction between the instrumental (normally economic) order and the expressive (normally social) order is common to a wide range of sociological theory from both conflict and functionalist perspectives, Habermas's distinction between the 'practical' (*praktisch*) and the 'purposive rational' (*zweckrational*) is particularly relevant to an understanding of the role of educational assessment.

Habermas defines the 'practical' as the basis for symbolic interaction within a normative order – the level of feeling, consciousness and volition and the associated level of ethics and politics (loosely, 'superstructure'). The 'purposive rational' is action which is directed towards specific purposes (loosely the economic and administrative 'base'). Habermas's *zweckrational* links closely with Weber's concept of rationality, which he used to define the form of capitalist economic activity, bourgeois private law and bureaucratic authority. Habermas (1970) argues that as social labour is increasingly industrialized, the criterion of rationality penetrates ever further into other areas of life through such developments as urbanization and the technification of transport and communication. Indeed, it may be argued that the growth of rationality has been of more importance than that of capitalist production itself and that the story of modern history is essentially that of the growth of bureaucracy: 'apart from the opaque line of technological rationality, social life is drift and habituation' (Gerth and Wright-Mills 1952: 165).

There is a clear Weberian legacy here. In *The Theory of Social and Economic Organization,* Weber draws a distinction between: the simple, undifferentiated society accepting the traditional authority which embodies prevailing social values; the charismatic leader able to inspire the kind of collective value consensus to which Durkheim attached such importance; and the 'routinization' of that value consensus into institutional structures and practices. Weber argues that such an active 'moral consensus' is a temporary phenomenon inevitably to he replaced by the much more enduring and essentially impersonal authority of institutional process and bureaucracy (Weber 1947).

But there is equally a Durkheimian legacy in Habermas's conception. Durkheim describes the gradual change from 'humanism' to 'realism' in the content of education from the seventeenth century onwards, a change in the legitimating ideology of education which has endured until the present day. Humanism in one or other of its forms, Durkheim argues, was the guiding spirit of all education in the Christian era until the early seventeenth century, or in France where change came later, the eighteenth century. In this perspective, he suggests,

> *Things* were not intrinsically interesting: they were not the object of a special study carried out for its own sake, but were only dealt with in connection with the human beliefs to which they had given rise. What people wanted to know about was not how the real world actually is but rather what human beings have said about it . . . Between the things of the world and the things of the mind falls the text, which acts as a partial veil between them.
>
> (Durkheim 1947: 279, author's emphasis)

The traditional, humanist paradigm, Durkheim suggests, resisted the incursion of any form of science, of finding out about the real world, into the curriculum. By contrast, the new perspective that Durkheim describes as being inspired by writers such as Comenius is designed to create good and useful citizens. It is 'realist', concerned with the study of things, with preparing men [sic] for every possible action and giving them insight into the world in which they live.

Although a complex and confused tradition, subject to many reinterpretations and changes of emphasis, it is still essentially the educational 'realism' of Comenius, Montaigne, Rousseau and others which provides the contemporary legitimating rhetoric of 'scientism' and hence of assessment.

At the same time, Durkheim suggests, the alternative, humanist tradition of the study of people, their interpretations and creations has never been eclipsed, the struggle between the two perspectives constituting a persistent theme in educational theory and educational policy.

Thus, the progression from feudalism to capitalism and, in particular, from entrepreneurial to corporate capitalism may be seen as one in which the ever increasing power of technical-scientific rationality not only structures the ideology and organization of production, but is more and more pervasive in the ideology and organization of social life as a whole. Reimer (1971: 19) puts the point with some force:

> School has become the universal church of a technological society, incorporating and transmitting its ideology, shaping men's minds to accept this ideology and conferring social status according to its acceptance. There is no question of man's rejecting technology. The question is only one of adaptation, direction and control. The role of the school teacher in this process is a triple one combining the functions of umpire, judge and counsellor.

As institutional life becomes more hierarchically and pervasively ordered, social life becomes correspondingly fragmented. High rates of social mobility serve to transform group conflict into individual competition, so that it is increasingly difficult for common interests and values to be identified as the basis for informal, democratic, collegial (that is, horizontal) forms of organization (Bates 1980a,b).

Habermas also suggests that, in advanced capitalist societies, deprived and privileged groups no longer confront each other *as* socio-economic classes. Although class distinctions still persist in the form of subcultural traditions, lifestyles and attitudes, the scope for normative activity – political initiatives, debates about the nature of the 'good life', the capability for conscious action as a class – are increasingly drowned in the technocratic consciousness.

> Today's dominant, rather glassy background ideology, which makes a fetish of science, is more irresistible and farther-reaching than ideologies of the old type. For with the veiling of 'practical' problems it not only justifies a particular class's interest in domination and represses another class's partial need for emancipation but affects the human's race's emancipatory interest as such . . . technocratic consciousness reflects . . . the repression of 'ethics' as such as a category of life.
> (Habermas 1970: 112)

The legitimation for this process, according to Marcuse, is the constantly increasing productivity which keeps individuals living in increasing comfort.

> In the universe, technology also provides the great rationalisation of the unfreedom of man and demonstrates the 'technical' impossibility of being autonomous, of determining one's own life. For this unfreedom appears neither as irrational nor as political, but rather as submission to the technical apparatus which enlarges the comforts of life and increases the productivity of labour.
> (Marcuse 1964)

What is being described here is the phenomenon of 'one-dimensional man' – the logical development of the process of individualization and rationalization associated with the development of capitalist economic relationships. As capitalism has itself become more and more institutionalized, into various kinds of state and corporate capitalism, its ideological legitimation has equally moved from the hegemonic domination of a particular class to the predominance of a common prevailing rationality *per se*, where science and technology are both base and superstructure. If, earlier, ownership and control of the means of production were crucial to effective domination, increasingly it is the bureaucracies of production and of administration which have become both controlling and self-determining. In this sense, class is not a tangible entity but rather the *form* of relations between interests and individuals (Hogan 1981). What started as a desire to understand and, hence, harness the material/natural world for the means of production is increasingly being extended by technocrats and bureaucrats alike into an attempt to extend 'technical' control into the realm of social life itself. This takes the form of new and more pervasive techniques for the surveillance, monitoring and control of both individuals and organizations.

> The economic take-off of Western Europe began with techniques that made possible capital accumulation, methods for the accumulation of men made possible a political take-off, as the traditional, ritual, costly, violent forms of power were superseded by a subtle calculated technology of subjection ... The establishment of a coded, formally egalitarian constitution supported by a system of representative government. But this 'Enlightenment' politics had its dark underside in the ever-proliferating network of disciplinary mechanisms.
> (Foucault 1977: 201)

Foucault suggests that the 'scientific method' of observation and evaluation was related to a growing post-enlightenment preoccupation with rules and normality. It was this tradition, heralded by earlier, more extreme attempts to impose a norm, as found for example in the Spanish Inquisition, which has also come to underpin the acceptability of making judgements on others in relation to prevailing norms and hence the acceptability of educational assessment.

More significant even than the evaluation of individuals according to some arbitrary social standard, disguised in the language of apparently objective science, is the bureaucratic style of administration that this makes possible. In practice, this means that issues which are in reality questions of alternative values are perceived as technical problems to which a 'right answer' – an 'optimum solution' – exists, waiting to be discovered.

Foucault and the Power Relations of Discourse

Foucault's theories have much in common with the emphasis of Marxist theory on the crucial role of false consciousness in the ideological legitimation of capitalism. Foucault differs strongly, however, in his identification of unequal power relations as the inevitable feature of any social intercourse, rather than a particular manifestation of capitalism (Donald 1981). His structuralist perspective is located between the freedom of interactionism and the determinism of much macro theory, as represented in the following quotation:

> Structuralism, then, involves deconstructing the subject. Certainly the individual remains at the centre of the analysis: what he or she 'knows' is the starting point. However, the subject is not seen as a free agent, centre of his own self creating and conferring meanings on the social world around him. Rather the approach effectively 'deconstructs' the subject, explaining meanings in terms of a structure which lies beyond the individual's comprehension and control . . . this necessitates a perception of the individual act as a representation of the underlying structure . . . a node through which language and the social formation speak.
>
> (Webster 1981: 6, 7)

One of the main strengths of Foucault's analysis in this respect is his commitment, like Weber's, to empirical study and his attempts to map in detail the outcomes of specific human actions. Straddling the normal boundaries of history, philosophy, politics, sociology and the history of science, Foucault's work grew in significance during the 1980s partly in response to the vacuum created, in France at least, by the discrediting of both Marxism and 'reformism'. There is no conspiracy theory in Foucault's work. His essentially phenomenological approach argues that all types of social form, from sexuality to penology and the law, are relationships of power. He thus locates power not in particular social structures, but as an effect of the operation of social relationships between groups and individuals. Hence power cannot be located as emanating from any particular point, such as 'the state', since Foucault sees the state as a composite of a multiplicity of centres and mechanisms of 'micro-powers', such as hospitals, schools and factories. The strategic aims of the state apparatus, in particular, must be understood in relation to these 'micro-powers'. Far from being the currency of the ideological superstructure in relation to the economic base, power and the political transformations it informs 'are not the result of some necessity, some imminent rationality but the responses to particular problems combining not in a totalised, centralised manner but by serial repercussion' (Sheridan 1980: 218).

> Political power from this perspective, is not the possession of a social class, but a proliferating, anonymous force which cannot be attributed to the ideological self-expression of a unified economic group . . . disseminated through many and varied discourses and institutions, power possesses no single determining centre and cannot be identified with a monolithic state apparatus which it largely outstrips . . . his [Foucault's] work invites a radical rethinking of such notions as the neutrality of scientific truth and the progressive acquisition of knowledge though trial and error, just as it challenges us to re-examine the idea that political power is increasingly centralised within the state and that power emanates from ideological oppression and ownership of the means of production.
>
> (Hill 1981: 7)

These now familiar arguments have proved extremely influential in recent years. Following the theoretical work of Foucault and others it is now widely accepted that power and knowledge are two sides of the same process; knowledge cannot be 'pure' but is necessarily political, not because it has necessarily political consequences or utility but because 'knowledge has its conditions of possibility in power relations . . . knowledge is not true or false but legitimate or illegitimate for a particular set of power relations' (Sheridan 1980: 20).

Thus, Foucault's work challenges the very basis of modern rationality and science, which have, according to this argument, the same ignoble origins as the lunatic asylum – one of Foucault's favourite subjects of study. People are only mad and in need of containment when they lack the power to assert the legitimacy of their version of reality, their knowledge, over that currently prevailing.

In Foucault's work there is no conception of historical determinism or of 'false' as opposed to 'true' consciousness. Although for him history is not simply the product of human interaction, it is nevertheless incomprehensible except as the outcome of human projects.

Clearly there are strong links here with Giddens's notion of 'structuration' (Giddens 1976), in which he conceives structures as existing 'out of time and space and impersonal for purposes of analysis but structures which (nevertheless) only exist as the reproduced conduct of situated actors with definite intentions and interests' (p. 127). Indeed in Volume 1 of his *Contemporary Critique of Historical Materialism* (Giddens 1981), he explicitly pursues Foucault's emphasis on covert domination as the basis for social control, identifying two of Foucault's principal themes – the commodification of time and the use of surveillance as a form of social control – as central in his own analysis of the characteristics of modern industrial society. It is the centrality of these themes to a sociological understanding of the specific topic of educational assessment which justifies the foregoing rather abstract discussion and the more specfic analysis that follows.

In his *Two Lectures* (Foucault 1976) Foucault argues that one of the great inventions of bourgeois society and of industrial capitalism was that of disciplinary power. In *Discipline and Punishment* (1977), he describes the emergence in France of a whole range of new 'disciplines' between 1760 and 1840 as an army of technicians – warders, doctors (and later), psychiatrists and teachers – came to replace the executioner, whose crude retribution is replaced by processes of assessment, diagnosis and normative judgement covering not only explicit offences but the 'whole range of passions, instincts, drives and desires, infirmities and maladjustments' (Sarup 1982: 15).

These new tactics of disciplinary power involve two principal techniques. The first, 'hierarchical observation', involves a 'permanent and continuous field of surveillance'. The second, 'normalizing judgement', involves the novel concept of a norm which serves as the basis for categorization. The initial, negative role of these emerging disciplines, which was simply to protect society, rapidly gave way, Foucault suggests, to a more positive emphasis on 'socialization' to reinforce the norm.

Foucault's analysis of the way in which 'delinquency' is 'neutralized' and deprived of any potential political content by the operation of total institutions, such as prisons, has some common ground with the work of Durkheim, who also stressed the significance of the public identification of deviation not so much for the protection of society but crucially for the reinforcement of social norms among the majority of the population. The two French scholars share a common interest in the techniques evolved by industrial society to provide for the division of labour and, at the same time, for social order. They have both been criticized for not distinguishing adequately in their analysis between the specific social configurations of France and its more general applications (O'Connor 1980; Sarup 1982).

Nevertheless, Foucault's preoccupation with the micro-processes of power as they emerge from the whole range of interactional discourse separates him fundamentally from Durkheim's statist and benign view. Although based on the specific micro-politics of France, Foucault's arguments offer insights which are generally applicable to societies undergoing an equivalent transformation of the social order to that of France. His description of the features of industrializing societies, which include the way in which the new 'disciplines' rapidly become attached to the new class power which developed with industrialization, the latter's central concern with reproducing national security and the power relations of the status quo through the maintenance of the expansion of production and the provision of a docile and appropriately skilled workforce, would appear to be valid for all such societies.

Crucially, though, Foucault rejects analyses which locate power within the economic relations of capitalist society. He explains the emerging disciplinary mechanisms through the technical requirements of mass production in industrial society *itself* (Sarup 1982: 24). His work is thus more in line with that of other more recent scholars, such as Marcuse, who, despite his Marxist orientation, emphasized the characteristics of social life under capitalism and the implications of these, which in his view transcend questions of class struggle and inequality. Thus Foucault argues, like Marcuse, that there is a:

> Proliferation of 'judges' who take the form of technical experts – teachers, doctors, psychologists, guards, social workers. As they operate in a sphere well protected from judicial or popular intervention, an antithesis has developed between discipline and democracy. Disciplinary power co-exists with democratic forms and undermines them from within. The roots of discipline are so deep in the organisation of modern society that the subordination of discipline to democratic control is increasingly difficult.
>
> (Sarup 1982: 24)

It is this emphasis on the significance of the form of social life itself, rather than on the specific balance of power relations, which makes Foucault's work so central to the exploration of the social roots of assessment. More particularly, Foucault has himself identified educational examinations (i.e. assessment) as one of the more significant disciplinary mechanisms to have emerged. For Foucault what might appear to be only a harmless technique of knowledge is in fact, simultaneously, a technique of power. By combining the two principles of hierarchical observation and normalizing judgement, the examination becomes one of the major instruments for locating each individual's place in society. In arguing that examinations both help to establish the 'truth' and deploy the force to maintain it, Foucault's work thus echoes the fundamental rationale for educational assessment given [earlier]. The student is controlled through a system of 'micro-penalties', the constant giving of marks which constitutes a whole field of surveillance.

Foucault's own analysis of the nature of this discipline is drawn predominantly from French examples. He describes a school of drawing for tapestry apprentices in 1737, emphasizing the detailed ordering of every minute of time, the regular, individual and carefully graded exercises, the supervision, assessment and subsequent allocation of individuals. The essentially monastic model of elaborate and detailed prescriptions for curriculum and pedagogy for each minute of the day is, and has remained, characteristically French. Although it made a significant, if relatively brief, appearance in England under Bell and Lancaster's tightly structured monitorial system, England has not typically provided generalized rules for such detailed curriculum structuring. More generally the commodification of time is, as Hargreaves (1989) has shown, an important apparatus of educational control which resonates with the core themes of technical rationality and individual control as these are addressed in this chapter.

Drawing on Jeremy Bentham's architectural concept of the 'panoptican', in which the isolated individual is constantly visible to a central authority, Foucault extends Bentham's idea that the perfection of surveillance makes the actual exercise of power unnecessary: the visible and unverifiable power will make the individual 'self controlling' as he is conscious of being observed, assessed and classified.

Very few individuals, except perhaps those in some prisons or mental hospitals, are now subjected to an explicit 'panoptism'. Although 'open-plan' schools were, arguably, a brief resurgence of the panoptic idea which characterized much of eighteenth- and nineteenth-century school architecture, the panoptic function is now largely symbolic, carried out pervasively and efficiently with little real opposition – not least by examinations and various other forms of assessment and accountability. As Foucault suggests, the age-based organization of the school, the graded curriculum, the marks for performance, produce an ensemble of compulsory alignments, some physical, some mental, by means of which individuals replace each other in a space 'marked off by aligned intervals' (Foucault, quoted by Sarup 1982: 18). The examination is the fixing, at once ritual and 'scientific', of individual differences.

Hoskin (1979) sets out in detail one example of how Foucault's theory may be applied to the empirical reality of the development of examinations in England. The advent of print and the explosion of knowledge was associated with the development of examinations based on individual questions, marks and syllabuses. The giving of marks for individual questions constituted a major step towards establishing a *mathematical* model of reality, a step which was in Hoskin's view arguably as important as the invention of the alphabet in that 'the science of the individual was now feasible, for the principle has now been articulated that a given "quality" could be assigned a quantitative mark' (p. 144). It was therefore possible to weigh up individuals and compare them to others.

Hoskin argues that the new technique of disciplinary power emerging from the fusion of traditional rationality and authority into 'rational authority' finds its archetypal form in the examination. It is the examination which lies at the heart of the control function of schooling. Equally, it is clear that the principles of examination – quantitative, particularistic, pseudo-scientific evaluation for specific purposes – are not confined to education, their growth in that sphere being reflexively related to a developing 'rational authority' in Western capitalist society as a whole. However, the recent trend towards hierarchical curriculum and assessment frameworks arguably represents an even more powerful manifestation of such symbolic control, in which the learner's identity is continuously defined by a series of categoric levels.

But, as well as being central, assessment is also necessarily flexible as an allocation and legitimation technique. Indeed, it is shot through with contradictions not only at the level of practice concerning the incompatibility of means which serve equally important ends (Eckstein and Noah 1993), but also at the fundamental level of purpose since, as has already been argued, it embodies the potential to be both liberating and controlling. [. . .].

References

Airasian, P. W. (1988) Symbolic validation: the case of state-mandated high states testing, *Educational Evaluation and Policy Analysis*, 10 (4): 301–15.

Banks, O. (1978) Macro and micro perspectives in the sociology of education, in L. Barton and R. Meighan (eds.) *Sociological Interpretations of Schooling and Classrooms*, Driffield, Nafferton.

Bates, R. (1980a) Educational administration, the sociology of science and the management of knowledge, *Educational Administration Quarterly*, 16 (2): 1–20.

Bates, R. (1980b) Bureaucracy, professionalisation and the control of knowledge. Paper presented to the National Conference of Professors of Educational Administration, Norfolk, VA.

Bernstein, B. (1977) *Class Codes and Control* (Vol. iii), London, Routledge & Kegan Paul.

Bernstein, B. (1982) Codes, modalities and the process of cultural reproduction: a model, in M. Apple (ed.) *Cultural and Economic Reproduction in Education*, London, Routledge & Kegan Paul.

Broadfoot, P. (1991) The significance of contemporary contradiction in educational assessment policies in England and Wales, in R. Stake (ed.) *Advances in Program Evaluation: Volume 1 (Part A)*, London, JAI Press.

Broadfoot, P. (1992) Assessment developments in French education, *Education Review*, 44 (3): 309–16.

Broadfoot, P. (1993) Assessment procedures in French education, in J. Nisbet (ed.) *Curriculum and Assessment*, Paris, Organization for Economic Co-operation and Development.

Cherkaoui, M. (1977) Bernstein and Durkheim: two theories of change in educational systems, *Harvard Education Review*, 47 (4): 156–66.

Chin, R. and Benne, K. (1978) General strategies for effecting changes in human systems, in W. G. Bennis, K. D. Benne, R. Chin and K. E. Corey (eds.) *The Planning of Change* (3rd edn), London, Holt, Rinehart & Winston.

Coleman, J. (1968) The concept of equality of educational opportunity, *Harvard Educational Review*, special issue, 38 (1): 7–22.

Collins, R. (1979) *The Credential Society*, New York, Academic Press.

Dallmayr, F. (1982) The theory of structuration: a critique, in A. Giddens (ed.) *Profiles and Critiques in Social Theory*, London, Macmillan.

Dawe, A. (1970) The two sociologies, *British Journal of Sociology*, 21 (2): 56–75.

Donald, J. (1981) Green paper: noise of crisis, in R. Dale, G. Esland, R. Ferguson and M. MacDonald (eds.) *Schooling and the National Interest*, Lewes, Falmer Press.

Durkheim, E. (1947) *The Division of Labour in Society*, New York, Free Press.

Durkheim, E. (1961) *Moral Education: A Study in the Theory and Application of the Sociology of Education*, New York, Free Press (trans. Wilson and Schnurer).

Eckstein, M. A. and Noah, H. J. (1993) *Secondary School Examinations. International Perspectives on Policies and Practice*, New Haven, CT, Yale University Press.

Foucault, M. (1976) *Two Lectures* (trans. A. Sheridan), London, Allen Lane.

Foucault, M. (1977) *Discipline and Punishment* (trans. A. Sheridan), London, Allen Lane.

Gerth, H. and Wright-Mills, C. (1952) A Marx for the managers, in R. K. Merton (ed.) *Bureaucracy*, New York, Free Press.

Giddens, A. (1976) *New Rules of Sociological Method*, London, Hutchinson.

Giddens, A. (1981) *A Contemporary Critique of Historical Materialism*, London, Macmillan.

Gintis, H. (1980) Theory, practice and the discursive structure of education. Paper given to the International Sociology of Education Conference, Westhill College, 3–5 January.

GNVQ Assessment Review Project (GARP) (1994) *Report No. 23* (final report), London, Research and Development Services, Department of Employment.

Gouldner, A. (1952) On Weber's analysis of bureaucratic rules, in R. K. Merton (ed.) *Bureaucracy*, New York, Free Press.

Habermas, J. (1970) Technology and science as ideology: for Herbert Marcuse on his seventieth birthday, in J. Habermas, *Towards a Rational Society*, London, Heinemann.

Habermas, J. (1976) *Legitimation Crisis*, London, Heinemann.

Hamilton, D. (1981) On simultaneous instruction – the early evolution of class teaching (mimeo), University of Glasgow, Department of Education.

Hargreaves, A. (1989) *Curriculum and Assessment Reform*, Milton Keynes, Open University Press.

Hargreaves, D. H. (1979) A sociological critique of individualism in education. Paper presented to the annual conference of the Standing Conference for Studies in Education, London, King's College.

Hill, L. (1981) Shades of the prison house, *The Times Higher Educational Supplement*, 2 January.

Hogan, D. (1981) Capitalism, liberalism and schooling, in R. Dale, G. Esland, R. Ferguson and M. MacDonald (eds.) *Schooling and the National Interest: Education and the State* (Vol. 1), Lewes, Falmer Press.

Hoskin, K. (1979) The examination, disciplinary powers and rational schooling, *History of Education*, 8 (2): 135–46.

Larson, M. (1981) Monopolies of competence and bourgeois ideology, in R. Dale, G. Esland, R. Ferguson and M. MacDonald (eds.) *Education and the State* (Vol. 2), London, Falmer Press/The Open University.

Marcuse, J. (1964) *One-Dimensional Man*, New York, Free Press.

Marshall, G. (1982) *In Search of the Spirit of Capitalism*, London, Hutchinson University Press.

Mills, I. (1979) Individuality and assessment. Paper presented to the annual conference of the Standing Conference for Studies in Education, London, King's College.

Munby, S. (1989) *Assessing and Recording Achievement*, Oxford, Blackwell.

Neave, G. (1980) Statements at 16+: a European perspective, in T. Burgess and E. Adams (eds.) *Outcomes of Education*, London, Macmillan.

Nisbet, J. (ed.) (1993) *Assessment and Curriculum Reform*, Paris, Organization for Economic Co-operation and Development.

O'Connor, J. (1980) The division of labor in society, *Insurgent Sociologist*, 10 (1): 60–8.

Organization for Economic Co-operation and Development (1989) *Education and the Economy in a Changing Society*, Paris, OECD.

Parsons, T. (1951) *The Social System*, New York, Free Press.

Pollard, A., Broadfoot, P., Croll, P., Osborn, M. and Abbot, D. (1994) *Changing English Primary Schools? The Impact of the Education Reform Act at Key Stage One*, London, Cassell.

Poulantzas, N. (1973) *Political Power and Social Classes*, London, New Left Books.

Reimer, F. (1971) *School is Dead*, London, Penguin.

Rodmell, D. (1977) The contribution of monitoring to educational policy-making, in R. Summer (ed.) *Monitoring Educational Achievement*, Slough, National Foundation for Educational Research.

Salaman, G. (1981) *Class and the Corporation*, London, Fontana.

Salter, B. and Tapper, T. (1981) *Education, Politics and the State*, London, Grant-McIntyre.

Sarup, M. (1982) *Education, State and Crisis – A Marxist Perspective*, London, Routledge & Kegan Paul.

Sheridan, A. (1980) *Michel Foucault: The Will to Truth*, London, Tavistock.

Smith, G. (1980) *Politics in Western Europe* (3rd edn), London, Heinemann.

Weber, M. (1923) *General Economic History*, London, Allen & Unwin.

Weber, M. (1947) *The Theory of Social and Economic Organization*, New York, Free Press (trans. T. Parsons and A. M. Henderson).

Webster, D. (1981) Attitudes to the world of work: the relation of theory to empirical data. Paper presented to the seventh annual conference of the British Educational Research Association, Crewe and Alsager College, 4–7 September.

Wilson, H. T. (1977) *The American Ideology*, London, Routledge & Kegan Paul.

SECTION 2
CULTURAL PERSPECTIVES

6

Values and Aims in Curriculum and Assessment Frameworks: A 16-Nation Review[1]

Joanna Le Métais

Introduction

International comparisons such as the Third International Maths and Science Survey (TIMSS) exert pressure on national education systems to score highly in a comparative context. However, learner performance in such surveys depends to a large extent on the overlap between national curricula and the content and nature of the survey tasks. The International Review of Curriculum and Assessment Frameworks (IRCAF) project was commissioned to identify national contexts which are crucial to an understanding of education policy and practice and of learner performance. Among the most important contextual factors are national values and educational aims. The IRCAF project has found that curricula and associated assessments differ between countries, both in the degree of centralized control and in the extent to which they are coherently linked to expressed values and aims, and the organization of education systems and institutions. Drawing on the project, this chapter explores

- values and their expression as educational aims;
- the extent to which governments explicitly state values and aims; and
- the ways in which values and aims are expressed in curriculum and assessment policies.

Values

Values are concerns about what ought to be. A value is a belief which need not rely upon facts or evidence, although a value position can be supported or challenged by knowledge propositions. Ryle (1949) talks of values as 'dispositions' which incline us towards specific structures, tasks and patterns of behaviour.

Basic values seek to monitor and maintain the system as a whole and include freedom, equity, the value of the unique individual, community, family and defence of society and social justice. They may be supported, or contradicted, by operational values which relate to the way in which policy is implemented at different levels. Examples of these are public burden (cost to the taxpayer), selectivity (for self-determination, élitism or equality), universality, participation, democracy, social control and residualism. Operational values may 'harden' or be promoted to basic values; for instance democracy may become an end in its own right instead of a means to achieve, say, equitable provision.

Tensions may arise between values or between their interpretation at various levels – for example choice and market forces on the one hand and economy and rational planning on the other. Moreover, the implementation of a single value, for example parental choice, can give rise to numerous internal conflicts, as follows:

diversity of provision	← →	parity of esteem
free market	← →	rational planning and use of resources
vouchers and privatization	← →	social justice
competing demands	← →	unmet needs

Reflecting values in education

In an ideal world, national values, clearly understood and shared by all, would form in clear steps a coherent thread through the education system from aims to outcomes (see Figure 6.1). This coherence would flow from

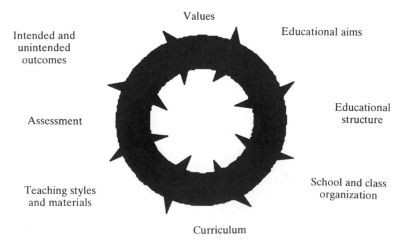

Figure 6.1   *Implementing values in education*

aims, through *educational structure* (duration of compulsory education, phases and types of schools), institutional *organization* of learners (grouping by age, general ability or curriculum choice), the selection and deployment of teachers (specialists or generalist; one per class or team teaching) and time. The *curriculum* (subject based or interdisciplinary, balance between breadth and depth, and common or differentiated content) would be consistent with aims and structure and supported by appropriate *teaching styles* (achieved through initial and in-service teacher education) and *materials*. Finally, the methods and frequency of *assessment* would be chosen to enable all learners to demonstrate the extent to which they had achieved the educational aims and internalized national values. Where discrepancies arose, deficiencies in any of the stages could be identified and addressed.

However, this model is too simple. National values may be neither national nor discrete. The aims of education as expressed in legislation or reforms may differ from, or even conflict with, those pursued by learners, teachers, parents, education administrators and others. Similar conflicts may arise with respect to internal organization, curriculum, teaching methods and materials and assessment. It is therefore not surprising that assessments reveal both intended and unintended outcomes and that the level of satisfaction with 'the system' or its components varies. Equally, within a context of limited resources, the most important of which is probably the amount of learning/teaching time, choices have to be made between different learning and teaching objectives. As a result, criticisms may variously be levelled at the system for failing to: instil basic values; teach basic skills; develop higher-order thinking and problem-solving skills; develop creativity, flexibility and co-operative working methods; prepare young people for today's jobs; prepare them for tomorrow's unemployment and life-long learning; and so forth. These criticisms reflect different expectations or different value positions.

There is also an important time dimension to the coherence between values and aims and curriculum and assessment systems (see Figure 6.2).

1. Education is a long-term project. It takes time to make and implement policy, build schools, train and recruit staff, develop curricula, materials and assessment instruments, and all this must be achieved before the first learner attends class. It takes a further 10–12 years for learners to complete their compulsory education.
2. The passing of time brings about political, economic and social changes which may affect the continuing relevance of educational aims. The time taken to establish or reform the infrastructure reduces the 'shelf-life' remaining once a new system becomes operational.
3. There is no point at which education can start with a clean slate: there are always inherited structures, learners part-way through the process and teachers with knowledge, skills and attitudes acquired to meet previous needs. The benefits of reforms in one aspect, for example, the curriculum, may not be fully achieved until other elements (for example

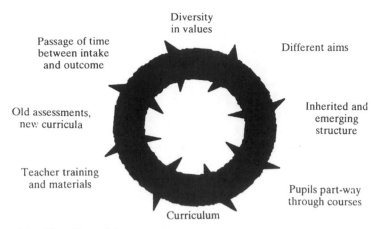

Figure 6.2　*The effect of time on coherence*

teaching styles, materials and assessment instruments) have been adapted.

4. In terms of measuring outcomes, whilst the achievement of some aims, such as functional literacy, may be assessed at specific points during compulsory education, success in others, such as achieving individual potential, developing positive attitudes to life-long learning and flexibility to deal with change, may not emerge until much later and the specific contribution of formal education, as distinct from other influences, may not be identifiable at all.

Thus, any education system is a combination of the past, the present and the future. The past is represented through aims, values, structures and teaching styles; for many teachers, the defining years are those in which they receive preservice training and first enter the profession. The present is represented, for example, in current assessment arrangements, which tend to have an immediate impact on curriculum practice. The future is often set out in the curriculum and learning targets, since curricula tend to embrace aspirations to optimize good practice. Understanding the effect of aims and values on education means understanding the interaction of these factors and successful implementation of reforms needs to take them into consideration.

Expressing values

The degree of detail in which *national* values underlying education are expressed or prescribed depends above all on whether the education system is subject to national or devolved control. There are further differences in the extent to which such values are made explicit.

National systems
National values are expressed in general terms in England, Hungary, The Netherlands, New Zealand and Spain. Within these national systems, there

may nevertheless be a commitment to pluralism and values may be expressed in the constitution and/or other statutes, which provide a framework for the expression of values through devolved educational structures.

England has no written constitution nor bill of rights and it is not customary to dwell on values nor to monitor the success of curriculum and assessment arrangements with specific attention to values. Basic values such as equality of opportunity, irrespective of gender, race and disability, are explicit in separate legislation such as the Sex Discrimination Act 1975, the Race Relations Act 1976 and the Disability Discrimination Act 1995. Expressed values underlying education legislation in England include respect for the individual through choice and equality of opportunity, quality, standards, early excellence and access.[2]

Until 1989, the *Hungarian* curriculum reinforced clearly stated Communist values. In 1990, the newly independent government *removed* explicit values statements from the curriculum and devolved decision-making powers to schools. The objectives of the new National Core Curriculum honour basic human rights, children's rights, freedom of conscience and religion and the values of school education, as well as minority rights.

In *The Netherlands*, the constitution prohibits state determination of educational values. It safeguards the individual's or group's right to transmit religious or moral values through education by granting them access to funding to establish schools on an equal footing with public sector establishments. The provisions ensure minimum input standards (such as teacher qualifications and numbers, accommodation) whilst fostering plurality by devolving management and financial responsibilities to the competent authority (that is, the municipality or the denominational or other body) which established the school and which determines its values and aims. Thus one may find very explicit, even prescriptive, values at institutional level.

Attitudes and values, along with knowledge and skills, are an integral part of the *New Zealand* curriculum. The curriculum does not prescribe specific values, recognizing that those held by individuals and by various groups may vary greatly, but it assumes that the values of individual and collective responsibility which underpin New Zealand's democratic society are supported by most people in most communities. The regulatory framework is intended to support and reward positive progress, promote the involvement of parents and communities and enable the government and the education sector to respond to change.

The post-Franco constitution of 1978 set a national framework in *Spain*, within which the new democracy would be reinforced through educational reform and also through the process of securing that reform 'which continually demands that it be argued and accepted by the whole of our society . . . progressively introduced over a sustained period . . . with the extensive support that must be assured for its prolonged survival [and] the active, motivated and reflexive participation of the personnel fundamental to education itself' (Spanish Ministry of Education and Science, 1990). This operational value means that values are centrally guided but not imposed. The powers granted to the autonomous communities offer further scope for regional diversity.

Countries which tend to express very detailed aims and clear educational and social values are exemplified by France, Japan, Korea, Singapore and Sweden. *France*, as part of a new initiative, explicitly promulgates the aims and objectives of schooling. These include equality of opportunity, minimum standards, access and involvement of the community in education.[3] *Italy's* constitution stresses the freedom of education and teaching and adds two rights and two duties with regard to education:

- The right of the state to issue general regulations on education.
- The right of private individuals to set up schools at no cost to the state.
- The state's duty to provide a network of education establishments of every type and level, open to everyone without distinction. Appropriate measures have to be taken to enable capable and deserving students to enter higher levels of education even if they lack the financial resources.
- The duty of parents to educate their children for at least eight years. This is free of charge in state schools.

In *Japan*, the Fundamental Law of Education 1949 enunciates explicit values: 'Education shall aim at full development of personality, at rearing a people, sound in mind and body, who love truth and justice, esteem individual values, respect labour, have a deep sense of responsibility and are imbued with an independent spirit as the builders of a peaceful state and society' (Kanaya, 1993).

The constitution of the *Republic of Korea* defines basic values which have changed little since their adoption some fifty years ago. Education legislation and the national curriculum provide more specific statements of values as they relate to education, and these are subject to regular review. Whilst wholesale change is uncommon, influences of the changing world make themselves felt through, for example, a growing materialism and the need to compete effectively on an international basis.

In *Singapore*, the government undertakes wide consultation to achieve consensus but, within the centralized system, there is diversity, especially between the denominational and non-denominational schools. Inspectors use school statements of values, aims and mission as a framework for inspecting the content and processes of teaching and learning.

Sweden prescribes, in considerable detail, the basic and operational values underpinning its education system and their transmission. These include the inviolability of human life, individual freedom and integrity, equal value, solidarity with the weak and vulnerable, understanding and compassion, open discussion, internationalization of Swedish society, and empathy with the values and conditions of others.

Federal systems, with responsibility devolved to subnational authorities

Five of the countries in the study (Australia, Canada, Germany, Switzerland and the USA) have federal structures and values which are therefore often expressed, in varying degrees of detail, in subnational legislation. Nevertheless, there may be over-riding values and operational principles which derive from national constitutions or which are promoted through nationally funded programmes.

In *Australia*, within a system of devolved authority to the states and territories, education legislation and practice are essentially based on the principle of equal access at all levels. The federal government, in co-operation with the state and territory governments, has played an increasing role in promoting equity and an education that reflects its commitment to social justice. Some value perspectives are supported by legislation not specific to education. Individual states and territories explicitly indicate values in their legislation and guidelines.

Responsibility for education in *Canada* is vested in the provinces and territories but the majority of Canada's citizens share an ethos of equal opportunity, and the provision of universal, free schooling to college or university level. Accordingly, the provinces and territories have developed diversified systems of education, designed to be universally accessible and to respond to

- increasing racial, cultural and linguistic diversity in Canadian society;
- greater equality for women;
- the needs of native Canadians and exceptional learners; and
- differing employment needs in an increasingly competitive world economy.

Detailed statements of values or principles may be made by subnational authorities, for example, Alberta: quality education, equity, flexibility, responsiveness and accountability, and 17 additional 'beliefs'.

In *Germany*, the basic law on education guarantees, among other things, 'the freedom of art and science, research and teaching, freedom of creed, conscience and to profess a religion, the freedom to choose one's occupation and place of study or training, equality before the law and the natural right of parents to care for and bring up their children'.[4]

The *Swiss* constitution requires that 'state education shall be available to children of all confessions without any restrictions being placed on their freedom of conscience or belief'.[5] Each *canton* has its own education legislation, with varying aims. The general principles laid down in one *canton* provide an example:

> State education shall promote the harmonious development of the abilities of the child within the framework of the democratic tradition of western civilisation, teach him tolerance and a sense of responsibility towards others and his environment, as well as respect for other languages and cultures. At the same time it shall instil in the pupil such knowledge and skills that will allow him to go on to vocational training and take up a cause.[6]

Despite the devolution of responsibility for education to states and districts, the *USA* constitution safeguards the rights of the individual with regard to matters of conscience, in a framework of individual and collective rights and responsibilities. The imposition of a national set of values would be perceived as a threat to individual and state liberties, but successive administrations seek to achieve a broad consensus concerning values and aims. These include civic morality, knowledge and a universal public education which teaches learners to think independently and creatively and to avoid subservience to the will of others, as the key to a truly democratic society. Where consensus on specific educational programmes or objectives is achieved, and carried through into (federal) legislation, federal resources may be allocated in support of their implementation.

More recently, national policy-makers believe that, as a result of devolved powers, schools, in particular, have become increasingly dominated by rules and procedures demanded by districts and states. A nationally integrated accountability system, with a strong emphasis on the setting of goals, especially those related to participation, retention and outcomes in terms of learner achievement, is designed to enhance the managerial and professional autonomy of schools, colleges and universities.[7]

Evolving values

Whilst basic values may alter little over time, political changes often serve as a stimulus for a major change, either in the expressed values themselves, or in the way in which they are expressed. The nature of this change varies. It may be linked to aspirations for national identity or for a break with the past, such as the Republic of Korea, where concern for democracy reflects its national history of conflict and competition with communist North Korea. In common with other central and eastern European countries, Hungary is striving to re-establish national, rather thǎn Soviet, values and to carry these through into its aims and systems. The Spanish reforms stress learner and parent involvement in the life and decision-making of the school, reflecting the relatively new democracy.

There are other, perhaps less dramatic, influences which nevertheless bring about change. Parental expectations have been a significant contributor to learner performance and lead to increasing competition for access to the most prestigious education institutions in many countries, but most strikingly in the Pacific Rim states. In the Republic of Korea, the material benefits of increased social and professional status now constitute a more powerful incentive for parents and learners than the intrinsic value traditionally placed on scholarship and education. By linking funding to the number of learners, two countries (England and The Netherlands) explicitly use choice and competition as a means to raise standards.

Another stimulus, explicitly stated in Singapore, comes from the realization that dependence on natural resources is not sufficient and that future employment and economic prosperity require highly developed human resources. This is highlighted by international indicators of educational and economic performance and employment. Employers in the USA enter into specific agreements with districts and schools concerning educational aims and targets, in return for providing employment for 'suitably trained' personnel.

Policy-makers in different countries are also becoming more aware of each others' approaches and outcomes and international studies of learner achievement increasingly influence education policy. With a primary focus on outcomes, these studies may cause (or reinforce) the value of educational competitiveness based on a limited range of measurable outcomes at the expense of processes and attitudes.

Finally, funding provides a powerful incentive for change, even in 'decentralized' countries where it has encouraged participation in 'national' initiatives such as promoting preschool education or adding a vocational dimension to general education.

Tensions between values

It is important to distinguish between the formal value system and the informal or implicit system espoused by practitioners, although it is not straightforward to measure values-in-use. For example, research in Korea reveals a reduction in the congruence between the stated values and values-in-use. Traditionally, obedience to and respect for elders were more highly valued than learner independence. Many parents wished to improve their children's social status and made considerable sacrifices to secure their children's success. In return, Korean children were expected to sacrifice play in favour of extra learning. Strong competition, reinforced by assessments and examinations, led to the establishment of many private institutions which provide tuition outside school. Surveys indicate that learners, like their teachers, strongly support 'values' or virtues such as 'basic etiquette' (defined as 'healthy living'), 'regular life', honesty and sincerity. However, more recently, individual pursuit of material and social advancement reflects a transfer from intrinsic to extrinsic motivation for educational success. The government also stresses individual creativity and diversity, as a means to national economic success in the twenty-first century, in contrast to teachers, for whom conformity facilitates the management of large classes. Thus, the situation may be more complex than research findings suggest.

Conflicts between individual and collective values are found in *Spain* where the constitutional right to education is expressed in terms of obligatory schooling, which is unacceptable to the gypsy community.

In the *USA*, conflicts can arise between different constitutional rights. For example, the insistence by certain fundamentalist groups on the teaching of 'creationism' (instead of Darwinian theories of evolution) opposes freedom of belief and the separation of church and school. It is important to remember that whilst constitutional rights (such as freedom of religion) can be defended in law, values cannot, and therefore fundamentalist challenges to values have implications for individual rights.

Aims

Value positions dispose us towards particular aims, structures and working methods. Aims may be expressed as objectives, goals and targets and they may be intrinsic (for example to contribute to life-long learning) or instrumental (preparing young people for work and contributing to the national economy). They may focus on developing individual qualities or capacities, or on promoting citizenship and a sense of community and safeguarding a cultural heritage.

Like values, aims reflect a country's historical context. The 1989 educational reform in *Spain* was preceded by extensive consideration of, and public consultation on, the values and aims of education. The reforms introduced a decentralized model whereby responsibility for education was devolved to the autonomous communities (although the transfer of responsibilities is not yet complete). However, time and political changes bring their influence to bear and the current government in Spain does not fully support its predecessor's reforms, which are still in the process of being implemented.

International comparisons such as TIMSS also exercise an influence on educational aims. Reactions to such surveys vary. Whilst some countries revise their provision to improve on their relatively poor performance, or include specific international performance targets in their aims (for example *New Zealand*, the *USA*), others seem able to distance themselves. *Korean* authorities apparently pay less attention to their country's position as a leading performer in the TIMSS survey because they are aware of the relative success of their *younger* learners; their concern is that this relative advantage diminishes as learners grow older.

Expressed educational aims in 16 countries

Aims may be general (to acknowledge or promote cultural, religious and social diversity) or expressed in relation to specific targets. The variation in detail is noticeable in the following examples,[8] where aims outlined by different countries are grouped in ten broad categories: artistic, cultural, developmental, economic, environmental, personal, political, social, moral/religious and physical. Not all countries specify aims for each category and there is some overlap between them.

Australia
An appreciation and understanding of, and confidence to participate in, the creative arts; understanding and respect for cultural heritage; a foundation

for further education and training, in terms of knowledge and skills, respect for learning and positive attitudes for life-long education; preparation for changing employment needs and the requirement for a 'productive work-force' in the current and emerging economic and social needs of the nation; an understanding of, and concern for, balanced development and the global environment; self-confidence, optimism, high self-esteem, respect for others, the achievement of personal excellence and the creative use of leisure time; knowledge, skills, attitudes and values which will enable individuals to parti-cipate as active and informed citizens in a democratic Australian society within an international context; a capacity for judgement in matters of moral-ity, ethics and social justice; physical and personal health and fitness.

Canada
To respond to the bilingual and multicultural character of society; to sus-tain and nourish cultural diversity, foster positive intergroup attitudes, break down cultural stereotypes and ensure equality of treatment and access for all minorities; preparation for further education, work and every-day life; to provide learners with opportunities for their fullest social and individual development; to teach all young people something about com-mon values and social behaviour and the intellectual and other traditions which support the common good in community, province and nation; and a positive lifestyle for all individuals, which includes maintaining physical health and psychological well-being (Saskatchewan Education, 1996).

England and Wales
To promote the spiritual, moral, cultural and mental development of learners at school and in society; preparation for the opportunities, respon-sibilities and experiences of adult life and increasing the relevance of learner achievement to the world of work to enhance the nation's interna-tional competitiveness; raising the standards of education of all, with par-ticular regard to literacy and numeracy; to reflect a clear national strategy for the development and improvement of information and communications technology in schools.

France
To provide the basic elements and tools of knowledge: oral and written expression, reading and mathematics; to exercise and develop the individ-ual's intelligence, sensitivity and manual, physical and artistic aptitudes; to develop awareness of time, space, the objects of the modern world and the human body; progressive acquisition of methodological knowledge; prepara-tion for the next phase of education and for work, not just for qualifications.

Germany
To further overall intellectual, emotional and physical development; to teach learners to be independent and make decisions and to bear their share of social responsibility; to further overall physical development.

Hungary
The drastic transformation of the wider political, social and economic environment has dramatically changed the education system. Key objectives include: to prepare learners for life in a modern market economy; to improve human resources, as well as the qualifications and flexibility of human resources for economic development; to prepare the country for full integration into Europe; to develop Hungary as a democracy.

Italy
Cultural literacy; to develop sensorial, perceptive, motor, linguistic and intellectual abilities; to promote independence; preparation for further study and employment; to promote the full development of the learner, with an emphasis on interaction with families and the broader social community; preparation for adulthood and citizenship; physical and psychodynamic capabilities.

Japan
To study the environment and natural and technological worlds; the capacity to cope positively with a changing society; self-reliant citizens of a peaceful and democratic state and community with a respect for human values; to promote international understanding; to teach community studies; through moral education in schools, to stop school violence and bullying, solve other behavioural problems and help children overcome school maladjustment problems; to rear a people, sound in mind and body.

Korea
To appreciate the arts, to preserve and develop natural culture, a respect for learning, a quest for truth and an ability to think scientifically; to help individuals lead creative and rational lives; to work diligently, be thrifty, be honest and responsible and become productive workers and wise consumers; a sense of originality; to appreciate nature; open-mindedness, creativity, independence and self-reliance and awareness of the individual; to promote patriotism and affection for others for the continuance and development of national independence as well as world peace; a sense of democratic citizenship; to teach learners to love freedom, observe a sense of responsibility and live harmoniously in society with a sense of human welfare; an ethical individual with sound morality; to acquire the knowledge and attitudes necessary for the sound growth and development of body and soul and to acquire courage and perseverance.

The Netherlands
To recognize that young people are growing up in a multicultural society; to develop understanding of and respect for cultural heritage; to contribute to the individual's upbringing on the basis of values acknowledged (notably by Christianity and humanism) as part of the Dutch tradition.

New Zealand
Respect for the diverse ethnic and cultural heritage of New Zealand people with acknowledgement of the unique place of the Maori; a broad education through a balanced curriculum covering essential learning areas and skills with high levels of competence in basic literacy and numeracy, science and technology, to enable successful participation in the changing technological and economic environment; to raise the educational achievement of all learners, including those at risk of failure; a highly skilled, adaptable and motivated workforce by promoting life-long learning; to prepare learners to participate as active and informed citizens in a democratic society, within an international context and to acknowledge New Zealand's role in the Pacific and as a member of the international community of nations; to create a community of shared values which include honesty, reliability, respect for others, respect for the law, tolerance (*rangimarie*), fairness, caring or compassion (*aroha*), non-sexism and non-racism.

Singapore
To develop literacy, numeracy, bilingualism, physical education, moral education and creative thinking.

Spain
Artistic and literary sensitivity; learning about the linguistic and cultural plurality of Spain; to acquire basic cultural skills and knowledge relating to oral expression, reading, writing and arithmetic, and progressive independence within the child's environment; acquisition of intellectual habits and working techniques, as well as scientific, technical, humanistic, historic and aesthetic knowledge; preparation for ongoing education and employment; full development of the learner's personality; individualized education comprising knowledge, skills and moral values in all areas of personal, family, social and professional life; knowledge of basic rights and liberties exercised in tolerance and freedom within the democratic principles of coexistence; training individuals to assume their responsibilities and to exercise their rights; promotion of peace, co-operation and solidarity between the different parts of the country; preparation for active participation in social and cultural life; critical analysis and evaluation of contemporary life; physical education and sports to enhance personal development.

Sweden
The ability to work independently and solve problems; to develop the personal qualities and competence necessary to enable all learners to achieve their potential in the labour market, built on continuous/life-long learning; to enable young people to keep their bearings in a complex reality, with a vast flow of information and rapid change; creative skills, the ability and will to change, communication skills; to teach learners to give of their best in responsible freedom; communicative abilities, language skills

and social competence; to instil those values on which society is based and to help learners to develop the ability to examine critically facts and relationships and appreciate the consequences of the various alternatives facing them.

Switzerland

To teach respect for other languages and cultures and to introduce learners to essential cultural and other values; to promote the harmonious development of the abilities of the child; to help learners acquire economic qualification; a sense of responsibility towards the environment; to promote personal development; to integrate the younger generation into the local, national and global society; within the framework of the democratic tradition of western civilization, to teach tolerance and a sense of responsibility towards others.

USA

To ensure that every adult US citizen will be literate; to teach learners to use their minds well, so they may be prepared for responsible citizenship, further learning and productive employment in the nation's modern economy; to recognize the influence of the environment; knowledge and skills necessary to exercise the rights and responsibilities of citizenship. An explicit aim for the *system* is to ensure that every school will be free of drugs, violence and the unauthorized presence of firearms and alcohol, and will offer a disciplined environment conducive to learning.

Values and Aims and the Curriculum

Similar values and aims can lead to the adoption of different curricular models. This section examines four dimensions of the values underlying different models of curricular provision.

Centralized/decentralized

This dimension deals with individual and group freedoms to impart values and educational philosophy and/or to reflect regional or local differences through education.

Centralized systems with a common form of publicly funded education for all learners exist, for example, in most of the non-federal countries. An exception is The Netherlands, where the establishment of schools is devolved to individual school management boards, to create a system of public (state-founded) and private (independently-founded) schools, reflecting different ideologies, but which receive equivalent levels of state funding and enjoy parity of esteem. As a result, the private sector consists of about 70% of schools in The Netherlands. Most other centralized states allow the establishment of schools by non-state bodies and subsidize them from public funds, but Italy requires private schools to operate at no cost to the state.

The decentralized systems (Australia, Canada, Germany, Switzerland and the USA) devolve decision-making to subnational authorities, to promote local accountability and responsiveness. The resulting diversity includes public and private sector schools and different schools to meet perceptions of regional need.

The benefits of centralization include equity, economies of scale and a common understanding of aims and purposes. A highly centralized system, with state control of the structure of the education system, teacher education, the curriculum and textbooks (for example Japan, the Republic of Korea, Singapore) would appear to support parity of esteem and coherence between values, educational aims and their implementation and outcomes. However, centralization may be seen to secure a minimum standard of provision at the expense of meeting the individual needs of the very able and less able learners, or of responding to local circumstances. Coherence may also be undermined by discrepancies between the official values and those of the teachers and learners. Furthermore, centralization may stifle responsiveness, creativity and innovation. In this context, the three countries mentioned above place the development of individual creativity high on their priorities for education in the twenty-first century. It will be interesting to see how this objective is achieved within systems which by tradition and organization are so strongly centralized.

Whilst diversity provides scope to address some of these issues, it is subject to other criticisms. It may be perceived as allowing or even promoting inequality between regions, schools or learners. Thus educational provision and resourcing in the USA can vary considerably between states and even between districts within states. Similarly, both government and non-government schools in Australia receive public sector funding for teachers' salaries, but non-government schools often pay their teachers at a higher rate than those employed in government schools.

One moderating strategy is the partnership model, where learners, parents, employers and other interested parties are actively involved in agreeing values and setting objectives. Such models may be introduced to secure greater understanding of, and support for, common values and aims. On the other hand, participation may be a time-consuming activity and, as is the case in Spain, the passing of time may diminish stakeholder support for reforms before they are fully implemented. A modified form of participation involves a requirement that the school explains aims and objectives to families and the broader social community (France, Italy, Sweden, the USA). Where such involvement is part of the accountability mechanism, as in England and Wales, there is special emphasis on the publication of learner and school outcomes.

Common core versus differentiated curricula

This dimension focuses on the nature of the individual's learning experience as controlled by the organization of teaching groups (separate schools, streams or sets) and curriculum content.

A *common curriculum* during the primary and the early secondary years is found in most of the countries in the study. This model is seen to secure a minimum entitlement for all learners, promoting a basic standard of knowledge, skills and understanding, and supporting social cohesion through shared experiences and values. Within the prescribed framework, certain flexibility may be allowed in the breadth or depth to which topics are treated, in teaching methods and in the textbooks and other resources which are used. Such diversity may reflect local contexts, learning styles and speeds, and different funding models. A broad commonality is cost-effective in terms of teacher training and the production of learning materials. The common curriculum model therefore contributes to the aims of equality, standards, social development and cost-effectiveness. A criticism of the model is that it assumes a common and predictable learning rate and, without appropriate targeted support, some learners may complete their education without reaching the expected levels of achievement. Such relative failure demotivates and sometimes alienates learners, and is expensive in financial and social terms. A number of other countries address differences in learning rate within a common curriculum by allowing or requiring learners to repeat or skip grades in line with their mastery of the knowledge, skills and understanding.

A *differentiated curriculum* (sometimes reinforced by selective school systems or by streaming/setting within schools) is explicitly provided for learners from age 10 in Singapore and from age 12 in Germany and The Netherlands. It is argued that the creation of homogeneous teaching groups is more cost-effective, and fairer for learners, allowing them to learn at their own pace without feeling a sense of failure. Opponents argue that explicit differentiation promotes competition, 'labels' learners and undermines the self-esteem of the less successful. It is difficult to compare the relative demotivating effects of streaming/setting, repeating a year or reaching the end of compulsory education without achieving the expected standards. However, the argument against explicit differentiation is countered, especially in The Netherlands and Singapore, by the argument that transfer between and access to alternative routes enable all learners to reach the highest levels of education, even if they take longer to do so.

A separate criticism arises when funding differs according to the curricular routes; in these circumstances differentiation is seen as élitist and discriminatory.

Flexibility/Stability

The degree of centralization of education systems also affects the extent to which curricula enjoy stability and/or flexibility to meet changing needs and circumstances. A set revision cycle, such as the ten-year programme in Korea, is rare. The majority of the countries in the study report a high degree of rapid change in different elements of their education systems, although the direction of such changes is not the same. Whilst some countries move away from centralized curricula, allowing more discretion to schools (for example, Hungary, Spain), others, such as England and The Netherlands, have introduced more centralized control.

Among the major forces for change are changes in government (national or regional) or in the national or local economy; parents' and learners' expectations of education, including its contribution to social and economic status; and technological changes in schools or in the world of work. Thus, the current reforms in Spain have raised the school leaving age and introduced a non-selective system which requires all learners to follow academic and vocational courses during the compulsory secondary phase with a view to deferring choices and raising the status of vocational courses. In contrast, parents in Pacific Rim countries resist the move away from content-based learning for fear that their child may not be admitted to the more prestigious schools and universities, which is a prerequisite for social and economic success.

International comparisons also trigger change, and the results of TIMSS have led to changes in the content and duration of mathematics learning in, for example, England and Australia. It is ironic that these changes are intended to improve learners' performance in computational skills to equal those of learners in Singapore and Korea, at a time when these latter countries are steering away from patterns of factual knowledge to higher-order thinking skills and creativity.

Stability is essential for the effective implementation of policies and to allow reliable evaluation. Rapid change is expensive in terms of professional development of teachers and the production of learning resources. On the other hand, flexibility is deemed desirable to tailor learning experiences to the changing needs of the learners and of the national economy. Decentralized systems sometimes envy the perceived ability of centralized systems to bring about structured, large-scale change, but the very conformity of those working within centralized systems may inhibit their flexibility.

Fostering desired attitudes through the curriculum

Broader values including *freedom, respect for the individual, social cohesion through diversity* and the *preservation of cultural heritage* are explicitly taught as part of the religious or moral education courses (England and Wales, Japan, Korea, Singapore, Sweden) or implicitly fostered through the content of other subjects, institutional organization and teaching styles.

In England, moral education is linked to religious education, which is compulsory for all school learners. The Republic of Korea and Japan have a clearly defined place for moral education, where theory is reinforced by practical activities. In Singapore, civic and moral education are compulsory throughout primary and secondary education, based on a structured syllabus and prescribed textbooks. This learning is reinforced through service programmes (for example voluntary work in hospitals) and by encouraging learners to participate in out-of-school club activities. Swedish legislation requires schools to represent and impart the equal worth of all people and solidarity with the weak and vulnerable, by fostering in the individual a sense of justice, generosity of spirit, tolerance and responsibility, and to inculcate values in terms of the development of skills and attitudes, as well as the acquisition of knowledge.

Elsewhere, moral and character education may be a cross-curricular dimension rather than a separate subject. For example, in The Netherlands, a crosscurricular theme concerned with the relationship between the person and the social environment (humanity and nature, the democratic citizen, gender differences, etc.) is expected to be reflected in all subjects of the basic curriculum.

Other examples of ways in which broader values are carried through into the curriculum include the following:

- *The active promotion of multicultural knowledge, skills and understanding for all* by including the study of other cultures in the curriculum (Australia, The Netherlands) or, more actively confronting xenophobia and intolerance with knowledge, open discussion and effective measures (Sweden).
- *Parity of provision* by supporting the establishment of religious schools (many countries) or those catering for specific groups such as specialist Maori-medium schools in New Zealand.
- *Support for the minority group* by providing facilities for a minority language community to run mother-tongue classes (several countries).
- *Compensatory programmes* for those perceived as disadvantaged in terms of the national culture or language, including language classes for immigrants (most countries).
- *The reassertion of national identity* following political upheavals (Germany, Hungary).
- *Promoting awareness of the national identity within a wider international framework* and mobility (Hungary, Japan, Korea and New Zealand).
- *Social cohesion*, as promoted in Singapore, by according priority explicitly to the needs of the community and the nation over those of the individual; and elsewhere by heterogeneous groupings.

Values, aims and assessment

Despite a high degree of similarity between expressed aims, there are wide variations in the extent to which learners are assessed during the compulsory education phase, and the nature of these assessments.

What is assessed
Most assessment focuses on readily measurable areas of knowledge, skills and understanding, such as the national language, mathematics, first foreign language and science. Assessment of values and attitudes is difficult, the more so because, whilst grades can be objectively awarded for the learner's ability to evaluate actions, their consequences and to develop moral judgement, the assumption that certain values are better than others conflicts with the freedom of thought and respect for individual differences enshrined in constitutions and other legislation. This has a backlash effect on the curriculum in that what is untested is less likely to be taught, particularly when there are financial consequences linked to learner performance.

Extent and frequency of assessment
Four countries (England, France, Germany and New Zealand) provide for assessment of learners at the beginning of compulsory schooling, and admission may be deferred in France and Germany if the child is not deemed ready for school. Thereafter, teacher assessment takes place throughout education for all learners, supplemented by compulsory national or standardized tests in England (age 7, 11, 14), France (age 8, 12, 15) and Korea (annually). Some other countries offer voluntary standardized tests.

The prevalence of school-leaving certificates increases with age; four countries have a compulsory primary school-leaving certificate (Hungary, Italy, Singapore and Spain); all except Australia, Sweden and Switzerland mark successful completion of lower secondary education (at age 14, 15 or 16) in this way; and all countries in the study have a formal certificate for those completing upper secondary education (normally age 18–19).

Purposes of assessment
All countries carry out diagnostic assessment of individual learners, to determine their learning needs and access to specialized programmes. Formative assessment is also common, usually conducted informally by teachers. France is unique in administering standardized tests at the *beginning* of key learning cycles to enable teachers to adapt their teaching to demonstrated learner needs.

Assessment to control the direction or speed of progression through education is common in many countries. Again, teacher evaluation predominates, with decisions being subject to parental approval. However, transfer to secondary school is controlled by primary school leaving examinations in the state of South Australia, Hungary, Italy, Singapore and Spain.

Whilst most assessment is used to inform and enhance the learning and teaching process in a relatively private way, assessment for accountability is becoming increasingly prevalent, placing pressure on learners, teachers and schools. Thus assessments are standardized, results are made public and used to set benchmarks and targets against which the effectiveness of individual teachers, schools and (in the case of international studies) systems are evaluated. Unfortunately such assessment may fail to give due consideration to differences in aims, cultures, structures and traditions. For example, to what extent can the education system be held accountable for failing to promote creativity within a centralized state such as Korea, or cooperation and teamwork to meet the demands of employers in the overtly competitive societies of most western countries?

The link between values and assessment
The link is not direct. As one example, Korean learners take standardized scholastic achievement tests annually throughout their education, but their Swedish counterparts are not externally assessed until the upper secondary phase. Both countries stress individual development, equal opportunity and the development of knowledge, skills and understanding amongst their aims, but their perceptions of how these aims are to be achieved clearly differs. Korean society stresses the work ethic, and competition to secure places at desired schools and colleges is high, exacting considerable sacrifices from both learners and their families. Regular assessment therefore provides essential feedback to identify weaknesses which need to be remedied before the crucial entrance examinations at ages 15 and 18. In contrast, in the Swedish system, respect for individuals must prevail and be *felt* to prevail; hence assessment which might be perceived as discriminatory is avoided.

In the international context of, say, upper secondary-school graduation rates, the nature of national assessments will affect performance. Thus the results of those countries where certificates are awarded largely on the basis of attendance and coursework within a modular system (such as Sweden) are more favourable than those where the upper secondary academic examinations are intended to safeguard a 'gold standard' and serve as an important criterion for competitive admission to higher education (such as England).

Conclusions

As the IRCAF study shows, there is no direct correlation between specific values and curriculum and assessment models; indeed, espousal of identical values may result in the adoption of wholly contradictory models. An understanding of the values underlying educational aims is nevertheless important in that it helps to explain the starting point of stakeholders, and may therefore provide a framework for reviewing alternative policies and practice.

Notes

1.   The countries in the review are Australia, Canada, England, France, Germany, Hungary, Italy, Japan, Korea, The Netherlands, New Zealand, Singapore,

Spain, Sweden, Switzerland, the USA. For further details, see O'Donnell *et al.* (forthcoming).

2.   For an analysis of conservative values underlying education, see Le Métais (1995).

3.   EURYDICE Unit France (1996).

4.   EURYDICE and CEDEFOP (1995).

5.   Switzerland Statutes, *The Federal Constitution* (Art. 27, Para. 3).

6.   BBW *et al.* (1995).

7.   HMI *et al.* (1991).

8.   For sources, see Sect. 1.2 of each of the national descriptions in O'Donnell *et al.* (forthcoming).

References

BBW/OFES/BIGA/OFIAMT/BFS/OFS/EDK/CPIP (1995) *Structures of the Education and Initial Training Systems in Switzerland.* Bern: BBW/OFES/BIGA/OFIAMT/BFS/OFS/EDK/CPIP.

Eurydice and Cedefop (second edition) (1995) *Structures of the Education and Initial Training Systems in the European Union.* Luxembourg: Office for Official Publications of the European Communities.

Eurydice Unit France (1996) Response to Official Eurydice Network question GB(L) 96 002 10 on curriculum and assessment frameworks. Paris: Ministère de l'Education Nationale, de l'Enseignement Superieur et de la Recherche. Unpublished document.

Her Majesty's Inspectorate, Department of Education and Science, the Scottish Office Education Department and the Welsh Office Education Department (1991) *Aspects of Education in the USA: Indicators in Educational Monitoring.* London: HMSO.

Kanaya, T. (1993) Japan, in T. N. Postlethwaite, *International Encyclopaedia of National Systems of Education.* Second edn. London: Pergamon.

Le Metais, J. (1995) *Legislating for Change: School Reforms in England and Wales, 1979–1994.* Slough: NFER.

O'Donnell, S., Le Metais, J., Boyd, S. and Tabberer, R. (forthcoming). *INCA: The International Review of Curriculum and Assessment Frameworks Archive* [CD-ROM]. London: Qualifications and Curriculum Authority.

Ryle, G. (1949) *The Concept of Mind.* London: Hutchinson.

Saskatchewan Education (1996) *Saskatchewan Education Indicators: Kindergarten to Grade 12. Update 1996.* Saskatchewan: Saskatchewan Education.

Spain. Ministry of Education and Science (1990) *The White Paper for the Reform of Educational System.* Madrid: Ministry of Education and Science.

Switzerland. Statutes. *The Federal Constitution* (Article 27, Paragraph 3).

7

'Quality' in Early Childhood Programmes – a Contextually Appropriate Approach[1]

Martin Woodhead

Questions about Quality

I take as my starting point two questions:

> What features of early child care and education programmes ensure quality in the lives of young children and their families?
> Is it feasible to prescribe a general framework for quality with relevance that extends beyond particular programmes and communities to national and international standards for early childhood?

These were amongst the fundamental questions examined by the Bernard van Leer Foundation between 1992 and 1995 as part of the 'Environment of the Child' project. The Bernard van Leer Foundation is a major international organisation based in the Netherlands providing financial support and professional guidance to low-cost, community-based initiatives in early childhood, care and education for socially and culturally disadvantaged children, from birth to eight years of age.

The 'Environment of the Child' project was an opportunity for reflection on the theories, knowledge and assumptions that inform the development of early childhood programmes within an international framework, with particular emphasis on the function of large-scale care/education programmes in impoverished communities, their impact on families and children, and directions for their development. Directed by Dr Horacio Walker, the project was neither purely a piece of academic research, nor was it mainly about the development of professional practice. Rather, it was about the interface between these two worlds and was targeted especially to people and organisations with a responsibility for programme planning, development and evaluation. Project activities included local and regional workshops (in Delhi, Mexico, Paris, Caracas, Madras and Nairobi) attended by programme specialists, project leaders and applied researchers.

Participants discussed the implications of a specially commissioned review of research on the impact of poverty in the environment of the young child (Nunes, 1994), as well as a series of local studies into diverse large-

---

This chapter has been edited.

scale programmes in Venezuela, India, Kenya and France (Gakuru & Koech, 1993; Paul, 1995; Teran de Ruesta *et al.*, 1995; Tijus *et al.*, 1995).

Visiting early childhood programmes in each of these countries, I was confronted by a paradox. Quality issues were uppermost in the minds of everyone I met, yet the programmes themselves seemed to have very little in common. The general label 'Early Childhood Programme' encompassed profound contrasts: in organisation, financing, buildings, facilities and equipment; staff training and ratios; approach to care and education; relative emphasis on health, nutrition, play and thinking, social learning, pre-academic skills; and relationship to families and community. In preparing the final report (Woodhead, 1996), I set myself two main challenges. First I wanted to make explicit the frameworks of thinking that underpin judgements of quality in particular settings, made by those involved in the programme as well as by experts and visitors (including myself). Second, I wanted to explore the possibility of working towards a common quality framework that is both context-sensitive, allowing for diversity, but is also recognisably consistent with universally recognised values and principles.

I was convinced of one thing from the outset. The quality assumptions that underpin standard-setting in the economically advantaged regions I know best (Europe and North America) are *not* the most appropriate starting-point for identifying indicators of quality relevant to most other regions of the world. To take just three most obvious contrasts.

1. The annual budget for a US Headstart programme is calculated to average about $2600 for each child. In India this sort of money would pay the annual salaries of at least 150 nursery workers.
2. Staffing ratios in British nursery education are calculated at around 15:1. Kenyan nursery classes (which include children as young as three) are regularly attended by 40 children, and it is not uncommon for there to be as many as 60 children, all in one classroom, under the supervision of one adult.
3. Preschool children in Europe and North America are surrounded with an abundance of play materials to support every conceivable form of play and learning, to which they generally have free access. In much of the rest of the world, early childhood programmes function with little or no manufactured equipment at all. Where a few wooden blocks or puzzles are available, children may only occasionally be given the opportunity to play with them – they are far too precious to permit unrestricted play.

The inappropriateness of blindly applying quality indicators from one context or country to another does not just apply to these most visible indicators of so-called 'basic standards'. There are numerous more subtle and arguably more significant dimensions of quality than resources, ratios and equipment, especially those about the goals and purposes of early childhood programmes, the emphasis given to play, discipline and teaching. For each of these dimensions there is a tendency to take quality

assumptions from the economically privileged, Minority World and assume they can be applied universally. But to do so amounts to condemning the quality of childhoods in the Majority World, where in most cases
these quality assumptions cannot be met. The question is, even if they
cannot be presently met, should they be taken as long-term goals, or
might altogether different expectations for early child development be
equally valid?

This debate is an expression of the philosophical dichotomy between
'universalism' and 'relativism'. Can universal standards be set for early
childhood, based on universally relevant knowledge and beliefs about what
is in children's best interests? Or is quality inevitably relative to particular
conditions, cultural values and practices? I believe that a universalist position is untenable, but I am also wary of falling into the 'black hole' of
extreme relativism. I signal this midway position by the principle that
quality in early childhood is 'relative but not arbitrary'. This means rejecting narrow, prescriptive, decontextualised views of early childhood development in favour of a more open, holistic, context-sensitive approach to
physical and social environments (including early childhood programmes)
that support children's growth.

Recognising the dangers of applying universal quality standards in early
childhood is especially important as we approach The Millenium. The
globalisation of economic and political life, the growth in high technology
communications, etc., are much discussed, but they are only part of the
story. Much less attention has been paid to the globalising influence of
universal schooling, widespread basic health and nutrition programmes,
and most recently, the regulatory promise of the UN Convention on the
Rights of the Child. Of course, these worldwide trends represent positive
progress to improve the lives of children. It would be wrong to romanticise
many of the experiences of childhood they have surplanted. Some childrearing practices have been detrimental to children's development, by any
humanitarian standards (Evans & Myers, 1994). My concern is that current
trends go beyond the elimination of universally unacceptable standards.
They also (often unwittingly) entail global promotion of particular beliefs
and values about the nature of early development, the needs of children
and the prerequisites for quality care and education (Boyden, 1990; Burman, 1996). Just as questionable modern dietary habits are being shaped
under the influence of multi-national fast food enterprises, are we in danger of promoting a uniformly bland, quality-controlled child development
product?

Quality and Child Development Theory

Theories of early child development and education have a key role to play
in this process. The science of psychology has constructed powerful norma-

tive models of development, based on a fundamental belief in the psychic unity of human kind (Stigler *et al.*, 1990). Shared features of childhood are emphasised. At best, differences are treated as 'variations on a theme'; at worst, as 'noise in the system'. Programme approaches, curriculum models and evaluation strategies are strongly informed by child development literature, which in turn becomes part of an export/import trade through books, international conferences, training programmes and commercial packages. With few exceptions, 'textbook' child development originates mainly in Europe and North America, and mainly within a fairly narrow socio-economic band within these Continents. Theories, programmes and evaluation strategies do not just convey well-researched knowledge about development, they also transmit hidden messages through rhetorical devices, notably about children's 'nature', their 'needs', what aspects of the 'environment' are 'harmful' or 'beneficial' for 'healthy development'. The problem is that much of this rhetoric has as much to do with particular socio-cultural contexts (of the research community as well as of the children they have studied) as with shared features of early human development (Kessen, 1979; Woodhead, 1990; Burman, 1994; Morss, 1996).

Developmentally Appropriate Practice?

The concept of Developmentally Appropriate Practice well illustrates this theme. Developmental appropriateness is a widely used indicator of quality in care arrangements for young children, drawing attention to the ways their play and learning is promoted, and the approach to teaching adopted by caregivers. It has been especially clearly elaborated by the US National Association for the Education of Young Children (NAEYC), in part as a response to pressure within the US public elementary school system for downward extension of school achievement expectations into the early years (Bredekamp, 1987). Within that context, the NAEYC document served a powerful function, offering a 'scientific' defence of informal play-based programmes for young children, based on the best available psychological knowledge about child development. Some features of this definition of developmental appropriateness were:

- Developmentally Appropriate Practice is based on universal, predictable sequences of growth and change;
- The teacher should take account of the age of the child and their individuality, in terms of growth pattern, personality, learning style and family background;
- Children learn best through play that is self-initiated, self-directed and self-chosen;
- The teacher's role is to provide a rich variety of activities and materials, support the children's play, and talk with children about their play.

The child-centred vision of Developmentally Appropriate Practice res-onates with very deep-rooted beliefs and ideals, widely shared amongst Western-educated child development specialists, and endorsed by domi-nant psychological theories, especially the individualistic constructivism elaborated by Jean Piaget (Walkerdine, 1984). Presuming universal applic-ability is highly problematic. Even within the USA, Developmentally Ap-propriate Practice has been challenged on the grounds that it is insensitive to the cultural diversity in children's family experiences and parenting practices, and it risks resurrecting discredited judgements about deprived environments and the need for compensation (Mallory & New, 1994). The NAEYC has now issued a position statement advocating responsiveness to linguistic and cultural diversity (NAEYC, 1996).

Developmentally Appropriate Practice illustrates the dangers of apply-ing universalistic, decontextualised views of what makes for quality in child development. It has much in common with approaches to evaluation that apply standardised psychometric measures of children's abilities, social competence and behavioural adjustment. Equally problematic are rating scales that attempt to measure the 'quality' in children's preschool environ-ment, For example, the Early Childhood Environment Rating Scale, ECERS (Harms & Clifford, 1980) has been widely used in national and international research (Phillips, 1987; Olmsted & Weikart, 1989; Brophy & Statham, 1994; Karrby & Giota, 1994).

The case for a more contextual, situated, cultural approach to develop-mental psychology is increasingly being recognised. There are universal features of development, but much that has been taken to be universal turns out to be cultural (Stigler *et al.*, 1990). I will offer four brief examples of psychological research that has significant implications for how quality is interpreted in child care and education.

A first example concerns the significance of infant attachments and the expression of separation distress. The emergence of specific attachments follows a similar developmental course for all societies studied (peaking between 10 and 13 months), but the numbers and patterns of attachment, the way caregivers respond to infant distress, and the way these close relationships are regulated within the family can vary considerably (Super & Harkness, 1982; van Ijzendoorn & Kroonenberg, 1988). Bowlby's origi-nal prescriptions for healthy emotional development reflect post-war fam-ily patterns and gender divisions as much as children's psychological needs (Woodhead, 1990; Tizard, 1991; Singer, 1992). More specifically, evalua-tions of day care that rely on the standard classifications of secure and insecure attachment prescribed by the 'Strange Situation' (Ainsworth *et al.*, 1978) may misinterpret the emotional adjustment of children for whom separation and reunion has been a daily occurrence (Clarke-Stewart, 1989; see also Dunn, 1993).

A second example relates to early 'teaching'. Purposeful adult activity designed to initiate young children into socially valued skills is a common feature of early relationships between toddlers and their caregivers. Comparing mother–child dyads in India, Guatemala, Turkey and the USA, Rogoff *et al.* (1993) found that collaboration in joint activity was universal, but there were important variations in the roles of adult and child, and in the extent to which these were embedded in a network of wider relations. While 'guided participation' was a feature in all these settings, the goals and processes of learning and teaching varied, which in turn was linked to the extent to which children's lives were segregated from the adult world of work. Each community expressed a particular pattern of adult–child relationship, which in its own terms can be considered 'developmentally appropriate'.

A third example elaborates on the way adult–child relationship patterns relate to learning, especially of language and communication. Close observation of Euro-American families has revealed the subtle parental strategies through which infants are encouraged to become partners in 'proto-conversations'. Their language learning is facilitated by the caregiver's adoption of so-called 'motherese', in which intonation is exaggerated, vocabulary and sentence structure simplified, and the child's utterances repeated and expanded (Snow, 1976). As before, there are dangers in interpreting these observations as part of a generalised theory of language acquisition (or worse still as prescriptive guidance about what style of caregiving is developmentally appropriate). Cross-cultural studies amongst the Kaluli of Papua New Guinea revealed that caregivers rarely engaged their infants in dyadic communicative exchanges, and when they did they tended to be directive rather than reciprocal. Yet these infants acquired their mother tongue quite 'normally' (Schieffelin & Ochs, 1983). It may be that Euro-American caregiving patterns are the exception rather than the norm; comparing child care in twelve societies, Whiting and Edwards (1988) concluded that the caregiving style observed in the USA was distinctively different from the eleven other societies in their study. Mothers in the USA were ranked highest in the extent of their sociability with their children, and in the number of playful interactions in which children were treated as equals.

A fourth and final example is most directly relevant to the NAEYC concept of Developmentally Appropriate Practice, which is largely founded on a Piagetian model of children progressing through a series of invariant stages of cognitive development, from initial egocentrism to mature, independent logical thought. Extensive reappraisal of Piagetian theory (Donaldson, 1978; Grieve & Hughes, 1990) suggests that young children are capable of logical thinking, especially perspective-taking, much younger than envisaged by Piaget, and that their thinking is much more dependent on social context and social meaning. Vygotsky's thinking has been especially influential in displacing a rigid view of individual progress through successive stages in favour of cognition embedded in social relationships and amplified by cultural tools, including language and literacy (Wertsch, 1983). On this theory, what children learn in the family and through early education, and at school, is not a universal form of logical reasoning. All cognition is 'embedded' or 'situated' cognition (Light &

Butterworth, 1992; Rogoff & Chavajay, 1995). Teaching processes are about cognitive socialisation and cannot be seen as 'developmentally appropriate' or otherwise, in any absolute sense.

Practice Appropriate to the Context of Early Development

This shift towards a more culturally sensitive developmental psychology has important implications for practice, demanding that the principle of 'Developmentally Appropriate Practice' (DAP) is complemented by an equally important principle of 'Contextually Appropriate Practice' (CAP). I have called the emergent hybrid 'Practice Appropriate to the Context of Early Development' (or PACED). Features of a PACED approach include:

- Contextually Appropriate Practice is based on local variations in children's experience of growth and change.
- The teacher/careworker should consider the age and individuality of children, as well as the social context of their care, the roles and responsibilities within their family and community, patterns of communication and language, approach to socialisation and so on.
- As far as possible, early childhood programmes should be consistent with and complementary to children's learning experiences within family and community. The goal should be mutual understanding, support and cooperation, and recognition of cultural difference.
- Young children can learn in a variety of ways: individual and social play, imitation of others, instruction by adults and other children, exploration, and group activity. Which is appropriate depends not only on their age and stage of development, but also on the goals and resources of the learning environment.
- The teacher/careworker's role is adapted to the resources at their disposal as well as their knowledge of learning opportunities in family and community. The role can include: serving as a model for children to imitate, structuring the environment for their learning, supporting their spontaneous play, teaching them culturally relevant skills, encouraging values and standards of behaviour expected in the community, and helping them interpret the complexities of their social environment (Woodhead, 1996, pp. 69–70).

In the rest of this article I want to elaborate on the steps that can be taken towards adopting a more contextual approach to issues of quality.

Steps Towards a Contextual Approach

Early childhood programmes are complex human systems involving numerous individuals and interest groups. There are many different potential criteria of quality, which are closely linked to beliefs about the goals and functions of programmes. These beliefs are in turn shaped by different perspectives on childhood and child development, different cultural patterns and personal values. We have to look towards a model of quality that accommodates multiple perspectives (Moss & Pence, 1995). A first step is to make explicit the perspectives of all those with a stake in the programme, including ourselves! We need to ask three key questions:

Who has a perspective on 'quality'?

There are numerous different interest groups (or stakeholders) in any early childhood programme, each with their own perspective on quality, for example programme managers, teachers, parents, community leaders, child development experts, not forgetting children themselves.

Who do these stakeholders perceive as beneficiaries from 'quality'?

The obvious answer is that programmes are for children, but most stakeholders would recognise that parents are also beneficiaries, in some programmes more than in others. There are also less explicitly identified beneficiaries, such as the careworkers or teachers who gain employment, and the community leaders who gain prestige. For some care programmes, older children are seen as major beneficiaries, because they are no longer required to care for their youngest siblings.

What do they take to be indicators of 'quality'?

Judgements about quality can focus on any number of things, from basic standards (e.g. physical space, staffing ratios, hygiene, nutrition), and resources for play activities and learning (e.g. toys, materials), to the quality of adult–child relationships, flexibility to parents working patterns, notions of cost-effectiveness and many more.

This model of quality accommodates diverse perspectives on the quality of an early childhood programme. It can be a vehicle for making explicit profound differences in perspective on quality in early childhood that might otherwise remain submerged. It can be the starting point for negotiating a shared understanding amongst key stakeholders in a particular community, notably between parents, and teachers or careworkers. For example, as part of the Bernard van Leer project, Venezuelan investigators asked both mothers and day care workers the question 'Which is most important for children's development – play or discipline?' Only 8% of mothers replied 'play', 52% replied 'discipline' and 23% thought they were equally important. The pattern for day care workers was similar, although they gave a little more emphasis to play (24%) and a little less to discipline (44%). The emphasis of both mothers and careworkers on discipline is surprising to the minds of those who have been educated to a belief in the pre-eminence of children's play. Parents especially remain unconvinced, as in the remark:

> An undisciplined child is ugly; discipline . . . is important in the life of the child . . . because they turn out obedient and don't make one look bad. (Teran de Ruesta *et al.*, 1995, p. 46)

These adults' emphasis on discipline does not mean that they were aloof and cold in their relationships with children. On the contrary, the emphasis on discipline was matched by an equal emphasis on the affectional aspects of relationships.

The low emphasis on play is reinforced by answers to a question about how to promote children's learning. Play was only mentioned by 9% of mothers and 13% of day care workers. Much greater emphasis was placed on the adult's role as a teacher:

> When the day care mothers and the children's mothers want the children to learn something . . . (most) . . . sit down and teach them, explain, repeat and speak to them, while others resort to different strategies: they motivate with patience and affection, give examples or invent 'things'. Very few set forth the possibility that children can learn by doing and playing. The child is seen as passive in relation to his or her environment. They do not consider of value, for the children's learning, the natural play situations or the spontaneous interactions which occur in the day care home/multihome. Rather they assign great value to words and advice. The majority handle situations such as stimulating learning, toilet training, and discipline in this way. (Teran de Ruesta *et al.*, 1995, p. 31)

In short, each of these stakeholder groups has a clear, and not always complementary, view about what counts as quality in the care, discipline and teaching of young children, which reflects their beliefs and priorities for childhood.

Another example of different stakeholder perspectives on what is 'developmentally appropriate' comes from a study carried out by High/Scope for IEA. Samples of parents and teachers in different countries were asked 'What are the most important skills for four-year-olds to learn?' In the USA, parents and teachers agreed that social and language skills are the highest priority, and gave much less emphasis to pre-academic skills. In a Nigerian sample, there was also agreement that language skills are important, but Nigerian parents and teachers identified pre-academic skills as the highest priority. In Hong Kong, the High/Scope study identified yet another pattern, including a discrepancy between teachers and parents. Once again, language skills featured highly, but whereas teachers gave low priority to pre-academic skills compared to self-sufficiency skills, amongst parents pre-academic skills were the highest priority (Olmsted & Weikart, 1989; High/Scope, 1995 personal communication).

These examples serve as an antidote to abstract claims about the universal developmental needs of young children. They draw attention to the dynamic, competing and sometimes contradictory perspectives on childhood that must be the starting-point for negotiating the development of a quality programme. So a first step is to make perspectives on quality explicit. A second step is to understand how these perspectives relate to the context of early development.

Quality and the Concept of 'Developmental Niche'

From the standpoint of Western 'expert' child development theory and practice it is tempting to attribute contrasting beliefs and practices with young children to shortages of resources, training, knowledge about children's needs and development, etc. This deficit approach risks alienating important stakeholders and is not likely to advance the development of early childhood programmes. A more constructive approach is to appreciate how parents and careworkers come to hold their beliefs about discipline, play and learning; how it relates to their circumstances, lifestyles and aspirations for their children. It may be that these beliefs are no longer functional to situations of social change. It may be that aspirations for childhood are out of step with processes of modernisation. Even so, respecting traditional values is a first step to introducing change. As a framework for considering these themes the Bernard van Leer project combined an ecological model (Bronfenbrenner, 1979) with the concept of developmental niche (Super & Harkness, 1986). It is common for Western-educated early childhood specialists to apply the idea of a development niche to practices and belief systems in rural Kenya, India or Latin America. It is not common to focus the social scientific lens on so-called 'modern' methods of child care and education, recognising their ecology. Expert beliefs and theories of child development are also part of a developmental niche, in so far as they inform (and are informed by) the way children are treated, how their behaviour is interpreted and what is considered 'quality' in early development (Goodnow & Collins, 1990).

Since the eighteenth century, Western childhoods have been progressively constructed as a period of extended economic dependency and protected innocence, a period of rapid learning regulated by natural growth processes and enhanced through universal schooling, which is largely separated off from economic and community life (James & Prout, 1990; Hockey & James, 1993). It is in this context that child development theory flourished, along with the principles of kindergarten and nursery education (Singer, 1992). Childhoods throughout the Majority World are strongly influenced by this 'modern' view of childhood, and by the process of modernisation itself, including the availability of creches, kindergartens and nursery schools. But there are other competing pressures on early childhood, that make for at best only a partial fit with social and economic realities. In rural subsistence economies, children are not just playful dependants, they are an essential trainable, economic resource. Hoffman (1987) asked parents in eight countries about the value they placed on their children. Only 6% of US parents referred to children's value as contributors to the family income, compared with 75% of Thai parents, 71% of parents in the Philippines and 54% in Turkey. These parents placed much less emphasis on the stimulation and fun of having children, which were major benefits to US parents. In a similar study carried out in Cameroon, parents valued children for their ability to do domestic chores (56%) and run errands (30%) (Nsamenang & Lamb, 1993).

Children's role in family and economy shapes attitudes to preschool quality. At one extreme are early childhoods that emphasise high levels of material resource, not just in terms of the buildings and equipment but especially in terms of play opportunities available to children. Material resources are plentiful and disposable and children are adept consumers. They are encouraged to feel confident in using material in a playful way, with limited regard to costs and outcomes. They are presented with choices – there is more than enough to go around – and encouraged to feel powerful in negotiating, consuming and owning property. Their play with manufactured materials serves important cognitive functions, in orienting children to a sense of mastery over basic principles of technology. This contrasts sharply with early childhoods where material resource (especially manufactured equipment) is scarce, for adults as well as for children. Much of children's play is social, or based on everyday objects. Children are taught to respect material resources as precious and difficult to replace. They feel privileged to use play equipment – few choices are available.

The impact of the developmental niche on early childhood values is vividly illustrated by LeVine's research amongst the Gusii of Kenya (Le Vine *et al.*, 1994). Traditionally, high birth and mortality rates placed a premium on early nurturance, with close physical contact, demand feeding and sleeping next to the mother. This nurturant style did not incorporate high levels of playful stimulation; mothers remained aloof, with little joint activity or verbal communication. At the same time, managing a large family as well as cultivating the fields put pressure on the mother as caregiver and necessitated a significant contribution from her children. The baby would be entrusted to the care of an older sibling, and by the age of three would already be expected to carry out small domestic chores. Deferrence to elders and obedience to instructions was emphasised; praise offered sparingly. LeVine *et al.* compares the Gusii infant's experience with a child in Boston, whose survival is virtually assured, and relationships are marked by reciprocity and mutual responsiveness. Children are provided with plenty of psychological space, they are encouraged to assert their individuality and clashes of will are at least expected, if not actively promoted. The power of these very different standards of quality care is conveyed in speculations about how one set of mothers might view the practices of the other. While a mother from Boston might view the Gusii practice of demand feeding as 'spoiling' the child, the demand for obedience as 'repressive' and the use of young children as caregivers as 'abusive', the traditional Gusii mother might view the Western practice of leaving infants to cry as 'abusive', tolerating a toddler's challenging behaviour as 'spoiling' and encouraging playful fun as 'over indulgent'.

Different orientations to childhood have repercussions for the kinds of learning that are valued, and the approach to socialisation. For the Cameroon families in Nsamenang and Lamb's study, good children were expected to display obedience and show respect, be hard working and helpful, honest and intelligent. Undesirable characteristics included laziness, fearfulness, playfulness and inquisitiveness (Nsamenang & Lamb, 1993). This is in sharp contrast with the image of parent-child relationships in Euro-American families, where inquisitiveness and playfulness are positively encouraged, and the assertiveness of the 'terrible twos', including challenging parental authority, is accepted as an inevitable and in some ways necessary part of growing up (see, for example, Dunn, 1988).

These differences reflect fundamental variations in belief about the purposes of childhood and about the status of the emerging personality. Western models of child development are premised on an individualistic view of personal development culminating in the separated, autonomous self. Kagitcibasi (1990, 1996) argues that much 'modern' early childhood thinking is an extension of individualism, with its emphasis on the psychological value of the child to parents, socialisation goals associated with independence, and a style of rearing encouraging autonomy and a strong emphasis on personal, cognitive and social development. This contrasts sharply with the interdependent outlook in traditional agrarian societies, where obedience training is emphasised and there is little place for encouraging play, for choice or for the exploration of ideas and beliefs (see also Markus & Kitayama, 1991). In the face of social change it could be argued that the sooner the Western model of child development is adopted the better, since child-centred, activity-based, individualistic programmes are most likely to serve the process of modernisation. Kagitcibasi proposes that this may not be the inevitable nor necessarily the most appropriate route to follow. She offers a third view, better characterising the experience of many developing societies, in which the child's development has acquired psychological value, but in the context of family patterns still emphasising interdependence and respect for parental authority.

The importance of resisting polarisation between so-called traditional and so-called modern conceptions of what makes for quality in early childhood is highlighted by another feature of the developmental niche – the school. This is now shaping childhood for virtually all the world's children. Beside family and work, school is becoming the principle agent of socialisation, and a powerful influence on what is viewed as quality in the early years. The influence need not be one-way. The quality of early childhood programmes should not be assessed just in terms of whether children show readiness for schooling. In the face of poorly staffed and resourced schools throughout much of the Majority World, we should also be asking about the 'readiness of schools for children' (Myers, 1992). But realistically, schooling is a powerful part of the developmental niche for childhood, shaping expectations of parents and early childhood workers alike, about what a preschool programme is for and what it should be teaching. For example, the van Leer study of a rural Kenyan community highlighted the pressures on families, and in turn on the nursery class teacher to prepare children for a highly competitive school system, which makes progressive demands on children to master not only their mother tongue (Kikamba) but also the national language (Kiswahili), and the language of instruction beyond the primary phase (English) (Gakuru & Koech, 1995). To evaluate the quality of preschool education without reference to this or any other key feature of the developmental niche would not do justice to the function of an early childhood programme within this particular child development system.

Planning for 'Quality' in Context-appropriate Ways

I began this article by drawing attention to the diversity of children's experiences encompassed by the general term 'Early Childhood Programme'. This diversity in practice has not been adequately reflected at the level of theory. All too often, students of child development and early education have been offered a relatively narrow vision of the parameters of socialisation, development, learning and teaching. This vision originates mainly in Western scientific and pedagogical traditions, but it has far-reaching influence on beliefs about what counts for quality in early childhood programmes. As Terezinha Nunes points out:

> An intervention programme that seeks to transform the children living in threatening environments into what one might call 'textbook children' risks losing sight of the strengths of those children on whose behalf it is acting . . . (Nunes, 1994)

A prerequisite of quality assessment is recognition that there is no single set of indicators that can prescribe for a quality environment in a once-and-for-all way. Even within a given setting, multiple factors shape children's experiences in ways which may be beneficial or detrimental, depending on the context of other influences in their lives, past, present and future. Most important, values for child development mediate the impact of any experience, the traditional interweaving with the modern, indigenous with imported, national with local. Taking account of different perspectives and negotiating a vision of childhood futures can be carried out in different ways at different levels in the child development system, from teachers and careworkers talking to parents, to state authorities preparing a policy statement.

Rejecting universalistic prescriptions about what constitutes quality in favour of a more open-ended, relativistic approach might appear self-defeating, inviting complacency about standards and uncertainty about what constitutes progress. This is not the case. I have argued that quality is relative, but it is not arbitrary. It is best understood within a framework of understanding about features of the developmental niche, and opportunities for sustainable improvement; it is best achieved through negotiation about the goals of development and approaches to play, discipline and learning. There are also limits – boundaries of adequacy in any early childhood environment, defined by children's basic needs and rights. But within those boundaries, there are numerous pathways to quality in early childhood.

Notes

1.   This article is based on a paper given at the Second Warwick International Early Years Conference, March 1996. It summarises the final report of the Bernard van Leer Foundation's 'Environment of the Child' project. The full report is: Woodhead, M. (1996) *In Search of the Rainbow: Pathways to Quality in Large-Scale Programmes for Young Disadvantaged Children* (The Hague, Bernard van Leer Foundation). It can be obtained on request from: Bernard van Leer Foundation, PO Box 82334, 2508 EH The Hague, The Netherlands.

References

Ainsworth, M. D. S., Blehar, M. C., Water, E. & Wall, S. (1978) *Patterns of Attachment: A Psychological Study of the Strange Situation* (Hillside, NJ, Erlbaum).
Boyden, J. (1990) Childhood and the policy-makers: a comparative perspective on the globalization of childhood, in: A. James & A. Prout (Eds) *Constructing and Reconstructing Childhood* (London, Falmer Press).
Bredekamp, S. (Ed.) (1987) *Developmentally Appropriate Practice in Early Childhood Programs Serving Children from Birth through Age 8* (Washington, DC, National Association for the Education of Young Children).
Bronfenbrenner, U. (1979) *The Ecology of Human Development* (Cambridge, MA, Harvard University Press).
Brophy, J. & Statham, J. (1994) Measure for measure: values, quality and evaluation, in: P. Moss & A. Pence (Eds) *Valuing Quality in Early Childhood Services* (London, Paul Chapman).
Burman, E. (1994) *Deconstructing Developmental Psychology* (London, Routledge).
Burman, E. (1996) Local, global or globalized? Child development and international child rights legislation. *Childhood* 3, pp. 45–67.
Clarke-Stewart, K. A. (1989) Infant day care: maligned or malignant? *American Psychologist.* 44, pp. 266–73.
Donaldson, M. (1978) *Children's Minds,* (London, Fontana).
Dunn, J. (1988) *The Beginnings of Social Understanding* (Oxford, Blackwell).
Dunn, J. (1993) *Young Children's Close Relationships: Beyond Attachment* (London, Sage).
Evans, J. L. & Myers, R. G. (1994) Childrearing practices: creating programs where traditions and modern practices meet, *Coordinators Notebook,* No. 15.
Gakuru, O. N. & Koech, B. G. (1995) The experiences of young children: a contextualised case study of early childhood care and education in Kenya. *Final Report to Bernard van Leer Foundation.*

Goodnow, J. J. & Collins, W. A. (1990) *Development According to Parents* (London, Erlbaum).

Grieve, R. & Hughes, M. (Eds) (1990) *Understanding Children* (Oxford, Blackwell).

Harms, T. & Clifford, R. (1980) *Early Childhood Environment Rating Scale* (New York, Teachers College Press).

Hockey, J. & James, A. (1993) *Growing-up and Growing Old* (London, Sage).

Hoffman, L. W. (1987) The value of children to parents and child rearing patterns, in: C. Kagitcibasi (Ed.) *Growth and Progress in Cross-cultural Psychology* (Berwyn, Swets N. America Inc.).

James, A. & Prout, A. (Eds) (1990) *Constructing and Reconstructing Childhood* (London, Falmer Press).

Kagitcibasi, C. (1990) Family and socialization in cross-cultural perspective: a model of change, in: J. Berman (Ed.) *Nebraska Symposium on Motivation,* Vol. 37, pp. 135–200 (Lincoln, Nebraska University Press).

Kagitcibasi, C. (1996) *Family and Human Development across Cultures: A View from the Other Side* (London, Erlbaum).

Karrby, C. & Giota, J. (1994) Dimensions of quality in Swedish day care centers – analysis of Early Childhood Environment Rating Scale. *Early Childhood Development and Care,* 104, pp. 1–22.

Kessen, W. (1979) The American child and other cultural inventions. *American Psychologist,* 34, pp. 815–20.

LeVine, R. A., Dixon, S., LeVine, S., Richman, A., Leiderman, P. H., Keefer, C. H. & Brazelton, T. B. (1994) *Child Core and Culture – Lessons from Africa* (Cambridge University Press).

Light, P. & Butterworth, G. (Eds) (1992) *Context and Cognition: Ways of Learning and Knowing* (London, Harvester Wheatsheaf).

Mallory, B. L. & New, R. S. (Eds) (1994) *Diversity and Developmentally Appropriate Practice* (New York, Teachers College Press).

Markus H. & Kitayama, S. (1991) Culture and the self: implications for cognition, emotion and motivation. *Psychological Review* 98, pp. 224–53.

Morss, J. R. (1996) *Growing Critical: Alternatives to Developmental psychology* (London, Routledge).

Moss, P. & Pence, A. (Eds) (1995) *Valuing Quality in Early Childhood Services* (London, Paul Chapman).

Myers, R. (1992) *The Twelve who Survive* (London, Routledge).

NAEYC (1996) Position statement: responding to linguistic and cultural diversity – recommendations for effective early childhood education. *Young Children,* January.

Nsamenang, A. B. & Lamb, M. E. (1993) The acquisition of socio-cognitive competence by Nso children in the Bamenda grassfields of Northwest Cameroon. *International Journal of Behavioural Development,* 16, pp. 429–41.

Nunes, T. (1994) *The Environment of the Child. Occasional Paper No. 5* (The Hague, Bernard van Leer Foundation).

Olmsted, P. & Weikart, D. (1989) (Eds) *How Nations Serve Young Children* (Ypsilanti, High/Scope Press).

Paul, R. (1995) Early Childhood Development and Environment. *Final Report to Bernard van Leer Foundation.*

Phillips, D. A. (Ed.) (1987) *Quality in Child Care: What Does Research Tell Us?* (Washington, DC, NAEYC).

Rogoff, B. & Chavajay, P. (1995) What's become of research on the cultural basis of cognitive development, *American Psychologist* 50, pp. 859–77.

Rogoff, B., Mistry, J., Goncu, A. & Mosier, C. (1993) Guided participation in cultural activity by toddlers and caregivers. *Monograph of the Society for Research in Child Development,* 58.

Schieffelin, B. B. & Ochs, E. (1983) A cultural perspective on the transition from prelinguistic to linguistic communication, in: R. M. Golinkoff (Ed.) *The Transition from Prelinguistic Communication* (Hillsdale, NJ, Erlbaum).

Singer, E. (1992) *Childcare and the Psychology of Development* (London, Routledge).

Snow, C. E. (1976) The language of the mother child relationship, in: M. Woodhead, R. Carr & P. Light (Eds) (1991) *Becoming a Person* (London, Routledge).

Stigler, J. W., Schneider, R. A. & Herd, G. (Eds) (1990) *Cultural Psychology* (New York, Cambridge University Press).

Super, C. & Harkness, S. (1982) Cultural perspectives on child development, in: D. Wagner & H. Stevenson (Eds) *Cultural Perspectives on Child Development* (San Francisco, W. H. Freeman).

Super, C. & Harkness, S. (1986) The developmental niche: a conceptualization at the interface of child and culture, *International Journal of Behavioral Development* 9. pp. 545–69.

Teran de Ruesta, M., Yanez, J., Tovar de Zarikian, A. & Diaz de Giannantonio, A. (1995) Environmental quality, culture and child development, Venezuela. *Final Report to Bernard van Leer Foundation.*

Tijus, C., Santolini, A. & Danis, A. (1995) Study of the environment of the disadvantaged child in parent-run preschools. *Final Report to Bernard van Leer Foundation.*

Tizard, B. (1991) Working mothers and the care of young children, in: E. Lloyd, A. Phoenix & A. Woollett (Eds) *Social Constructs of Motherhood* (London, Sage).

Van Ijzendoorn, M. H. & Kroonenberg, P. M. (1988) Cross-cultural patterns of attachment: a meta-analysis of the Strange Situation. *Child Development,* 59, pp. 147–56.

Walkderdine, V. (1984) Developmental psychology and the child-centred pedagogy: the insertion of Piaget's theory into primary school practice, in: J. Henriques *et al.* (Eds) *Changing the Subject* (London, Methuen).

Wertsch, J. V. (1985) *Culture, Communication and Cognition* (Cambridge University Press).

Whiting, B. & Edwards, C. (1988) *Children of Different Worlds – The Formation of Social Behavior* (Cambridge, MA, Harvard University Press).

Woodhead, M. (1990) Psychology and the cultural construction of children's needs, in: A. James & A. Prout (Eds) *Constructing and Reconstructing Childhood* (London, Falmer Press).

Woodhead, M. (1996) *In Search of the Rainbow: Pathways to Quality in Large Scale Programmes for Young Disadvantaged Children* (The Hague, Bernard van Leer Foundation).

8

Valid Knowledge and the Problem of Practical Arts Curricula

Theodore Lewis

Introduction

One of the more resilient and contentious issues in the realm of school curricula has been the epistemological claim of the practical arts. Whatever the nature of their claim, subjects of this class have historically enjoyed no more than a marginalized existence in schools, and in the discourse on curriculum. Technology education with its intrinsic bent and general-education purpose has enjoyed no higher status than vocational education with its overtly instrumental purpose. Quite clearly, *purpose* in the curriculum does not provide a satisfactory explanation for the historic difficulties that have beset these subjects.

The contention of this chapter is that the practical arts have languished because as a class they do not conform to the traditional view of what constitutes valid knowledge. The chapter holds that until the existential circumstances of humans can be universally accepted as a valid source of knowledge, the practical arts, whatever their form or purpose, will continue to find disfavor in the curriculum. To expand upon these basic notions, the issue is discussed first from a historical perspective, then as it has played out in contemporary educational policy and practice. The rest of the chapter is organized along the following lines: (a) views of the nature and worth of knowledge, (b) valid knowledge, industrial culture, and schooling, (c) contemporary difficulties (e.g., the British prevocational debate; the US educational reform debate; the problem of introducing technology into the school and university curricula; and the peculiar difficulties of professional schools, and of subprofessional education in US community colleges), (d) discussion, and (e) conclusion.

Views of the Nature and Worth of Knowledge

The discussion on the nature and worth of knowledge begins appropriately with a consideration of Plato's distinction between *episteme* (knowledge) and *doxa* (opinion) – or between rational and irrational thought – in *The*

This chapter has been edited.

Republic (Lee 1974, 310). One arrived at pure truth through *episteme*, that is, through intelligence and reason. One could not arrive at ultimate truth via the realm of *doxa*, which included the visible physical realm. In this realm one could arrive only at shadows and illusions. As Egan (1987, 445) points out, 'true knowledge' in Platonic culture could be arrived at only by 'sight, speculation, contemplation'.

Consistent with this view of what constituted true or valid knowledge, Plato set forth that the object of education was 'to teach us to love what is beautiful' (Lee 1974, 165). One could find this beauty in the study of poetry, mathematics, literature, or music. The purpose of education was to train character, along with moral and aesthetic judgment: 'Good Literature, therefore, and good music, beauty of form and good rhythm, all depended on goodness of character' (162). However, in Plato's estimation, 'The more practical forms of skill (did not) seem very elevating' (327).

Here, Plato was echoing a theory that was common to Greek thought. This theory held that 'art', being imitative for the most part, had, particularly in its performance, no redeeming transcendent aspect. Art included all human practices. As Dewey (1958) notes, it was a 'commonplace of Greek observation – that the fine arts as well as the industrial technologies are affairs of practice' (355). In describing the Greek view of the nature of art, Lodge (1953) notes the following:

> It is applied indifferently to the trades of the carpenter and builder, or of the smith, potter, weaver, etc., on the one hand, and to the trades of the flautist, lyrist, or other musician, or of the painter, poet, or prose rhetorician, on the other. All are alike in being primarily professional activities: forms of manipulative dexterity acquired by practice, by repeated pushings and pullings applied to moving objects in a world of motions. (p. 52)

Art transmitted defective knowledge. Seeking to unravel Plato's theory of art, Lodge (1953) muses: 'Just what is this "knowledge", which artists should have, but apparently do not? Will Socrates kindly tell us?' (285). He posits two possibilities: 'In a word, Socrates recognizes (1) a best, i.e., an ideally best, and (2) a second-best' (285). The 'best' is transcendent. It is pure knowledge. The 'second best' is the knowledge of practice – empirically derived, and based upon observation and tentative generalizations. Among the 'human knowledge' situations Lodge includes in his analysis are the fields of social psychology, sociology, agriculture, and medicine. Such knowledge falls short of the fourth level of Plato's hierarchy of artistic development as set forth by Lodge. This is the level of 'dialectical or metaphysical insight into the principle of ideality', where 'philosopher-artists' attempt to 'apply the idea of good to the whole of human life in the closest realizable approximation to human perfection' (160).

On this same theme, Dewey (1958) noted that to the Greeks

> labor, production, did not seem to create form, it dealt with matter of changing things so as to furnish an occasion for incarnation of antecedent forms of matter. To artisans form is alien, unperceived and unenjoyed; absorbed in laboring with material, they lie in a world of change and matter, even when their labors have an

end in manifestation of form. Plato was so troubled by the consequences of this ignorance of form on the part of all who live in the world of practice, industrial and political, that he elaborated a plan by which their activities might be regulated by those who, above labor and entanglement in change and practice, provide in laws forms to shape the habits of those who work. Aristotle escaped the dilemma by putting nature above art, and endowing nature with skilled purpose that for the most part achieves ends or completions. Thus the role of the human artisan whether in industry or politics became relatively negligible, and the miscarriages of human art a matter of relative insignificance. (p. 92)

Thus, according to Dewey, science (that is, theory or philosophy or knowledge) has been handed down from Greek culture as 'the only *authentic* expression of nature, in which case art must be an arbitrary addition to nature' (355).

The Platonic ideal was theory that supported the sharp cleavage in Greek society between citizen and slave. Knowledge derived from the culture of the leisured class, not from the toil of subservients. Epistemological notions in the Greek Platonic tradition have had a nagging resiliency through the ages, transported through time especially via the medium of the great English universities, and the instrument or the concept of liberal education.

What made the ancient universities fertile ground for the inculcation and transmission of the Platonic tradition was that they catered to the elite – the leisured class, and further, that the liberal curriculum featuring theology, 'the Queen of the sciences', had the sponsorship of the Church of England. Religious virtue and the liberal education curriculum went hand in hand, attaching to the latter its enduring transcendent aura.

Reviewing education and economic and social change in England in the period 1780–1870, Sanderson (1983) dwells on the reactions of Oxford and Cambridge. These universities, he claims, 'reposed in a social and curricular inertia that limited their value to society. These limitations arose partly from a network of institutional arrangements and partly from assumptions arising from the concept of liberal education' (41). Their doctrinaire matriculation requirements excluded nonconformists, and thus, the possibility of attracting a new clientele of nonconformist business families enriched by the industrial revolution. The social class of the intake continued to be narrow, and stable, in the period in question – weighted heavily by the families of the landed gentry and the clergy [. . .].

In the first half of the nineteenth century, amid pressures on Oxbridge to yield to the professional education requirements of an age becoming increasingly more industrial, there ensued a great liberal education debate, the origin of which Sanderson (1983) traces to the publication by R. L. Edgeworth in 1809 of *Essays on Professional Education*. The protagonists included John Henry Newman, Matthew Arnold, and John Stuart Mill on the one hand, and T. H. Huxley on the other. In *The Modern Idea of the University*, Thompson (1984) frames the debate as follows:

> Newman, Arnold, Huxley, and Mill all sought to define the nature of 'liberal education' as the goal of university education, with each offering a variation on the theme of ideal education. For each of these men was concerned with the

impact of the scientific and technological revolution taking place around them – a revolution that eventually rendered the standard classical education of Oxford and Cambridge not merely inadequate but obsolete. New approaches to the sciences and humanities, in light of these discoveries, were required; new philosophies for integrating them all into the curriculum essential. The great classicists – Newman, Mill, Arnold – sought to justify the preeminence of humane letters as the much-needed unifying, elevating force in the curriculum. The great scientist, Huxley, would attribute this quality to science. (p. 14)

[. . .]

Amid the ferment that led eventually to the erosion of the resistance of the universities to what they viewed as a vulgar professionalism came Spencer's challenge to the Platonic view of knowledge, as epitomized in the ideas of Newman. In an 1860 treatise entitled 'What knowledge Is of Most Worth?' (see Spencer [1860] 1914), Spencer advanced the view that the practical could be a source of knowledge. He argued that to arrive at a 'rational curriculum', it was necessary first to determine the 'relative value of knowledges' (11). Rejecting tradition, Spencer proposed that knowledge should be hierarchically organized in terms of 'the leading kinds of activity which constitute human life', as follows:

> 1. Those activities which directly minister to self-preservation; 2. Those activities which, by securing the necessaries of life, indirectly minister to self-preservation; 3. Those activities which have for their end the rearing and discipline of offspring; 4. Those activities which are involved in the maintenance of proper social and political relations; 5. Those miscellaneous activities which make up the leisure part of life, devoted to the gratification of the tastes and feelings. (p. 14)

He called attention to the theory/practice imbalance in the school curriculum, observing for example that 'while the great bulk of what else is acquired has no bearing on the industrial activities, an immensity of information that has a direct bearing on the industrial activities is entirely passed over' (27).

Spencer's basic ideas – his rejection of the Platonic view of knowledge – were to gain a new legitimacy in this century, notably, when they were echoed in the educational philosophy of Alfred North Whitehead. In his *Aims of Education*, Whitehead (1929) held that indeed practical affairs were of epistemological consequence. He recognized three main sources of knowledge deriving from 'the way of literary culture, the way of scientific culture, *the way of technical culture*' [my emphasis] (84). In setting forth these three sources of knowledge, Whitehead acknowledged no hierarchy. He insisted that 'no one of these methods can be exclusively followed without grave loss of intellectual activity and of character' (84). All three, equally, were valid sources of knowledge. Like Spencer before him, Whitehead saw the purveyance of knowledge derived from industrial practices as an important role of schools. He called this technical education. Noted Whitehead:

> An evil side of the Platonic culture has been its total neglect of technical education as an ingredient in the complete development of ideal human beings. This neglect has arisen from two disastrous antitheses, namely, that between mind and body, and that between thought and action. (p. 77)

In Whitehead's view, technical education necessarily had a scientific aspect, but it could also be in the realm of the aesthetic. Such education satisfied 'our deep natural instinct to translate thought into manual skill, and manual activity into thought' (80).

But Whitehead did not have the last word here. The inertia of tradition, and the attendant elitism, would not allow the notion that the practical affairs of humans could be the basis of valid knowledge to take hold. The tenacity of the status quo is evident in the landmark *General Education in a Free Society* (Harvard University 1945), and in the seminal offerings of Phenix (1969) and Hirst (1975).

Although acknowledging that 'methods of knowledge' (59) would be a more pleasing way to divide school learning than would the traditional natural science, humanities, and social studies, the Harvard Committee, authors of *General Education in a Free Society*, did not go on to suggest an expansion of the realm of knowledge as suggested by Whitehead. They would concede only that 'shop training' was of educative value. Such training should center around 'simple hand tools and the execution of simple basic operations' (160).

Phenix (1969) contended that 'all curriculum content should be drawn from the disciplines . . . only knowledge contained in the disciplines is appropriate to the curriculum' (188). A discipline is 'knowledge organized for instruction' (188). This knowledge would be based upon 'a synthetic structure of concepts' (193). While Phenix did not overtly suggest the exclusion of the practical arts from the curriculum, the fact that these subjects have traditionally failed the critical test of discipline structure tacitly means that they do not belong. They do not qualify as valid knowledge.

Hirst (1975) posited that a liberal education seeks to shed light on the 'forms of knowledge'. These forms of knowledge are 'distinct disciplines' – namely, 'mathematics, physical sciences, human sciences, history, religion, literature and the fine arts, philosophy, morals' (18). Beyond the distinct disciplines of knowledge, Hirst saw possibility for the development of 'fields' of knowledge. It is here that knowledge derived from practice could be accommodated. For example, 'engineering' could be a field. Fields are applied in nature, and while they could shed light on the forms of knowledge, they clearly lack the purity of disciplines. They are not seen as purveying knowledge in their own right.

But to conceive of knowledge purely in traditional terms – in terms of traditional disciplinary packages – is to constrict the curriculum artificially. The curriculum would not be totally inclusive of what there is to know. The advent of industrial society only served to highlight this curricular shortcoming.

Valid Knowledge, Industrial Culture, and Schooling

When conceived in terms of purveyance of the culture, knowledge in the Platonic mold is found to be deficient. Since the dawn of the industrial revolution, practical people have been suggesting that knowledge should admit to new forms. But always there has been inertia and a strong press for retention of the traditional view. The practical arts have nonetheless been able to make inroads, though tentative, into popular thinking about the curriculum.

English reaction

In nineteenth-century England the growth of science and industry, and the threat of foreign inventive and economic competition, raised concerns about the efficacy of the ancient universities. Beecham (1982) postulates that from antiquity the ancient English universities had acknowledged only *speculative* knowledge – knowledge that 'assists the forming of conjectures . . . without experiment or intention to experiment' (59). They had distanced themselves from *applicable* knowledge or *applied* knowledge (59). According to Beecham, the lure of speculative knowledge is its intrinsic nature – 'putting the acquired knowledge to use is considered to be de-meaning of knowledge' (59). He explains that as the Industrial Revolution beckoned, neither the universities nor the State could react, or were inclined to react, to the urgent demand for technical education – knowledge pertaining to industrial culture. It was left to working-class agencies such as the Mechanics Institute Movement to step in to fill the breach. When the State eventually did assume responsibility for technical education in 1853, by setting up the State Science and Art Department, clear lines were drawn between science, which was to be taught in established schools of science, and technical instruction, which was to be had in workshops. The State, notes Beecham, was 'not prepared freely to involve itself with the technical education of the industrial classes' (63).

Armytage (1955) traces official concern for the need for technical education in England to the Great Exhibition of 1851, at which the country gave a creditable showing but was left impressed by the French and German contributions. The need for an industrial university was being whispered. By the Paris Exhibition of 1867, at which the English showing was poor, it became clear that the State had to become more openly supportive of technical education. This led to two decades of investigations into the link between science, industry, and education, and beyond 1890, to improvements in technical education.

A more concrete and direct response to the 1867 Paris Exhibition was the establishment of alternative universities in the provinces (Leeds University being the first), geared to teaching the sciences related to industries (such as engineering and woolen dyeing), and of Polytechnics (out of charities and philanthrophies, and fueled by the advocacy of concerned industrialists).

American reaction

At the dawn of the American Industrial Revolution, following the end of the Civil War, the colonial legacy of elitism and preference for liberal studies, epitomized by the Harvard curriculum, was deemed unsatisfactory by the state. Higher education needed to be democratized, and the curriculum needed to be reformed to reflect new, everyday realities.

Like the ancient universities upon which it was patterned, Harvard had to come to terms with new social and economic realities. There was need 'to define anew liberal education' (Eliot 1901, 89). To this end the curriculum was expanded by its new president, Charles William Eliot, to include English Language and Literature, History, German, French, Political Economy, and Natural Science. Eliot, assuming his position in 1869, also brought about the reform of the medical and law schools, which, not unlike their counterparts in the great English universities, had to that time been grossly neglected and not given to scholarship (see Morison 1964, 339). Eliot had his work cut out in getting professional education at Harvard to the point where it could gain academic respectability in the university. But the society at large was not going to wait on Harvard. The push of nascent industrialism and the concomitant demand for knowledge that could explain or inform everyday practice was irrepressible. The solution was the passage of the Morrill Act of 1862, giving rise to the establishment of land grant colleges in which the curricular focus would be upon agricultural and mechanic arts. In the American context, this was a watershed in the quest to recognize practical arts as a valid source of knowledge. Waterous (1989) argues that Utopian principles were foundational to the land grant ideal. Underlying these principles was 'a utilitarian ethic of practicality for social progress' (368).

[. . .]

Also responding to the new industrialism, commercial arts found their way into the US curriculum, provoking resistance among traditionalists. Weiss (1982) indicates that despite popular appeal, these subjects had their opponents. According to Weiss, these opponents were

> the old-guard educators, the academics who resolutely maintained that education's prime purpose was mental discipline. To them, practicality was a minor concern at best: in fact, subject matter was in a sense secondary. What counted was whether the subject stretched students' minds, exercised their intellects and developed their mental faculties like muscles. Among the devotees of this theory, it was generally agreed that the ideal subjects for the purpose were the classics, philosophy, mathematics, and the like. (p. 619)

Weiss continues, 'To convince such skeptics, commercial education advocates argued . . . that commercial education really did contribute to mental discipline' (619).

Interestingly, Jackson and Gaskell (1987) point to similar difficulties in establishing commercial arts as a school subject in Canada in the latter part of the nineteenth century. Despite popular acceptance, there were still attempts to establish a curricular hierarchy in the schools in such a manner as to denude their status.

[. . .]

Reflection

It cannot be denied that with the coming of the Industrial Age, knowledge derived purely from human practices increased drastically. Such knowledge has spanned virtually all spheres of human endeavor. In the circumstances, it would seem not unreasonable to argue that the purely Platonic defense of the curriculum must now be untenable. And yet, that is not the reality. The biases continue and, as will be shown in the next section of the article, inform much of the curricular debate today in industrial societies on both sides of the Atlantic.

Contemporary Difficulties

Thus far, this chapter has dwelled upon the historical struggle of the practical arts for recognition as valid knowledge, and for space in the curriculum. The focus of the chapter now shifts to the contemporary scene – to the way in which the historical problem of the practical arts alluded to above has persisted, remaining ineluctably a part of today's educational policy and practice. For illustrative purposes this section of the paper looks at (a) the debate in the United Kingdom over the merits of the prevocational curriculum, (b) the debate in the United States as to what knowledge is most likely to lead to competitive edge in the global economy, (c) attempts to introduce the study of technology into the curriculum of schools and universities, and (d) the peculiar problems of professional schools, and of subprofessional training in community colleges. In each case, the chapter attempts to show that at issue, whether explicitly or implicitly, is the question of the validity of practical affairs as knowledge – the notion that such knowledge would at best be second-rate – inferior to the traditional academic subjects.

The British prevocational debate

Traditional British aversion for the practical arts, exemplified by the attitude of the traditional universities, has been alluded to earlier in this chapter, pointedly so in the account of Beecham (1982). In contemporary times, this issue has remained, and is evidenced in the ongoing prevocational education debate, out of which was borne the Education for Capability movement.

The current debate in Britain over the so-called prevocational curriculum is agreed to have begun with Prime Minister Callaghan's famous 1976 speech at Ruskin College, Oxford, when he suggested that schooling should fit recipients for a place in society, and for a job of work. Schools could do so by deliberately linking with industry through work experience programs, by teaching positive attitudes towards industry, and so on. The debate that began in the Callaghan term of office carried over into the Thatcher government. In 1982, Prime Minister Thatcher launched a £7 million sterling project consisting of a series of pilot projects designed to stimulate the interest of youth ages 14–18 in technical and vocational education. These projects are generically referred to as the Technical Vocational Education Initiative (TVEI). As conceived, they feature a balance of general and technical and vocational education, problem solving, and a planned work experience (see Atkins 1984 for a case study account). Completion of a prevocational course leads to an array of certificates including the Certificate of Pre-Vocational Education (CPVE), and the City and Guilds of London Institute (CGLI).

The TVEI has sparked wide-ranging debate, much of which has had to do with resentment over the politicization of the curriculum, but much also of which (and here Beecham is instructive) has had to do with the traditional British distaste for nonliberal intrusions into the curriculum. In setting forth the issues involved in the prevocational debate, Atkins (1986) was able to discern that the question of the 'worth of the prevocational curriculum' (45) was paramount. She pointed to the concern of some that this curriculum would provide a 'second-class education' to disadvantaged groups. Indeed, prevocational qualifications did not count as much as '0' levels (48). As described by Atkins, the prevocational curriculum typically offers 'a common core of general educational competencies compulsory for all students, complemented by a limited choice of more vocational modules, including some skills training and work experience' (46).

The general education component includes new educational 'basics' such as information skills, computer literacy, microelectronics, and technology. But Atkins points out that there are those who view this curriculum as being invalid. They are of this persuasion because

> the emphasis on practical, applied knowledge and skills related to everyday life is an emphasis on the second-rate. The knowledge and skills which have traditionally been highly valued do not appear in the prevocational curriculum . . . there is little theoretical knowledge, little emphasis on the mastery of abstract symbolic reasoning, and little attention paid to written argument, analysis and synthesis. (p. 50)

[. . .]

One important source of such opinion has been the Royal Society of Arts (RSA), which in 1980 set forth its *Education for Capability* manifesto. Signatories to the manifesto spanned a wide cross-section of the society, inclusive of academics, politicians, and industrialists. Following is an excerpt, which appears in Burgess (1986):

> There is a serious imbalance in Britain today in the full process which is described by two words 'education' and 'training' . . This imbalance is harmful to individuals, to industry and to society . . . A well-balanced education should, of course, embrace analysis and the acquisition of knowledge. But it must also include the exercise of creative skills, the competence to undertake and complete

tasks and the ability to cope with everyday life . . . There exists in its own right a culture which is concerned with doing, making and organizing the creative arts. This culture emphasizes the day-to-day management of affairs, the formulation and solution of problems and the design, manufacture and marketing of goods and services. Educators should spend more time preparing people in this way for a life outside the education system. (p. ix)

In the RSA publication *Education for Capability*, the concerns and philosophy of key architects of the movement are set forth. In it, Nuttgens (1986) explains his perspective thus:

The most far-reaching characteristic of education in this country in the last 150 years has been the dislike and fear of technology – and therefore of the modern world. The new technology of the Industrial Revolution was fundamental to that world; it changed the social and economic status quo, upset many of the conventions of the mind and created the urban and industrial environment of today. Yet, in a rather British way, the attitude of the people developing the educational system was not to exploit it but in some way to correct it. In that sense it was a development, not of excitement and wonder, but of fear. (p. 25)

He argued that the time had come to dispel the old belief that the practical diminished the curriculum. To him the challenge lay in forging a new curriculum 'in which thinking and doing and making are fused together in a new concept of living and learning' (32).
[. . .]
As the British debate over the introduction of the TVEI and prevocationalism has shown, acceptance of the practical as valid knowledge remains firmly a matter of intense philosophical debate. For many, what is at stake is the purity of the curriculum. They deem as invalid any claim that the practical arts belong in their own right.

Global competition, which education? The US debate

Unlike in Great Britain, where the decline of international competitiveness has led to deliberate policy shifts toward practical education [. . .], in the United States concern for lack of competitive edge has led to a strong official push towards academics, and thus to retreat from practical arts programs.

Current US educational policy, and the ongoing reform of the secondary curriculum, derives largely from the recommendations set forth in an official document, *A Nation at Risk* (National Commission on Excellence in Education 1983). The authors of this report made it clear that the overarching goal of US education was to restore the country's economic preeminence. They wrote:

America's position in the world may once have been reasonably secure with only a few exceptionally well-trained men and women. It is no longer. The risk is not only that the Japanese make automobiles more efficiently than Americans and have government subsidies for development and export. It is not just that the South Koreans recently built the world's most efficient steel mill, or that American machine tools, once the pride of the world, are being displaced by German products. It is also that these developments signify a redistribution of trained capability throughout the globe . . . If only to keep and improve on the slim competitive edge we will retain in world markets, we must dedicate ourselves to the reform of our educational system for the benefit of all. (p. 6)

It ought to be recalled here that a typical argument of critics of prevocationalism in the United Kingdom (see, for example, Holt 1987; Bailey 1988) has been that its rationale is economic. The higher purpose of schooling was thereby being subverted by utilitarian, extrinsic considerations. In the US case, as can be seen from the above excerpt from *A Nation at Risk*, there is no transcendent, liberal rationale for proposed curricular reforms. The dominant considerations are utilitarian. The aims are extrinsic. What is different here is that utilitarian and extrinsic ends are expected to be attained via the *liberal*, not the practical, curriculum. This then leads to *less*, not more, vocational education. Education for capability in the United States is academic, not practical, education. Vocational education has been downgraded, but vocationalism drives the new reforms. This is the irony.

The primary curricular reform recommended in *A Nation at Risk* excluded practical arts subjects. Instead, what was proposed was adherence to the 'basics'. Following is a relevant excerpt from *A Nation at Risk*:

We recommend that State and local high school graduation requirements be strengthened and that, at a minimum, all students seeking a diploma be required to lay the foundations in the Five New Basics by taking the following curriculum during their four years of high school: (a) 4 years of English; (b) 3 years of mathematics; (c) 3 years of science; (d) 3 years of social studies; and (e) one-half year of computer science. For the college-bound, 2 years of foreign language in high school are recommended in addition to those taken earlier. (National Commission on Excellence in Education 1983, 24)

The way to prepare a workforce that could compete with German, Korean, and Japanese manufactures was through excellence in academic, not practical, education. Even in its traditional preserve – preparation for work – vocational education had become marginalized.

The authors of *A Nation at Risk* were, in fair measure, yielding to criticism leveled by American business interests against the quality of public schooling. Workers were lacking so-called basic skills, and schools were to blame. But in Japan and Germany, unlike in the United States, firms assume the responsibility for job-specific education and training (see, for example, Cantor 1985; Schmidt 1985). As Kirst (1991) observes, American businesses and industries invest very little on upgrading their workers, relying on the contribution of the massive postsecondary system of trade and industrial schools, community colleges, and universities. On this theme, Robert Reich (1990) points out that foreign firms in the United States seem to pay more attention (than do domestic firms) to the quality of their workers. 'They emphasize on-the-job training and the continuous development of new skills to a greater extent than do American firms' (84).

Blaming the schools, and invoking liberal education, has its appeal, but can American businesses and industries survive without the vocationalism of the postsecondary system? Japan, Germany, and South Korea all value liberal education highly. But they find ways, through apprenticeships (in the case of Germany), through in-plant education and training, and particularly in South Korea, through vocational and technical high schools (see Kang and Im 1983), to complement it with practical arts education.

It had become fashionable in the years following publication of a *A Nation at Risk* to accept the hypothesis that schools were indeed at fault, and that subjects not obviously college-track should be excised from the curriculum. But scholars such as Bracey (1991) and Kirst (1991) have introduced compelling new contrary arguments regarding the nature of American education. They are asking for a reexamination of the evidence, suggesting that there have been distortions in the approach to international comparisons, especially because postsecondary schooling tends to be discounted. This is a refreshing new movement, away from the emotionalism engendered by *A Nation at Risk*, and perhaps it will help to relieve the somewhat unreasonable political pressure placed upon schools, allowing them to take as broad a perspective of knowledge as possible in the search for truth.

[. . .]

Technology education – overcoming difficulties

Though its curricular claim has been along intrinsic lines, technology education too, like vocational education, has had difficulty finding expression and acceptance in school curricula (see Lewis 1991). When one looks at the problem from an international perspective it becomes clear that the difficulties are shared. In the United Kingdom Allsop and Woolnough (1990) report that given 'the high status of the existing sciences . . . technology fought vainly for acceptance' (128). This was not unlike an earlier account in which Heywood (1978) pointed to the sharp craft/engineering dichotomy perceived in British universities and schools: 'Both universities and schools took a poor view of traditional metalwork. Some university teachers felt craft subjects gave engineering a poor image' (139). Lindblad (1990) speaks of difficulties involved in trying to make technology a compulsory subject in Sweden. Teachers could not coherently set forth its subject matter.

In the United States, technology education holds the place in the curriculum traditionally held by industrial arts, and despite a history traceable to Woodward's manual training movement in the late decades of the last century, and to the thought of John Dewey, that place remains insecure. In the current climate of reform, technology education, like vocational education, must give way to more valued subjects. This is evident in the report of the Project 2061 panel (Johnson 1989):

Although the primary charge to the Technology Panel was to consider content in future curricula, the panel concluded early in its deliberations that technology, unlike science and mathematics, currently has little or no place in elementary and secondary school programs. Thus the panel believed it should start by suggesting how technology should be integrated into future elementary and secondary school programs. (p. 3)

Why is technology not an established subject even in highly industrialized, technological countries? One reason is that historically technology has not had a coherent conceptual structure, a criterion demanded by Phenix (1969). But philosophers of technology (e.g., Rapp 1989; Downey, Donovan, and Elliot 1989) argue that absence of structure derives from the fact that technology has historically been deemed as not being suited to philosophical speculation.

Difficulties notwithstanding, important recent attempts to make the structure of technological knowledge more coherent can be identified, in the work of Savage and Sterry (1990a, b). Savage and Sterry (1990a) have these views about technological knowledge:

The body of knowledge for technology must be identified based upon content that is unique to the study of the human-made world . . . technological knowledge can be classified as bio-related technology, communication technology, production technology, and transportation technology. (p. 8)

Inherent in this way of thinking is the rejection of the notion that technology is merely applied science and support for the notion that technology is an autonomous, valid sphere of knowledge. But whether this view would become a commonplace in education remains doubtful.

[. . .]

Discussion

Why has the Platonic legacy been so enduring? One cannot of course answer this definitively, but it may have to do with its claim of transcendence. Newman's claim that liberal education of itself conferred omnibus utilitarian capabilities upon its recipient still resonates. It brings a kind of parsimony to the way we might think about the curriculum. Schools could simply take the high ground, concerning themselves with matters of mind and holding to a universe of knowledge that is uncluttered by the mere everyday.

But the Platonic culture was a slave-owning culture. The high ground of philosophy was reserved for the leisured class. The toil of slaves, artistic or otherwise, could be valid – of epistemological consequence – only in the abstract, never of itself. Thus another explanation of the tenacity of the Platonic conception is that it provides a seemingly rational explanation for social inequalities – it validates the meritocracy. In the secondary school, the liberal curriculum has become an efficient, convenient way to sort children for their roles in society. Those who apparently cannot cope with this curriculum – who cannot pass the attendant examinations – have the practical arts school subjects as their alternative. But ability to cope with the liberal curriculum often has much to do with the social circumstances into which one was born. Privilege and valid knowledge still go together.

This leaves seemingly unexplained the fact that spheres of life that clearly are to be included among the practical arts (such as engineering, journalism, law, medicine, and agriculture) today enjoy popular prestigious status and occupy the top rungs of the occupational ladder. As indicated above, and elsewhere in this article, these endeavors must make adjustments to be accommodated in academe. But more to the point, within these practical arts distinctions have emerged, between engineer and mechanic, doctor and midwife, agronomist and farmer, dentist and dental technician, and so on. These distinctions have to do with the ever-increasing division of labor in contemporary society, and their basis (wittingly or unwittingly) is the Platonic model. Knowledge workers are distinguished increasingly from skill workers, the very distinction attesting to the notion that skill and knowledge are mutually exclusive. Not coincidentally, these distinctions mirror the class structure of the society.

The case for the practical arts as valid knowledge

The case for the practical arts as knowledge in its own right has been made by others, but notably by Whitehead (1929). The basis of this case, from this author's own perspective, is that an important purpose of schooling is transmission of the culture. Culture includes the sum of human practices cutting across all spheres of existence. Whether these practices are in the realm of speculation, contemplation, or solution of existential problems such as the need for clothing or shelter; the need to preserve food, to travel, to remedy affliction, to assure social cohesion, or to gaze into the heavens, they constitute genuine human expression and important ways of knowing. That many of these practices have in common an empirical basis ought not to detract from their validity. In large measure, they account for our very existence, and for our quality of life. Bertrand Russell (1972) has argued that the importance of industrialism was that it transformed the way men thought. It conferred 'an immense increase in the sense of human power' (728). The contemporary curriculum ought not to deny this. To be authentic, the curriculum must view the practical arts as being important sources of knowledge, crucial to human advance.

[. . .]

Education ought not to be disconnected from everyday existence. It ought to be a central role of institutions of learning – schools, colleges, universities – that they seek to shed further light upon the day-to-day. And formal education is well placed to do that. It cannot be disputed, for example, that the training of doctors, lawyers, carpenters, and mechanics was substantially rationalized when such training evolved from the hold of apprenticeship, and the mysteries that attended it, to formal classrooms and shared knowledge. Trial and error was not completely abandoned but became less fortuitous by incorporating sciencelike problem-solving approaches. A result of the involvement of formal education in practical affairs has been to improve practice, to create more reflective practitioners, to change practice, and to widen the pool of practitioners. This has not in any way been an ignoble contribution.

It remains the lot of practical affairs, unfortunately, that the standard against which they are measured when they take their place in the curriculum is the traditional Platonic one. This chapter has argued, however, that the Platonic standard serves only to marginalize this quite valid source of human knowledge.

Conclusion

It has been my contention through this chapter that practical arts subjects, being the antithesis of the Platonic conception of knowledge, have tended to exist somewhat at the fringes of the curriculum. The chapter has argued that the bias against these subjects has endured perhaps because the Platonic model now provides convenient explanation for the rationing of curriculum on what amounts to a class basis. But bias against the practical arts leads to an inauthentic curriculum, since it suggests, erroneously, that knowledge thus derived cannot be as ennobling as knowledge derived through contemplation.

Appendix A: Definition of Terms

Practical arts

The term *practical arts* is used generically in this chapter to include affairs of everyday existence that are utilitarian in character and that are based upon efficient human action. The term subsumes areas of the curriculum such as vocational education and technology education, along with professional education. Discrete spheres of human existence (such as agriculture, medicine, construction, law, manufacturing, homemaking, or commerce) all have their own peculiar practices. Practical experience leads to conclusions and generalizations that can illuminate future practice, making for ever more efficient action (see Kotarbinski 1965 for more elaborate treatment).

Vocational education

The term *vocational education* is used in the chapter to mean education for and about work. In the United States, consistent with the provisions of the

Smith-Hughes Act of 1917, the term refers to such education that is less than university level. Typical divisions in the curriculum include Trade and Industrial, Business and Marketing, Home Economics, and Agriculture.

Technology education

Technology education is the term now being accepted internationally to describe the curriculum that is replacing traditional industrial arts. Instead of tool skills and drawing, the new focus is on design and problem solving; manufacturing, construction, transportation, communication, power and energy; technological choice; and critical study of the impact of technology. Technology education is taught as part of the general education curriculum. Its purpose is not preparation for jobs.

Professional education

Professional education is used to mean university-based vocational preparation for the more prestigious occupations (law, medicine, journalism, etc.).

Notes

This paper benefited from the comments on earlier drafts by the editorial staff of *Curriculum Inquiry* and five anonymous reviewers. Shortcomings remain the responsibility of the author.

References

Allsop, T. and Woolnough, B. (1990) The relationship of technology to science in English schools, *Journal of Curriculum Studies*, 22(2): 126-36.
Armytage, W. H. G. (1955) *Civic Universities: Aspects of a British Tradition*, London, Ernest Benn Limited.
Atkins, M. J. (1984) Pre-vocational courses: tensions and strategies, *Journal of Curriculum Studies*, 16(4): 403–15.
Atkins, M. J. (1986) The pre-vocational curriculum: a review of the issues involved, *Journal of Curriculum Studies*, 19(1): 45–53.
Bailey, C. (1988) What hopes for liberal education? *Cambridge Journal of Education*, 18(1): 27–37.
Beecham, J. (1982) The universities and technical education in England and Wales, *Journal of Further and Higher Education*, 6(1): 59–74.
Bracey, G. W. (1991) Why can't they be like we were? *Phi Delta Kappan*, 73(2): 105–17.
Burgess, T. (1986) New ways to learn. In *Education for capability*, ed. T. Burgess, Philadelphia, NFER-Nelson.
Cantor, L. (1985) Vocational education and training: the Japanese approach, *Comparative Education*, 21(1): 67–76.

Dewey, J. (1958) *Experience and Nature*, New York, Dover.

Downey, G. L., Donovan, A. and Elliot, T. J. (1989) The invisible engineer: how engineering ceased to be a problem in science and technology studies. In *Knowledge and Society: Studies in the Sociology of Science Past and Present*, ed. L. Hargens, R. A. Jones and A. Pickering, Greenwich, CT, JAI Press.

Egan, K (1987) Literacy and the oral foundations of education, *Harvard Educational Review*, 57(4): 445–72.

Eliot, C. W. (1901) *Educational Reform – Essays and Addresses*, New York, Century.

Harvard University (1945) *General education in a Free Society – Report of the Harvard Committee*, Cambridge, MA, Harvard University Press.

Heywood, J. (1978) Factors influencing attitudes to technology in schools, *British Journal of Educational Studies*, 26(2): 137–49.

Hirst, P. H. (1975) Liberal education and the nature of knowledge. In *Education and Reason*, ed. R. F. Dearden, P. H. Hirst, and R. S. Peters, London, Routledge & Kegan Paul.

Holt, M. (1987) Vocationalism on the hoof: observations on the TVEI. In *Skills and Vocationalism: The Easy Answer*, ed. M. Holt, Milton Keynes, Open University Press.

Jackson, N. S., and Gaskell, J. S. (1987) White collar vocationalism: the rise of commercial education in Ontario and British Columbia, 1870–1920, *Curriculum Inquiry*, 17(2): 177–97.

Johnson, J. R. (1989) *Technology: Report of the Project 2061 Phase 1 Technology Panel*, Washington, DC, American Association for the Advancement of Science.

Kang, M. S., and Im, C. S. (1983) *The Current Status and the Prospect of Vocational Education and Training in the Republic of Korea*, Korean Educational Development Institute.

Kirst, M. W. (1991) The need to broaden our perspective concerning America's educational attainment, *Phi Delta Kappan*, 73(2): 118–20.

Kotarbinski, T. (1965) *Praxiology: An Introduction to the Sciences of Efficient Action,* trans. O. Wojtasiewicz, New York, Pergamon Press.

Lee, D. (1974) *Plato: The Republic*, New York, Penguin Books.

Lewis, T. (1991) Introducing technology into school curricula, *Journal of Curriculum Studies*, 23(2): 141–54.

Lindblad, S. (1990) From technology to craft: on teachers' experimental adoption of technology as a new subject in the Swedish primary school, *Journal of Curriculum Studies*, 22(2): 166–75.

Lodge, R. C. (1953) *Plato's Theory of Art*, London, Routledge & Kegan Paul.

Morison, S. E. (1964) *Three Centuries of Harvard: 1636–1936*, Cambridge, MA, Harvard University Press.

National Commission on Excellence in Education (1983) *A Nation at Risk*, Washington, DC, US Department of Education.

Newman, J. H. [1852] (1917) *The Idea of a University*, New York, Dover Publications Inc.

Nuttgens, P. (1986) The educational failure. In *Education for Capability,* ed. T. Burgess, Philadelphia, NFER-Nelson.

Phenix, P. H. (1969) The disciplines as curriculum content. In *Theory of Knowledge and Problems of Education*, ed. D. Vandenberg, Chicago, University of Illinois Press.

Rapp, F. (1989) Introduction: General perspectives on the complexity of philosophy of technology. In *Philosophy of Technology*, ed. P. T. Durbin, Boston, Kluwer Academic Publishers.

Reich, R. B. (1990) Metamorphosis of the American worker, *Business Month*, 135(9): 58–66.

Russell, B. (1972) *A History of Western Philosophy*, New York, Simon & Schuster.

Sanderson, M. (1983) *Education, Economic Change and Society in England, 1780–1870*, London, Macmillan.

Savage, E. and Sterry, L. (1990a) A conceptual framework for technology education, *The Technology Teacher*, 50(1): 6–11.

Savage, E. and Sterry, L. (1990b) A conceptual framework for technology education part II, *The Technology Teacher*, 50(2): 7–11.

Schmidt, H. (1985) Vocational retraining and structural change in West Germany. In *Economic Dislocation and Job Loss*, ed. B. G. Lall, Tallahassee, FL, Rose Printing.

Spencer, H. [1860] (1914) *Education – Intellectual, Moral, and Physical*, New York, D. Appleton & Company.

Thompson, J. A. G. (1984) *The Modern Idea of the University*, New York, Peter Lang Publishing.

Turner, G. L'E. (1984) The physical sciences. In *The History of the University of Oxford*, ed. L. S. Sutherland and L. G. Mitchell, Oxford, Clarendon Press.

Waterous, F. B. (1989) From salomon's house to the land grant college: practical arts education and the utopian vision of progress, *Educational Theory*, 39(4): 359–72.

Weiss, J. (1982) The advent of education for clerical work in the school: a reconsideration of the historiography of vocationalism, *Teachers College Record*, 83(4): 613–38.

Whitehead, A. N. (1929) *The Aims of Education and Other Essays*, New York, Macmillan.

9

Culture, Mind, and Education

Jerome Bruner

I

[. . .] Fundamental changes [. . .] have been altering conceptions about the nature of the human mind in the decades since the cognitive revolution. These changes, it now seems clear in retrospect, grew out of two strikingly divergent conceptions about how mind works. The first of these was the hypothesis that mind could be conceived as a computational device. This was not a new idea, but it had been powerfully reconceived in the newly advanced computational sciences. The other was the proposal that mind is both constituted by and realized in the use of human culture. The two views led to very different conceptions of the nature of mind itself, and of how mind should be cultivated. Each led its adherents to follow distinctively different strategies of inquiry about how mind functions and about how it might be improved through 'education'.

The first or *computational* view is concerned with *information processing*: how finite, coded, unambiguous information about the world is inscribed, sorted, stored, collated, retrieved, and generally managed by a computational device. It takes information as its given, as something already settled in relation to some preexisting, rule-bound code that maps onto states of the world. This so-called 'well-formedness' is both its strength and its shortcoming, as we shall see. For the process of knowing is often messier, more fraught with ambiguity than such a view allows.

Computational science makes interesting general claims about the conduct of education, though it is still unclear what specific lessons it has to teach the educator. There is a widespread and not unreasonable belief that we *should* be able to discover something about how to teach human beings more effectively from knowing how to program computers effectively. One can scarcely doubt, for example, that computers provide a learner with powerful aids in mastering bodies of knowledge, particularly if the knowledge in question is well defined. A well-programmed computer is especially useful for taking over tasks that, at last, can be declared 'unfit for human production'. For computers are faster, more orderly, less fitful in remembering, and do not get bored. And of course, it is revealing of our own minds and our human situation to ask what things we do better or worse than our servant computer.

This chapter has been edited.

It is considerably more uncertain whether, in any deep sense, the tasks of a teacher can be 'handed over' to a computer, even the most 'responsive' one that can be theoretically envisioned. Which is not to say that a suitably programmed computer cannot lighten a teacher's load by taking over some of the routines that clutter the process of instruction. But that is not the issue. After all, books came to serve such a function after Gutenberg's discovery made them widely available.

The issue, rather, is whether the computational view of mind itself offers an adequate enough view about how mind works to guide our efforts in trying to 'educate' it. It is a subtle question. For in certain respects, 'how the mind works' is itself dependent on the tools at its disposal. 'How the *hand* works', for example, cannot be fully appreciated unless one also takes into account whether it is equipped with a screwdriver, a pair of scissors, or a laser-beam gun. And by the same token, the systematic historian's 'mind' works differently from the mind of the classic 'teller of tales' with his stock of combinable myth-like modules. So, in a sense, the mere existence of computational devices (and a theory of computation about their mode of operating) can (and doubtless will) change our minds about how 'mind' works, just as the book did.

This brings us directly to the second approach to the nature of mind – call it *culturalism*. It takes its inspiration from the evolutionary fact that mind could not exist save for culture. For the evolution of the hominid mind is linked to the development of a way of life where 'reality' is represented by a symbolism shared by members of a cultural community in which a technical-social way of life is both organized and construed in terms of that symbolism. This symbolic mode is not only shared by a community, but conserved, elaborated, and passed on to succeeding generations who, by virtue of this transmission, continue to maintain the culture's identity and way of life.

Culture in this sense is *superorganic*. But it shapes the minds of individuals as well. Its individual expression inheres in *meaning making*, assigning meanings to things in different settings on particular occasions. Meaning making involves situating encounters with the world in their appropriate cultural contexts in order to know 'what they are about'. Although meanings are 'in the mind', they have their origins and their significance in the culture in which they are created. It is this cultural situatedness of meanings that assures their negotiability and, ultimately, their communicability. Whether 'private meanings' exist is not the point; what is important is that meanings provide a basis for cultural exchange. On this view, knowing and communicating are in their nature highly interdependent, indeed virtually inseparable. For however much the individual may seem to operate on his or her own in carrying out the quest for meanings, nobody can do it unaided by the culture's symbolic systems. It is culture that provides the tools for organizing and understanding our worlds in communicable ways. The distinctive feature of human evolution is that mind evolved in a fashion that enables human beings to utilize the tools of culture. Without those tools, whether symbolic or material, man is not a 'naked ape' but an empty abstraction.

Culture, then, though itself man-made, both forms and makes possible the workings of a distinctively human mind. On this view, learning and thinking are always *situated* in a cultural setting and always dependent upon the utilization of cultural resources. Even individual variation in the nature and use of mind can be attributed to the varied opportunities that different cultural settings provide, though these are not the only source of variation in mental functioning.

Like its computational cousin, culturalism seeks to bring together insights from psychology, anthropology, linguistics, and the human sciences generally, in order to reformulate a model of mind. But the two do so for radically different purposes. Computationalism, to its great credit, is interested in any and all ways in which information is organized and used – information in the well-formed and finite sense mentioned earlier, regardless of the guise in which information processing is realized. In this broad sense, it recognizes no disciplinary boundaries, not even the boundary between human and non-human functioning. Culturalism, on the other hand, concentrates exclusively on how human beings in cultural communities create and transform meanings.

I want to set forth in this [. . .] chapter some principal motifs of the cultural approach and explore how these relate to education. But before turning to that formidable task, I need first to dispel the shibboleth of a necessary contradiction between culturalism and computationalism. For I think the apparent contradiction is based on a misunderstanding, one that leads to gross and needless over-dramatization. Obviously the approaches are very different, and their ideological overspill may indeed overwhelm us if we do not take care to distinguish them clearly. For it surely matters ideologically what kind of 'model' of the human mind one embraces. Indeed, the model of mind to which one adheres even shapes the 'folk pedagogy' of schoolroom practice [. . .]. Mind as equated to the power of association and habit formation privileges 'drill' as the true pedagogy, while mind taken as the capacity for reflection and discourse on the nature of necessary truths favors the Socratic dialogue. And each of these is linked to our conception of the ideal society and the ideal citizen.

Yet in fact, neither computationalism nor culturalism is so linked to particular models of mind as to be shackled in particular pedagogies. Their difference is of quite a different kind. Let me try to sketch it.

The objective of computationalism is to devise a formal redescription of *any* and *all* functioning systems that manage the flow of well-formed information. It seeks to do so in a way that produces foreseeable, systematic outcomes. One such system is the human mind. But thoughtful computationalism does *not* propose that mind is like some particular 'computer' that needs to be 'programmed' in a particular way in order to operate systematically or 'efficiently'. What it argues, rather, is that any and all systems that process information must be governed by specifiable 'rules' or procedures that govern what to do with inputs. It matters not whether it is a nervous system or the genetic apparatus that takes instruction from DNA and then reproduces later generations, or whatever. This is the ideal of Artificial Intelligence, so-called. 'Real minds' are describable in terms of the same AI generalization – systems governed by specifiable rules for managing the flow of coded information.

But, as already noted, the rules common to all information systems do not cover the messy, ambiguous, and context-sensitive processes of meaning making, a form of activity in which the construction of highly 'fuzzy' and metaphoric category systems is just as notable as the use of specifiable categories for sorting inputs in a way to yield comprehensible outputs. Some computationalists, convinced a priori that even meaning making can be reduced to AI specifications, are perpetually at work trying to prove that the messiness of meaning making is not beyond their reach. The complex 'universal models' they propose are sometimes half-jokingly referred to by them as 'TOEs', an acronym for 'theories of everything'. But though they have not even come near to succeeding and, as many believe, will probably never in principle succeed, their efforts nonetheless are interesting for the light they shed on the divide between meaning making and information processing.

The difficulty these computationalists encounter inheres in the kinds of 'rules' or operations that are possible in computation. All of them, as we know, must be specifiable in advance, must be free of ambiguity, and so on. They must, in their ensemble, also be computationally consistent, which means that while operations may alter with feedback from prior results, the alterations must also adhere to a consistent, prearranged systematicity. Computational rules may be contingent, but they cannot encompass unforeseeable contingencies. Thus Hamlet cannot (in AI) tease Polonius with ambiguous banter about 'yonder cloud shaped like a camel, nay 'tis backed like a weasel', in the hope that his banter might evoke guilt and some telltale knowledge about the death of Hamlet's father.

It is precisely this clarity, this prefixedness of categories that imposes the most severe limit on computationalism as a medium in which to frame a model of mind. But once this limitation is recognized, the alleged death struggle between culturalism and computationalism evaporates. For the meaning making of the culturalist, unlike the information processing of the computationalist, is in principle interpretive, fraught with ambiguity, sensitive to the occasion, and often after the fact. Its 'ill-formed procedures' are like 'maxims' rather than like fully specifiable rules. But they are hardly unprincipled. Rather, they are the stuff of *hermeneutics*, an intellectual pursuit no less disciplined for its failure to produce the click-clear outputs of a computational exercise. Its model case is text interpretation. In interpreting a text, the meaning of a part depends upon a hypothesis about the meanings of the whole, whose meaning in turn is based upon one's judgment of meanings of the parts that compose it. But [. . .] a wide swath of the human cultural enterprise depends upon it. Nor is it clear that the infamous 'hermeneutic circle' deserves the knocks it gets from those in search of clarity and certainty. After all, it lies at the heart of meaning making.

Hermeneutic meaning making and well-formed information processing are incommensurate. Their incommensurability can be made evident even in a simple example. Any input to a computational system must, of course, be encoded in a specifiable way that leaves no room for ambiguity. What happens, then, if (as in human meaning making) an input needs to be encoded according to the context in which it is encountered? Let me give a homely example involving language, since so much of meaning making involves language. Say the input into the system is the word *cloud*. Shall it be taken in its 'meteorological' sense, its 'mental condition' sense, or in some other way? Now, it is easy (indeed necessary) to provide a computational device with a 'look-up' lexicon that provides alternative senses of *cloud*. Any dictionary can do it. But to determine *which* sense is appropriate for a particular context, the computational device would also need a way of encoding and interpreting all contexts in which the word *cloud* might appear. That would then require the computer to have a look-up list for all possible contexts, a 'contexticon'. But while there are a finite number of words, there are an infinite number of contexts in which particular words might appear. Encoding the context of Hamlet's little riddle about 'yonder cloud' would almost certainly escape the powers of the best 'contexticon' one could imagine!

There is no decision procedure known that could resolve the question whether the incommensurability between culturalism's meaning making and computationalism's information processing could ever be overcome. Yet, for all that, the two have a kinship that is difficult to ignore. For once meanings are established, it is their formalization into a well-formed category system that *can* be managed by computational rules. Obviously one loses the subtlety of context dependency and metaphor in doing so: *clouds* would have to pass tests of truth functionality to get into the play. But then again, 'formalization' in science consists of just such maneuvers: treating an array of formalized and operationalized meanings 'as if' they were fit for computation. Eventually we come to believe that scientific terms actually were born and grew that way: decontextualized, disambiguated, totally 'lookuppable'.

There is equally puzzling commerce in the other direction. For we are often forced to interpret the output of a computation in order to 'make some sense' of it – that is, to figure out what it 'means'. This 'search for the meaning' of final outputs has always been customary in statistical procedures such as factor analysis where the association between different 'variables', discovered by statistical manipulation, needed to be interpreted hermeneutically in order to 'make sense'. The same problem is encountered when investigators use the computational option of parallel processing to discover the association between a set of coded inputs. The final output of such parallel processing similarly needs interpretation to be rendered meaningful. So there is plainly some complementary relationship between what the computationalist is trying to explain and what the culturalist is trying to interpret, a relationship that has long puzzled students of epistemology.

[. . .] Suffice to say that in an undertaking as inherently reflexive and complicated as characterizing 'how our minds work' or how they might be made to work better, there is surely room for two perspectives on the nature of knowing. Nor is there any demonstrable reason to suppose that without a single and legitimately 'true' way of knowing the world, we could only slide helplessly down the slippery slope that leads to relativism. It is surely as 'true' to say that Euclid's theorems are computable as to say, with the poet, that 'Euclid alone has looked on beauty bare'.

II

To begin with, if a theory of mind is to be interesting educationally, it should contain some specifications for (or at least implications bearing on) how its functioning can be improved or altered in some significant way. All-or-none and once-for-all theories of mind are not educationally interesting. More specifically, educationally interesting theories of mind contain specifications of some kind about the 'resources' required for a mind to operate effectively. These include not only instrumental resources (like mental 'tools'), but also settings or conditions required for effective operations – anything from feedback within certain time limits to, say, freedom from stress or from excessive uniformity. Without specification of resources and settings required, a theory of mind is all 'inside-out' and of limited applicability to education. It becomes interesting only when it becomes more 'outside-in', indicating the kind of world needed to make it possible to use mind (or heart!) effectively – what kinds of symbol systems, what kinds of accounts of the past, what arts and sciences, and so on. The approach of computationalism to education tends to be inside-out – though it smuggles the world into the mind by inscribing bits of it in memory, as with our earlier dictionary example, and then relies on 'look-up' routines. Culturalism is much more outside-in, and although it may contain specifications about mental operations *eo ipso*, as it were, they are not as binding as, say, the formal requirement of computability. For the approach of the computationalist to education is indeed bound by the constraint of computability – that is, whatever aids are offered to mind must be operable by a computational device.

When one actually examines how computationalism has approached educational issues, there seem to be three different styles. The first of these consists in 'restating' classical theories of teaching or learning in a computable form. But while some clarity is gained in so doing (for example, in locating ambiguities), not much is gained by way of power. Old wine does not improve much for being poured into differently shaped bottles, even if the glass is clearer. The classic reply, of course, is that a computable reformulation yields 'surplus insight'. Yet 'association theory', for example, has gone through successive translations from Aristotle to Locke to Pavlov to Clark Hull without much surplus yield. So one is justifiably impatient with new claims for veiled versions of the same – as with many so-called PDP 'learning models'.

But in fact, computationalism can and does do better than that. Its second approach begins with a rich description or protocol of what actually transpires when somebody sets out to solve a particular problem or master a particular body of knowledge. It then seeks to redescribe what has been observed in strict computational terms. In what order, for example, does a subject ask for information, what confuses him, what kinds of hypotheses does he entertain? This approach then asks what might be going on computationally in devices that operate that way, for instance, like the subject's 'mind'. From this it seeks to reformulate a plan about how a learner of this kind might be helped – again within limits of computability. John Bruer's interesting book is a nice example of what can be gained from this fresh approach.[1]

But there is an even more interesting third route that computationalists sometimes follow. The work of Annette Karmiloff-Smith[2] provides an example if taken in conjunction with some abstract computational ideas. All complex 'adaptive' computational programs involve redescribing the output of prior operations in order both to reduce their complexity and to improve their 'fit' to an adaptation criterion. That is what 'adaptive' means: reducing prior complexities to achieve greater 'fitness' to a criterion. An example will help. Karmiloff-Smith notes that when we go about solving particular problems, say language acquisition, we characteristically 'turn around' on the results of a procedure that has worked locally and try to redescribe it in more general, simplified terms. We say, for example, 'I've put an s at the end of that noun to pluralize it; how about doing the same for *all* nouns?' When the new rule fails to pluralize *woman*, the learner may generate some additional ones. Eventually, he ends up with a more or less adequate rule for pluralizing, with only a few odd 'exceptions' left over to be handled by rote. Note that in each step of this process that Karmiloff-Smith calls 'redescription', the learner 'goes meta', considering how he is thinking as well as what he is thinking about. This is the hallmark of 'metacognition', a topic of passionate interest among psychologists – but also among computational scientists.

That is to say, the rule of redescription is a feature of *all* complex 'adaptive' computation, but in the present instance, it is also a genuinely interesting *psychological* phenomenon. This is the rare music of an overlap between different fields of inquiry – if the overlap turns out to be fertile. So, REDESCRIBE, a TOE-like rule for adaptive computational systems that also happens to be a good rule in human problem solving, may turn out to be a 'new frontier'. And the new frontier may turn out to be next door to educational practice.

So the computationalist's approach to education seems to take three forms as noted. The first reformulates old theories of learning (or teaching, or whatever) in computable form in the hope that the reformulation will yield surplus power. The second analyzes rich protocols and applies the apparatus of computational theory to them to discern better what might be going on computationally. Then it tries to figure out how the process can be helped. This, in effect, is what Newell, Shaw, and Simon did in their work on the General Problem Solver,[3] and what is currently being done in studies of how 'novices' become 'experts'. Finally there is the happy fortuity where a central computational idea, like 'redescription', seems to map directly onto a central idea in cognitive theory, like 'metacognition'.

 The culturalist approaches education in a very different way. Culturalism takes as its first premise that education is not an island, but part of the continent of culture. It asks first what function 'education' serves in the culture and what role it plays in the lives of those who operate within it. Its next question might be why education is situated in the culture as it is, and how this placement reflects the distribution of power, status, and other benefits. Inevitably, and virtually from the start, culturalism also asks about the enabling resources made available to people to cope, and what portion of those resources is made available through 'education', institutionally conceived. And it will constantly be concerned with constraints imposed on the process of education – external ones like the organization of schools and classrooms or the recruitment of teachers, and internal ones like the natural or imposed distribution of native endowment, for native endowment may be as much affected by the accessibility of symbolic systems as by the distribution of genes.

Culturalism's task is a double one. On the 'macro' side, it looks at the culture as a system of values, rights, exchanges, obligations, opportunities, power. On the 'micro' side, it examines how the demands of a cultural system affect those who must operate within it. In that latter spirit, it concentrates on how individual human beings construct 'realities' and meanings that adapt them to the system, at what personal cost, with what expected outcomes. While culturalism implies no particular view concerning inherent psychobiological constraints that affect human functioning, particularly meaning making, it usually takes such constraints for granted and considers how they are managed by the culture and its instituted educational system.

Although culturalism is far from computationalism and its constraints, it has no difficulty incorporating its insights – with one exception. It obviously cannot rule out processes relating to human meaning making, however much they do not meet the test of computability. As a corollary, it cannot and does not rule out subjectivity and its role in culture. Indeed, as we shall see, it is much concerned with *inter*subjectivity – how humans come to know 'each other's minds'. In both these senses, culturalism is to be counted among the ·'sciences of the subjective'. And, in consequence, I shall often refer to it as the 'cultural psychological' approach, or simply as 'cultural psychology'. For all that it embraces the subjective in its purview and refers often to the 'construction of reality', cultural psychology surely does not rule out 'reality' in any ontological sense. It argues (on epistemological grounds) that 'external' or 'objective' reality can only be known by the properties of mind and the symbol systems on which mind relies.

A final point relates to the place of emotion and feeling. It is often said that all 'cognitive psychology', even its cultural version, neglects or even ignores the place of these in the life of mind. But it is neither necessary that this be so nor, at least in my view, is it so. Why should an interest in cognition preclude feeling and emotion? Surely emotions and feelings are represented in the processes of meaning making and in our constructions of reality. Whether one adopts the Zajonc view that emotion is a direct and unmediated response to the world with subsequent cognitive consequences, or the Lazarus view that emotion requires prior cognitive inference, it is still 'there', still to be reckoned with.[4] And as we shall see, particularly in dealing with the role of schools in 'self' construction, it is very much a part of education.

III

Let me now set out some tenets that guide a psycho-cultural approach to education. In doing so I shall commute back and forth between questions about the nature of mind and about the nature of culture, for a theory of education necessarily lies at the intersect between them. We shall, in consequence, constantly be inquiring about the interaction between the powers of individual minds and the means by which the culture aids or thwarts their realization. And this will inevitably involve us in a never-ending assessment of the fit between what any particular culture deems essential for a good, or useful, or worthwhile way of life, and how individuals adapt to these demands as they impinge on their lives. We shall be particularly mindful of the resources that a culture provides in making this fit possible. These are all matters that relate directly to how a culture or society manages its system of education, for education is a major embodiment of a culture's way of life, not just a preparation for it.

Here, then, are the tenets and some of their consequences for education.

1. The perspectival tenet. First, about meaning making. The meaning of any fact, proposition, or encounter is relative to the perspective or frame of reference in terms of which it is construed. A treaty that legitimizes the building of the Panama Canal, for example, is an episode in the history of North American imperialism. It is also a monumental step in the history of inter-ocean transportation, as well as a landmark in man's effort to shape nature to his own convenience at whatever cost. To understand well what something 'means' requires some awareness of the alternative meanings that can be attached to the matter under scrutiny, whether one agrees with them or not.

Understanding something in one way does not preclude understanding it in other ways. Understanding in any one particular way is only 'right' or 'wrong' from the particular perspective in terms of which it is pursued. But the 'rightness' of particular interpretations, while dependent on perspective, also reflects rules of evidence, consistency, and coherence. Not everything goes. There are inherent criteria of rightness, and the possibility of alternative interpretations does not license all of them equally. A perspectival view of meaning making does *not* preclude common sense or 'logic'. Something that happens a century after an event cannot be taken as a 'cause' or 'condition' of that event. I shall return to this issue of common-sense, logic, and reason in a later tenet.

Interpretations of meaning reflect not only the idiosyncratic histories of individuals, but also the culture's canonical ways of constructing reality. Nothing is 'culture free', but neither are individuals simply mirrors of their culture. It is the interaction between them that both gives a communal cast to individual thought and imposes a certain unpredictable richness on any culture's way of life, thought, or feeling. There are, as it were 'official' versions of all of these – 'Frenchmen are realistic', for example – and some of them are even inscribed in the law or in widely accepted kinship practices. And of course, they are also portrayed (often ambiguously and even problematically) in a culture's literature and its folk theories.

Life in culture is, then, an interplay between the versions of the world that people form under its institutional sway and the versions of it that are products of their individual histories. It rarely conforms to anything resembling a cookbook of recipes or formulas, for it is a universal of all cultures that they contain factional or institutional interests. Nonetheless, any particular individual's idiosyncratic interpretations of the world are constantly subject to judgment against what are taken to be the canonical beliefs of the culture at large. Such communal judgments, though often governed by 'rational' and evidentiary criteria, are just as often dominated by commit ments, tastes, interests, and expressions of adherence to the culture's values relating to the good life, decency, legitimacy, or power. In consequence of all of the foregoing, a culture's judgments about the idiosyncratic construals of its members are rarely univocal. And to cope with this ever-present cultural multivocality, every society requires some 'principle of tolerance', a phrase that David Richards has used to characterize the way in which constitutional systems cope with contending interests and their interpretive claims.[5]

An 'official' educational enterprise presumably cultivates beliefs, skills, and feelings in order to transmit and explicate its sponsoring culture's ways of interpreting the natural and social worlds. And as we shall see later, it also plays a key role in helping the young construct and maintain a concept of Self. In carrying out that function, it inevitably courts risk by 'sponsoring', however implicitly, a certain version of the world. Or it runs the risk of offending some interests by openly examining views that might be taken as like the culture's canonically tabooed ones. That is the price of educating the young in societies whose canonical interpretations of the world are multivocal or ambiguous. But an educational enterprise that fails to take the risks involved becomes stagnant and eventually alienating.

It follows from this, then, that effective education is always in jeopardy either in the culture at large or with constituencies more dedicated to maintaining a status quo than to fostering flexibility. The corollary of this is that when education narrows its scope of interpretive inquiry, it reduces a culture's power to adapt to change. And in the contemporary world, change is the norm.

In a word, the perspectival tenet highlights the interpretive, meaning-making side of human thought while, at the same time, recognizing the inherent risks of discord that may result from cultivating this deeply human side of mental life. It is this double-facing, Janus-like aspect of education that makes it either a somewhat dangerous pursuit or a rather drearily routine one.

2. The constraints tenet. The forms of meaning making accessible to human beings in any culture are constrained in two crucial ways. The first inheres in the nature of human mental functioning itself. Our evolution as a species has specialized us into certain characteristic ways of knowing, thinking, feeling, and perceiving. We cannot, even given our most imaginative efforts, construct a concept of Self that does not impute some causal influence of prior mental states on later ones. We cannot seem to accept a version of our own mental lives that denies that what we thought before affects what we think now. We are obliged to experience ourselves as invariant across circumstances and continuous across time. Moreover, to pick up a theme that will concern us later, we need to conceive of ourselves as 'agents' impelled by self-generated intentions. And we see others in the same way. In answer to those who deny this version of selfhood on philosophical or 'scientific' grounds, we reply simply, 'But that's how it is: can't you *see*?' All this despite the fact that there have always been rhetorically compelling philosophers (or in more recent centuries, psychologists) who have denied this 'folk psychological' view and even called it mischievous.

Indeed, we even institutionalize these so-called folk beliefs. Our legal system takes it as a given and constructs a *corpus juris* based upon notions like 'voluntary consent', 'responsibility', and the rest. It does not matter whether 'selfhood' can be proved scientifically or whether it is merely a 'fiction' of folk psychology. We simply take it as in the 'nature of human nature'. Never mind what critics say. 'Common sense' asserts it to be so. To be sure, we bend slightly for the critics. The law, typically, meets its critics by enunciating 'principled exceptions' – as in the extension and clarification of the *mens rea* doctrine.

Such intrinsic constraints on our capacities to interpret are by no means limited only to subjective concepts like 'selfhood'. They even limit our ways of conceiving of such presumably impersonal, 'objective' matters as time, space, and causality. We see 'time' as having a homogeneous continuity – as flowing evenly whether measured by clocks, phases of the moon, climatic changes, or any other form of recurrence. Discontinuous or quantal conceptions of time offend common sense to such an extent that we come to believe that continuous time is the state of nature that we experience directly. And this despite the fact that Immanuel Kant, one of the most highly honored philosophers in the Western tradition, made so strong a case for time and space as categories of mind rather than facts of nature. Faced with the fact, adduced by anthropologists, that there are local cultural variations in conceptions of time and space, and that these have practical implications in a culture's ways of life and thought, we tend to 'naturalize' them by labeling them exotic. It seems to be a human universal that we nominate certain forms of interpreted experience as hard-edged, objective realities rather than 'things of the mind'. And it is widely believed, both among lay people and scientists, that the 'nominees' for such objective status reflect certain natural or native predispositions to think and interpret the world in a particular way.

These universals are generally considered to constitute the 'psychic unity of mankind'. They can be considered as limits on human capacity for meaning making. And they require our attention because they presumably reduce the range of the perspectival tenet discussed in the preceding section. I think of them as constraints on human meaning making, and it is for that reason that I have labeled this section 'the constraints tenet'. These constraints are generally taken to be an inheritance of our evolution as a species, part of our 'native endowment'.

But while they may reflect the evolution of the human mind, these constraints should not be taken as man's *fixed* native endowment. They may be common to the species, but they also reflect how we represent the world through language and folk theories. And they are not immutable. Euclid, after all, finally altered our way of conceiving of, even looking at space. And in time, doubtless, Einstein will have done the same. Indeed, the very predispositions that we take to be 'innate' most often require shaping by exposure to some communally shared notational system, like language. Despite our presumably native endowment, we seem to have what Vygotsky called a Zone of Proximal Development,[6] a capacity to recognize ways beyond that endowment. The famous slave-boy in Plato's *Meno* was indeed capable of certain 'mathematical' insights (at least in response to the questions posed by the masterful Socrates). Would his insights have been possible without the queries of Socrates?

The educational implications that follow from the foregoing are both massive and subtle. If pedagogy is to empower human beings to go beyond their 'native' predispositions, it must transmit the 'toolkit' the culture has developed for doing so. It is a commonplace that any math major in a halfway decent modern university can do more mathematics than, say, Leibniz, who 'invented' the calculus – that we stand on the shoulders of the giants who preceded us. Obviously, not everybody benefits equally from instruction in the culture's toolkit. But it hardly follows that we should instruct only those with the most conspicuous talent to benefit from such instruction. That is a political or economic decision that should never be allowed to take on the status of an evolutionary principle. Decisions to cultivate 'trained incompetencies' will concern us presently.

I mentioned *two* constraints on human mental activity at the start of this discussion. The second comprises those constraints imposed by the symbolic systems accessible to human minds generally – limits imposed, say, by the very nature of language – but more particularly, constraints imposed by the different languages and notational systems accessible to different cultures. The latter is usually called the Whorf-Sapir hypothesis[7] – that thought is shaped by the language in which it is formulated and/or expressed.

As for the 'limits of language', not much can be said with any certainty – or with much clarity. It has never been clear whether our ability to entertain certain notions inheres in the nature of our minds or in the symbolic systems upon which mind relies in carrying out its mental operations. Is it in mind or in language that it is 'necessary' that something cannot be both A and not-A? Or is it 'in the world' – except for the part of the world covered by quantum theory? Is it in the structure of natural language that the world divides into subjects and predicates, or is this a reflection of how human attention works naturally?

Some have gone to the fanciful length of likening language to an instinct. But that dubious claim relates only to the formal syntax of language and is belied, in the main, by the profusion of expressive forms that mark its *use* – the pragmatics of language. The crafts of the storyteller, the orator, the gossip, or the poet/novelist, while caught in the web of syntax, hardly seem constrained by that fact. And as literary linguists continue to remind us, novelists keep surprising us by inventing new genres, still using the 'old' language.

As for the Whorf–Sapir hypothesis, its power and reach are also still not clearly understood. But as with the 'limits of language' question, it poses an interesting question for the cultural psychology of education. All that is known for sure is that consciousness or 'linguistic awareness' seems to reduce the constraints imposed by any symbolic system. The real victims of the limits of language or of the Whorfian hypothesis are those least aware of the language they speak.

But as the greatest linguist of our century, Roman Jakobson, long ago noted,[8] the *metalinguistic* gift, the capacity to 'turn around' on our language to examine and transcend its limits, is within everybody's reach. There is little reason to believe that anybody, even the speech-disabled, cannot be helped to explore more deeply the nature and uses of his language. Indeed, the spread of literacy may itself have increased linguistic awareness just by virtue of externalizing, decontextualizing, and making more permanent 'what was said', as David Olson has recently argued.[9]

The pedagogical implications of the foregoing are strikingly obvious. Since the limits of our inherent mental predispositions can be transcended by having recourse to more powerful symbolic systems, one function of education is to equip human beings with the needed symbolic systems for doing so. And if the limits imposed by the languages we use are expanded by increasing our 'linguistic awareness', then another function of pedagogy is to cultivate such awareness. We may not succeed in transcending all the limits imposed in either case, but we can surely accept the more modest goal of improving thereby the human capacity for construing meanings and constructing realities. In sum, then, 'thinking about thinking' has to be a principal ingredient of any empowering practice of education.

3.The constructivism tenet. This tenet has already been implied in all that has gone before. But it is worth making explicit. The 'reality' that we impute to the 'worlds' we inhabit is a constructed one. To paraphrase Nelson Goodman,[10] 'reality is made, not found'. Reality construction is the product of meaning making shaped by traditions and by a culture's toolkit of ways of thought. In this sense, education must be conceived as aiding young humans in learning to use the tools of meaning making and reality construction, to better adapt to the world in which they find themselves and to help in the process of changing it as required. In this sense, it can even be conceived as akin to helping people become better architects and better builders.

4. The interactional tenet. Passing on knowledge and skill, like any human exchange, involves a subcommunity in interaction. At the minimum, it involves a 'teacher' and a 'learner' – or if not a teacher in flesh and blood, then a vicarious one like a book, or film, or display, or a 'responsive' computer.

It is principally through interacting with others that children find out what the culture is about and how it conceives of the world. Unlike any other species, human beings deliberately teach each other in settings outside the ones in which the knowledge being taught will be used. Nowhere else in the animal kingdom is such deliberate 'teaching' found – save scrappily among higher primates. To be sure, many indigenous cultures do not practice as deliberate or decontextualized a form of teaching as we do. But 'telling' and 'showing' are as humanly universal as speaking.

It is customary to say that this specialization rests upon the gift of language. But perhaps more to the point, it also rests upon our astonishingly well developed talent for 'intersubjectivity' – the human ability to understand the minds of others, whether through language, gesture, or other means. It is not just words that make this possible, but our capacity to grasp the role of the settings in which words, acts, and gestures occur. We are the intersubjective species par excellence. It is this that permits us to 'negotiate' meanings when words go astray.

Our Western pedagogical tradition hardly does justice to the importance of intersubjectivity in transmitting culture. Indeed, it often clings to a preference for a degree of explicitness that seems to ignore it. So teaching is fitted into a mold in which a single, presumably omniscient teacher explicitly tells or shows presumably unknowing learners something they presumably know nothing about. Even when we tamper with this model, as with 'question periods' and the like, we still remain loyal to its unspoken precepts. I believe that one of the most important gifts that a cultural psychology can give to education is a reformulation of this impoverished conception. For only a very small part of educating takes place on such a one-way street – and it is probably one of the least successful parts.

So back to the innocent but fundamental question: how best to conceive of a subcommunity that specializes in learning among its members? One obvious answer would be that it is a place where, among other things, learners help each other learn, each according to her abilities. And this, of course, need not exclude the presence of somebody serving in the role of teacher. It simply implies that the teacher does not play that role as a monopoly, that learners 'scaffold' for each other as well. The antithesis is the 'transmission' model first described, often further exaggerated by an emphasis on transmitting 'subject matter'. But in most matters of achieving mastery, we also want learners to gain good judgment, to become self-reliant, to work well with each other. And such competencies do not flourish under a one-way 'transmission' regimen. Indeed, the very institutionalization of schooling may get in the way of creating a subcommunity of learners who bootstrap each other.

Consider the more 'mutual' community for a moment. Typically, it models ways of doing or knowing, provides opportunity for emulation, offers running commentary, provides 'scaffolding' for novices, and even provides a good context for teaching deliberately. It even makes possible that form of job-related division of labor one finds in effective work groups: some serving pro tem as 'memories' for the others, or as record keepers of 'where things have got up to now', or as encouragers or cautioners. The point is for those in the group to help each other get the lay of the land and the hang of the job.

One of the most radical proposals to have emerged from the cultural-psychological approach to education is that the classroom be reconceived as just such a subcommunity of mutual learners, with the teacher orchestrating the proceedings. Note that, contrary to traditional critics, such subcommunities do not reduce the teacher's role nor his or her 'authority'. Rather, the teacher takes on the additional function of encouraging others to share it. Just as the omniscient narrator has disappeared from modern fiction, so will the omniscient teacher disappear from the classroom of the future.

There is obviously no single formula that follows from the cultural-psychological approach to interactive, intersubjective pedagogy. For one thing, the practices adopted will vary with subject: poetry and mathematics doubtless require different approaches. Its sole precept is that where human beings are concerned, learning (whatever else it may be) is an interactive process in which people learn from each other, and not just by showing and telling. It is surely in the nature of human cultures to form such communities of mutual learners. Even if we are the only species that 'teaches deliberately' and 'out of the context of use', this does not mean that we should convert this evolutionary step into a fetish.

5. The externalization tenet. A French cultural psychologist, Ignace Meyerson,[11] first enunciated an idea that today, a quarter-century after his death, now seems both obvious and brimming with educational implications. Briefly, his view was that the main function of all collective cultural activity is to produce 'works' – *oeuvres,* as he called them, works that, as it were, achieve an existence of their own. In the grand sense, these include the arts and sciences of a culture, institutional structures such as its laws and its markets, even its 'history' conceived as a canonical version of the past. But there are minor oeuvres as well: those 'works' of smaller groupings that give pride, identity, and a sense of continuity to those who participate, however obliquely, in their making. These may be 'inspirational' – for example, our school soccer team won the county championship six years ago, or our famous Bronx High School of Science has 'produced' three Nobel Laureates. Oeuvres are often touchingly local, modest, yet equally identity-bestowing, such as this remark by a 10-year-old student: 'Look at *this* thing we're working on if you want to see how *we* handle oil spills.'

The benefits of 'externalizing' such joint products into oeuvres have too long been overlooked. First on the list, obviously, is that collective oeuvres produce and sustain group solidarity. They help *make* a community, and communities of mutual learners are no exception. But just as important, they promote a sense of the division of labor that goes into producing a product: Todd is our real computer wonk, Jeff's terrific at making graphics, Alice and David are our 'word geniuses', Maddalena is fantastic at explaining things that puzzle some of the rest of us. One group ... even devised a way to highlight these 'group works' by instituting a weekly session to hear and discuss a report on the class's performance for the week. The report, presented by a 'class ethnographer' (usually one of the teaching assistants), highlights *overall* rather than individual progress; it produces 'metacognition' on the class's oeuvre and usually leads to lively discussion.

Works and works-in-progress create *shared* and *negotiable* ways of thinking in a group. The French historians of the so-called *Annales* school, who were strongly influenced by Meyerson's ideas, refer to these shared and negotiable forms of thought as *mentalités,* styles of thinking that characterize different groups in different periods living under various circumstances. The class's approach to its 'weekly ethnography' produces just such a *mentalité.*

I can see one other benefit from externalizing mental work into a more palpable oeuvre, one that we psychologists have tended to ignore. Externalization produces a *record* of our mental efforts, one that is 'outside us' rather than vaguely 'in memory'. It is somewhat like producing a draft, a rough sketch, a 'mock-up'. 'It' takes over our attention as something that, in its own right, needs a transitional paragraph, or a less frontal perspective there, or a better 'introduction'. 'It' relieves us in some measure from the always difficult task of 'thinking about our own thoughts' while often accomplishing the same end. 'It' embodies our thoughts and intentions in a form more accessible to reflective efforts. The process of thought and its product become interwoven, like Picasso's countless sketches and drawings in reconceiving Velasquez's *Las Meninas*. There is a Latin motto, 'scientia dependit in mores', knowledge works its way into habits. It might easily be retranslated as 'thinking works its way into its products'.

All viable cultures, Ignace Meyerson noted, make provisions for conserving and passing on their 'works'. Laws get written down, codified, and embodied in the procedure of courts. Law schools train people in the ways of a 'profession' so that the *corpus juris* can be assured for the future. These 'hard copy' externalizations are typically supported as well by myth-like ones: the indomitable Lord Mansfield bringing the skepticism of Montaigne and Montesquieu into English law, the equally indomitable Mr Chief Justice Holmes injecting a new, Darwinian 'realism' into American jurisprudence, and even John Mortimer's fictional Rumpole struggling commonsensically against the legal pedants. What finally emerges is a subtle mix of starchy procedures and their informal human explication.

Obviously, a school's classroom is no match for the law in tradition-making. Yet it can have long-lasting influence. We carry with us habits of thought and taste fostered in some nearly forgotten classroom by a certain teacher. I can remember one who made us relish as a class 'less obvious' interpretations of historical happenings. We lost our embarrassment about offering our 'wilder' ideas. She helped us invent a tradition. I still relish it. Can schools and classrooms be designed to foster such tradition-inventing? Denmark is experimenting with keeping the same group of children and teachers together through all the primary grades – an idea that goes back to Steiner. Does that turn 'work' into 'works' with a life of their own? Modern mobility is, of course, the enemy of all such aspirations. Yet the creation and conservation of culture in shared works is a matter worth reflecting upon. Nor are we without good examples in our own time. Sarah Lightfoot has documented how certain public high schools create a sense of their enduring meaning,[12] and Michael Cole's 'computer networking' seems to yield the interesting by-product of widely separated groups of children finding a wider, more enduring, and palpable world through contact with each other by e-mail.[13]

Externalizing, in a word, rescues cognitive activity from implicitness, making it more public, negotiable, and 'solidary'. At the same time, it makes it more accessible to subsequent reflection and metacognition. Probably the greatest milestone in the history of externalization was literacy, putting thought and memory 'out there' on clay tablets or paper. Computers and e-mail may represent another step forward. But there are doubtless myriad ways in which jointly negotiated thought can be communally externalized as oeuvres – and many ways in which they can be put to use in schools.

6. The instrumentalism tenet. Education, however conducted in whatever culture, always has consequences in the later lives of those who undergo it. Everybody knows this; nobody doubts it. We also know that these consequences are instrumental in the lives of individuals, and even know that, in a less immediately personal sense, they are instrumental to the culture and its various institutions (the latter are discussed in the following tenet). Education, however gratuitous or decorative it may seem or profess to be, provides skills, ways of thinking, feeling, and speaking, that later may be traded for 'distinctions' in the institutionalized 'markets' of a society. In this deeper sense, then, education is never neutral, never without social and economic consequences. However much it may be claimed to the contrary, education is always political in this broader sense.

There are two pervasive considerations that need to be taken into account in pursuing the implications of these hard-edged facts. One has to do with *talent;* the other with *opportunity.* And while the two are by no means unrelated, they need to be discussed separately first. For, as in the recent book by Herrnstein and Murray,[14] the two are often confounded – as if opportunity followed talent like its shadow.

About talent, it is by now obvious that it is more multifaceted than any single score, like an IQ test, could possibly reveal. Not only are there many ways of using mind, many ways of knowing and constructing meanings, but they serve many functions in different situations. These ways of using mind are enabled, indeed often brought into being, by learning to master what I earlier described as a culture's 'toolkit' of symbolic systems and speech registers. There is thinking and meaning making for intimate situations different in kind from what one uses in the impersonal setting of a shop or office.

Some people seem to have great aptitude in using certain powers of mind and their supporting registers, others less. Howard Gardner has made a good case for certain of these aptitudes (he calls them 'frames of mind') having an innate and universal basis – like the ability to deal with quantitative relations, or with linguistic subtleties, or with skilled movement of the body in dance, or with sensing the feelings of others.[15] And he is engaged in constructing curricula for fostering these differing aptitudes.

Beyond the issue of differing native aptitudes, however, it is also the case that different cultures place different emphasis upon the skilled use of different modes of thought and different registers. Not everybody is supposed to be numerate, but if you occupy the role of engineer, you're something of a queer duck if you're not. But everybody is supposed to be passingly competent in managing interpersonal relations. Different cultures distribute these skills differently. The French even have an expression that refers to the 'shape' of one's trained capabilities, 'professional deformation' in literal translation. And these very rapidly get 'typed' and consolidated through training and schooling: girls used to be considered more 'sensitive' to poetry, were given more experience in it, and more often than not *became* more sensitive. But this is a harmless example of the kinds of considerations that affect the *opportunity* young people have for developing the skills and ways of thinking that they will later trade for distinctions and rewards in the larger society.

There are many uglier features of opportunity that blight lives far more profoundly. Racism, social-class entitlements, and prejudice, all of them amplified by the forms of poverty they create, have powerful effects on how much and how we educate the young. Indeed, even the so-called innate talents of children from 'socially tainted' backgrounds are altered before they ever get to school – in ghettos, barrios, and those other settings of poverty, despair, and defiance that seem to suppress and divert the mental powers of the young who 'grow up' in them. Indeed, it was principally to counteract these early blighting effects of poverty (and, of course, racism) that Head Start was founded [. . .]. But schools themselves, given that they are locally situated, also tend to continue and perpetuate the subcultures of poverty or defiance that initially nipped or diverted children's 'natural' talents of mind in the first place.

Schools have always been highly selective with respect to the uses of mind they cultivate – which uses are to be considered 'basic', which 'frills', which the school's responsibility and which the responsibility of others, which for girls and which for boys, which for working-class children and which for 'swells'. Some of this selectivity was doubtless based on considered notions about what the society required or what the individual needed to get along. Much of it was a spillover of folk or social class tradition. Even the more recent and seemingly obvious objective of equipping all with 'basic literacy' is premised on moral-political grounds, however pragmatically those grounds may be justified. School curricula and classroom 'climates' always reflect inarticulate cultural values as well as explicit plans; and these values are never far removed from considerations of social class, gender, and the prerogatives of social power. Should girls, to take a case pending before the US Supreme Court, be admitted into state-supported military academies formerly reserved for young men? Is affirmative action a covert form of discrimination against the middle class?

Nothing could be more expressive of a culture than the conflicts and compromises that swirl around quasi-educational questions of this order. What is striking in most democratic states is that the compromises that emerge initially get buried in the rhetoric of official blandness, after which (and partly as a result of which) they become candidates for bitter and rather poorly considered attack. All children should have the same curricula? Of course. And then there is an exposé of what 'the same' means in the schools, say, of a South Bronx ghetto and those in suburban Forest Hills. With increased community awareness, formerly innocent issues like curriculum soon become political ones – and quite appropriately so. The trouble, of course, is that purely political debate specializes in oversimplification. And these are not simple issues.

So the 'underground curriculum' continues to loom larger – a school's way of adapting a curriculum to express its attitudes toward its pupils, its racial attitudes, and the rest. And in the community's politicized reaction, political slogans become at least as determinative of educational policy as do theories about the cultivation of the multiple powers of mind.

Surely one of the major educational tenets of a cultural psychology is that the school can never be considered as culturally 'free standing'. *What* it teaches, what modes of thought and what 'speech registers' it actually cultivates in its pupils, cannot be isolated from how the school is situated in the lives and culture of its students. For a school's curriculum is not only *about* 'subjects'. The chief subject matter of school, viewed culturally, is school itself. That is how most students experience it, and it determines what meaning they make of it.

This, of course, is what I mean by the 'situatedness' of school and school learning. Yet, for all its pervasiveness, there is little question that, with thought and will, it can be changed. Change can occur even by little symbolic innovations – like creating a chess club in a ghetto school, and providing real coaching. Joining the chess club (indeed, *having* a chess club) in a mainly black Harlem middle school creates a quite different communal self-image than joining one (or having one) in Cincinnati's well-to-do Walnut Hills. And winning the National Junior High School Chess Team Championship for Mott High Middle School in Harlem is no ho-hum matter. In some cryptic way it can mean 'beating the oppressor at his own brainy games'. But bits of symbolism scarcely touch the problem at large.

None of this is new. What does the cultural psychologist have to say about such matters? Certainly one general thing: education does not stand alone, and it cannot be designed as if it did. It exists in a culture. And culture, whatever else it is, is also about power, distinctions, and rewards. We have, in the laudable interest of protecting freedom of thought and instruction, officially buffered schools against political pressures. School is 'above' politics. In some important sense, this is surely true – but it is a threadbare truth. Increasingly, we see something quite different. For, as it were, the secret is out. Even the so-called man in the street knows that how one equips minds matters mightily later in our postindustrial, technological era. The public, to be sure, has a rather unformed sense of this – and certainly the press does. But they are aware. The *New York Times* carried as front-page news in the spring of 1995 that achievement levels had gone up in the city's schools; and Dublin's *Irish Times* in the summer of that same year carried on its front page the news that Irish students had scored 'above the average' in a comparative study of reading ability in European schools.

Why not, then, treat education for what it is? It has always been 'political', though cryptically so in more settled, less aware times. There has now been a revolution in public awareness. But it has not been accompanied by a comparable revolution in our ways of taking this awareness into account in the forging of educational policies and practices. All of which is not to propose that we 'politicize' education, but simply that we recognize that it is already politicized and that its political side needs finally to be taken into account more explicitly, not simply as though it were 'public protest'. I will return to this issue in more detail later in this chapter.

7. *The institutional tenet.* My seventh tenet is that as education in the developed world becomes institutionalized, it behaves as institutions do and often must, and suffers certain problems common to all institutions. What distinguishes it from others is its special role in preparing the young to take a more active part in other institutions of the culture. Let us explore now what this implies.

Cultures are not simply collections of people sharing a common language and historical tradition. They are composed of institutions that specify more concretely what roles people play and what status and respect these are accorded – though the culture at large expresses its way of life through institutions as well. Cultures can also be conceived as elaborate exchange systems, with media of exchange as varied as respect, goods, loyalty, and services. Exchange systems become focalized and legitimized in institutions which provide buildings, stipends, titles, and the rest. They are further legitimized by a complex symbolic apparatus of myths, statutes, precedents, ways of talking and thinking, and even uniforms. Institutions impose their 'will' through coercion, sometimes implicit as in incentives and disincentives, sometimes explicit as in restriction backed by the power of the state, such as the disbarring of a lawyer or the refusal of credit to a defaulting merchant.

Institutions do the culture's serious business. But for all that, they do so through an unpredictable mix of coercion and voluntarism. I say 'unpredictable' because it remains perpetually unclear both to participants in a culture and to those who observe it from 'outside' when and how the power of enforcement will be brought to bear by those delegated or otherwise thought privileged to use it. So if it can be said that a culture's institutions do 'serious business', it can equally be said that it is often ambiguous and uncertain business.

It is also characteristic of human cultures that individuals rarely owe allegiance to any single institution: one 'belongs' to a family of origin and one by marriage, an occupational group, a neighborhood, as well as to more general groups like a nation or a social class. Each institutional grouping struggles to achieve its distinctive pattern of rights and responsibilities. This adds further to the inherent ambiguity of life in culture. As Walter Lippmann and John Dewey long ago pointed out,[16] how any given individual forms his interpretation on issues of public concern will usually involve him in a conflict of interests and identities. For while institutions may complement each other functionally, they also compete for privilege and power. Indeed, the power of a culture inheres in its capacity to integrate its component institutions through a dialectic of conflict resolution.

Institutions, as Pierre Bourdieu has suggested,[17] provide the 'markets' where people 'trade' their acquired skills, knowledge, and ways of constructing meanings for 'distinctions' or privileges. Institutions often compete in getting their 'distinctions' prized above those of others, but the competition must never be 'winner take all', for institutions are mutually dependent upon each other. Lawyers and businessmen need each other as much as patients and doctors do. So, as in Diderot's delightful *Jacques le fataliste et son maître*, bargaining for distinction becomes a subtle game, often a source of sly humor. The struggle for distinction seems to be a feature of all cultures.

While all this may at first seem remote from schools and the process of education, the remoteness is an illusion. Education is up to its elbows in the struggle for distinctions. The very expressions *primary, secondary*, and *tertiary* are metaphors for it. It has even been argued recently that the 'new' bourgeoisie in France after the Revolution used the schools as one of their principal tools for 'turning around' the system of prestige and distinction previously dominated by the aristocracy and gentry of the *ancien régime*. Indeed, the very concept of a meritocracy is precisely an expression of the new power that schools are expected to exercise in fixing the distribution of distinctions in contemporary bureaucratic society.

It was the 'tug' of institutional competition that mainly concerned us in the preceding section, often converted into a more conventionalized political form. I commented there that there had been an 'evolution in awareness' about education. Let me pursue that now. Few democracies today are short of cultural critics who bring educational issues before the public, sometimes vividly: a Paulo Freire in Latin America, a Pierre Bourdieu in France, a Neil Postman in America, or an A. H. Halsey in Britain. There is lively public discussion of education in virtually every developed country of the world. Despite that, most countries still lack public forums for informed consideration of educational issues. I believe such forums are crucial for responding to and, indeed, informing the kinds of politicized debates discussed earlier. But they are emerging. And though they may not turn out to be as stately or noncontroversial as Her Majesty's Inspectorate of Education in Queen Victoria's class-dominated days, they at least are bringing education out from behind its screen of 'neutrality'. We already have some foretaste of what is to come, as when the President of the United States discusses educational issues on television with a selected forum of experts and participants, or when Shirley Williams, formerly Britain's Minister of Education, instituted widely covered broadcasts of regional discussions. Many regional Italian teachers' unions now hold annual discussion meetings on the state and progress of education, with provincial ministers and leading researchers actively in attendance. In the United States, where sectarian acrimony often increases faster than responsible and informed discussion, many state governors have established quasi-official groups at whose meetings pending state policy decisions on education get discussed. The goals of education seem again to have become a topic worthy of study as well as debate.

But there is more to the matter than public opinion and the need to inform it. For, as I remarked at the outset, educational systems are themselves highly institutionalized, in the grip of their *own* values. Educators have their own usually well informed views about how to cultivate and how to 'grade' the human mind. And like other institutions, education perpetuates itself and its practices: by establishing graduate schools of education, *grandes écoles* like the École Normale Supérieure in France, even elite academies like the chartered National Academy of Education in America and the informal All Souls Group in Britain. And as often happens, it invents durable ways of distributing skills, attitudes, and ways of thinking in the same old unjust demographic patterns. A reliable example of this can be found in procedures for examining students that, somehow, long outlive exposés of their unfairness to less privileged groups in the population. In consequence, the goodness of fit between school practices and society's demands comes increasingly under scrutiny.

Yet, in a sense, the public discussions that occur in consequence of this scrutiny are by no means strictly about 'education'. It is not simply that we are trying to reevaluate the balance between schools as a fixed Educational Establishment, on the one side, and a set of well-established needs of the culture, on the other. The issues are much broader than that. They have to do with the emerging role of women in society, with the vexing problem of the ethnic loyalties of the children of guest workers, with minority rights, with sexual mores, with unmarried mothers, with violence, with poverty. The Educational Establishment, for all its fingertip expertise in dealing with educational routines, has little by way of established doctrine for dealing with such problems. Nor do other institutions within the culture, though they nonetheless seem always tempted to 'blame education' for its particular set of troubles – whether it be the falling competitiveness of the auto industry, the increase in births out of wedlock, or violence on the streets.

It is astonishing how little systematic study is devoted to the institutional 'anthropology' of schooling, given the complexity of its situatedness and its exposure to the changing social and economic climate. Its relation to the family, to the economy, to religious institutions, even to the labor market, is only vaguely understood. But suggestive work is beginning. I find it encouraging that one distinguished contributor to this current debate on the role of education in the economy is no less a figure than the serving Secretary of Labor in the Clinton administration. His discussion of the place of symbolic 'meta-skills' in *The Work of Nations* could serve as a policy document in our times. And one wonders, indeed, whether the institutional challenges of our changing society might call not only for the proverbial New Man, but also for some New Institutions (as Daniel Bell suggests).[18]

Let me offer two such institutions, though entirely in the spirit of illustration. Each is intended to address the range of institutional questions just discussed – both very much in the spirit of the culturalist approach. Each takes for granted that there is a reciprocal relation between education and the other major institutional activities of a culture: communication, economics, politics, family life, and so on. The first is designed to recognize the shortage of useful information on such crucial matters, the second that we lack a deliberative apparatus that can convert useful knowledge into wise policy alternatives.

In connection with the first of these, gathering useful information, what I envision is something that might be called an 'anthropology' of education, a term that for me goes far beyond the collection of 'classroom ethnographies', however helpful such exercises have been. This kind of 'anthropology' should be dedicated to work on the situatedness of education in the society at large – to its institutions, as just noted, but also to 'crisis' problems like poverty and racism. Or, in a word, what role does schooling play in coping with or exacerbating the 'predicament of culture' that James Clifford has described so vividly?[19]

Well, there is no such 'field' as this one, really: only a lot of scattered investigators working in different academic departments. So, one invents a field and even legitimizes it by granting a broad charter to, say, a National Institute of Education, to be financed (in the interest of maintaining the 'compromise control' mentioned earlier) by federal, state, and private foundation support and sponsorship. And since these are all thoughts that come even before a 'drawing board' gets involved, I will also suggest that such an institute not be exclusively for research, but also for consultation. But let me turn to the other institutional invention, this one concerned principally with forging possible policy alternatives in a setting of competing institutions.

We still have reason to celebrate Clemenceau's remark that war is too important to leave to the generals. Not generals alone – too many other interests and constituencies are affected. In this same sense, as I've tried to make clear in this [. . .] chapter, education is too consequential to too many constituencies to leave to professional educators. And I'm sure most thoughtful professionals would agree. Thus, to bring judgment, balance, and a broader social commitment to the educational scene in America, we would need to engage 'the best and the brightest' as well as the most publicly committed to the task of formulating alternative policies and practices. I know this is not easy, but imagine a task force or a board whose members were recruited from many 'walks of life', as we like to put it. It might take many different forms: its only requirement is that it be made up of those who have achieved a reputation for their acumen, their fair-mindedness, and their public commitment. Imagine such a body as a White House Board, say, in the spirit of the Board of Economic Advisers or the National Security Council, with the function of advising the President of the United States on educational issues in the broad sense, including the impact of federal policy generally on the conduct of education, and vice versa. Or a more vigorous model might be the Federal Reserve Board, though obviously such a model would violate the American constitutional mandate of leaving education to the 'several states'. In any case, I offer these suggestions in the spirit of recognizing that education is not a free-standing institution, not an island, but part of the continent.

Having offered these rather grandiose examples, I must conclude this discussion of 'institutionalization' on a more homely note. Improving education requires teachers who understand and are committed to the improvements envisioned. So banal a point would scarcely be worth mentioning were it not so easily overlooked by many efforts at educational reform. We need to equip teachers with the necessary background training to take an effective part in reform. The people who run them make institutions. However thoughtful our educational plans may become, they must include a crucial place for teachers. For ultimately, that is where the action is.

8. The tenet of identity and self-esteem. I have put this tenet late in the list. For it is so pervasive as to implicate virtually all that has gone before. Perhaps the single most universal thing about human experience is the phenomenon of 'Self', and we know that education is crucial to its formation. Education should be conducted with that fact in mind.

We know 'Self' from our own inner experience, and we recognize others as selves. Indeed, more than one distinguished scholar has argued that self-awareness requires as its necessary condition the recognition of the Other as a self. Though there are universals of selfhood – and we will consider two of them in a moment – different cultures both shape it differently and set its limits in varying ways. Some emphasize autonomy and individuality, some affiliation; some link it closely to a person's position in a divine or secular social order, some link it to individual effort or even to luck. Since schooling is one of life's earliest institutional involvements outside the family, it is not surprising that it plays a critical role in the shaping of Self. But I think this will be clearer if we first examine two aspects of selfhood that are regarded as universal.

The first is *agency*. Selfhood, most students of the subject believe, derives from the sense that one can initiate and carry out activities on one's own. Whether this is 'really' so or simply a folk belief, as radical behaviorists would have us believe, is beyond the scope of this inquiry. I shall simply take it as so. People experience themselves as agents. But then too, any vertebrate distinguishes between a branch *it* has shaken and one that has shaken *it*. So there must be something more to selfhood than the recognition of simple sensorimotor agentivity. What characterizes human selfhood is the construction of a conceptual system that organizes, as it were, a 'record' of agentive encounters with the world, a record that is related to the past (that is, 'autobiographical memory', so-called) but that is also extrapolated into the future – self with history and with possibility. It is a 'possible self' that regulates aspiration, confidence, optimism, and their opposites. While this 'constructed' self-system is inner, private, and suffused with affect, it also extends outward to the things and activities and places with which we become 'ego-involved' – William James's 'extended self'. Schools and school learning are among the earliest of those places and activities.

But just as important as the inner psychodynamics of selfhood are the ways in which a culture institutionalizes it. All natural languages, for example, make obligatory grammatical distinctions between agentive and patientive forms: *I hit him; he hit me.* And even the simplest narratives are built around, indeed depend upon, an agent-Self as a protagonist with his or her own goals operating in a recognizable cultural setting. There is a moral aspect to selfhood as well, expressed simply by such ubiquitous phenomena as 'blaming yourself' or 'blaming another' for acts committed or outcomes that result from our acts. At a more evolved level, all legal systems specify (and legitimize) some notion of *responsibility* by which Self is endowed with obligation in regard to some broader cultural authority – confirming 'officially' that we, our Selves, are presumed to be agents in control of our own actions.

Since agency implies not only the capacity for initiating, but also for completing our acts, it also implies *skill* or *know-how*. Success and failure are principal nutrients in the development of selfhood. Yet we may not be the final arbiters of success and failure, which are often defined from 'outside' according to culturally specified criteria. And school is where the child first encounters such criteria – often as if applied arbitrarily. School judges the child's performance, and the child responds by evaluating himself or herself in turn.

Which brings us to a second ubiquitous feature of selfhood: *evaluation*. Not only do we experience self as agentive, we evaluate our efficacy in bringing off what we hoped for or were asked to do. Self increasingly takes on the flavor of these valuations. I call this mix of agentive efficacy and self-evaluation 'self-esteem'. It combines our sense of what we believe ourselves to be (or even hope to be) capable of and what we fear is beyond us.

How self-esteem is experienced (or how it is expressed) varies, of course, with the ways of one's culture. Low esteem sometimes manifests itself in guilt about intentions, sometimes simply in shame for having been 'found out'; sometimes it is accompanied by depression, even to the point of suicide, sometimes by defiant anger. In some cultures, particularly those that emphasize achievement, high self-esteem increases level of aspiration; in others it leads to status display and standing pat. There may even be an individual temperamental component in how people deal with threatened self-esteem – whether one blames oneself, others, or circumstances.

Only two things can be said for certain and in general: the management of self-esteem is never simple and never settled, and its state is affected powerfully by the availability of supports provided from outside. These supports are hardly mysterious or exotic. They include such homely resorts as a second chance, honor for a good if unsuccessful try, but above all the chance for discourse that permits one to find out why or how things didn't work out as planned. It is no secret that school is often rough on children's self-esteem, and we are beginning to know something about their vulnerability in this area. Ideally, of course, school is supposed to provide a setting where our performance has fewer esteem-threatening consequences than in the 'real world', presumably in the interest of encouraging the learner to 'try things out'. Yet radical critics, like Paulo Freire,[20] have argued that school often metes out failures to those children the society would later 'exploit'. And even moderate critics, like Roland Barthes and Pierre Bourdieu, make the provocative case that school is principally an agent for producing, say, 'little Frenchmen and Frenchwomen' who will conform to the niche where they will end up.[21]

Obviously there are other 'markets' where even school children can 'trade' their skills for distinctions, to use Bourdieu's interesting terms again. And these 'markets' often compensate for sensed failure in school – as when 'street smarts' are traded on the market of petty crime, or when defiance of the majority community earns black teenagers respect among their peers. School, more than we have realized, competes with myriad forms of 'anti-school' as a provider of agency, identity, and self-esteem – no less at a middle-class suburban mall than on the ghetto streets.

Any system of education, any theory of pedagogy, any 'grand national policy' that diminishes the school's role in nurturing its pupils' self-esteem fails at one of its primary functions. The deeper problem – from a cultural-psychological point of view, but in workaday common sense as well – is how to cope with the erosion of this function under modern urban conditions. [. . .] Schools do not simply equip kids with skills and self-esteem or not. They are in competition with other parts of society that can do this, but with deplorable consequences for the society. America manages to alienate enough black ghetto boys to land nearly a third of them in jail before they reach the age of thirty.

More positively, if agency and esteem are central to the construction of a concept of Self, then the ordinary practices of school need to be examined with a view to what contribution they make to these two crucial ingredients of personhood. Surely the 'community of learners' approach mentioned earlier contributes to both. But equally, the granting of more responsibility in setting and achieving goals in all aspects of a school's activities could also contribute – everything from maintenance of a school's physical plant to a share in decisions about academic and extracurricular projects to be undertaken. Such a conception, earlier so dear to the progressive tradition in education, is also in the image of the constitutional principle that (in a democracy) rights and responsibilities are two sides of the same coin. If, as I noted at the outset, school is an entry into the culture and not just a preparation for it, then we must constantly reassess what school does to the young student's conception of his own powers (his sense of agency) and his sensed chances of being able to cope with the world both in school and after (his self-esteem). In many democratic cultures, I think, we have become so preoccupied with the more formal criteria of 'performance' and with the bureaucratic demands of education as an institution that we have neglected this personal side of education.

9. The narrative tenet. I want finally to leapfrog over the issue of school 'subjects' and curricula in order to deal with a more general matter: the mode of thinking and feeling that helps children (indeed, people generally) create a version of the world in which, psychologically, they can envisage a place for themselves – a personal world. I believe that story making, narrative, is what is needed for that, and I want to discuss it briefly in this final tenet.

I still hold firmly to the views expressed in my earlier work about subject-matter teaching: the importance of giving the learner a sense of the generative structure of a subject discipline, the value of a 'spiral curriculum', the crucial role of self-generated discovery in learning a subject matter, and so forth. The issue I want to address now has to do more directly with the issue of how growing children create meanings from school experience that they can relate to their lives in a culture. So let me turn to narrative as a mode of thought and as a vehicle of meaning making.

I shall begin with some basics. There appear to be two broad ways in which human beings organize and manage their knowledge of the world, indeed structure even their immediate experience: one seems more specialized for treating of physical 'things', the other for treating of people and their plights. These are conventionally known as *logical-scientific* thinking and *narrative* thinking. Their universality suggests that they have their roots in the human genome or that they are (to revert to an earlier tenet) givens in the nature of language. They have varied modes of expression in different cultures, which also cultivate them differently. No culture is without both of them, though different cultures privilege them differently.

It has been the convention of most schools to treat the arts of narrative – song, drama, fiction, theater, whatever – as more 'decoration' than necessity, something with which to grace leisure, sometimes even as something morally exemplary. Despite that, we frame the accounts of our cultural origins and our most cherished beliefs in story form, and it is not just the 'content' of these stories that grip us, but their narrative artifice. Our immediate experience, what happened yesterday or the day before, is framed in the same storied way. Even more striking, we represent our lives (to ourselves as well as to others) in the form of narrative. It is not surprising that psychoanalysts now recognize that personhood implicates narrative, 'neurosis' being a reflection of either an insufficient, incomplete, or inappropriate story about oneself. Recall that when Peter Pan asks Wendy to return to Never Never Land with him, he gives as his reason that she could teach the Lost Boys there how to tell stories. If they knew how to tell them, the Lost Boys might be able to grow up.

The importance of narrative for the cohesion of a culture is as great, very likely, as it is in structuring an individual life. Take law as an illustration. Without a sense of the common trouble narratives that the law translates into its common law writs, it becomes arid. And those 'trouble narratives' appear again in mythic literature and contemporary novels, better contained in that form than in reasoned and logically coherent propositions. It seems evident, then, that skill in narrative construction and narrative understanding is crucial to constructing our lives and a 'place' for ourselves in the possible world we will encounter.

It has always been tacitly assumed that narrative skill comes 'naturally', that it does not have to be taught. But a closer look shows this not to be true at all. We know now, for example, that it goes through definite stages, is severely impaired in brain damage of certain kinds, fares poorly under stress, and ends up in literalism in one social community while becoming fanciful in a neighboring one with a different tradition. Observe law students or young lawyers preparing their final arguments for litigation or mock court and it will quickly be plain that some people have the knack more than others – they have simply learned how to make a story believable and worth thinking about.

Feeling at home in the world, knowing how to place oneself into self-descriptive stories, is surely not made easier by the enormous increase in migration in the modern world. It is not easy, however multicultural your intentions, to help a ten-year-old create a story that includes him in the world beyond his family and neighborhood, having been transplanted from Vietnam to the San Fernando Valley, from Algeria to Lyons, from Anatolia to Dresden. If school, his *pied-à-terre* outside the family, can't help him, there are alienated countercultures that can.

None of us know as much as we should about how to create narrative sensibility. Two commonplaces seem to have stood the test of time. The first is that a child should 'know', have a 'feel' for, the myths, histories, folktales, conventional stories of his or her culture (or cultures). They frame and nourish an identity. The second commonplace urges imagination through fiction. Finding a place in the world, for all that it implicates the immediacy of home, mate, job, and friends, is ultimately an act of imagination. So, for the culturally transplanted, there is the imaginative challenge of the fiction and 'quasi-fiction' that takes him or her into the world of possibilities – as in the novels of a Maxine Hong Kingston or the poems of a Maya Angelou. And for any schoolboy pondering how it all came about, there is a Simon Schama narratively restoring the human plights to the 'dead certainties' of the past, to use his telling phrase.[22]

Obviously, if narrative is to be made an instrument of mind on behalf of meaning making, it requires work on our part – reading it, making it, analyzing it, understanding its craft, sensing its uses, discussing it. These are matters much better understood today than a generation ago.

All of which is not intended to undervalue the importance of logical-scientific thinking. Its value is so implicit in our highly technological culture that its inclusion in school curricula is taken for granted. While its teaching may still be in need of improvement, it has become strikingly better since the curriculum reform movements of the 1950s and 1960s. But it is no secret that for many of the young now in school, 'science' has come to seem 'inhuman' and 'uncaring' and 'off-putting' – despite the first-class efforts of science and mathematics teachers and their associations. Indeed, the image of science as a human and cultural undertaking might itself be improved if it were also conceived as a history of human beings overcoming received ideas – whether Lavoisier overcoming the dogma of phlogiston, Darwin rethinking respectable creationism, or Freud daring to look under the smug surface of our self-satisfaction. We may have erred in divorcing science from the narrative of culture.

[. . .]

Notes

1. J. Bruer, *Schools for Thought: A Science of Learning in the Classroom* (Cambridge, Mass., MIT Press, 1993).
2. A. Karmiloff-Smith, *A Functional Approach to Child Language: A Study of Determiners and Reference* (Cambridge, Cambridge University Press, 1979); A. Karmiloff-Smith, *Beyond Modularity: A Developmental Perspective on Cognitive Science* (Cambridge, Mass., MIT Press, 1992).
3. A. Newell and H. A. Simon, *Human Problem Solving* (Englewood Cliffs, N.J., Prentice-Hall).
4. R. B. Zajonc, Feeling and thinking: preferences need no inferences, *American Psychologist*, 35 (1980): 151–75; R. S. Lazarus, A cognitivist's reply to Zajonc on emotion and cognition, *American Psychologist*, 36 (1981): 222–3; R. S. Lazarus, Thoughts on the relations between emotion and cognition, *American Psychologist*, 37 (1982): 1019–24; R. B. Zajonc, On the primary of affect, *American Psychologist*, 39 (1984): 117–23; R. S. Lazarus, On the primary of cognition, *American Psychologist*, 39 (1984): 124–9.
5. D. A. J. Richards, *Toleration and the Constitution* (New York, Oxford University Press, 1986); D. A. J. Richards, *Foundation of American Constitutionalism* (New York, Oxford University Press, 1989).
6. Vygotsky, *Thought and Language* (Cambridge, Mass., MIT Press, 1962).
7. B. L. Whorf, *Language, Thought, and Reality: Selected Writings* (Cambridge, Mass., Technology Press of MIT, 1956).
8. R. Jakobson, Poetry of grammer and grammar of poetry, in R. Jakobson, *Selected Writings, III: Poetry of Grammar and Grammar of Poetry* (The Hague, Mourton, 1981).
9. D. A. Olson, *The World on Paper: The Conceptual and Cognitive Implications of Writing and Reading* (Cambridge, Cambridge University Press, 1994).
10. N. Goodman, *Ways of Worldmaking* (Indianapolis, Hackett, 1978).
11 I. Meyerson, *Les Fonctions Psychologiques et les Oeuvres* (Paris, J. Vrin, 1948); I. Meyerson, *Écrits, 1920–1983: Pour une Psychologie Historique* (Paris, Presses Universitarires de France, 1987).
12. S. L. Lightfoot, *The Good High School: Portraits of Character and Culture* (New York, Basic Books, 1983).
13. M. Cole and A. V. Belayeva, Computer-mediated joint activity and the problem of mental development, *Soviet Journal of Psychology*, 12 (1991): 133–41.
14. R. J. Herrnstein and C. Murray, *The Bell Curve: Intelligence and Class Structure in American Life* (New York, Free Press, 1994).
15. H. Gardner, *Frames of Mind: The Theory of Multiple Intelligences* (New York, Basic Books, 1983).
16. W. Lippmann, *Public Opinion* (New York: Harcourt, Brace, 1927); J. Dewey, *The Public and its Problems* (Chicago, Swallow Press, 1954).
17. P. Bourdieu, *Language and Symbolic Power* (Cambridge, Mass., Harvard University Press, 1991).
18. R. B. Reich, *The Work of Nations: Preparing Ourselves for Twenty-first-Century Capitalism* (New York, Knopf, 1991); D. Bell, *The Coming of Post-Industrial Society: A Venture in Social Forecasting* (New York, Basic Books, 1976).

19. J. Clifford, *The Predicament of Culture: Twentieth-Century Ethnography, Literature and Art* (Cambridge, Mass., Harvard University Press, 1988).

20. P. Freire, *Pedagogy of the Oppressed* (new rev. 20th anniversary ed) (New York, Continuum, 1994).

21. P. Bourdieu, *Distinction: A Social Critique of the Judgment of Taste* (Cambridge, Mass., Harvard University Press, 1984); R. Barthes, Toys, in R. Barthes, *Mythologies* (New York, Hill & Wang, 1982).

22. S. Schama, *Dead Certainties: Unwarranted Speculations* (New York, Knopf, 1991).

SECTION 3
CHANGE PERSPECTIVES

10

Vision and Constraint in Curriculum Change: A Case Study of South African Secondary School Principals

Ken Harley and Volker Wedekind

Introduction

About this chapter

Experience in many countries, as well as theoretical insight since Durkheim (1977), suggests that major curriculum change occurs most readily in response to major social change or crisis.

In this chapter we explore the responses of secondary school principals to state policy change in South Africa. To anyone who had grown up in this country after 1948, recent policy change was so dramatic, and of such a fundamental nature, that it would previously have been almost unthinkable. But by the late 1980s a deteriorating economy and prolonged political resistance had made *apartheid* unworkable. In February 1990, then-President F. W. de Klerk announced the birth of a 'New South Africa', and by the end of that year legislation was enacted that made it possible for hitherto segregated 'white', 'Indian' and 'coloured' schools to admit children of 'other' races. By September of that year, 'white' schools were in a position to determine their own admissions policies within a number of policy options provided by the state, provided the parent body supported the changes by voting for the opening of admissions. Given the rapidity of the change, it is not surprising that formal education systems and key personnel within them were totally unprepared for change.

This chapter draws on interviews conducted with secondary school principals before the new ANC government was voted into power in April 1994. This period covers a time of anticipation of change when, for the vast majority of South Africans, anxiety about the future was replaced by hope. For educators, there was an exciting prospect of education serving to unite, rather than divide, the country's people.

179

Under the separate *apartheid* education departments, principals had fulfilled little more than a controlling bureaucratic function to ensure that directives from the educational authorities were carried out. Even before 1994, however, it was clear that the new educational dispensation was to create a far greater autonomy for principals as managers of their schools, responsible for key activities such as staff and curriculum development. It was for this reason that principals had been targeted for interview. Interrogation of the interview data for the present study was guided by the following questions:

a) How did principals react to the prospect of desegregated schools and a new democratic social order?
b) What sorts of changes did they plan or wish to introduce in their schools as a consequence of (a)?
c) To what extent was (b) shaped by historical conditions 'given' to principals?

Background to the study

It is a truism that there are as many definitions of the curriculum as there are writers on the subject. Generally, definitions occupy nuanced gradations between two polarities. At one extreme, curriculum is viewed as no more than a documented blueprint; and at the other, it is conceptualised as what learners actually experience when the blueprint is mediated in particular contexts.

South African definitions of curriculum carry the imprint of the country's history. Given a uniquely legislated, racially-segregated past, it is not surprising that South African writers rely on broader definitions of the curriculum in highlighting its political and contested character. For example, Maurice (1982), with obvious reference to the widespread resistance to *apartheid* that was played out in schools, includes 'whether those to whom it is taught want it to be taught' in his definition.

The social and political dimensions of curriculum are captured in the views of this country's two foremost curriculum writers. Pam Christie (1993) argues that '. . . the curriculum can never be neutral or stand outside of patterns of power'. Jonathan Jansen (1995) writes that:

> . . . the school curriculum is not simply a technical document outlining intended learning outcomes or specifying content to be covered or teaching or assessment strategies to be used. It is, fundamentally, a political document which reflects the struggles of opposing groups to have their interests, values, histories and politics dominate the school curriculum.

The South African story of curriculum is one of power, exercised formally by power elites, and resisted informally by dominated social groups. Curriculum motifs are *domination* and *resistance* (see, for example, Cross and Chisholm 1990, Harley 1992, 1994, Christie 1995). The history of the curriculum is one of increasing differentiation for different racial groups, a trajectory which reached its apex in 1984 with the entrenching of racially exclusive education bureaucracies.

Our account is set in the Msunduzi metropolitan area – which includes the City of Pietermaritzburg – in the province of KwaZulu-Natal. It has the second largest urban concentration in the province. The majority of the population lives in Edendale, a black township on the fringe of the metropolitan area. The province itself has the second largest population of the nine provinces in South Africa, but is amongst the poorest in terms of rural infrastructure, health care, education, and per capita income. It is also the province in which political conflict has been most complex and severe. While violence subsided markedly throughout the rest of South Africa after the April 1994 election, KwaZulu-Natal remained locked into a complex spiral of violence.

The city had traditionally been regarded as a centre for good quality state education for 'whites'. Additionally, a number of its private schools have national standing. The 'Indian' population had achieved a comparatively good standard of provision, with the 'coloured' population not far behind. Education for Africans had been very badly affected by political instability and violence (see Gultig and Hart 1990; Nzimande and Thusi 1992). In the discussion that follows the privileged sector comprising private schools, and those for 'coloureds', 'whites', and 'Indians', will be grouped together for purposes of convenience and referred to as the '*open schools*'. The schools administered by the Department of Education and Training (DET) were much more homogeneous in that their pupil population was exclusively black. We shall refer to these as the '*DET*' schools.

Principals' Views on Schooling and the New Social Order

Social change and desegregated schooling: 'a good thing'

All principals applauded the prospect of social change and the desegregation of schools. Most importantly, the emergence of 'open' schools represented an important symbolic victory for anti-*apartheid* sentiment, for the principle of social justice.

As a new orthodoxy, the 'open' schools were regarded almost uncritically by principals as a 'good thing'. Nevertheless, principals in the 'open' and 'DET' sectors of schooling emphasised somewhat different reasons for their enthusiasm for 'open' schools. These differences are best described separately.

'Open' school principals: principle and pragmatism

There can be little doubt of the strength of goodwill and the need to 'do the right thing' with respect to the victims of discrimination. Principals had in many instances taken great pains, sometimes against the odds, to secure the vote necessary to open their enrolments. Some had campaigned for the opening of their schools despite opposition from members of their own staff and parents.

The actions of the white education authority had varied between a position of offering no support, and an attitude of obstructionism. Certain officials reportedly even warned school principals 'not to engage in politics'.

There was, however, a layer of complexity to the 'open' school principals' support for opening their enrolments. Their sense of what was morally right was not untrammelled by pragmatism and economic expediency at different levels. Enrolments in several of these schools had been falling. This had implications for the school's staff allocation and meant possible redundancies.

A mix of morality and other concerns is captured in the following interchange:

> *Interviewer:* Now, what would you say was the actual rationale behind the, you know, the opening of the school, or the decision to open the school?
> *Principal:* Well, I think if this country is going to provide skilled manpower to drive your economy . . . you can't just allow the white people to do that. The white people when you look at demographics, are declining very fast in terms of their numbers, whereas the black populations are increasing, so it stands to reason that if you want to maintain the high standard of living actually . . . you have to open up your system. Education I think is the most important place. It's got to start there. And I think it's clear common sense and it's also humanitarian – it's the right thing to do.

'DET' principals: integration and social healing

Black principals were markedly optimistic about the prospect of political change and the potential benefits that this would have for the education system in South Africa. In a political era with strong messages of reconciliation emerging from the major political figures, principals placed strong emphasis on healing relationships between people divided by the racial classification system of *apartheid*. However, the physical 'mixing' of races was viewed unproblematically, and self-evidently, as a noble enterprise.

A common theme focussed on the benefits of pupils of different races being able to play together and learning to understand each other:

> . . . When a white child [looks] at a black child, she would run away from him because he's the enemy . . . And a black child who looks at a white child, she or he sees nothing but an oppressor. You see, it's that twisted idea, as far as I'm concerned.

Justification for integration was frequently made with reference to the past:

> [Pupils] . . . have grown up in a society where we are racially divided and perhaps put, ah, they were put in different schools, just for, for reasons of colour and nothing else.

Now there was a need to integrate schools to avoid 'nasty incidents'. It was thus necessary for schools to prepare young people for 'the future dispensation', and it was maintained that this process should begin early in the primary school.

Realising the Vision: A Disjunction

We turn now to the question of what was actually happening in schools, and what principals who believed that social integration was a 'good thing' were planning to do in order to support their vision of a new social order.

Again it is analytically useful to discuss separately views from the 'DET' and 'open' schools.

'Open' school principals: curriculum maintenance

Although they had 'openness' in common, the 'open' schools in fact included a variety a diverse schools with differing intersections along the lines of history, ethos, and socio-economic standing. Given these differences, one would expect to find diverse perspectives, and indeed this was so. Tensions were evident within and between schools:

- There was a long-term vision of developments, but also a desire to effect appropriate day-to-day management decisions. While principals may have wished to ponder their overall policy regarding integration, pupils were already sitting in their classes, and effective programmes had to be designed for them. Faced with this demand, institutions appeared to rely on what had worked for them in the past.
- There was a general desire to be pro-active, but the demands of integration were forcing schools to be re-active. Schools were ill-prepared for the changes and opportunities that had arrived at short notice. They had been given little or no support from their respective education authorities, and although a referendum had been required at least in the white sector, for schools in the coloured and Indian sectors, these changes had been instituted by fiat.
- There was an inconsistency between the internal locus of control, with schools being required to act on their own account, while tight external control was continued through the provision of staff salaries, syllabi, examinations, and inspection.
- Culture and ethnicity were seen in reified terms, but there was also a desire to see them in dynamic evolutionary terms. Terms like 'them' and 'us' were used frequently, which together with the strong assimilationist-incorporationist philosophies in respect to both short and long-term goals, indicated a strong containment as distinct from a change orientation.

These tensions were each aspects of a central tension, namely that between curriculum maintenance and curriculum change. However, the most powerful theme was *curriculum maintenance*. Even amongst the strongest supporters of desegregation, there was an overriding concern for *academic standards and the ethos of the school*. (Since *apartheid* education had been designed to nurture 'own cultures' – the culture supposedly unique to each racial group – concerns about ethos and standards were almost inevitable.)

In sum, while the 'open' school principals were strongly supportive of desegregating their schools, they wished to achieve this in ways that did not threaten their ethos or the 'standards' in their schools. To do this, it was necessary for them to seize the opportunity to control the process of admission on their own terms. The less affluent schools enjoyed a greater measure of freedom in making decisions; but the more powerful state schools, and most notably the private schools, were best placed to manage change in such a way that their ethos and standards were not assaulted.

The non-negotiable nature of standards had implications for practice. Major dimensions of this are:

A policy of social and academic assimilation

It was a social imperative that pupils should 'fit in'. Admission policies were built around the commonsense view that younger pupils would 'fit in' more easily than their senior pupils. A typical comment:

> I don't like taking boys later than Std. 7. We've tried some aged about 15, 16. They don't . . . there are problems, you've got social problems. They don't integrate.

The dominant cultural standards were most commonly described as 'western', as in the following statement:

> Okay. One of the problems that you always have to face is which culture is the culture that you should follow . . . There's no doubt in my mind that we aim at the western culture. We aim at what they are doing in Australia, the rest of the world. So the boys coming to my dining room, they are taught table manners that would be acceptable to any of the modernized western countries, and all the social graces that go with that. But at the same time the boys are taught to respect the cultural differences of other people, and to actually maybe assimilate some of them, because some of the boys here bring different types of habits which are actually better than we find elsewhere, and that becomes part of it. So we aim to take the best of each of the cultures, but predominantly it's the western culture that dominates.

This was the typical pattern: dominant 'western' cultural standards, but with 'respect' being accorded to other cultures. At no institution was a clear account provided of what was actually being done, as part of the school curriculum, to develop respect for other cultures. It appeared rather as if principals were of the view that an inherent part of 'western' culture was the bestowal of respect to other cultures. It was almost as if principals felt they could rely on western 'social graces' in this regard, and that the necessary cultural recipe was already embedded in the school ethos in a way that rendered explicit programmes dealing with issues of culture and ethnicity unnecessary.

Similarly, the academic roots of assimilation lay in a confident belief that particular forms of knowledge were universal. Views on socially constructed knowledge were not evident here, and of course personal views on what was worthwhile knowledge were consonant with the entire curriculum and assessment edifice of the 'own affairs' departments.

Social and academic assimilation meant that beyond the level of cultural artefacts, differences were not viewed with much sympathy. If a cultural standard is universal, deviation from that standard constitutes 'deprivation':

> . . . if a child has come from a deprived background where they haven't had the things that we take for granted, electricity, and everything that goes with electricity, etc., yes, their perceptions are different.

And if they're different they need remediation:

> Standards are going to be a problem. One has to understand that, but I think a heavy, hard remedial programme is needed, but all of us, and here I'm talking to an expert, know the importance of praise and encouragement – boost them, 'well done', 'fantastic' . . .

In the majority of settings, assimilation and remediation was synonymous with 'bringing pupils up to standard' in the basics, as is evident in this explanation offered by the principal of a 'coloured' school:

> . . . at the beginning of this year, for the first two months in standard six, we only taught English and mathematics. We didn't have the other subjects, of course without the approval of my department, if they knew they might have hammered me for it, but I did it because I taught in Zambia 1967–74 and I knew the children coming from the primary schools in Zambia had the same problem when they only learnt in the vernacular and when they came to high school, and we did that for a whole term and it was very successful in Zambia and I couldn't see why it wasn't going to be successful here.

Assimilation was unchallenged because 'It's what they want'

Principals were clear that pupils of other races wished to be inducted into the cultural and academic standards of the 'open' schools. This view found its strongest expression in the private schools:

> First of all, just to say recently, and I didn't do this, the senior staff did it, they interviewed each child of colour at the school. Now this is very interesting. That first of all the African children, they probably told us what we wanted, what they thought we would like to hear, but every one of them said that they were happy in the Eurocentric type school, the parents sent them here specifically because they wanted our type of education and they didn't want to see an African type education, whatever that might be.

Apart from concessionary gestures to the standards of other cultures, there was widespread agreement that all pupils would be able to accommodate to the 'Eurocentric' type of school provided they were keen and had the right attitude. If they were, they would adapt and do well. Some successful instances of this were cited, particularly by the principals of private schools which had had experience of some years of 'open' schooling:

> *Principal:* . . . well here. And I use that as an example, where there was potential hidden and given the opportunity, and out it came . . . we've got a boy who came, and they said 'ooh, brilliant mathematician!' Did well enough in our entrance exam, but had never put studded boots on. And had never held a rugger ball. And he's now a star in our wing for our Under 15 side.
> *Interviewer:* Yes.
> *Principal:* And he just learnt the skill – never caught a rugger ball, loved Kaiser Chiefs or something like that, realised that he couldn't play soccer here, put his mind to his rugger, and has done fantastically

Assimilation works if numbers are controlled

One of the stock expressions in South African educational jargon is 'critical mass': the desired result is achievable if there are sufficient numbers of competent actors available to serve the cause.

'Open' school principals – particularly those from the higher status schools – showed a keen awareness of the possible effects of an uncontrolled 'critical mass' of children from different ethnic or racial groups entering their schools. Standards and ethos could be compromised by sheer weight of numbers:

> Obviously, if you're going to have a massive influx of people who've come from a deprived background, yes, the style of teaching is going to change . . .

Control measures took the form of admission tests, almost universally in English and Mathematics. Here is an example of more liberal practice in a less affluent school:

> Uh, basically, I asked my English teacher to set an English test for standard 6, standard 7, standard 8, and we've tried to make it as elementary as possible, so that, it's not an unfair test to the pupils. The same with Mathematics, standard 5 level and we, we even accepted pupils with 30%.

More powerful schools were more cautious:

> *Principal:* English and Mathematics. Those are the two that we really look at. Afrikaans if they do Afrikaans at any sort of level, but English and Mathematics are the two that we –
> *Interviewer:* Now obviously those tests you use as a screening device?
> *Principal:* Right.
> *Interviewer:* Do you go beyond that, and say, well, hang on now, within those somebody's quite good at maths, but look, his English is not so good, or vice versa. And then do you attempt to try to offer some support system when they arrive here?
> *Principal:* Yes, well, first of all, let's go back to selection. We also look at home background. Very important. We ask things like 'Do you have television at home, where do your parents work, what brothers and sisters do you have', and we get some sort of feel of the home background. Have they, have they ever had a colouring-in book at home, do they cut things out with scissors, etc. etc. So that's how we do it. Then we do have a back-up system, we do have a lady coming in to help again with English comprehension, and she'll help with Mathematics
> . . .

'DET' schools

How open were the DET schools?

It has already been mentioned that the role played by the departmental authority in the 'open schools' had been unhelpful and occasionally obstructive. This was not the case in the DET, which simply played no role whatsoever.

Although the DET had officially declared itself to be an 'open' department, two principals were in fact unaware of this development, and three others expressed reservations about their educational authority being 'open'. One principal commented:

> I do not think the DET is racially open because there is no institution where this can be supported or demonstrated, and the DET has not given us any guidance as to how we can prepare for an integrated school.

Even had the DET played an active role with respect to school integration, this would have been no more than a symbolic gesture. There was no realistic prospect of black schools attracting pupils of other races. As victims of discriminatory resourcing and political turbulence, township schools had little that was visible to offer. Geographically they were also isolated from the metropolitan areas in which pupils of other races resided, and poorly served by public transport.

While no 'white', 'Indian' or 'coloured' students had enrolled at black schools, there had been a movement of black pupils to 'open' schools. Principals could not be certain of exact numbers, but estimates in the various schools ranged from 4 to 22 per annum since 1991, with one school reporting a figure of 50. It was speculated that migrations would have been prolific were it not for transport difficulties and costs of travel to the 'open' schools. 'Well-to-do' was an expression frequently used in describing the families who were moving into town and enrolling their children in the 'open' schools. More significantly, 8 of the 10 principals specifically mentioned that it was teachers' children who were moving to the 'open' schools.

> *Interviewer:* In terms of teachers here at [name of school], are there any that have sent their kids there [to 'open' schools]?
> *Principal:* Yes, most of them!

Indeed, principals themselves were prominent amongst those who had moved their own children to 'open' schools.

Integrated schooling, for the principals of DET schools, had a meaning circumscribed by the realities of the situation. It meant that black children able to move to the 'open' schools, did move.

Principals' views

Unlike the 'open' schools which had been faced by pupils of other races, 'DET' schools had not been confronted with change. In character, the DET schools presented far greater uniformity than did the 'open' schools. Common understanding was a prominent feature of the responses of black principals.

Views on curriculum   When pressed on curriculum issues, principals addressed both pedagogy and subject content. When dealing with subject content, principals did not easily outline specific changes necessary to sustain their broader aims of a transformed society. Some of the most concrete suggestions involved the correction of inaccuracies. Distortions resulting from the political past were reported in subjects such as History and Afrikaans. Beyond that, one principal argued for the facilitation of the passage from school to tertiary education by the 'matching' of content. In similar vein, other arguments were proposed for the inclusion of essential life skills, for relevance to the work situation, and for 'practicality'. Some proposed technical adjustments in the form of modernising the syllabus:

> I think it's a good thing that we look at the syllabi, for some of them I think are very outdated. If I go and look at my Woodworking, and things like that, there are things in there that you don't see any more. No modern methods are used. And now the children are learning things that are 30, 40, 50 years old.

'Modernist' rather than transformatory orientations were evident.

Not one of the principals interviewed felt that DET schools should address issues of culture and race within their curriculum. While they recognised a need for multi-cultural and anti-racist programmes within the 'open' schools, the fact that they were unlikely to find students of other race groups attending their schools meant that such interventions were not necessary. Clearly then, issues of integration in the broader South African society were not seen as central concerns of the school curriculum, irrespective of whether the schools were integrated or not. The vision of open schooling supported by the principals did not translate into direct changes within the curriculum and remained a vision of a primarily demographic integration.

With respect to pedagogy there was remarkable consensus. With one exception, principals were committed to the canon of respectable, professional discourse: 'spoon-feeding' had to go; creativity had to be encouraged; activity should be pupil-centred and empowering; and there should be less reliance on textbooks.

> • By traditional methods of teaching I mean the methods which would assume that the student knows nothing, and the teacher has all the information. So the student would sit there being passive, while the teacher poured the information into the kids. And I personally believe that we have to change that soon, that method.
> • . . . teachers usually employ the traditional type of teaching where the teacher talks and the children are always passive, they listen to the teacher and you find that there is very little pupil activity in the classroom.

Accounts of pedagogy carried two main points of significance. Firstly, black principals revealed little optimism that these practices were achievable in their own schools.

Secondly, it was clear that the 'open' schools served as a powerful reference point with respect to both pedagogy and content. The dominant image of desirable curriculum change was, in the words of one principal, 'syllabuses on the same lines as those in the Indian schools and coloured schools and white schools'.

What then is the role of a black school in the face of existing disparities? It is to prepare pupils for 'open' schools.

> Our students have left [name of school] and gone to these Model B and C schools. What is encouraging is that we have received feedback from them and they are saying that they found nothing new in these schools. They have adjusted very well. Some of them are even leading in these schools, they are getting top positions, position one in other instances.

That a principal was able to derive encouragement from losing his best pupils is a significant commentary on the process of affirmation taking place. If the 'open' schools served as a benchmark, transformation was achieved to the extent that one's 'products' were successful in those schools. There was some irony in this. As we have seen, the 'open' schools were scarcely transformational.

Responsibility for curriculum change   Principals had been accustomed to working in an authoritarian department:

- . . . we are under the DET and the only thing that happens is instructions and work that should be done . . .
- They expect you to adhere to the subject management policy and there is no leeway.

Principals were united in condemning this 'top-down' form of governance as inappropriate and outmoded. However, when identifying subject matter in need of being 'put right', responsibility for change was located within the bureaucratic hierarchy: '*they* must change the syllabus'; 'change should filter down from policy level'; 'teachers must be informed about new developments'; and 'they [teachers] must know what is expected of them'.

Clearly, schools were conceptualised as 'curriculum receivers' (Marland 1978). Principals were concerned not so much with the *process* of the top-down mode of curriculum decision making, as with its *source*. The source with which they had become familiar was the DET with its illegitimacy and unacceptable political baggage. But now indications were strong that centralised prescription from the new 'legitimate' authority would not only be acceptable, but expected. This was probably more than a case of simple 'legitimacy'. As has been noted in other third world contexts, bureaucratic forms of control reduce uncertainty in the eyes of principals and provide a framework of security (Fuller, 1991).

A more sympathetic (and realistic) view of the principals' perspectives leads to consideration of the situational constraints in their working environments. One of the characteristics of teaching is 'immediacy' (Delamont, 1975). This useful term describing the overwhelming nature of unavoidable day-to-day issues to which one must respond hardly does justice to the position of DET principals. Their difficulties in the day-to-day management of their schools were such that long- and even medium-term planning would have been an unattainable luxury. 'Crisis management' was the norm. Changes in pupil population alone would bedevil planning. The attrition rate in these schools was such that the number of pupils in standard 10 as a percentage of the standard 6 enrolment ranged from 27% to 53%, with a mean of 39%. But pupil migration emerged as an even more disruptive factor. Non-educational difficulties included violence and pupils' relocating to different areas:

> When there's more violence like we had at the beginning of the year, then we find that pupils run away to other areas. Especially this year, we had a situation where there were two gangs fighting in the township, and as a result of that many of our pupils fled, especially those in the lower classes.

The corollary of schools such as this losing cohorts of pupils is that others experienced unanticipated influxes:

> Edendale has become a sanctuary. Everybody who is affected by riots and killings, they all run to Edendale. As a result we have large numbers of students coming in here.

'Squatter camps that are coming up like mushrooms' was cited as a further source of pressure. Principals of the 'safe' African schools spoke of 'shouldering the burdens of other schools' in surrounding peri-urban and rural areas.

Despite the pressure of these situational constraints, there seemed to be another perhaps more complex issue constraining the principal's ability to innovate. Principals were trapped by the image of the well-resourced and seemingly effective 'open' schools, an image so far removed from the reality of their own schools that the distance between the two types of schools seemed unbridgeable. The picture of the 'open' schools held the principals captive, making it difficult to begin any realistic innovation in their schools. Principals' notions of education and transformation were essentially conservative, with a vivid disjuncture emerging between progressive educational rhetoric (often based on their contact with 'open' schools) and political rhetoric, and adherence to new right thinking around efficiency, expert-driven systems, and resourcing.

Table 10.1 is a tabulation of the key differences discussed thus far.

Discussion on Curriculum Change

In the present case study we have seen that all principals supported the vision of a new social order. Consistent with that position, the 'open' schools had revealed considerable goodwill in opening up their enrolments. However, the view we have seen of principals' practices and plans in the years preceding the 1994 elections is one of limited demographic change, but curriculum stasis.

Table 10.1   *A comparative summary of issues in the 'open' schools and the black schools*

Issue	Black schools	Open schools
Disposition towards democratisation, social transformation, integrated schools	Overwhelmingly supportive	Overwhelmingly supportive
Reason for opening of enrolment to all races	Unsure if schools were indeed officially 'open'; negligible probability of other races enrolling	Complex and varied: • Moral imperatives • Falling rolls • Strategic thrust to manage control on own terms
Pressure to change	Still mono-racial: little immediate pressure for change	Some pressure for change: • Symbolic importance of broadening demographic composition of school • How to cope with 'new' pupils from different cultural backgrounds?
Admission policy	No entrance tests: accommodate all pupils insofar as possible	• Key concern to protect school ethos and standards • Entrance tests, almost invariably in English and Maths
Intake of other races	Nil	Limited • Higher status schools able to control the process more stringently • Preference for junior pupils
View of how to accommodate new intake of other races	Not seen as applicable – schools have no responsibility for preparing pupils for an integrated society	Assimiliationist – to protect standards and ethos
View of necessary curriculum change	• The 'open' schools were a powerful reference group • Greater technical efficiency	Bridging courses for newcomers: bring them 'up to speed'
Situational constraints	• Day-to-day governance • Lack of infrastructure and support • Entrenched traditional teaching practices • Violence, pupil migration	• Staff and parental opposition (varied) • Maintain standards and ethos of school

Attempts to account for this disjunction between educational vision and educational practice call into consideration both school principals' sense of personal agency, and social constraint.

The importance of personal agency in South African schools has recently been highlighted. In her school-based research, Christie (forthcoming) identifies factors which enabled some black schools to remain stable, while others around them collapsed. The former – depicted as 'resilient schools' – were characterised by a sense of agency and responsibility, and had flexible and purposive leadership. Dysfunctional schools did not acknowledge their responsibilities and agency potential: they saw themselves as victims of an oppressive system.

In the present case study, would the visions of principals have been realised had they had a more developed sense of agency? Some sense of agency was evident, most notably in 'open' schools. In spite of '. . . working in the dark – just sort of fumbling in the dark' (in the words of one principal), a degree of change had been achieved. In the rather limited demographic sense, some schools had at least become integrated. Other instances of agency are difficult to find. If schools are sites of both constraint and promise (Hargreaves, 1988), principals' accounts suggested that constraint loomed very much larger than promise. The picture that emerges from this analysis is one of people making their own history, but very much in terms of conditions that were given to them. We have already discussed a number of situational and contextual constraints that emerged from the interviews, and it would be tedious to repeat these here. However, there are three additional social constraints worthy of mention. These were not embedded in the data, but formed a backdrop to many of the issues principals spoke about. In dealing with these issues, the question of future change is also addressed.

Firstly, principals had no transformatory curriculum model that they could refer to, either in theory or in precedent. If 'social healing' were one's vision, what type of curriculum would one construct to bring it about in one's school? It is notable that forces opposed to what is often loosely characterised as 'Bantu Education' had done little to provide substance to an alternative vision of education. Opponents of *apartheid* tended to celebrate the role of the school in terms of its potential for resistance to an oppressive state. While a concept of 'People's Education' was certainly popularised, this was more of a mobilising rallying cry than an articulated view of educational practice. At best, schools had constituted sites for political mobilisation, and unlike their counterparts in Mozambique or Cuba, had never been sites of educational progressivism.

At the time of the interviews even the political commitment to 'People's Education' was disappearing from the discourses on formal education (Wolpe, 1993/94). It is little wonder that principals of black schools drew their images of desirable practice from the 'open' schools, thus implicitly validating curriculum practices that were rooted in what was essentially curriculum maintenance. In this regard, little has changed in recent years.

The ministry has introduced an ambitious outcomes-based curriculum design called 'Curriculum 2005'. But this is essentially an assessment framework (Young, 1996). Although gilded with much rhetoric about imputed transformatory effects, the new model tells principals little about what they should actually *do* to effect curriculum change in their schools.

Secondly, and related to the above point, there is the importance of a supportive educational bureaucracy. As we saw in the Pietermaritzburg case study, there was much evidence of principals needing support that was simply not available. At the present time the bureaucracy is far more likely to support new policy rather than to subvert it or adopt the default position, as was the case prior to the 1994 elections. However, the incapacity of the massive state bureaucracy to support 'Curriculum 2005' has led to the adoption of an inappropriate 'cascade training' model being contracted to a non-governmental agency. Policy making appears to have been context blind to the limitations of its own bureaucracy.

Thirdly, there is an interesting and complex political question. In South Africa there are high expectations of schooling, and schools are very powerful symbols of modernity in Africa (Fuller, 1991). While some expectations of schooling fall easily into line with the perceived common interest – such as development, democracy, nationhood, and equity – other interests may reside at the more personal level. In a modernising state individual aspirations are expressed through education, the pre-eminent route to personal social mobility.

The delicate balance of forces in the third world is captured admirably in Fuller's (1991) theory of the 'fragile state'. Fuller argues that the state, while attempting to modernise society, must at the same time keep the conflicting demands of both its popular support base and that of the 'new elite' in some sort of balance. Should the 'fragile state' wish to introduce reform (which it must for its own political survival) it will have to balance carefully the conflicting interests of the majority of parents whose children are attending poorly resourced schools with the expectations of the middle classes. Furthermore, Fuller argues that the school as an institution presents a further difficulty in any reform initiative: the local principals and teachers have the capacity to undermine any initiative by the state through processes of interpretation in the light of their own needs and expectations. Thus, while the state may not simply represent the interests of the middle class, innovation which is not in the perceived interests of the 'new elites' is likely to face grave challenges.

The Pietermaritzburg case study provides a clear picture of the migration of the more affluent blacks to the 'open' schools. This is understandable because, in at least the medium term, black schools will not be in a position to meet the expectations of the emerging black middle class. Equally clear was the perception of at least some black principals that the mission of their schools was to make this migration both possible and successful. The 'open' schools appeared to be intent on receiving this new elite and assimilating it into old elite in the interests of 'maintaining standards'.

This tendency towards a two-tiered school system has, if anything, gained momentum in the years since the interviews with school principals were carried out. Ideologically, a two-tiered system is an embarrassment for the present egalitarian state. However, if we turn from the egalitarian state to Fuller's 'fragile state', an unlikely sounding but plausible possibility becomes apparent. Is it possible that a two-tiered educational system has a certain functional value to the 'fragile state'? It certainly caters for the elites, old and new, which cluster into the 'open' schools; for the broader population with expectations of higher levels of schooling, mass schooling is available. The tension is symbolised by the teachers who worked in the ex-DET schools, but who sent their own children to the 'open' schools. If teachers can live with that tension, perhaps the 'fragile state' can accommodate to it as well.

Finally, our case study demonstrates what everybody knows: curriculum change is not easy. In a complex setting like South Africa, struggles and contestations around curriculum are not resolved once curriculum policy documents have been written. They are continually re-enacted in daily practices in educational settings.

References

Christie, P. (1990) *Open Schools: Racially Mixed Catholic Schools in South Africa, 1976–1986*, Johannesburg, Ravan.

Christie, P. (1993) Equality and curriculum policy in post-apartheid South Africa, *Journal of Education*, 18 (1): 4–15.

Christie, P. (1995) Transition tricks? Policy models for school desegregation in South Africa, 1990–94, *Journal of Education Policy*, 10 (1): 45–55.

Christie, P. (forthcoming) Schools as (dis)organisations: the 'breakdown of the culture of learning and teaching' in South Africa, *Cambridge Journal of Education*.

Cross, M. and Chisholm, L. (1990) The roots of segregated schooling in twentieth century South Africa, in M. Nkomo (ed.) *Pedagogy of Domination*, New Jersey, Africa World Press.

Delamont, S. (1975) *Interaction in the Classroom*, London, Methuen.

Durkheim, E. (1977) On education and society, in J. Karabel and A. H. Halsey (eds.) *Power and Ideology in education*, New York, Oxford University Press.

Fuller, B. (1991) *Growing-up Modern: The Western State Builds Third-World Schools*, New York, Routledge.

Gultig, J. and Hart, M. (1990) 'The world is full of blood': youth, schooling and conflict in Pietermaritzburg, 1987–1989, *Perspectives in Education*, 11 (2): 1–19.

Hargreaves, A. (1988) Teaching quality: a sociological analysis, *Journal of Curriculum Studies*, 20 (3): 211–31.

Harley, K. L. (1985) Aspirations and opportunities: perspectives of black pupils and matriculated school leavers, *Journal of Education*, 17: 47–57.

Harley, K. L. (1992) African education and social control in colonial Natal, *Perspectives in Education*, 13 (2): 27–52.

Harley, K. L. (1994) Landmarks in the history of 'open' schooling in Natal: the search for social control, *Journal of Education* 19 (1): 37–51.

Jansen, J. D. (1995) Understanding social transition through the lens of curriculum policy, *Journal of Curriculum Studies* 27 (3): 245–61.

Marland, P. (1978) *Curriculum Theory*, Townsville, College of Advanced Education.

Maurice, E. (1982) The curriculum crisis in schools, in A. P. Hunter, M. J. Ashley and C. J. Millar (eds.) *Education, Curriculum and Development: Papers Presented at Conferences at the University of Cape Town and the University of Witwatersrand*, Cape Town, Centre for Continuing Education.

Molteno, F. (1987) Students take control: the 1980 boycott of coloured education in the Cape Peninsula, *British Journal of Sociology of Education*, 8 (1): 3–22.

NEPI (1992) *Curriculum: Report of the National Education Policy Investigation Curriculum Research Group*, Cape Town, Oxford University Press.

Nzimande, B. and Thusi, S. (1992) *Children of War: The Impact of Political Violence on Schooling in Natal*, Durban, Education Projects Unit.

Penny, A., Appel, S., Gultig, J., Harley, K. and Muir, R. (1993) 'Just sort of fumbling in the dark': a case study of the advent of racial integration in South African schools, *Comparative Education Review*, 37 (4): 412–33.

Wedekind, V., Lubisi, C., Harley, K. and Gultig, J. (1996) Political change, social integration, and curriculum: a South African case study, *Journal of Curriculum Studies*, 28 (4): 419–36.

Wolpe, A. (1993/94) Guest editors' introduction, *Perspectives in Education*, 15 (1), 1–12.

Young, M. F. D. (1996) The outcomes approach to education and training: theoretical grounding and an international perspective. Paper presented at NQF launch, 22–24 April 1996.

11

Recent Curriculum Change in Post-Pinochet Chile

Ruth Aedo-Richmond and Mark Richmond

Introduction

Recent years have in many advanced industrialised countries witnessed the emergence of a national educational debate of some prominent and public kind. Apart from the significant fact that the educational system and educational issues appear to have acquired a heightened salience on the political agenda, there is the further consideration that the curriculum has often figured centrally in these debates. Moreover, this interest typically has focused on the need or demand for curriculum change of some form if the nation is to grapple successfully with the multiple challenges it faces, especially those emanating from rapid technological transformation and economic restructuring.

The pervasiveness of curriculum change, as revealed by his survey of trends and issues in curriculum reform and pedagogy across OECD member states, has prompted Malcolm Skilbeck (1990, p. 79) to ask: 'Are we at a watershed in school curriculum development and pedagogical practice?' Though Skilbeck is wary of giving an unqualified affirmative judgement or prediction, he proceeds to report that, as far as curriculum is concerned, 'in practically all education systems there is, at the very least, a quickening of interest and, in several, major transformations are under way' (Skilbeck, 1990, p. 79). Clearly, curriculum change is most definitely on the agenda, and not just in the 'North'.

Had his survey included Chile, for example, Skilbeck may have been induced to edge closer towards an unequivocal answer to his question. [This chapter] has as its main purpose the development of a clearer understanding of the curriculum-related changes introduced into Chilean primary education since March 1990, when the democratically-elected coalition government of Patricio Aylwin took office and thereby peacefully replaced Pinochet's military regime which had dominated Chile since the violent *coup* of September 1973. We shall maintain that Chile has embarked upon a distinctive change in its approach to curriculum and that this change promises to mark a genuine watershed in the country's educational history

---

This paper has been edited.

and development. Moreover, we believe the Chilean case is likely to commend itself to the attention of other countries addressing comparable situations or problems. Particularly noteworthy in regard to Chile, for example, is the important role accorded to educational policy in the attempt to overcome the adverse social legacy of prolonged authoritarian rule and the strong influence of extreme neoliberalism on the determination of policy. In view of this inheritance, which other countries may share in whole or in part, Chile's new approach to curriculum may be expected to attract and merit wider interest.

At the heart of that new approach is a form of curricular and pedagogical decentralisation. Its emergence, design and significance cannot be explained satisfactorily without reference to a complex interaction of factors internal and external to the educational system. It is important to recognise that the 'external' factors, such as the particular circumstances of Chile's transition to (and consolidation of) democracy, the shifting relationship between the state and civil society, and the requirements and constraints imposed by a free market, export-oriented economy, are not merely broadly contextual in character for they penetrate deeply and directly into the educational and curricular changes which have been introduced. However, to reveal the full meaning and implications of these changes it will be necessary to focus upon the specifically educational reforms and policies of the Pinochet years and upon the critique which they stimulated (Aedo-Richmond *et al.,* 1985; Cox, 1990).

[. . .]

Continuity and Change

In order to appreciate the distinctiveness of the approach adopted by Aylwin's educational team, it will be useful to identify what it considered its priority goals and tasks compared with those of previous administrations. The push for quantitative expansion and increased coverage, for example, was the *sine qua non* of educational policy in Chile throughout the twentieth century, but since March 1990 this form of educational democratisation ceased to constitute a priority concern. Increased access and school-age enrolment were perceived by the Aylwin Government as no longer requiring the kind of emphasis, energies and resources they once attracted, in large part because satisfactory levels of achievement had been reached and maintained. Thus, well over 90% of children aged between 6 and 14 years were attending school, as were 80% of young people between 15 and 19 years of age (Espinola, 1991, p. 148). The Aylwin Government's shift of emphasis has been summarised neatly by Gracia Huidobro (1990, p. 165):

> Until today State responsibility has been centred on ensuring that Chilean children attend school; from now on the State must guarantee that the children learn in school.

In addition, the organisation and institutional structuring of the school system in post-Pinochet Chile were not under serious review: the decentralisation reforms of the early 1980s, involving processes of regionalisation, municipalisation and privatisation, were not dismantled.

Instead of expansion and institutional restructuring, the chief concerns of Aylwin's educational policy were the quality and equity of education. Quality was understood in relation to the actual learning outcomes being generated by schooling processes, that is, the acquisition and mastery of *las destrezas culturales básicas* (basic cultural skills) necessary for the child's personal, social and intellectual development. Equity, meanwhile, referred to the distribution of those learning outcomes within the school population; again, Garcia-Huidobro (1990, p. 165) has provided a clear encapsulation of the term's meaning and implications:

> Until now, the application of the principle of equality of opportunities has insisted that all children receive a similar education; in future one must look for a differentiated education in order to achieve similar results. This implies flexibility in order to spend more resources on the schools and programmes which are attended by the poorest children, young people and adults in the countryside and the city.

As subsequent discussion will show, other basic orientations shaping the educational policies of the Aylwin Government included: the cultivation of a consensus spanning as much as possible of the social and political spectrum; the encouragement of greater participation by a diversity of social actors; the achievement of curricular and pedagogical decentralisation as well as administrative decentralisation; greater efficiency in the operation of the educational system; and the opportunity for continuous improvement of the schooling experience through an open design permitting flexibility and adaptation (Chile, Ministerio de Educación, 1991a, pp. 5–9). Together, these priorities and orientations signify a substantial departure from the tradition of the *estado docente* and from the model of state-directed, system-wide educational reform. In both respects, the new approach in educational policy has been a disappointment to some opponents of Pinochet.

In the years and months leading up to the hoped-for democratic transition in Chile, the architects of what was to become the Aylwin Government's educational policy sought to prepare the ground for the type of educational strategy and programmes they had in mind. One danger they perceived was that opposition to Pinochet would take the form of a desire to restore the educational status quo before 1973; many teachers, for example, felt that only through such a restoration would they recover the professional status, collective protection and terms of employment which Pinochet had taken from them. However, for Ivan Núñez, once a key figure in Allende's Ministry of Education, any attempt to overhaul the educational system completely and reverse Pinochet's educational reforms in their entirety would not only court disaster but also was unwarranted. Núñez was convinced that a new comprehensive educational reform would polarise public opinion and would risk provoking a second military intervention; educational controversy, after all, had played a not-inconsiderable role in the destabilisation and eventual downfall of the Popular Unity government in 1973 (Farrell, 1986; Núñez, 1987, pp. 11–12). He also denied that such a large-scale reform was necessary: the decentralised structure of the educational system was acceptable in principle, for example, even if aspects of its design, operation and results could be criticised. For Núñez and others persuaded by the new educational thinking, acceptance of administrative decentralisation could not be separated from the need to re-appraise other aspects of centralisation associated with the *estado docente* tradition, according to which education ought to be a monopoly of the state:

> *Estado docente* was literally a 'teaching state', responsible for the education of all its citizens. *Estado docente* involved rigid central control and national uniformity in all aspects of instruction: curriculum, syllabuses, school texts and evaluation. (Cox, 1990, p. 175)

[. . .]

In recent years, there has emerged a different conception of the role of the state, especially the central state, and a changed understanding of the means of securing democracy for Chile, a country now rather different in character from that to which the old *estado docente* tradition corresponded. That tradition has not been totally abandoned; rather, it has been re-defined in such a way as to offer a reduced and amended role for the central state, thereby permitting greater scope for the actors comprising civil society to exercise freedom, creativity and power. [. . .] The new curriculum-related changes in Chile, therefore, may be seen as one mani-festation of the breaking of the spell cast by grand, state-directed social reform: the response to Pinochet's educational policies, in other words, is scrupulously *not* a reform (at least, not yet). Our analysis turns next to more detailed examination of Pinochet's educational policies, especially those relating to curriculum.

Curriculum Change under the Pinochet Regime

Over the period of the Pinochet regime (1973–1990), quite a number of decrees, regulations and circulars touching directly or indirectly on ques-tions of curriculum were issued (Magendzo, 1988, pp. 9–41). However, it is possible to identify two broad phases for purposes of characterising policy shifts and developments.

The first phase was that between 1973 and 1979, during which the mili-tary regime's educational policy was based upon a blend of repression, exclusion and demobilisation, on the one hand, and ideologisation and control, on the other. The Pinochet regime sought to remove all sources of opposition, resistance and overt discontent from the educational system. This involved the 'purging' of educational institutions of persons associated with the Allende Government and with the left in general; all signs of

Marxism–Leninism, a 'contamination' held responsible for Chile's difficulties, were targeted for elimination. The institutional mechanisms for
participation in the running of the education system were abolished or
banned, such as elected municipal governments, parent–teacher associations and the teachers' trade union (McGinn & Street, 1986, p. 481). Many
educational institutions, in fact, were placed under the direct control of
military forces.

At the same time, the military regime began in 1974 to impose its own
ideological vision through measures affecting programmes of study,
especially in such subject areas as geography, history and social science
(Aedo-Richmond, 1978). As Cox points out,

> The direction of the changes is the exclusion of certain topics and the introduc-
> tion of new ones, in accordance with the vision of the military and of traditional
> Catholic sectors on the right which articulated a new concept of nation in which
> 'the social', the pillar of the previous vision, is made invisible. (Cox, 1991, p. 21)

Consequently, the military's favourite themes began to appear in programmes of study, especially at the secondary level: order, national security, hierarchy, the nation and its symbols, obedience, individualism,
family and tradition. However, it may be noted that the structure of the
plans and programmes of study installed by the Frei Government's educational reform of 1965 remained intact.

[. . .]

The policies of educational decentralisation enacted by Pinochet's Government formed part of a wider attack, inspired by neoliberal principles
and arguments, upon the central apparatus of the state, which was accused
of being too powerful, inflexible and over-bureaucratised. While there had
been earlier efforts, in the mid-1970s, in the direction of a decentralised
structure, the decentralisation drive from 1980 onwards was more thorough
and far-reaching. The process of educational decentralisation was essentially administrative and managerial in character, involving the decon-
centration of certain Ministry of Education functions down to regional,
provincial and municipal levels. The key development was the decision to
transfer pre-primary, primary and secondary schools from the hands of the
central Ministry of Education directly to the municipalities, except in the
case of technical-vocational schools which were turned over to associations
of private enterprises. Three important changes occurred in tandem with
the municipalisation process. First, a new system of educational financing
was introduced based on a subsidy calculated according to pupils' daily
attendance. Second, privatisation was encouraged; indeed, the new system
of financing encouraged the rapid growth of private subsidised schools.
Third, there was the transfer of teachers from the position of being employees of the central state to becoming employees of either municipalities
or private (subsidised or fee-paying) schools, with all that this meant in
terms of status, pay, years of continuous service, security of employment
and career progression (Latorre *et al.*, 1991, pp. 24–36). In association with

these and other changes, the decentralisation policies enacted by Pinochet altered Chile's educational landscape dramatically, particularly in the perspective of the centralist traditions of public responsibility represented by the *estado docente*.

Pinochet sought to weaken those traditions still further through the application of the principle of curricular flexibility, which has been charac- terised by Cox as the educational correlative of the ascendant neoliberal groups' ideas favouring state de-regulation and the celebration of local and individual initiative (Cox, 1986, p. 56). The military regime's interest in the notion of curricular flexibility was evident as early as 1974 but it was not until the early 1980s that substantial changes were enacted in the form of Decree 4002 (May 1980) regarding basic education and Decree 300 (December 1981) regarding secondary education. In formal terms, the principle of curricular flexibility was put forward as a means of improving the quality and relevance of education by reducing the amount of central determination of the curriculum and by opening up opportunities for adap- tation at school-level. Two main aspects of curricular flexibility may be identified: first, the adaptation of the curriculum to each region and school, and second, the adaptation of the curriculum to the capacities of the pupils in each class (Espinola, 1989, p. 48). We shall now consider briefly the main changes affecting the plans and programmes of study in basic and second- ary education, as designed by the Pinochet Government.

At the level of basic education, Decree 4002 introduced a form of flexi- bility into the plans of study by declaring that the number of hours per week to be devoted to different subjects could be varied by the head- teacher in the light of pedagogical needs and the resources of the school. [. . .]

At the secondary education level, Decree 300 determined there would be a common plan of study (32 hours per week) for the first cycle (grades 1 and 2) but in the second cycle (grades 3 and 4) an elective plan was introduced. This elective plan of 9 hours per week would contain subjects not available in the common plan; the latter would be pursued during the remaining 21 hours of the school week. Flexibility would take two major forms: first, the students' opportunity to choose subjects suited to their interests and, second, the school's opportunity to adapt its curricular offer- ings in accordance with its resources, regional location and parental/ community views (Magendzo, 1988, p. 40). [. . .]

Two further aspects of the Pinochet regime's approach to curriculum may be identified. First, there was the introduction, through Decree 2099 (March 1980), of the opportunity for schools to apply to the Ministry of Education for the approval of special plans and programmes of study. The Decree derived from Pinochet's Presidential Directives on national educa- tion which he issued in 1979; here, Pinochet seemed to privilege private schools as having an experimental character and a recognised role for the generation of curricular and pedagogical innovations, though this was not stipulated in Decree 2099 (Magendzo, 1988, p. 58). Second, the Pinochet

Government declared its formal commitment, in Decree 300 (December 1981), to a curriculum 'centred on the person', i.e. pupil-centred. All pedagogical and curricular activities were to revolve around the formative development of each pupil; in this regard, the character of the elective plan in the second cycle of secondary education may be explained, viz. the attempt to adapt schooling to the pupils' interests and needs.

Critical Reaction to Pinochet's Curriculum Changes

At the risk of simplifying a complex and unevenly unfolding process, the pattern of critical response to the Pinochet regime's educational reforms may be seen to divide into three main phases. The first two phases clearly correspond to the shifting priorities of educational policy during the 1973–1979 and post-1980 periods, while the final phase has elements of a summative and prospective character, shaped by considerations of the legacy of the Pinochet years *in toto* and the particular circumstances, possibilities and requirements of the forthcoming democratic transition. In suggesting this periodisation, we do not wish to deny the existence of certain continuities of criticism and opposition; rather, we wish to show that the preoccupations of the critics understandably shadowed the shifts in Pinochet's educational policies and, to that extent, their approach was largely reactive in nature. However, the prospect of a transfer of power and the acquisition of responsibility for the nation's educational system served to focus energies upon the need to devise an alternative educational vision appropriate to a post-Pinochet Chile. For those involved, the elaboration of this vision demanded a further reappraisal of Pinochet's educational legacy and an acceptance that some continuities might be not only necessary but also justifiable.

Criticism of Pinochet's educational policies focused initially upon their repressive and ideological features. The imprisonment, torture, disappearance and killing of teachers, lecturers and pupils, along with large-scale, politically motivated sackings and transfers and the intimidatory presence of military personnel within educational establishments, appalled many Chileans but open protest and resistance were acutely dangerous in the circumstances. The brutality of the regime's methods, the ideological 'cleansing' of certain curricular subjects, and the imposition of blatantly ideological precepts and values associated with military authoritarianism were seen to restrict drastically the 'space' available for a diversity of views within the curriculum. Together, they may be taken to represent a crude attempt to endow educational processes with an overtly indoctrinatory function.

However, while the ideological framing and underpinning of educational policy under Pinochet should always be kept in view, the pressure to impose a detailed and explicit ideologisation of the curriculum, especially in terms of indoctrinatory classroom practices, was not maintained at the same pitch or intensity. Cox (1987, p. 40) draws attention to the way Chilean teachers, most of whom were imbued with values and ideological orientations different from those of the military, had the capacity to interrupt the transmission of the regime's 'regulative discourse', thereby impeding or frustrating indoctrination in any simple sense.

[. . .]

With reference to the curriculum changes introduced in 1980–1981, it is clear that Pinochet's critics have not been persuaded that curricular flexibility was achieved or that centralised control of the curriculum was substantially reduced. Pinochet's policy was condemned as merely flexibility by decree, involving little or no consultation in advance with those who would have to implement the changes. Teachers were supposedly encouraged to be creative, adaptable and innovative but they were not granted the authority to make their own professional decisions. Their freedom was curtailed and hindered by the high level of political and ideological control to which they were subjected, especially by a municipalisation process which had not so much decentralised the educational system as brought the centre down to the locality: the *alcalde* (mayor) and his appointees (headmasters) were inhibiting, controlling presences for teachers, whose autonomy in the classroom and the school was further constrained by fewer legal rights and increased economic insecurity. In addition, the great majority of teachers lacked the appropriate training (pre-service or in-service) which would have prepared them for a more active, innovative approach towards the curriculum.

[. . .]

Further criticism of Pinochet's curriculum reforms focused upon the sheer incompetence of those who drafted the new regulations. According to one of Chile's leading curriculum experts, the reforms introduced in the early 1980s brought 'permanent changes in a scheme of conceptual instability' (Magendzo, 1988, p. 9). There was a distinct impression that the curricular changes had simply not been thought through. As a result, they were subjected to serious professional criticisms and were later amended or supplemented (though not always with any noticeable improvement). [. . .]

The greatest contradiction, however, was that between educational decentralisation and curricular flexibility, on the one hand, and the authoritarian, undemocratic and anti-participatory context affecting the educational system and the country as a whole. Under Pinochet, the curriculum remained centralised, hierarchical, narrow and ill-adapted to the needs and circumstances of pupils' lives. Ultimately, however, criticisms of Pinochet's educational record in general and his curriculum reforms in particular coalesced around a recognition that educational quality was not only not improving but it was also barely being addressed. This, coupled with a greater sensitivity to the disparities affecting children's learning in Chile's schools, formed the point of departure for the new educational thinking associated with the anti-Pinochet forces which gained power in March 1990.

Towards a New Synthesis

One of the common trends among OECD countries identified in Skilbeck's survey is the following:

> the treatment of school curriculum in strategic terms by governments seeking to restructure or firmly steer their economies. This reflects both public concern with the outcome of schooling and a rekindled interest in human capital theory. (Skilbeck, 1990, p. 76)

Skilbeck, however, sounds a strong note of caution against the temptation to subordinate 'long-term concerns for access, opportunity, equity and fairness in education' (1990, p. 79) to short-term economic exigencies. With regard to curriculum and pedagogy, he calls for a 'new synthesis' which directly and simultaneously engages with the challenge of economic restructuring, the ongoing scientific-technological revolution, and 'the universalist principle embedded in the claim that every person has educational rights and freedoms' (Skilbeck, 1990, p. 79). Distinct echoes of Skilbeck's terms of analysis and his championing of a new synthesis are discernible in Chile's new approach to curriculum. At the beginning of an Aylwin Government policy document concerning the *Programa MECE* (Programa de Mejoramiento de la Calidad y Equidad de la Educación), a section dealing with the policy context of the programme places the Government's commitment to education in the following framework: the needs of personal growth and the requirements of moral and cognitive integration; the affirmation of democracy; and the country's economic growth and competitiveness within a global market in which the addition of intellectual value to export goods and services is of strategic importance (Chile, Ministerio de Educación, 1991a, p. 6). [. . .]

Several points may be noted concerning these matters. It is clear, for example. that the essential features of the economic model or strategy inherited from the Pinochet regime were not abandoned. [. . .] According to Cox (1991), the economic growth undoubtedly inaugurated under Pinochet could not be sustained by his economic policies, for at least two main reasons. First, economic policy during the Pinochet years was pursued without regard to its differential social impact; as a result of the marginalisation of the question of social justice, trouble was being stored up which sooner or later would disrupt economic growth and perhaps threaten the economic system itself. Second, Pinochet's economic strategy was not supported by effective mechanisms for invigorating Chile's productive capacity with the stimuli of scientific-technological advance and innovation. In particular, the modest quality of Chilean education and the perceived irrelevance of the curriculum to the economic tasks facing the country were unreliable foundations for continued economic growth. In a nutshell, Pinochet's economic policies were doomed because they were not linked to appropriate social and educational policies. This judgement, in conjunction with the widespread desire for a return to acceptable norms of democratic citizenship and political participation, proved to be persuasive not only to broad sections of the Chilean electorate but also to a national and international business community anxious to see Chile's economic success story continue.

It is against this background that we must consider the Aylwin Government's search for a 'new synthesis' which would embrace the kind of broad themes identified by Skilbeck and the specificities of the Chilean situation. Included in the latter are the legal and constitutional constraints under which the new civilian government was required to operate (Aedo-Richmond *et al.*, 1990). [. . .]

However, it would be wrong to dismiss the Aylwin Government as being simply reactive or as responding passively to a highly restrictive agenda set by Pinochet and the circumstances facing Chile in the early 1990s. Such an interpretation would fail to accord appropriate recognition to the realignment of educational thinking which occurred among certain anti-Pinochet forces during the 1980s. In the historical context of Chilean educational development, this new educational thinking can be seen to be creative, adaptive and critical. It emerged and developed, moreover, within a distinctive institutional and intellectual environment which rested not on the traditional universities but on independent research institutes, non-governmental organisations, and international networks of academic exchange and support (Richmond, 1992, p.6; Hojman, 1993). [. . .]

Educational Priorities under the Aylwin Government

After March 1990, there was no dramatic intervention to transform the plans and programmes of study in Chilean schools in a comprehensive manner, and yet the curriculum-related changes which were introduced represent a genuinely significant departure from past practices and established traditions. Eschewing 'reform' in favour of 'improvement', the Aylwin Government's educational policies were constructed around deliberately chosen or at any rate accepted continuities, selective amendments and partial alterations, plus specific innovations. Moreover, the pace, direction and extent of change varied from one part of the educational system to another. In our judgement, primary education was the chief beneficiary of the Aylwin Government's educational efforts and it is upon this sector that our analysis will concentrate. This is not intended to deny or downplay the significance of policy developments affecting other levels and types of education; rather, we hope that by examining primary education in particular, in which the new educational orientations were more fully elaborated and implemented, changes elsewhere in the educational system will become more readily understood. Those orientations were summarised in 1991 by the then Minister of Education Ricardo Lagos when he stated that the principal aims of the Aylwin Government's educational policy were 'to improve the quality of education, to achieve equity in its distribution and to improve the participation of the various social actors in the educational task' (Chile, Ministerio de Educación, 1991b, p. 1). We shall now consider three important educational developments introduced in the first years of the Aylwin Government which illustrate how these principles were put into practice.

The '900 Schools Programme'

Arising from a diagnosis of the serious weaknesses and problems affecting many primary schools in the most poor urban and rural areas (see, for example, Garcia-Huidobro & Zúñiga, 1990), this programme was regarded as an urgent priority of the new Government and also as a potentially useful learning experience for those who might design other, perhaps larger, schemes of educational help. Drawing upon the evidence of national tests, around 10% of the worst-performing primary schools in Chile were identified and targeted for special assistance. The main objective was to improve the quality of learning of children in the first four grades in regard to the basic skills of reading, writing and mathematics. In the 969 schools initially targeted, both quality and equity were addressed in practical ways, with a clear focus upon actual learning rather than upon, say, attendance rates. Through regular in-service training workshops, efforts were made to improve the teachers' capacity to develop the children's learning, in conjunction with the help of 'community monitors', typically local young people who offered extra assistance and personal attention to third and fourth grade pupils through after-school workshops. Vital elements of the 900 Schools Programme were the improvements to the physical infrastructure of the schools; the provision of specially designed educational materials for mathematics, reading and writing; increased educational resources (school books, classroom libraries, teaching materials); and additional resources to address the pupils' problems concerning health and nutrition.
[. . .]

The Estatuto Docente *(Teaching Statute)*

Properly called the *Estatuto de los Profesionales de Ia Educación* (Statute of Professionals in Education), this piece of legislation was published on 1 July 1991 with a view to addressing some of the main grievances of teachers (for example, pay) while at the same time drawing them towards a fuller professionalisation of their role than had existed under Pinochet and even during the pre-Pinochet years. For the first time, teachers in the public and private sectors of schooling were covered by the same legislation, though recognition was given to the different conditions of each sector. Teachers in municipal schools were accepted as being members of the broad field of public service and they recovered many of the norms and entitlements attaching to that status. Particularly important in this respect were the guarantees of greater job security and less arbitrariness of treatment by employers, the provision for open and fair competition for teaching posts, and the promise of a professional career ladder with rewards for experience, further training, and posts involving difficult working conditions. In keeping with the Aylwin Government's commitment to the idea of pedagogical decentralisation and some form of school-based curriculum development, Article 16 of the Statute itemised the main areas of professional autonomy and responsibility in which teachers in Chile will operate. It is clear from this piece of legislation that teachers are expected to embrace a more developed notion of professionalism, one which is geared towards a more active and creative role, but one bearing clearer responsibility for the effectiveness of pupil learning. [. . .]

The MECE Programme

The *Programa de Mejoramiento de la Calidad y Equidad de la Educación* (Programme of Improvement of the Quality and Equity of Education) was the most important and ambitious feature of the Aylwin Government's educational policy. Scheduled to run over six academic years (1992–1997) and costing US$243 million (two-thirds of which derives from a World Bank loan), the MECE Programme at once embraced and further developed many of the themes inaugurated under the 900 Schools Programme. The four objectives of the MECE Programme were:

1. To improve in substantive terms the quality of learning in basic education and the equity of the distribution of that learning;
2. To widen the coverage and improve the quality of pre-school education;
3. To improve and strengthen the organisational capacity of the Ministry of Education;
4. To evaluate alternative institutional and curricular reforms in secondary education with a view to improving its relevance, quality and equity.

By far the most important of these objectives was the first, as was reflected in the fact that basic education was scheduled to attract over 70% of the Programme's total funding (Chile, Ministerio de Educación, 1991a, p. 19). The quest for greater quality was focused upon the systematic improvement in the learning of basic cultural competences by the country's children. These competences relate to the mother language and mathematics, along with learning how to learn. Two major lines of action for tackling the question of improved quality were identified. The first involved substantive improvements to the material context which impacts directly upon the effectiveness of learning: books, guides and teaching materials; classroom libraries; school infrastructure; increased health care; and in-service teacher training. The second line of action related to innovations in pedagogical practice: pedagogical decentralisation; rural education; a pilot project regarding an inter-school network in educational computing; and a diagnostic study of the use of computers in basic education. Meanwhile, the quest for greater equity focused upon the progressive improvement in the social distribution of learning, as oriented by the principle of equality of opportunity and by positive discrimination directed towards those groups at greatest educational risk. The lines of action for securing greater equity included the 'focalization' or channelling of extra resources towards the worst performing schools and towards rural schools.

As well as quality and equity, the MECE Programme rested upon four other basic orientations (participation, decentralisation, efficacy and open design), all of which found expression in the proposals for basic education. The concept of 'open design', for example, was judged appropriate to an educational strategy based on continuous improvement rather than reform. Improvement of the quality of learning was expected to flow out of school-level initiatives rather than from a rigid adherence to a centrally designed methodological or curricular recipe imposed from above. In support of this orientation were the plans for in-service training of teachers so that they could strengthen their command of the substantive areas of the curriculum which were to be improved: language, mathematics, social sciences and natural sciences. In-service training was also considered vital for achieving pedagogical decentralisation. This idea, which best expressed the spirit of the new educational thinking embodied in the MECE Programme, was designed to be fulfilled by means of three kinds of initiatives which would raise the level of pupil learning through an activation of teachers' capacities for innovation and pedagogical autonomy [. . .].

In order to illustrate the change of orientation represented by the MECE Programme, it may be useful to focus on its plans for rural education. Traditionally, the specific needs of rural schooling in terms of teaching–learning strategies and curriculum had been either overlooked or deliberately denied. The official commitment to a uniform national curriculum for all Chilean school-children had meant that adaptations to the rural environment were construed as offering a second-class, deficient education or one which would restrict equality of opportunity by tying the educational experience too tightly to a narrow rural context. By way of contrast and criticism, the thinking behind the MECE Programme regarded these traditional justifications of an unadapted curriculum as a recipe for neglect and irrelevance, weaknesses much more damaging to the educational experience of rural pupils than a departure from national uniformity would be. Thus, for the first time in Chilean education, the Ministry of Education was authorised to design and distribute school textbooks (for Grades 1–6) especially tailored for the rural context. The MECE Programme included provision for in-service training of rural teachers in regard to the new curriculum contents and the different teaching methods and learning strategies to be utilised; in relation to the latter, a *Manual of Curriculum Development* was envisaged for use in rural schools with just one, two or three teachers. Moreover, five schools were to be selected to operate as demonstration centres for sharing ideas and new experiences in terms of curriculum, teaching methods, school organisation, use of textbooks and the application of innovations in rural schooling so that learning could be enhanced. Finally, measures to improve the infrastructure of rural schools were to be financed through the MECE Programme; it was projected that 500 classrooms would be built and equipped especially to give 'incomplete' rural schools the opportunity to offer the full 8 years of basic education (Chile, Ministerio de Educación, 1991a, pp. 26–27).

While rural schooling clearly was scheduled to receive special and targeted attention, the general orientation of the MECE Programme was applied throughout Chilean primary schooling. As far as the curriculum was concerned, this meant that rigid, uniform and nation-wide changes to curriculum contents were not introduced; instead, efforts were being directed towards modifying and improving, indeed generating, the school-based capacity for curriculum development through practical measures of support and the stimulation of pedagogical decentralisation. [. . .]

The Projects of Educative Improvement (PMEs) have represented an exciting and promising innovation in the Chilean context, furnishing a point of intersection between many tendencies and orientations evident in the new educational thinking: the preference for incentives rather than compulsion; decentralisation in pedagogical, not merely administrative terms; the encouragement of teachers to exercise autonomy and creativity as essential aspects of their professionalism; recognition of and adaptation to local circumstances; the provision of material measures of support and technical–pedagogical guidance; and the involvement of the school community and local social actors. [. . .]

Concluding Remarks

As the foregoing outline of the Aylwin Government's policies and initiatives regarding primary schooling hopefully shows, there is much of interest in the new direction being pursued in Chilean education. The possibilities for successfully pursuing this new direction were always highly dependent on two key factors: the reaction and responsiveness of teachers, on the one hand, and the sustainability of consensus, on the other. It was by no means certain, for example, that teachers would respond positively and enthusiastically, or that they would understand what the Government's plans would mean for them in practice. On this latter point it should be noted that teachers in Chile have had no tradition or experience of school-based curriculum innovation to draw upon. Their initial training and subsequent teaching careers hardly prepared them for exercising choice, initiative or autonomy in relation to the curriculum. Certain attitudes and preconceptions, especially those pertaining to Chile's statist and centralist past, could be assumed to be deep-rooted. In addition, the demoralisation of the teaching force as a consequence of its treatment under Pinochet was a difficult inheritance to overcome. However, most Chilean teachers appear to have responded positively to the Aylwin Government's educational policies, despite some initial doubts and suspicions. Some credit for this must go to the consultative approach adopted, and especially to the *Estatuto Docente* which, in conjunction with the incentives offered by the MECE Programme and the provision of in-service training and guidance, helped assuage teachers' fears.

The pursuit of consensus was a new departure for Chile, where educational policy traditionally has been 'governmental' or 'party-political' rather than 'national' in character. It was by no means certain that the consensus present at the beginning of Aylwin's term of office would be able to withstand the push and pull of democratic politics or, for that matter, intra-governmental and intra-departmental conflicts. However, the forces within the coalition government did hold together, as did the consensus on educational policy. The continuity represented by the Frei administration which succeeded that of Aylwin in 1994 bears witness to this. The Aylwin Government's conspicuous efforts to consult widely and publicly, to actively cultivate consensus and to promote the idea of education as a national priority, transcending political and ideological differences, were vital for this achievement.

On balance, the changes brought into Chilean basic education since March 1990 have been innovative, sensitively handled and well-adapted to the delicate conditions of the transition period and involved no small amount of ingenuity. The curriculum remains one which has been centrally defined, of course, but there are now genuine opportunities for school-level, teacher-led adaptation and innovation to take place. The post-Pinochet educational changes have not invented flexibility or legitimised teacher initiative so much as produced the framework of material support, guidance and official encouragement to enable greater curricular and pedagogical freedom to be exercised.

Editor's Note

The authors wish to make it clear that this article represents a personal view and not necessarily that of UNESCO.

References

Aedo-Richmond, R. (1978) The teaching of social science in Chilean schools. Unpublished, diploma dissertation, University of Hull.
Aedo-Richmond, R., Noguera, I. & Richmond, M. (1985) Changes in the Chilean educational system during eleven years of military government, 1973–1984, in: C. Brock & H. Lawlor (Eds) *Education in Latin America*, London, Croom Helm.

Aedo-Richmond, R., Noguera, I. & Richmond, M. (1990) Education, law and democratic transition in Chile. Paper presented to the Annual Conference of the British Comparative and International Education Society, Wolfson College, University of Cambridge, 14–16 September.

Casassus, J. (1988) The state and education in Latin America, *Bulletin of the Major Project in tile Field of Education in Latin America and the Caribbean*, No. 17, December, pp. 32–41.

Chile, Ministerio de Educación (1991a) *Programa de Mejoramiento de la Calidad y Equidad de la Educación 1992–97. Orientaciones Básicas. Objectivos y Componentes*, Santiago, MINEDUC, July.

Chile, Ministerio de Educación (1991b) *Programa de Mejoramiento de la Calidad en Escuelas Básicas de Sectores Pobres*, Santiago, MINEDUC.

Chile, Ministerio de Educación (1994) *Proyectos de Mejoramiento Educativo en el Desarrollo de Ia Educación Básicas Chilena. Programa MECE/Básica*, Santiago, MINEDUC.

Cox, C. (1986) *Políticas Educacionales y Principios Culturales. Chile 1965–1985*, Santiago, CIDE.

Cox, C. (1987) *Education under Military Rule in Chile: Authoritarian and Laissez Faire Strategies of Cultural Control*, Santiago, CIDE.

Cox, C. (1990) The structuring of schooling in different political contexts: the case of Chile, in: N. Entwistle (Ed.) *Handbook of Educational Ideas and Practices*, London, Routledge.

Cox, C. (1991) *Sociedad y Conocimiento en los 90': puntos para una agenda sobre curriculum del sistema escolar*, Santiago. FLACSO.

Espinola, V. (1989) Los resultados del modelo económico de la enseñanza basica, in: J. E. Garcia-Huidobro (Ed.) *Escuela, Calidad e Igualdad*, Santiago, CIDE.

Espinola, V. (1991) Decentralización de la gestión pedagógica: una cuestion pendiente, *Cuadernos de Educación*, No. 205, Año XXI, Julio, pp. 148–53.

Farrell, J. P. (1986) *The National Unified School in Allende's Chile*, Vancouver, University of British Columbia Press.

Garcia-Huidobro, J. E. (1990) Educación y Democracia. in: *PIIE Las Reformas Educativas en las Transiciones Democraticas*, Santiago, PIIE.

Garcia-Huidobro. J.E. & Zúñiga, L. (1990) *Qué pueden esperar los pobres de la educación?*, Santiago, CIDE.

Guttman, C. (1993) *All Children Can Learn. Chile's 900 Schools Programme for the Underprivileged*, Paris, UNESCO.

Gysling, J. (1991) Descentralización del curriculum, *Cuadernos de Educación*, No. 205, Año XXI, Julio, pp. ii–iii.

Hojman, D.E. (1993) Non-governmental organisations (NGOs) and the Chilean transition to democracy, *European Review of Latin American and Caribbean Studies*, No. 54, June, pp. 7–24.

Latorre, C. L., Núñez, I., Gonzalez, L. E. & Hevia, R. (1991) *La Municipalización de la Educación: una mirada desde los administradores del sistema*, Santiago. PIIE.

McGinn, N. & Street, S. (1986) Educational decentralization: weak state or strong state? *Comparative Education Review*, Vol. 30, pp. 471–90.

Magendzo, A. (1988) *Desarrollo de las Normativas Curriculares Bajo el Régimen Militar (1973–1987): un análisis crítico*, Santiago, PIIE.

Núñez, I. (1987) *La Gobernabilidad Democrática del Sector Educación: relación entre investigación y política*, Santiago, PIIE.

Núñez, I. (1991) Política educacional: realizaciones y futuro, *Revista de Educación*, No. 194, Marzo, pp. 10–15.

Richmond, M. (1992) Democratic transition and educational change in Chile: the Programa MECE. Paper presented to the Regional BCIES Conference 'Education in Latin America', University of Humberside, Hull, 30 May.

Skilbeck, M. (1990) *Curriculum Reform. An Overview of Trends*, Paris, OECD.

12

Curriculum Development and New Information Technology

Robert McCormick

[. . .]

Curriculum Change and National Systems

It is not my intention here to try and give a comprehensive overview of curriculum change across national systems, but rather to draw out some aspects of curriculum change that relate to the new information technologies. In this section I will merely catalogue the important aspects of curriculum change, in a later section I will make the links with the new information technologies. These aspects are: the use of education to improve the economy; the resulting government initiatives; the influences on curriculum change; the place of the teacher and the school in central initiatives; and teacher development. In the final sub-section I will then draw a few lessons from this account.

The economic imperative

The first aspect is the widespread emphasis on education for economic development, reflecting an embracing of human capital theory more common in developing than developed countries. This leads to policies emphasising education for working life, and a concern to make sure young people can function in an industrial world dominated by modern technological developments. Along with this is a concern for methods of learning appropriate to this new world, emphasising problem solving and the application of knowledge, flexibility, creativity, and an ability to continue learning after schooling. However, there are a number of policies that contradict this concern for the methods of learning: a curriculum that is increasingly subject centred, accompanied by a 'back to the basics' movement and an increase in assessment and testing at a national level.

This chapter has been edited.

Central initiatives

The increased emphasis on the effect of education on the economy has been related to cuts in education and calls for efficiency and value for money. Simultaneously to these cuts and calls for efficiency governments have increased their interventions and initiation of curriculum change, in part to try to ensure that education is more responsive to the needs of the economy. Indeed there is an internationalisation of change with similar initiatives being carried out in various national systems. This is reinforced by the activities of international organisations such as OECD and UNESCO (Moon, 1986, p. 232). The initiatives can have similar characteristics across national systems, whether curriculum control is centralised or decentralised. Skilbeck (1990, p. 25) and Moon (1986, p. 201) both conclude that whether a system is centralised or decentralised is not the crucial element in determining or explaining change. This is in part because systems are not simply centralised or decentralised in decision making but are made up of shared roles and responsibilities within an educational system with a mixture of types of agencies involved. It is also in part because some movements such as 'educational accountability' are found in both types, irrespective of the form of control actually exercised. Finally the school is remarkably similar across all systems and the reality of school life is such that the formal system can be by-passed.

Influences on curriculum change

There are a number of influences that are important in change in various types of systems, irrespective of the location of decision making. These influences are interest groups, commercial curriculum resource providers (e.g. textbook publishers) and international organisations, and I will deal with each of these in turn. National agencies also constitute one kind of interest group; however, these tend to be very peculiar to specific changes, and I will deal with these specifically in the context of the new information technologies.

Within particular national education systems it is evident that interest groups, often based on various school subject traditions, have a strong influence on the course of events, as Moon (1986) has shown in his study of 'new mathematics' across a number of European countries. Indeed there is a tradition of research on curriculum history focusing upon school subjects that shows the effect of such interest groups acting within various countries. This research has led to hypotheses about the development of subjects: that they are not monolithic entities but a shifting amalgamation of sub-groups and traditions; in the process of establishing a school subject it moves from promoting pedagogic and utilitarian traditions to an academic one; curriculum debate can be seen as a conflict between subject groups over status, resources and territory (Moon, 1986, p. 29). Moon (1986, p. 232) adds an international dimension to such developments and concludes that because of the role of UNESCO and OECD in providing important fora for advocates of reform it is difficult to see curriculum change in mathematics in nationalist terms alone. Part of the internationalisation was the role of textbook publishers, and Moon (1986, pp. 220–1) shows what a significant role they played within and across national boundaries. Their publishing policy, which did not always follow national policy, had a reforming role and responded to the changing fortunes of the various groups who were active in the reforms. However, he notes the difficulty in collecting evidence in this secretive area of commercial operation. Moon's conclusion on the interaction of the various interest groups, particularly the professionalised ones related to subject areas related to mathematics, is that:

> curriculum change is a long-term, interpersonal process, based upon the establishment of subject paradigms via networks of communication and apprenticeship (Moon, 1986, p. 223).

Teachers and central initiatives

All types of education systems recognise the central role of teachers and of supporting them to ensure change in the classroom. It is recognised by those involved in comprehensive initiatives that they should involve teacher training if they are to have a universal impact, whether the system be centralised or decentralised (Skilbeck, 1990, p. 71). But that does not mean, however, that the resources are made available to adequately fund this training and support; indeed often such funds are cut at the very time that curriculum change is at its peak.

The international tendency towards central initiatives dominating curriculum change leads to national policies on the curriculum, whether in general (i.e. the whole or core curriculum) or in particular areas (e.g. social studies and information technology). The policies rely upon documentation and legislation to define the curriculum, but teachers often do not read them (Skilbeck, 1990, p. 26), or circumvent them in the privacy of their own classrooms (Beattie, 1990). Skilbeck (1990, p. 71) details the requirements for project-based curriculum development (e.g. one that comes from a central initiative):

- adequate staffing at the centre and the periphery to support the project;
- teacher expertise in the schools to be linked through some kind of network;
- adequate provision for staff development and project evaluation;
- real potential for adoption of the change by schools in the mainstream and not just in specially endowed schools.

Although there are some important general lessons of this type that can be learnt, there remain some uncertainties: what should be the balance of central guidelines and local development, or central materials and locally produced ones? Nevertheless as I will show below, wherever the initiatives come from, teacher development is necessary, even if that is unpalatable at a time of restraints in educational spending. This remains no less true when these restraints are accompanied by increased accountability and concern for value for money.

The place of the school

The problem of change at the level of schools (not just classrooms) needs to be addressed. This is not to argue that only change that emanates from the school is good, but that change that does not address the issues faced by a school will fail to have any profound impact. As Skilbeck (1990, p. 57) put it:

> It is difficult to avoid the conclusion that there is a real risk, if such approaches are not complemented by equal attention to the processes of change within the schools themselves, of a widening gap between policy directions and the classroom reality.

Sadly there is little published research on what happens in schools as a result of curriculum change. There are few parallels of the curriculum histories represented in the work of Goodson (1983) and Moon (1986) at the level of the school to indicate whether the interactions of interest groups etc., are replicated at this level. However, Weston (1979) carried out an important and detailed case study of a secondary school partly focusing upon the fortunes of an innovatory science curriculum based upon a curriculum project initiated nationally. She developed the idea of the negotiation of the curriculum, a process 'through which any curriculum comes into being, emphasising that this negotiation is not a regrettable concession to the "real" world but an integral part of the business of teaching and learning' (Weston, 1979, p. 265). Three conditions of success for the negotiation are necessary: common interest among the parties strong enough to override or at least to set against their differing and conflicting priorities; a social system with its own rules and norms within which negotiation can take place; each party to the negotiation must have power to back its demands. The negotiation takes place at two levels: in the interaction among teachers; in the interaction among teachers and pupils. This identifies the importance of both the school and the classroom level. She shows how it is possible for a planning team of heads of subject departments to subordinate whole curriculum considerations to their subject concerns in allocating scarce resources such as time and space (p. 266). But the negotiation has informal aspects, that individual teachers encounter in their day-to-day dealings with each other, where they develop common understandings about a curriculum innovation in the *specific context of their school* (pp. 267–8). However, these informal aspects need to be complemented by formal reflections of teachers as a group in which they can learn about new approaches to learning (p. 270). Without this she says, ·tellingly, 'it is not surprising if innovatory programmes . . . tend to be recast into more familiar classroom patterns' (Weston, 1979, p. 270).

I have dwelt on this particular study because it provides the school-level parallel with the ideas on the role of subjects in curriculum development from the work of Goodson (1983) and Moon (1986). But also because it focuses upon some of the mechanisms within the school that central initiatives must address. It justifies the concern for teacher development showing that teachers must reflect on practice, but also shows that school structures, formal and informal, are crucial to the fortunes of curriculum change. The situation in primary schools will be different, but there is evidence that informal interactions are an important aspect of curriculum development (Nias, 1989; Pollard, 1985; Richards, 1988).

Professional development

An alternative approach is to insist that the school or teacher is the source of innovation and change, a view that became popular in the period of the 1970s when faith in central curriculum projects was on the decline. This led to ideas of the 'teacher-as-researcher' (Stenhouse, 1975), the 'creative school' (CERI, 1978) and 'school-based curriculum development' (Skilbeck, 1976).

Although these approaches have continued to have their advocates, the central policy initiatives sketched out above have tended to dominate the debate. Indeed Skilbeck himself notes the waning of school-based curriculum development in his OECD review (Skilbeck, 1990, pp. 72–4). But this school-based tradition and that of in-service training have put the same focus upon professional development implied by Weston (1979), one that Skilbeck's review neglects. This focus sees professional development as an essential element in curriculum change, wherever the initiative comes from. This is evident in Skilbeck's plea not to just assume that providing documents and information will by itself change teacher behaviour. In the jargon of change a normative-re-educative strategy is required to enable teachers to change their attitudes, beliefs, values, knowledge, skills, roles and relationships so that curriculum change can take place. This contrasts with the empirical-rationalist strategy that assumes that teachers will change if shown, through research, that a particular practice or idea is effective, or a strategy that simply coerces them by legal authority. There are points of dispute in these ideas, for example the relative importance of individual professional development and institutional development, but it seems likely that the two are intimately linked (McCormick & James, 1988, p. 43).

Lessons to learn

There are many lessons to be learnt by all those involved in curriculum change, be they teachers, administrators at various levels in education, educationalists who are involved in (or study) curriculum change, or government policy makers. First and foremost we all have to recognise the complexity of curriculum change, and our failure to either understand or successfully implement it. Teachers and educationalists cannot ignore or simply reject central initiatives, even those that stem from the economic imperative and hence conflict with their own beliefs and ideologies. Neither can policy makers and administrators think that all they have to do is spell out the requirements of a curriculum innovation and that change will then take place in schools. More important they should not see teachers as an obstacle to change. In many cases teachers enthusiastically embrace considerable change and go to great efforts to implement it, often at great personal cost to their family life and indeed health. Teacher training cannot be seen as a one-off 'quick shot' of information about new curricula. Rather it must be seen as part of teacher development, where teachers can learn and debate the ideas and concepts underlying the change, and to find their resolution of such conflicts as meeting the needs of the economy and at the same time utilising modern teaching and learning methods. This also means addressing not just individual teachers and their classrooms, but the school as a whole.

The Case of Technology Education

This area of the curriculum is now being established in many countries in the world, although its focus varies. In some countries, for example the USA, it is seen as an effort to educate young people in the range of technologies that confront them in everyday life, either as citizens or as workers. In others, such as the UK, it is seen as an opportunity to involve children in the practical problem solving that is part of technological activity, in particular designing and making. Despite the differences in approach both in content and the way change is carried out, there is a growing international consensus and communication among those involved in technology education.

The motivations for developing this area of the curriculum are fourfold:

1. that it will improve the economy by producing young people able to work in modern industry and commerce (the economic imperative);
2. that it involves activities that accord with progressivist or constructivist views of learning (its value to learning);
3. that it has some intrinsic value through its unique concepts and processes that are essential to the development of all individuals, in the same way as the study of mathematics, science, history, humanities, etc. (its intrinsic value);
4. a modern citizen has to have an understanding of technology to be able to function, and to be collectively in control of the development of society that is increasingly driven by technology (education for citizenship).

This area of the curriculum has not just appeared on the scene with the advent of electronics, computers or biotechnology, but has a history going back to the nineteenth century. Various interest groups in education have contributed to this development including craft teachers, design and art educators, science teachers, science–technology–society teachers, and those with a concern for industry and work. Each of these groups has brought to the development different views of the nature of technology education, different reasons for teaching it, and different pedagogic traditions. In recent years a number of governments and professional organisations have made proposals, and indeed legislation, for the inclusion of technology education in the curriculum of all children. What actually happens in schools does not, however, necessarily match the proposals no matter how detailed these proposals are. Thus we have:

- a conflict between those who see 'design' as a central feature and focus upon processes rather than, say, scientific knowledge;
- craft teachers who feel that skills in working wood or metal are important and yet can see no place for their approach in new curriculum proposals;
- home economics teachers who are unclear where their focus on the home and food fits in to technology, and who in any case may feel less than qualified to deal with food technology;
- primary school teachers who see in technology education, not a subject but a process that helps to provide a focus for active learning which children clearly enjoy.

The list of such conflicts and views could be enumerated for many groups of teachers who find themselves faced with what they see as either the opportunity or obligation to teach technology. The different views contribute to different definitions of technology education and different approaches to teaching it. How each school deals with technology education depends on a number of factors such as the skills and background of the teachers, the particular curricular organisation of the school, personality and power conflicts within the school, and the facilities and where they are situated. At a national level policies of resource provision and teacher training are necessary to ensure that curriculum change can take place. But it has to be remembered that if, for example, there are a variety of differing views of technology education at national level, there will be a similar range at school level. The senior management of a school have to appreciate these views if they are to make sensible decisions about the curriculum and the personnel associated with technology education. These views will be embedded within departmental and curriculum structures, and the associated distribution of resources, and change will only take place when all these have been attended to at the school level. The conditions for change at a national and school level are the same whether or not the change to teaching technology education is implemented through centralised or local decision making as teachers in both the USA and the UK can attest.

All of the features of the case for technology education are in line with that outlined earlier for curriculum change in general, and I have given some details of this case for two reasons. Firstly, there is considerable overlap between curriculum developments in technology education and the new information technologies. To illustrate this take the cases of both the USA and the UK. A prestigious project in the USA, Project 2061, included electronics and computer technology in describing the technologies that were part of technology education (Johnson, 1989), both of which have featured in programmes for the development of new information technologies. In the UK a new 'subject' was created within the national curriculum that included capability in 'design and technology' and 'information technology' (DES, 1990), a clear case of overlap. Secondly, it is an example of a recent innovation in the school curriculum that could both create a new subject and affect existing subjects. The parallels, that should already be evident from my brief description of developments, are instructive for the introduction of the new information technologies into schools, albeit that technology education has a slightly longer pre-history. These parallels remind us that despite the special features of the new information technologies there are similarities related to change that are common and that should inhibit us from always trying to 're-invent the wheel', or from failing to learn from experience.

An Overview of Development Strategies in the New Information Technologies

Introduction

My intention here is to survey the findings of others who have examined the developments in new information technologies in a number of countries, as a context for a consideration, in the next section, of how they relate to the views on change outlined in the first section. What is striking is the remarkable convergence of the general approach to the new information technologies that has been adopted by countries, although they may be at different stages in their development of policy and its implementation. I take a wide view of what is included in new information technologies, although focus on those based on the computer. Similarly with the educational uses I include learning about the computer (including its social implications) and information technology, using general-purpose software tools such as spreadsheet and wordprocessing, and computer-assisted learning from drill and practice, to problem-solving simulations and individualised learning.

Motivation and overall strategy

This similarity is evident both in the motivation for change and the way that change has been encouraged. Governments have seen the need for encouraging the use of the new information technologies as a way of ensuring that information technology is exploited in the economy, and for preparing young people for a world that will be permeated with this technology. Because it has been in the interests of the economy, and because of the special needs of this kind of development (e.g. for computer hardware), governments have taken the initiative. This has usually involved using a central agency which overlooks and co-ordinates the whole process: for example, in the UK initially the Microelectronics Programme and latterly the National Council for Educational Technology, and in France the Agence pour le Développement de l'Informatique. These two examples from the UK and France illustrate the fact that this kind of strategy is independent of the degree of centralisation of the education system. The role of such central initiatives extends to several areas: the supply of hardware; the development and supply of software; the development of the curriculum; the training of teachers.

There have been differences of emphasis with some initiatives taking a more vocational thrust and putting resources into computer science in preparation for employment (e.g. taking the computer as the subject of study). Others have a comprehensive policy that adds to the vocational thrust more general concerns for promoting computer literacy and improving teaching and learning generally by using the new information technologies. However, countries appear to be moving towards the comprehensive policy (Duguet, 1990, p. 167). As I will indicate later these differences have important curriculum implications, that are not simply avoided by having a comprehensive policy. Some governments will see the importance of new ways of learning as part of their desire to prepare young people for a future where handling information using the new technologies will be a central activity. This has rarely given rise to a desire to reduce the role of the teacher, although there are examples of governments wanting to see gains in efficiency. Differences of approach also occur over whether all, or only pilot, schools are included in the national programme. Although this is discussed in terms of cost and the possibility of reaching a critical mass to test effectiveness (CERI, 1986, p. 105; Duguet, 1990, p. 167), nothing is said about how development occurs subsequent to a central initiative. For example, how are the lessons of the pilot schools put into practice in all schools without incurring the high costs similar to those in the pilots?

International agencies have rarely been part of a national strategy, but have been important in supporting and in sharing information. The Nordic Committee on Educational Software and Technology, established in 1985, is unique, drawing together Denmark, Finland, Iceland, Norway and Sweden in a permanent organisation to share information and to develop software. The OECD through the Centre for Educational Research and Innovation (CERI) has carried out investigations and held conferences to share information across member countries, though has not taken any specific initiatives in development work. The European Community through its 'Forecasting and Assessment in Science and Technology' programme and 'Development of European Learning through Technological Advance' project carries out similar but more developmental tasks to the OECD (Aston & Templeton, 1988).

[. . .]

Impact of the new information technologies

This impact can only be described as disappointing. Despite the dispensing of large sums of money through programmes the impact on education systems as a whole has been limited. What success stories there were have stopped, and yet much remains to be done (Gwyn, 1988a, p. 299). The major failure seems to be with the impact on teaching and learning, and the efficiency savings that were hoped for by some have yet to be conclusively demonstrated in most areas (Congress of the USA, 1988, p. 81; POST, 1991, p. 43). The fact is that, although there have been school-subject related developments, there is little evidence of changes in schools that might reflect shifts in teaching and learning styles; certainly none of the dramatic changes in the organisation of learning, for example, that are based upon an individualised curriculum. Thus as noted earlier 'computer studies' and 'information technology' as subjects have been established and the use of applications within existing subjects has increased. Some argue that primary schools show more success because they do not have the confines of subject barriers (Boyd-Barrett, 1990, p. 181). Even here the impact on teaching and learning has often been in the form of drill and practice programs.

The general barriers to change are seen to be both the 'system', by which is meant the organisation of the school, and teachers. Nothing specific is identified as at the root of the 'system' problems, except that the classroom remains unchanged, that is, teacher dominated. It is argued that the amount of hardware available may need to be massively increased to bring courseware onto the market (CERI, 1986, p. 86), but no particular connection is made between this and the ability of a school to transform its operation to say an individualised curriculum. Fullan *et al.* (1987), quoted in Plomp *et al.* (1990, pp. 169–70), identify ten factors affecting the implementation of innovation involving the new information technologies. Seven of them are connected with the local conditions of the school, the remaining three being characteristic of the innovation itself. The local conditions include central office direction, commitment and support, the process of implementation and institutionalisation, professional development and assistance, implementation monitoring and problem solving, the principal's leadership, community support and environmental stability. France has recognised the need for more research on the effect of the new information technologies on the functioning of the school indicating that there are no clear views on this (CERI, 1986, p. 110), and it is likely that we have much to learn about just how the school as an institution affects change.

The barriers that relate to teachers include their attitudes, motivation, personality and training. The lack of training, and the fact that it is rudimentary and geared towards computer skills, must in part be responsible for this barrier. The inappropriateness of training courses with respect to pedagogic principles explains why some teachers are resistant to using computer simulations, for example, in their classrooms. The evidence is that teachers are keen to attend courses, so their lack of motivation alone cannot be the source of the barrier, although an OECD report talks of them being resistant to change (CERI, 1986, p. 27). Wellington (1990, p. 60) argues that human-factor elements have been ignored, and hence some teachers may feel that computers represent a threat. I shall argue below that it may be that it is the institutional (system) factors that are the main barrier.

The Case of Curriculum Change and the New Information Technologies

Applying the lessons from other areas

Here I am not setting out to explain why the development of the new information technologies has turned out the way it has. Instead I want to reflect on how the lessons from the literature on curriculum change in general, and technology education in particular, might relate to the case of the new information technologies.

The parallels with curriculum change in general should by now be evident:

- the importance of the economic imperative and associated with it central initiatives that rely upon a central agency;
- the fact that similarities in strategies exist across national systems that have centralised or decentralised control of the curriculum;
- the disappointment with changes at the level of schools;
- the central role of teacher development and the need for a strategy that deals with their attitudes, motivation, etc. (i.e. a normative-re-educative strategy);
- the relative lack of attention to the school compared to classrooms;
- the curtailment of government expenditure
- accompanied by concern for efficiency or value for money;
- the growing importance of international agencies.

My earlier account of curriculum change in general noted the import-ance of the school, as well as the classroom, as a focus for change. The programmes for the new information technologies have been particularly poor at addressing the school level, with for example little in the way of training for senior management. Few studies focus on this level, con-centrating instead on national programmes or at the detailed level of the pupil–computer (or software) interaction and the whole-classroom use of a computer. Some who address innovation and the new information tech-nologies take an action-research approach arguing for the involvement of the teacher in the development process (e.g. Candy, 1988). This answers the possibility of teacher attitude change, etc., as required by the 'normative-re-educative' strategy, but ignores the role of the school as an institution in sustaining and spreading the innovation. Goodson and Mangan (1991) give a collection of studies in this tradition, with only one article dealing with a group of teachers acting as researchers, but even here the focus is on the work in their individual classrooms. Initiatives that focus on the classroom only consider one level of teacher negotiation of the curriculum (Weston, 1979, p. 266), namely that of teacher and pupils, but ignore the second level of negotiation among teachers. This, in the case of the new information technologies, implies a school-level activity.

Not only do the processes of change in the new information technologies have much in common with those in general curriculum change, but the aims of change overlap. This is particularly true with the conflict of, on the one hand, a concern for modern teaching and learning methods and, on the other, a desire to match the content of learning to the needs of the economy. The latter aim is evident in the general concern for the basics of mathematics, language, and more recently science, or the particular concern for computer skills of use to industry. This is of course only one of the conflicts the new information technologies are faced with. In the following sub-sections I will consider how conflicts are evident in differences of intentions and meanings among teachers involved with the new information technologies, and consider other groups that are also involved. These considerations lead to a focus on the idea of negotiating the curriculum.

Differences of intentions and meaning

Fothergill (1988b, p. 25) laments the conflicts that exist in the UK between those who have advocated computer studies and those concerned for the development of computers across the curriculum, as an unnecessary polarisation. However, in taking this 'rational view' of the world he is ignoring the importance of how differing aims and meanings exist among those who are involved in any curriculum change. These differences cannot be wished away, at best they can be talked out over a period of time and lead to consensus among a group, at worst they will remain profound ideological differences about the purposes of education. Moreover, it is evident that the economic imperative has been responsible for the initiatives that have done so much to increase the opportunities to exploit the new information technologies in schools. The objectives may clash (CERI, 1986, p. 19), as they do in the case of technology education, but they will be used by various groups within education to further their own causes. This is true at all levels, including the school, as Weston (1979) illustrated in her concept of negotiation.

Let me explore briefly how these conflicts are evident through the various interest groups that exist in the area of the new information technologies. I do this somewhat speculatively as I know of no 'curriculum history' that gives an account of the players in the development of these technologies within education. Because of this I will also concentrate on the school level, where these interest groups have their most graphic manifestations.

The idea of computer studies teachers as an interest group is appealing. Their development from mathematics teachers and the establishment of a separate identity with equal academic status resembles that of other school subjects, although perhaps not following the stages identified by Goodson (1983), namely from pedagogic and utilitarian to academic. Indeed the development from computer studies to information technology as a subject would offer an interesting case study to perhaps challenge this view of curriculum change. Computers in education have included more disparate groupings, but Goodson's idea of subjects being shifting amalgamations of sub-groups and traditions has some force, especially when seen in the context of the process of negotiation described by Weston (1979). The change from computer studies to information technology as a subject, and the reduction in programming as an element, for example, are likely to be indicative of the shifting fortunes of various groups. The success of the establishment of computer studies and then of information technology as subjects indicates that a cohesive group can get hold of the status, resources and territory. Their cohesiveness as a group may explain why they do better than those who have a non-subject view of the use of the new information technologies. In the UK, however, the business studies tradition has a stake in information technology related to office practice, and at a school level this offers a different power base, one of the conditions of success put forward by Weston (1979, p. 265).

Areas like microelectronics and control technology do not fit easily with either computer studies or information technology and are part of the more general problems of the development of technology education referred to earlier. There are, for example, pedagogic differences evident in a 'bottom-up' or 'top-down' approach to teaching reflecting the subject traditions of science and craft (latterly technology) respectively. But there are also problems about where microelectronics and control will be dealt with and who is seen to have the expertise to teach them. The teaching of these has considerable resource and accommodation implications and could be the subject of contentious negotiation within schools. In the UK teachers who have an interest in these areas have used the resources made available by the Technical and Vocational Education Initiative (TVEI), which was a government initiative motivated by the economic imperative. This parallels computer studies and information technology teachers who used the funding of this initiative, and that of the national information technology initiatives, to build up their 'computing empire'.

Those who see in the new information technologies a way of improving learning do not by definition have a subject base around which to form an interest group. Educational technology is the nearest 'subject' that could represent them, but this is only found in higher education. Even within this latter group there are different interests, with some being concerned to develop the use of the new information technologies to promote independent learning and problem-solving approaches. Others are more concerned with the computer as an environment to study learning, and investigate how children's science concepts are formed and developed by posing problems simulated in the computer environment. Neither of these two interests, which are of course not exclusive, have constituents in schools. The nearest that does exist are those who advocated resource-based learning, and who in happier times were responsible for resource centres in schools. However, when faced with the established subjects within schools such constituents are at a disadvantage in the negotiation that makes up curriculum development. [. . .] While there may be no competing interests between educational technology and say computer studies interests at school level they can exist at local authority level. Fothergill (1988b, p. 26) notes that within the local authority advisory staff there are conflicts between those who support computer studies and those concerned with educational technology.

Although the educational technology interest group is not strong within schools, the impact of the new information technologies on teaching and learning is evident through conventional subjects to varying degrees. Subject teachers may do this in a fashion that does not require a fundamental change in teaching and learning arrangements. Equally it may be that they are not able to implement change because of a lack of control over computing resources. Thus technical drawing using a board and paper is replaced by computer-aided drafting, or manual collecting and analysis of experimental data by data logging and spreadsheets. This can improve learning, and is an important addition to the subject teaching, but an addition it remains. Any more profound change may need a more serious look at what it means to teach and learn a particular subject. This is the very kind of reflection that Weston (1979, pp. 269–70) thought was so important when teachers are faced with innovatory programmes.

Most of the above observations apply to secondary schools, so what of the primary sector? Moon (1986, pp. 216–8), in the context of the development of new mathematics, showed how primary school teachers moved from the utilitarianism of arithmetic to the academic tradition of mathematics. In the context of the new information technologies it is difficult to see any parallels, because the adoption of computer-based learning at this level stems from a pedagogic concern. The absence of 'computer studies', and the associated interest group in the school, does of course help to ensure that all resources are focused upon teaching and learning. But if teachers are to go beyond the obvious uses of drill and practice or wordprocessing, then they too will need the structures to allow collective reflection.

Other groups

The manufacturers of computers and publishers of software and courseware, could be seen as other groups at work in the process of curriculum change. Again I can only speculate, in an area which is likely to involve more commercial secrecy than Moon (1986) found among textbook publishers. The fact that governments supported local manufacturers gave these companies considerable hold over schools, one that in the UK they have not released. It is not possible to speculate what difference in price or in availability of software might have occurred if such support had not been given by governments. Would, for example, the local home-grown software production by individual teachers have occurred, or would publishers have put more investment into it with the possibility of an international market? All computer manufacturers try to lock their customers into their products, but have the recent moves by some education computer manufacturers to move their products into the mainstream MS-DOS base, while following the power inflation of ever bigger machines, isolated schools from a wider and cheaper range? Given the central problem of the quantity of machines available, and the software to follow them, such questions are important to a consideration of curriculum change. The answers to these questions are unknown, and more significantly the implications for future action are even more unclear. However, they must be important, even if only as negative examples of opportunities lost.

The curriculum as a result of negotiation

What I have been trying to draw attention to in the last two sections is the fact that different groups with different interests are at work in determining the curriculum. Some of these work at a national, and indeed an international, level and all have some influence at the school level. So, while national policies will be drawn up and programmes initiated to implement the change in the curriculum to use the new information technologies, the course of events will be an interaction of these groups with the policies and programmes. I make no claim for knowing just what the nature of the interaction is, but the lessons from the curriculum change literature, and from technology education in particular, indicate their importance. In the case of technology education, as I have argued elsewhere (McCormick, 1990), teachers need time to develop their understanding, and this applies equally well in the case of the new information technologies and how they are used in schools. At the school level some of the groups will be involved in negotiations for status, resources and territory, and this negotiation will be used to interpret the policies and programmes that come from outside the school.
[. . .]

Acknowledgement

I would like to thank my colleagues Oliver Boyd-Barrett, Michael Harrison and Peter Scrimshaw for their comments and suggestions on an earlier draft of this paper.

References

Anderson, J. (1987) Information technology and in-service education: a change of emphasis, *British Journal of Educational Technology*, 18, pp. 199–205.

Aston, M. H. & Templeton, R. (1988) Prospects & problems: a pan-European perspective on technological innovation and educational practice, in F. Lovis & E. D. Tagg (Eds) (1988) *Computers in Education*, Proceedings of the IFIP TC 3, 1st European Conference on Computers in Education – ECCE 88 Lausanne, Switzerland, 24–29 July, Amsterdam, North-Holland.

Batista, J. B. A. E. (1990) Can technology advance education?, *International Journal of Educational Development*, 10, pp. 231–44.

Beattie, N. (1990) The wider context: are curricula manageable?, in T. Brighouse & B. Moon (Eds) *Managing the National Curriculum: Some Critical Perspectives*. Harlow, Longman, in association with British Educational Management and Administration Society.

Beynon, J. & Mackay, H. (1989) Information technology into education: towards a critical perspective, *Journal of Education Policy*, 4, pp. 245–57.

Bigum, C. (1990) Computers and the curriculum: the Australian experience, *Journal of Curriculum Studies*, 22, pp. 63–7.

Boyd-Barrett, O. (1990) Schools' computing policy as state-directed innovation, *Educational Studies*, 16, pp. 169–85.

Candy, L. (1988) Computers and curriculum change: an action research perspective, *Journal of Computer Assisted Learning*, 4, pp. 203–13.

Casmir, G. (1988) In-service training in the NVIO-project in The Netherlands, *European Journal of Education*, 23, pp. 315–21.

Centre for Educational Research and Innovation (CERI) (1978) *Creativity of the School: Conclusions of a Programme of Enquiry*, Paris, OECD.

Centre for Educational Research and Innovation (CERI) (1986) *New Information Technologies: A Challenge for Education*, Paris, OECD.

Centre for Educational Research and Innovation (CERI) (1989) *Information Technologies in Education: The Quest for Quality Software*, Paris, OECD.

Collis, B. (1990) Using information technology to create new educational situations, *Prospects*, 20, pp. 173–86.

Collis, B. A. & Oliveira, J. B. (1990) Categorizing national computer-related educational policy: a model and its applications, *Information Technology for Development*, 5, pp. 45–68.

Congress of the USA (1988) *Power On! New Tools for Teaching and Learning*, Washington, DC, Office of Technology Assessment, US Government Printing Office.

Conlon, T. (1989) Educating educators: the computing experience, in T. Conlon & P. Cope (Eds) *Computing in Scottish Education: The First Decade and Beyond*, Edinburgh, Edinburgh University Press.

Department of Education and Science (DES) (1989) *Survey of Information Technology in Schools*, London, HMSO.

Department of Education and Science and the Welsh Office (DES) (1990) *Technology in the National Curriculum*, London, HMSO.

Duguct, P. (1990) Computers in schools: national strategies and their extension to the international level, *Prospects*, 20, pp. 165–72.

Ennals, R., Gwyn, R. & Zdravchev, L. (1986) *Information Technology and Education: The Changing School*, Chichester, Ellis Horwood.

Fothergill, R. (1988a) The problem of innovation: the British experience, *European Journal of Education*, 23, pp. 305–13.

Fothergill, R. (1988b) *Implication of New Technology for the School Curriculum*, London, Kogan Page.

Fullan, M., Miles, M. M. & Anderson, S. A. (1987) *A Conceptual Plan for Implementing the New Information Technology in Ontario Schools*, Toronto, Ministry of Education.

Gardner, J. & Salters, J. (1990) Information technology in education and teacher education in France, *European Journal of Teacher Education*, 13, pp. 161–71.

Goodson, I. F. (1983) *School Subjects and Curriculum Change*, London, Croom Helm.

Goodson, I. F. & Mangan, J. M. (1991) *Computers, Classrooms, and Culture: Studies in the Use of Computers for Classroom Learning*. London, Ontario, The Research Unit on Classroom Learning and Computer Use in Schools, Faculty of Education, University of Western Ontario.

Greffe, X. (1988) France 'Informatique Pour Tous' or the lessons of innovation, *European Journal of Education*, 23, pp. 329–43.

Gwyn, R. (1988a) The new information technologies and educational policy: lessons learned, lessons unthinkable (editorial), *European Journal of Education*, 23, pp. 299–300.

Gwyn, R. (1988b) Teacher education and change: the first decade of IT, *European Journal of Teacher Education*, 11, pp. 195–205.

Hodson, D. (1990) Computer-based education in New Zealand: a time of transition and uncertainty, *Journal of Curriculum Studies*, 22, pp. 67–72.

Johnson, J. R. (1989) *Technology: Report of the Project 2061 Phase I Technology Panel*, Washington, DC, American Association for the Advancement of Science.

Lovis, F. & Tagg, E. D. (Eds) (1988) *Computers in Education*, Proceedings of the IFIP TC 3, 1st European Conference on Computers in Education – ECCE 88 Lausanne, Switzerland, 24–29 July. Amsterdam, North-Holland/Elsevier.

McCormick, R. (1990) Technology and the National Curriculum: the creation of a 'subject' by committee?, *The Curriculum Journal*, 1, pp. 39–51.

McCormick, R. (1991) The evolution of current practice in technology education, in M. Hacker, A. Gordon & M. de Vries (Eds) *Integrating Advanced Technology into Technology Education*, Berlin, Springer-Verlag, in co-operation with NATO Scientific Affairs Division.

McCormick, R. & James, M. (1988) *Curriculum Evaluation in Schools*, 2nd edn, London, Croom Helm.

McDonald, S. (1991) Information technology in the National Curriculum: a view from Scotland, *Journal of Computer Assisted Learning*, 7, pp. 34–41.

Mallatratt, J. (1990) Needs and provision, *Computer Education*, 64, pp. 25–7.

Moon, B. (1986) *The 'New Maths' Curriculum Controversy: An International Story*, London, Falmer Press.

National Curriculum Council (NCC) (1990) *Non-Statutory Guidance: Information Technology*, York, NCC.

Nias, J. (1989) *Primary Teachers Talking: A Study of Teaching as Work*, London: Routledge.

North, R. (1990) Managing IT across the whole curriculum, *Management in Education*, 3, pp. 14–16.

Nydahl, G. (1988) The Swedish approach to introducing computers into education, *European Journal of Education*, 23, pp. 323–7.

Parliamentary Office of Science and Technology (POST) (1991) *Technologies for Teaching: The Use of Technologies for Teaching and Learning in Primary and Secondary' Schools*, London, POST.

Plomp, T., Pelgrum, W. J. & Steerneman, A. H. M. (1990) Influence of computer use on schools' curriculum: limited integration, *Computers and Education*, 14, pp. 159–71.

Pollard, A. (1985) *The Social World of the Primary School*, London, Holt, Rinehart & Winston.

Psacharopoulos, G. (1988) Special issue – Vocational education, *International Review of Education*, 34, pp. 141–8.

Ransley, W. (1989) Towards a framework for analysis of country action in the field of information technologies and education, *Journal of Education Policy*, 4, pp. 125–48.

Richards, C. (1988) Primary education in England: an analysis of some recent issues and development, in M. Clarkson (Ed) *Emerging Issues in Primary Education*, Lewes, Falmer Press.

Skilbeck, M. (1976) School-based curriculum development and teacher education, in Open University *Supporting Curriculum Development* (Course E203, Units 24, 25 and 26), Milton Keynes, Open University.

Skilbeck, M. (1990) *Curriculum Reform: An Overview of Trends*, Paris, OECD.

Stenhouse, L. (1975) *An Introduction to Curriculum Research and Development*, London, Heinemann.

Stern, B. E. (1991) Technology education as a component of fundamental education: a national perspective, in M. Hacker, A. Gordon & M. de Vries (Eds) *Integrating Advanced Technology into Technology Education*, Berlin, Springer-Verlag, in co-operation with NATO Scientific Affairs Division.

Wellington, J. J. (1990) The impact of IT on the school curriculum: downwards, sideways, backwards and forwards, *Journal of Curriculum Studies*, 22, pp. 57–76.

Weston, P. B. (1979) *Negotiating the Curriculum: A Study in Secondary Schooling*, Windsor, NFER.

13

Race, Culture and Curriculum Development in the USA: A Study of the Process of Introducing a Multicultural Dimension into the Curriculum

Crain Soudien

[. . .]

Introduction

Of the many issues which vex and divide US society, few invoke as much passion as race and culture. Predictably, schools and universities, long the pre-eminent vehicles for the transmission of US identity, are frequently at the centre of the discord which has seen Americans calling into question each other's sense of 'Americaness'. Key in the various appeals and claims which are being made are questions of representation. Who are American people and how are schools and universities to assist their young in representing themselves, their society and the world in which they live? Vying for the high moral ground in the argument are a number of positions. For the purposes of this paper, particularly its interest in issues of race and culture, two stand out: that which insists that the USA is a single coherent culture made up of subsidiary streams, and that which acknowledges only its common social boundaries but sees within it many disparate and indeed discontinuous cultures (see Asante, 1991, p. 270).

This paper arises out of my involvement and work as a researcher in a project which sought to develop a curriculum which was sensitive to the cultural interests of students of colour. Set in the school district (hereafter simply the 'School District') of a large north-eastern city, the project, officially called the Multicultural Education Program, grew out of the disillusionment of African-American parents and the African-American community with a school system which seemed to be punishing their children by referring them for special education placement and placing their young men on suspension. At the heart of parental and community concern was the perception that the School District had failed to comprehend, and

This chapter has been edited.

230

was even exacerbating, the social conditions which produced alienation amongst African-Americans. This chapter is a critical study of the School District's attempt to address the issues raised by the African-American community. The positions I take in it are, not unexpectedly, influenced by my own insights and experiences as a South African of colour.

The data are derived from copious notes gathered during my participation in meetings, during interviews conducted with individuals and groups and my observation of the process over a period of 9 months.

The Background to this Study

The School District in which this work is set is large, serving a population of approximately 300,000 people. During the 1990–91 school year, the public schools reported an enrolment of 47,660 students, more than 60% of whom were children of colour, with African-Americans constituting the great majority of these. A publication of the Council of Great City Schools reported that the District had more poor children than the average for its state. Against a national average of $5512 (. . . News, September 24 1994), the District spent approximately $5200 per student in the 1990–91 school year.

In the mid-1980s, in the wake of pressure from parents and the community, the School District decided to focus its attention on the high referrals of African-American children to special education and the suspension of African-American males. Two task forces were appointed by the Superintendent to investigate the problem, one the *Task Force on Handicapping Conditions*, and another the *Task Force on Suspensions*. Independently, the two task forces came to the conclusion that African-American curriculum content should be introduced into the school curriculum throughout the grade levels. Absent from the curriculum, it was concluded, were positive representations of people of colour, and the contributions of Africans and African-Americans in particular to the making of the modern world. *The Task Force on Suspensions*, for example, urged that,

> African and African-American History are a must in terms of their educational, social and moral value for all students. Such course offerings should span the entire curriculum and not be limited to Social Studies and Language Arts Classes. (Quoted in Evaluation Document, 1991, p. 5 with emphasis in the original.)

A policy was developed in the District which required its teachers to infuse African and African-American content into the school curriculum. Called the Curriculum Infusion Project (CIP), it was intended that the project would correct the Eurocentric bias in the messages, images and symbols of schooling and help young African-American people to feel a greater sense of ownership of that which they learnt.

With discussion beginning in 1986–87, it was intended to have a programme in place by the start of the 1988–89 school year. Preparatory to this, and based on the recommendations of the two task forces, an advisory committee made up of community members and a consultant, well-known for his work in helping school districts rewrite their curricula, was appointed in the 1987–88 school year. These developments, widely heralded in the media, unfortunately stalled as quickly as they began. Just when it appeared that the community was poised to make an input into the education of its children, it effectively fell out of the reform process. As an evaluator of the CIP explained, 'the advisory committee withered away amidst seemingly irreconcilable differences among its members over the direction the CIP should take' (Evaluation Document, 1991). In March of 1989, after 2 years, disillusioned with the lack of support from the District, the consultant himself resigned.

The project took a significant turn in direction at this stage. Begun through, and projected as a community initiative, it found itself the subject of contestation, and was drawn into the bureaucracy of the District. This signalled an important shift in the ownership of the reform. The project was placed under the guidance of the District's Curriculum Evaluation and Development Department and a new consultant in the 1988–89 school year. The consultant produced a curriculum guide for teachers called *Materials Set 1*. The guide consisted mainly of 'infusible facts' which teachers were asked to integrate into their regular planning and instruction. Concurrently, to help teachers in this process, monthly in-service training sessions were held for liaison teachers who volunteered to serve as 'turnkey trainers' in their buildings. At a more intensive level, two pilot schools were selected at the beginning of 1990 to implement the CIP throughout the curriculum. In-service training was made available for all the teachers at the two schools.

To assess the success of the implementation of the CIP, the District appointed a professor from a local university to conduct an evaluation in 1990. After a systematic series of interviews with participants in the programme, he came to the conclusion that the initiative had overlooked the input and skills of teachers. He also concluded that most teachers saw the CIP as a vehicle for changing African-American students; the students had deficits 'which needed mending'. Crucially too, he showed, the District had not developed a policy statement for the CIP. As a result few teachers were able to articulate the goals of the CIP clearly. Two key recommendations were made; that the programme draw on the experience and knowledge of teachers and use them as trainers of other teachers; and that in response to prevailing perceptions which saw the children as 'being the problem', the programme address the issue of racism in the District. In the evaluation, the Professor reported, 'I could not help but notice the failure of anyone we interviewed, teachers or administrators, to address racism as a phenomenon to study and understand in terms of its practice, effects and perpetuation. In fact, use of the term 'racism' was virtually taboo'.[1]

As a consequence of the evaluation and the discussions which accompanied and followed it, the programme went into a second phase at the beginning of the 1992–93 school year under the joint auspices of a team of education professors (one an African-American and the other a white American) from a local university and the District's Department of Curriculum Evaluation and Development (CED). A grant was procured which enabled the programme to make good the absence of teachers in the previous stage of its implementation. As a result, teachers were incorporated into the design and implementation of the programme from the start. Where the previous stage, too, had been characterised by in-servicing of teachers by 'experts' in a didactic ambience, in keeping with the recommendations from the evaluation, the role of the university faculty and the CED was proposed to be essentially facilitative.

Of key importance, and I will return to discuss this in the conclusion, in the course of the transition from the first to the second phase of the project, the District changed the name of the programme from the CIP to Multicultural Education in the . . . Public Schools (MCE). The District's argument, essentially, was that the MCE should provide all children in the District with the opportunity to view their worlds through less Eurocentric perspectives. The goal, rationale and expected student outcomes of the District are important to note:

District Goal
The goal of the multicultural education program in . . . Public Schools is to develop, implement, and evaluate a comprehensive multicultural curriculum throughout the District.

Rationale
The limitations imposed by membership within a specific community or nation have been eroded over the years by the emergence of today's global interaction. Narrow community boundaries have been broadened because of current worldwide trade and communication. There is heightened international awareness, progressive dismantling of colonialism, and dissolution of political barriers. Media coverage, new independent nations, and the dramatic worldwide shift of political power have become major factors in our daily lives. These have combined with advancing technology and increasing environmental concern. Added to the emergence of today's global economy, all of these factors mandate an active understanding by all persons of a multicultural world.

The role of the United States in this global drama has emphasized the need for multicultural awareness within its own borders. Through America's history, the cultures of diverse nations and peoples have become interwoven. Cultural diversity has provided the strength of America. Study of this diversity becomes a reaffirmation of the belief in America's national goals and identity.

Related Student Outcomes

1. Students will learn about, understand, appreciate, and value their own cultures and the cultures of others, thus enabling them to live in, work in, and enjoy the diverse global environment that will increasingly become the home of all people in the 21st century.
2. Students will be aware of and able to evaluate the cultural assumptions that underlie our individual beliefs and influence our individual and group actions.
3. Students will be able to apply critical and reflective thinking skills to the specific issues of racism, stereotype, and prejudice in relation to historical events as well as everyday life.

4. Students will have a greater awareness and appreciation of the contributions and roles of all ethnic groups to the development of civilization.
5. Students will demonstrate positive self-esteem through a greater awareness of their specific cultural heritage and its complementary relationship to other cultural traditions.

(*The African and African-American Curriculum Program Newsletter,* November, 1991)

A Narration of the Project

The first three months

The second phase of the MCE programme began with the opening of the 1992–93 school year. The faculty of the CED team met several times in preparing the scene for the programme. For the two members of the university faculty, both of whom had an interest in helping teachers link their classroom practice with community and social concerns, the project was much more than about developing a cadre of trainers who could articulate multicultural messages in the schools.

For both members of faculty, the work of developing a new approach to the curriculum was a slow reconstructive process. Developing the curriculum was not something which could result from legislation from the top. While they were reluctant to spell out a blueprint or prescribe a model for change, they were to rely heavily on the action research (AR) approach. Central to AR was the idea of teachers researching their practice and taking responsibility for their own knowledge. This above all implied a willingness to reflect critically on the positions they took to issues in the classroom and how they taught. The faculty member responsible for developing the AR component of the programme made the point in an early meeting that, 'I believe in what I say, and I reserve my right to change it'. Both she and the other faculty member tried hard to emphasise that they did not have the answers to the problems of the District. Everybody had to be open-minded but honest and ready to engage in a critical dialogue about their various assumptions and to learn that 'one is not necessarily better than another'. 'We want', said one of them, 'the teachers and the liaisons when they go out into the school to see that they can get as well as give information.' The difficulty of doing this was to become apparent later.

Members of the CED brought a somewhat different set of interests to the project. Burdened by requests for workshops and material from schools in the District which they could not always meet, they were concerned that the project develop presentational skills for teachers so that a larger pool of 'personal power' was available in the District. The plan which evolved out of the faculty members' (FMs) and CED's discussions was that two layers of teachers would be organised. A first layer was identified which came to be known as the 'Support Team' (ST). These teachers, selected by the

CED from a list of volunteers on the basis of experience, were to be involved with approximately 80 others who, largely, had volunteered to serve as liaison teachers (LTs) for their schools in a series of meetings to plan and implement the new programme. Many of the STs had been involved in the previous phase of the programme as LTs, and were to bring those experiences into play.

The STs consisted mainly of women, of whom five were African-American and the remainder white American. In the beginning there were two men, both white American, one who was present at every meeting and another who dropped out after a few months. The LTs were overwhelmingly represented by women, the vast majority of whom were African-American. Amongst the handful of men amongst the LTs, one was African-American. The members, who spanned the whole age spectrum of the school experience, were all experienced teachers.

The first few meetings of the ST were important for the programme. Constructed around tight agendas, they were, nonetheless, marked by a tone of informality which the FMs used to illustrate the problem-solving approach which they hoped would become intrinsic to the style of operation of the programme. With the entire ST seated around a table, discussions were fluid. 'People are tired of one-way communication', said an FM, 'There's been too much talking at people (referring to the previous phase of the programme). People had a lot of feelings, but not the opportunity to talk about them, [and] the different reasons for [doing] what they're doing.'
[. . .]

Developing a sense of confidence in the ST for such members was more easily said than done. For some who had been involved with the previous phase of the programme, it was a hard question of, 'is this project really going to be different?' While the first meeting gave everyone a sense of the ethos which the planners hoped would inhere in the project, for a long time afterwards many remained unsure that the structure would transform into a meaningful vehicle for change. To illustrate, I had an opportunity to speak with two key members of the ST after what I had considered to be an important breakthrough in a discussion. The discussion in the project had turned to the topic of racism, and had, I felt, begun opening up for consideration an issue which had been skirted around. Both, however, remained cautious. 'We'll see how far this goes,' both said in different ways.

In fact, they had themselves been instrumental in facilitating this development as early as the second meeting. Evaluating a meeting which the ST members had had with the LTs, the opportunity arose for generalising themes which came out of LTs' discussions. Some members of the ST reported that LTs were being challenged by white Americans about the accuracy of information which was being presented in classes:

> It's uncomfortable. When we discussed Ancient Egypt having been developed by black Africans, the comment was made that African-Americans came from West Africa. They were trying to refute the information, and questioning the authority of the sources. So I said, 'you've never questioned other things'.

One of the aspects of the whole dynamic is that you provide them with sources, you prove the question which is being asked. It becomes then, 'I don't like this, I'm being threatened'. The question in our group was 'is it really about accuracy?'
Or is it racism?
It's racism. Racism is grounded in fear.

Wary as these two women were, a tone had undoubtedly been set for the project, and the next few meetings were to build on this development. In the two meetings which followed, one with the LTs, the discussion was dominated by issues of race and racism. While white American voice was not absent from these discussions, it was the African-American teachers who took the lead and participated most. The meeting of the ST and LT members, in particular, was entirely devoted to questions of racism. Fortuitously, the local newspaper was running a series of articles on race relations in the city which highlighted many of the issues which were being addressed. Pointing to the pervasiveness and depth of segregation, the articles stimulated a great deal of passion amongst African-American teachers. Discussion ranged freely in both small groups and plenary sessions, and saw issues being raised from institutional racism to racism in television imagery. Interestingly too, but not unexpectedly, many different perspectives on the situation of African-Americans in the schools came out of these discussions, ranging from assimilationism at one end, and the accompanying plea for mutual tolerance, to strident denunciations of the failed integrationist policies of the authorities. 'We didn't ask to be integrated anyway,' said a teacher. There was much discussion of how to deal with racism in the schools. Often teachers encouraged their colleagues to work together at schools. There were ways of beating the system, but it was difficult to do it by oneself. The tone of the discussions and the frankness with which people participated marked something of a watershed.
[. . .]
A clear distinction appeared in the language and vocabularies of African-Americans and white Americans. While there was hardly a single perspective amongst African-Americans, with some considerably more disturbed by the events in the District than others, they tended to be far more cautious in their expectations of the programme. Once, when a teacher commented on how helpful her principal was, some in her small group nodded politely. Others, however, disagreed vehemently, saying that they had totally contrary experiences, suggesting that racism was often the reason. While these did not indicate tension in the ST, they were suggestive of distinct discourses within the group which were to become somewhat contentious later.
The role of the FMs through these experiences was crucial. The interpretive framework which they offered for the discussion was that of individuals coming together, making a personal commitment to the initiative and becoming a part of a group.
[. . .]

As the project developed it became clear that a course was being evolved which placed some strain on some of the participants. The ability of everybody in the ST to talk and communicate their feelings was not equal. Many of the white American members of the ST did not participate in some of the discussions. Those that did, clearly found the tone of the discussions not easy to deal with. Where many of the African-Americans teachers spoke from the experience of being persecuted as a group and articulated their grievances in those terms, generally, white members of the ST approached the discussions from personal standpoints. In an early meeting, when some African-American teachers questioned the capacity of the project to make a difference in the context of an obstructive District, a white teacher commented, 'Nobody's going to keep me from doing what I need to with my children'. The difference is important in illustrating the very disparate discourses which were emerging in the ST. The identity African-Americans were presenting was refracted through their experience as an oppressed group. White people generally did not have those kinds of resources, and, given the parameters of the discussions, particularly the burden of responsibility their African-American colleagues were placing on white people for the social ills of the country, were unable to present themselves as a collective, or to talk of themselves as white people. When they participated they did so as individuals with specific experiences of interaction with children of colour in the classroom.

[. . .]

Three more months

The next 3 months were eventful ones. The STs met several times, sometimes by themselves and on other occasions with the LTs. There was a great deal of discussion about introducing and implementing the AR component of the programme and because this was new to most people, it required a great deal of explanation and preparation.

The first meeting in this second period was devoted entirely to introducing the idea of AR to the STs. Based on intensive planning the strategy evolved was to introduce AR to the STs in a two-step process; in the first instance, teachers were to work through an example of a lesson in which a teacher was critiquing her own practice, and in the second, in the context of a group (called the Study and Practice Group [SPG]), to choose a theme which several teachers could collaboratively develop. In the broader framework of the project, the intention was to turn the SPGs into the dynamic cells of the project. The SPGs would help individuals create networks of support and trust. Within the SPGs they would find a collective identity and develop the confidence to share their ideas and criticisms. And with time and experience, it was hoped that they would engender shared visions which could 'become a way of creating changes in institutions'.

[. . .]

What the project was supposed to be doing, this did indeed suggest, was not at all clear to many people. While much water had flowed under the bridge, and individuals were being exposed to new and interesting ways of looking at the worlds of their schools, the project was different things to different people, a way of expanding the curriculum for some, and for others, a vehicle for completely redrafting it. The project had, for example, brought in a visiting speaker who was received well. She spoke of her own work with teachers, and in the collaborative style of the project itself, proceeded to share her thoughts with the STs. Valuable as her participation was in helping teachers to reflect on their cultural assumptions in their SPGs, the question of the identity of the ST itself continued to be a problem. Reflecting the difficulty which many were experiencing with coming to terms with AR, many members in the ST were not making the connections between the visitor's workshop and the key questions which brought to the fore the purpose of the project.

The project leaders, aware of a growing sense of malaise, made several attempts to overcome this sense of disparateness in the ST. At meetings which followed, they continuously tried to bring the whole initiative into focus. Summaries of what individual groups were doing were shared. At one meeting, much of the first session was devoted to CED and FMs critiquing work which they themselves were working on. *Materials Set II*, the follow-up to *Materials Set I*, was subjected to a great deal of dissection and analysis. Many useful insights on how to engage in critical thinking came out of this exercise. Elements of *Materials Set II*, for example, were usefully evaluated by many of the STs. Nonetheless, in the course of doing the exercise, a teacher, one of the African-American women who had previously played an influential role in raising the issue of racism, made the comment that she thought that the MCE project was still extremely circular. 'I have a question,' she said, 'in all these years that I have been involved with this project I still don't know what is happening to support liaisons . . .' Elaborating, she went on to make it clear that she herself did not need permission from anyone to teach that which she thought was important. Her real concern was the absence of a clear policy with respect to issues of culture, 'I want the question spoken to of the reality of where everybody is'.

[. . .]

The Discourse of Multiculturalism and Reform

The idea of multicultural education has seized the American imagination. A vast literature on the subject has been generated in the last 20 years. It has, variously, been embraced as the solution to problems schools have encountered in desegregating themselves (see Green and Heflin, 1989), to the growing representation of people of colour in the American polity (see

Banks & Lynch, 1986), and to the globalisation of world political and economic relations (see Noffke, 1994 and Corner, 1984).

Multiculturalism has risen to the prominence it has, to be sure, because of the attention accorded it by the dominant order. At the same time, one must emphasise its deep roots in oppositional movements. In the last two decades there has been an eruption of claims by individuals and groups of their difference from the putative mainstream. Crichlow *et al.* (1990, p. 101) make the point that, 'throughout the world, a wide range of resurgent cultures are asserting their privilege to represent themselves, their histories, realities and voices in their own cultural tones'. Against the homogenising stream of Western discourse seeking to redefine the world in the narrow image of white, middle-class men, people of colour, women, gays and lesbians and many others have begun to argue that the politics of difference articulated in that discourse is fundamentally hierarchical and oppressive. Seeking to decentre Western precepts governing, *inter alia*, behaviour, personal relations and aesthetics, they have assisted in bringing to the front of the stage the politics of representation. As Crichlow *et al.* (1990, p. 101) say, who defines whom, who interprets, how, in what ways, and toward what ends, are some of the major questions this politics has posed.

While public discourse has privileged a particular understanding of these issues, multiculturalism, by its very nature, is fiercely contested. Several attempts have been made to classify the contending parties in this fray. Sleeter and Grant's (1987) work, however, is known best. They identify five categories of multicultural education, viz., the human relations approach, teaching the culturally different, multicultural education or multicultural democracy, single group studies and multiculturalism for reconstruction. Within this spectrum, the first two approaches are generally perceived as falling within the domain of benign policy choices for confronting social inequality, with the last three providing more scope for challenge. Noffke's (1994) conceptualisation of policies which deal with social difference amends the Sleeter and Grant framework somewhat, introducing dimensions which include anti-colonial struggle and challenge to the hegemony of the Eurocentric.

These categories are useful in so far as they help us understand what policy-makers are doing and where they wish to go. The trouble, however, is that policy-makers seldom develop their manuals and mission statements on the basis of options clarified for them by academics. They are far more likely to develop policies on the basis of the material conditions which define the terms on which they are allowed to govern. Considerations of how much or how little they should change standing orders are far more likely to reflect the parameters of their thought. In their analysis, so well-defined is the basic core of knowledge which every child and adult needs to possess who wishes to be educated, that they are outraged that there are people who dare to presume that other knowledges and other ways of knowing can have real legitimacy. Indeed, the work of Ravitch (1990) expresses this phenomenon of what I call parameter manipulation best. In this understanding, the 'mainstream' is sometimes presented as a tolerant order which permits people the choice of 'maintain[ing] their cultural heritage or to assimilate . . . the choice is theirs, not the state's'. More often, however, particularly when challenged for the deep and now imperceptible conceit embedded within it, it is portrayed as the canonical order assailed and polluted – the 'politicization of all curricula . . . which throws into question the very idea of American education' (Ravitch, 1990, pp. 339–51). The American way of life is given an organic character which has evolved naturally. Its tale is a hymn and testament to the achievement of this character.

A basic element of this approach is its self-assuredness, or its sense of certainty. This characteristic of certainty, buttressed by almost three centuries of 'empirical evidence' – the entire Western canon – is engrained or naturalised in its content, grammar and presentation. How all of these, as specific human and social representations of being, have come into existence are rendered opaque in the telling of its story. The story in the forms it takes in classrooms, at virtually all levels, is a complete narrative, seamless and uninterrupted. Humans are depersonalised within it. They have no frailties, eccentricities or quirks. They tell no lies and are fearless in the face of calamity.

The threat which people outside of the 'mainstream' present resides in their interruption of that narrative. It is this interpretation, I would like to argue, which explains how much 'interruption' the authorities will tolerate. 'Interruptions' for them, become political and undesirable when they attempt to show that the narrative has an underside. It is, for example, not only in bad taste to point out that the 'founding fathers' were notorious slave-holders, but also politically mischievous. One version of the tale is 'truth', another version is 'political'. My basic approach in seeking to understand the politics of the CIP and the MCE comes out of this perspective.

The difficulties of developing a common discourse in the District derive, in large measure, from the politics of challenging the hegemonic common sense. This common sense, represented in the practices of most teachers and the District itself, essentially pivots on the axis of the *status quo* or what is out there as knowledge. In this perspective, knowledge and culture are invariably understood as products which are already finished and complete. As products they are available in a commodified sense. Students are consumers who require regular doses of this commodified knowledge. It is how much of this knowledge they have which determines how successful they will be in the real world. Before the advent of the multicultural discourse, the remedy most popularly applied to students perceived to be in academic danger was simply that of finding ways of giving them more of the same. If they were failing, it was because they were not receiving enough educational medicine. There was little enquiry about the suitability and appropriateness of the medicine. The remedy of multicultural education is inspired by the same thinking. The students are still perceived to be deficient. The ingredients of the medicine have been adjusted, but the treatment protocol is unchanged. In the District the point of view most frequently taken is that all children are culturally deficient. They now all require additional information to help them to learn within the expanded frame of US society. Multiculturalism's mission is to enlarge the story which is told. For example, inventors were not always whites. Crucially, children need to know that there were African-Americans, too, who contributed to the making of the technological and scientific society.

In the District, the dominant motif for the MCE is culture as commodified knowledge. It is materials with new facts which dominate perceptions of whether a culturally sensitive programme is in place or not. Whether or not the school has a box for African-American materials is the framing question in interrogating the progress of the programme. The presence of materials is undoubtedly of great importance, and can determine the quality of the pedagogy of a reform-minded teacher. The basic problem with this approach, is that by itself it has the potential for being a political placebo. It is in this regard that African centred pedagogy, and indeed pedagogies centred in the experience of other marginalised groups, is deeply important. Its objective is not only infusing fact, but fundamentally interrogating the social relations embedded in the making of fact. It asks questions such as by and for whom were 'facts' developed and under what circumstances (Asante, 1991; Fry, 1989; Ladson-Billings, 1990 and 1992). This kind of approach uses materials in a way which is subversive of the certainty of the Eurocentric vision. In Eurocentric models, facts are neutral artefacts which have a disembodied and decontextualised existence. They exist as free-floating signifiers which are available whenever one needs them. Telling the multicultural story, therefore, is calling on that which is available; all one has to do is to substitute one set of facts with another. As McCarthy (1990, p. 54) says, this approach promotes a form of multiculturalism which hinges 'almost exclusively upon the reorganization of the content of the school curriculum'. The proponents of this approach tend to ignore the reality that information and knowledge are implicated in a powerful web of socio-economic power. The process of expanding the curriculum to include more sensitive cultural material does not impact on the unequal relations that continue to exist between white and black people.

Hilliard (1988, p. 37) argues that inequality, or privilege and oppression, to use his terms, are articulated through six major interrelated functions: ideology, political control, uses of history and culture, uses of group identity, uses of financial and human resources and physical segregation. He continues to make the point that schools throughout the USA have moved to address some of these difficulties, but that, in general, they have failed to understand the interrelated nature of the oppression which children of colour and others not accepted into the so-called mainstream are experiencing. As a result, we have seen cosmetic conversions of programmes or additions to curricula, but seldom the commitment to coming to terms with the way in which racial privilege, and other forms of privilege, are constructed as deliberate social projects.

What one is left with, at the end of a reform process, is a new curriculum which has revised only on one or two dimensions of the interrelated problem. The system remains fundamentally inequitable in the sense that its operators have tinkered with some of the barriers which obstruct full equality, but left the complex which generated the problem unchallenged. Amongst other things, reformers neglect to inquire into the larger context in which schools find themselves. To develop an approach which is equitable, Fry (1989) argues that multiculturalism must examine the relationship between school and society. Schools, she says, can help students to participate in social change by introducing them to discussions of oppression and inequality. They could begin to define and then confront their own unfair practices. Involving students in these exercises could be central in helping everyone concerned to understand the meaning of equity.

Achieving equity in the schools of the USA is a profoundly complex process, for inherent in reform processes, as several commentators tell (see Young, 1985; Apple, 1988; Garcia & Pugh, 1992), are power structures with deep roots in the prevailing order. These work hard to inhibit the scope of fundamental change in the classroom and the school. At the same time, one needs to recognise that the political and economic structure is not all-powerful. Groups on the margins of US society have forced it to make changes. In the schools, struggles have been won and have been inspired by political struggle from community and civic groups. It is their capacity to organise and mobilise which has forced new interpretations and new meanings into the public discourse.

The discourse of multiculturalism in the USA must be seen against this perspective. Its essential mission is that of developing what McCarthy (1990) calls harmonious group relations. It is not interested in addressing the social relations which produce those mindsets and practices which in turn are responsible for the oppression and inequities experienced by people of colour. The kind of multiculturalism it tends to gravitate towards is that which denies the political nature of schooling. In the District, amongst some teachers and administrators, it is this form which is dominant. As Hilliard says (1988, p. 39), its tendency is to develop euphemisms which 'reduce psychological and social tension. It does this in two ways: the euphemism may reduce the perceived scope of the domain being considered, or it may reduce the negative intensity of the perception of the topic'.

Fundamentally, however, as we saw, this is not the only discourse on offer in schools. Present in the District is an approach which is insistently oppositional. To the language of multiculturalism, it brings the charge of white supremacy and a determination to unveil the social relations which inform ways of speaking, ways of knowing and ways of being. As we have seen, several impediments stand in the way of such a discourse. To quote Hilliard (1988, p. 39) once more, people such as these have little of the preparation that is necessary to 'mount a comprehensive assault on the problem of privilege and oppression in the schools'. Even the knowledge which they add to correct biases can be rejected or neutralised by those in power. However, it is their sense of community which they share with each other, their conceptual analysis of the problems which they confront and a strategy for making change which presents, for all to see, the possibility that the world can make alternative choices in the way in which it conducts itself. To be sure, the mere existence of such a moral community by no means suggests a battle won. People who subscribe to alternative visions of justice and equality are vulnerable, psychologically, socially and in other ways, to the idealised standards of the hegemonic order which will always seek to present them as deviants. But they are daily reminders for the world that alternative communities can exist.

Note

1. For reasons of anonymity I am not providing references either in terms of authorship or title to participants in the project.

References

Apple, M. (1988) Social crisis and curriculum accords, *Educational Theory*, 38, pp. 191–201.
Asante, M. K. (1991) Multiculturalism: an exchange, *American Scholar*, 60, pp. 267–76.
Banks, J. A. & Lynch, J. (Eds) (1986) *Multicultural Education in Western Societies*, New York, Holt, Rinehart & Winston.
Billings, J. (1989) Top down/bottom up curriculum development, *Thrust*, 18, pp. 18–19.
Corner, T. (1984) *Education in Multicultural Societies*, London, Croom Helm.
Crichlow, W., Goodwin, S., Shakes, G. & Swartz, E. (1990) Multicultural ways of knowing: implications for practice, *Journal of Education*, 172, pp. 101–17.
Fry, P. G. (1989) A vision for multicultural education, *Equity and Excellence*, 25, pp. 139–44.
Garcia, J. & Pugh, S. L. (1992) Multicultural education in teacher preparation programs. A political or an educational concept?, *Phi Delta Kappan*, November, pp. 215–19.
Green, T. G. & Heflin, J. F. (1989) State government and multicultural education policy, *Equity and Excellence*, 25, pp. 145–50.
Hilliard, A. (1988) Conceptual confusion and the persistence of group oppression through education, *Equity and Excellence*, 24, pp. 36–42.
Ladson-Billings, G. (1990) Culturally relevant teaching. Effective instruction for black students, *The College Board Review*, 55, pp. 20–5.
Ladson-Billings, G. (1992) I don't see color, I just see children. Dealing with stereotyping and prejudice in young children, *Social Studies and the Young Learner*, November/December, pp. 9–12.
McCarthy, C. (1990) *Race and Curriculum*, London, Falmer Press.

Noffke, S. (1994) Multicultural education, curricula for, in T. Husen & N. Postleth-waite (Eds) *International Encyclopaedia of Education*, 2nd edn, Oxford, Pergamon Press.

Ravitch, D. (1990) Multiculturalism. E pluribus plures, *American Scholar*, 59, pp. 337–54.

Sleeter, C .E. & Grant, C. A. (1987) An analysis of multicultural education in the United States, *Harvard Educational Review*, 57, pp. 421–44.

Young, J. H. (1985) Participation in curriculum development: an inquiry into the responses of teachers, *Curriculum Enquiry*, 15, pp. 387–414.

14

Principles for Reflecting on the Curriculum

Pierre Bourdieu

Preamble

At the end of 1988 a committee was formed by the Minister of Education, chaired by Pierre Bourdieu and Francois Gros, with a brief to reflect on the curriculum and to plan a revision of it, bearing in mind the importance of the coherence and unity of knowledge. Other members included Pierre Baqué, Pierre Bergé, Rene Blanchet, Jacques Bouveresse, Jean-Claude Chevallier, Hubert Condamines, Didier Da Cunha Castelle, Jacques Derrida, Philippe Joutard, Edmond Malinvaud, François Mathey.

In the first instance the members of the committee resolved to formulate principles which would guide them in their work. They were conscious and aware of the practical implications and applications of these principles, particularly as they related to pedagogical issues. They strove, therefore, to establish principles on the basis of strict intellectual rigour derived from the intrinsic logic of knowledge and from definable assumptions and questions. The committee was not expected to intervene directly and rapidly in curriculum design. They wished to delineate the main objectives for *gradual* change in the compulsory curriculum. These changes would take time if they were to follow, or perhaps anticipate, the evolution of science and society.

Specialist working groups will later continue a deeper reflective process for each of the main areas of knowledge. They will attempt to suggest, through regular reports which will be completed in 1989, a number of precise observations that draw out the implications of the principles proposed in this paper. They will not define the ideal content of an ideal curriculum. The proposals will, in the main, consider the restructuring of the division of knowledge, a new definition of the transmission of knowledge, the elimination of outdated or outmoded notions, and the introduction of new knowledge that stems from research as well as economic, technical and social changes. These will then be discussed at an international gathering of experts.

If, in the educational system, or elsewhere, it is essential to reflect on the notion of change it is out of the question to contemplate abolishing the past. The majority of innovations introduced in recent years were justified. Although important to ensure that what is inherited from the past is not rejected outright it is not always possible, *at any one time and in any one area*, to determine the importance given to items that are 'out of date' as opposed to those that are still 'valid'. It is necessary to consider constantly a new balance which reflects the influence of the past and the necessity of adaptation for the future.

The necessary abstract and generalized shape of the principles thus defined can only be justified by the work to come. This work will need to be guided by the rigour of these principles, while also testing them to determine and differentiate the content.

First Principle

Course content must be regularly reviewed so that new knowledge demanded by scientific progress and changes in society (European unification being a prime example) can be introduced. Any addition of knowledge must be **compensated** *for by a reduction elsewhere in the programme.*

To reduce the breadth or difficulty of a part of the programme should not lower the standard or level. On the contrary, if such a reduction is cautiously achieved it should raise standards, provided the time required for study is reduced and the work improved by substituting passive learning for active reading – and here we refer to audio-visual as well as literary texts. A discussion of practical approaches should give more room for creativity and imagination. This implies, among other things, that the testing of learning and the evaluation of achievements must be radically transformed. An evaluation of standards reached should no longer be based on a heavy and haphazard examination. Continuous assessment and an end-of-course examination focused on essential knowledge should reflect the importance of putting into practice knowledge acquired in different contexts. This would, for example in the case of experimental science, involve practical tests aimed at evaluating creativity, critical abilities and the practical knowledge acquired.

Second Principle

Education must give priority to all the areas which can lead to a way of thinking which is endowed with a validity and applicability of a general nature as opposed to areas where knowledge could be acquired just as efficiently (and sometimes more pleasantly) through other means. It is important to ensure that education does not leave unacceptable gaps which could endanger the success of pedagogic objectives. Most notably, attention should be given to fundamental ways of thinking or knowledge that **are supposed to be taught by everyone and yet may never be taught by anyone**.

It is absolutely necessary to give priority to those areas where the objective is to ensure that fundamental processes are thoughtfully and critically assimilated. These processes – the deductive, the experimental, the historical as well as the critical and reflective – should always be included. In order to redress the balance, the uniqueness of the experimental thinking process should be made clearer. The outcome will be a positive reassessment of qualitative reasoning, a clear recognition of the temporary nature of explanatory models and an appraisal of the need constantly to train for practical forms of research enquiry. It will also be necessary to examine whether and how each main area of knowledge (and each of the 'disciplines' within which they have been more or less adequately interpreted) can contribute to the different thought processes. The logic and traditions of certain specialisms might involve a re-examination of where they are located in the curriculum.

An appropriate place should also be found for certain techniques that are given tacit acknowledgement at the present time but are seldom transmitted methodically, for example the use of dictionaries, the use of abbreviations, the rhetoric of communication, the setting up of a filming system, the creation of an index, the use of a 'ficher signalétique' or of a data bank, the preparation of a manuscript, the search for documents, the use of computer data, the reading of numerical or graphical tables. If *all* pupils were given the technology of intellectual enquiry, and if in general they were given rational ways of working (such as the art of choosing between compulsory tasks or of spreading them over time), then an important way of reducing inequalities based on cultural inheritance would have been achieved.

Third Principle

Open, flexible and changeable programmes are a framework not a prison. There should be fewer and fewer constraints the more you go up the hierarchy of the educational process. Teachers need to collaborate in order to define and implement programmes. There must be progression – vertical connections and coherence – and horizontal connections within specialist areas and equally at the whole programme level (for each class or year group).

The programme should not be dictatorial. It operates as a guide for teachers, pupils and parents who need clear objectives and an understanding of the requirements of the level of knowledge being considered. (Teachers could be asked to talk to their pupils about this at the beginning of the school year.) This is why it has to be seen alongside a review of underlying *philosophy*, the objectives sought, the prerequisites and requirements necessary, and it should also include examples of where it has been applied.

Objectives and content of different specialisms and at different levels must be perceived and defined through their interconnections. Programmes must predict *explicitly* the places where they repeat part of other programmes and this should *only* occur where it is necessary to ensure that fundamental knowledge is acquired. Although it can be useful to address the same question from different viewpoints (for example, the law of perspective from the viewpoint of mathematics and the history of art), we should strive to abolish, when it has been established that no purpose is served, all undesirable overlaps and double usages. This would be true both between successive levels of the same specialist areas and between different subjects within one level.

In order to require and obtain progressive and coherent curriculum courses we must predetermine, *as accurately as possible, the level expected at the beginning* (avoiding systematically vague titles which can be interpreted loosely) and the level to be reached *at the end* of the year in question. Programmes must be piloted to ensure that they can be completed by the majority of pupils (to ensure success they must be accompanied by indications of the study time required at each stage). Every fundamental specialism must be taught through a process planned over years, which guides the learner from a simple initiation through to a mastery of the thought processes and requirements which are unique to the specialism.

Coherence and complementarity between courses offered by different specialist areas must be methodically investigated at each level and it will be necessary to establish a committee for common courses (at each level) to ensure coherence and avoid repetition.

While there would be no wish naively to copy foreign models it is possible that a critical inspiration could be found in a methodical comparison of the curriculum offered in other countries, notably within Europe. The comparison could provide a means of bringing to light gaps and omissions and ought to permit the *discarding* of remnants from an outdated historical tradition. Not only would this increase the compatibility of the French with other European systems, it would also reduce any disadvantage faced against eventual competitors. It would as well lead to a conscious and explicit redirection of established programmes.

Fourth Principle

A critical review of the compulsory curriculum must always reconcile two variables, compulsoriness and transmittability. On the one hand the acquisition of an area of knowledge or of a thought process is more or less **indispen-**

sable *for scientific or social reasons at certain levels; on the other hand, its transmission is more or less difficult depending on the ability that the children have to assimilate and the training of the teachers involved.*

This principle should lead to the exclusion of any premature transmission of knowledge. It should lead to the mobilization of all the necessary resources (for example, in terms of *time* allocated and teaching methods) to ensure efficient transmission and assimilation of the areas of knowledge deemed to be essential (to have a better idea of the real transmittability, at a given level of a knowledge area or thought process we should take account of research that would evaluate mastery of the knowledge taught in different specialisms to pupils of different levels of attainment and from different social strata). The eventual transformation of the content of courses and the final modifications to a course should be established after a trial run in a real situation. This should be done in collaboration with teachers who have received appropriate training. The demands for adaptation by teachers should be supported through sabbaticals and through long secondments which would allow them to prepare for new thinking processes and areas of knowledge. They should acquire new qualifications in the process of developing these new approaches.

On a more general note, new systems would have to be erected with the objective of drawing together and analysing the reactions and reflections of teachers who would be asked to criticize and suggest improvements (the minitel system could be useful for that purpose). A permanent search for methodical and practical teaching research which would bring teachers together and directly involve them in innovation would be put in place.

Fifth Principle

In order to improve the effectiveness of knowledge transmission through a diversification of teaching methods *(while at the same time taking account of the real rather than theoretical* knowledge that has to be assimilated) *it will be necessary to distinguish between specialisms as well as within specialisms what is* **compulsory** *and what is optional. Teachers responsible for different specialisms would come together to develop collective and group learning* through, for example, enquiry or field work approaches.

The increase in knowledge renders invalid the concept of encyclopaedism. It is impossible to teach all the specialisms or the whole of a specialist area – besides which, new specialisms appear which connect fundamental science and technical application (information technology is within each subject as well as existing as a subject in its own right). These areas would not be merely added to the curriculum. Sooner or later the divisions of the curriculum will need redefinition.

It is necessary to substitute for the actual, encyclopaedic, additive and compartmentalized teaching a system of defined compulsory and optional subjects, directly adapted to the intellectual orientation of the pupils and planned to ensure the assimilation of essential knowledge. Alongside this would be a range of optional and interdisciplinary areas allowing the teachers to take the initiative. This diversification of pedagogical structures, and of the status of different areas, will take account of the specific nature of each 'discipline'. This represents a move away from the mere totalling-up of subjects which, as practised, is one of the major obstacles to any real transformation of the curriculum. The redefinition would create alternative theoretical and practical applications, compulsory and optional courses, individual and group learning (and individualized programmes for pupils). This would have the effect of *reducing the number of hours on pupils' timetables without increasing the number of classes allocated to each teacher*. It would increase *teacher autonomy* since, within each defined *programme of study*, they would organize their own study plan before the beginning of the school year. It should also lead to a more flexible and intensive use of apparatus and buildings (the relevant authority – department or commune – should involve teachers in the building or renovation of schools to ensure that education takes place in a setting which is adapted for quality and need).

Group and multidisciplinary activities would best fit into the afternoon. This is the case, for example, in the teaching of languages where the study of discourse, oral and written, and the image are brought together. Language is at the junction of a number of specialisms, presupposing that good use is made of technical materials, leads to relationships with *outside partners* (artists, the media, industries, etc.) necessitating practical as well as analytical activity.

Sixth Principle

Concern to reinforce the coherence of teaching should lead to the enhancement of team teaching, that brings together teachers from different disciplines. It should lead to a rethinking of the divisions within disciplines and a re-examination of certain historical regroupings. It might succeed, although always gradually, in bringing closer together the different areas created in the evolution of science.

Everything should be done to encourage teachers to co-ordinate their actions through workshops aimed at exchanging information on content and teaching method. These would also give them the means (in adapted buildings and with new equipment, etc.) to enrich, diversify and broaden their teaching and leave behind, in the context of team teaching, the strict frontiers of their discipline. (It would be desirable to have certain teachers who have a formal proportion of hours allotted to them for the co-ordination and organization of meetings, the printing of documents, communicating with colleagues, etc.)

Teaching sessions calling on teachers of two (or more) different special-isms, put together because of their affinity, should have the same status as other lessons (each hour taught in that way would, in practical terms, have to be acknowledged as one hour teaching for each teacher). These sessions would be targeted at groups of pupils assembled on the basis of criteria different from those currently used. These could be on the basis of attain-ment, or common interest, or a particular theme. An allocation of hours, whose use would be freely and annually determined by the teachers in-volved, might officially be put aside for that purpose. All means – enriched and modernized libraries, audio-visual techniques and so forth – would be mobilized to reinforce the attraction and efficiency of the approach. The care taken to rethink and surmount the 'frontier' between the disciplines and corresponding teaching units should not be to the detriment of the identity of fundamental subject teaching. It should, rather, bring out the coherence and problematic areas of the thinking process which is the char-acteristic of each specialism.

Seventh Principle

The search for coherence should be accompanied by a search for balance and integration between the different specialisms and, as a consequence, between different forms of excellence. It would be especially important to reconcile the universalism which is inherent in scientific thought and the relativism taught through the historical sciences and it should reflect the plurality of lifestyles and cultural traditions.

Everything should be done to reduce the conflict between theory and technical, between formal and concrete, between pure and applied. Practi-cal features of the curriculum should be reintegrated within fundamental teaching areas. The need to balance the room given to what we shall call, for the sake of convenience, the 'conceptual', the 'sensitive' and the 'corpo-ral' is obvious at all levels, particularly in the early years. The weight given to technical requirements and to theoretical requirements will be deter-mined according to criteria which are unique to each level of the pro-gramme. They will therefore take account of career interests, the pupils' power of abstraction and the time they will be entering working life.

Modern education should in no way sacrifice the history of languages and literature, of culture and religion, of philosophy and science. It must, rather, reassess itself and work ceaselessly towards these histories in an increasingly subtle and critical manner. For this very reason it must not be based on a representation given by those who reduce 'humanism' to a fixed image of 'humanities'. The teaching of languages can, and must, provide the opportunity to learn logic, just as much as the teaching of physics or ·biology. The teaching of mathematics or physics, as much as the teaching of philosophy or history, can and must prepare the learner for the history of ideas in science or technology (provided, of course, the teachers are trained accordingly).

On a more general note, access to scientific methods derives from the acquisition of elementary logic and ways of thought – in other words techniques or cognitive tools which are totally indispensable in promoting rigorous and reflective reasoning. The opposition between art and science which continues to dominate the organization of schooling and the mentality of teachers, pupils and pupils' parents can and must be surmounted. The curriculum should be capable of addressing simultaneously science and the history of science or epistemology. It should also promote art and literature, and aesthetic reflection and forms of logic that these subjects can develop. Finally, it will be necessary to teach not only a mastery of language and literature, philosophy and science, but also the active process of logical procedures and rhetoric that engagement with these subjects requires. The apparent abstractness of these areas could be removed if common programmes were developed where the teacher of mathematics (or physics) and teachers of language or philosophy made clear that general competencies were required in the reading of scientific texts, technical briefs or approaches to argument and discourse. A similar effort should be made to articulate thinking processes which are part of the natural human sciences, to inculcate the rational, critical-thinking mode which all sciences teach, and to ensure that these are based on historical and cultural roots which reflect the range of scientific and cultural knowledge. In this way the pupil should develop a comprehensive respect for diversity in time and space and for civilization, lifestyles and cultural traditions.

The National Council for developing all aspects of the curriculum and school programmes will be expected to put into practice all the principles outlined above. Membership will be on a personal basis rather than through representation of teachers, institutions or associations. The National Council will operate on a permanent basis (which presupposes that members will be freed from a proportion of their other duties) for a period of five years. Changes will only be introduced every five years, with the jurisdiction of the National Council embracing all trends and types of education.

15

Getting to Scale with Good Educational Practice

Richard F. Elmore

[. . .]

The Problem of Scale in Educational Reform

Why do good ideas about teaching and learning have so little impact on US educational practice? This question, I argue, raises a central problem of US education: A significant body of circumstantial evidence points to a deep, systemic incapacity of US schools, and the practitioners who work in them, to develop, incorporate, and extend new ideas about teaching and learning in anything but a small fraction of schools and classrooms. This incapacity, I argue is rooted primarily in the incentive structures in which teachers and administrators work. Therefore, solving the problem of scale means substantially changing these incentive structures.

Changing the core: students, teachers, and knowledge

The problem of scale in educational innovation can be briefly stated as follows: Innovations that require large changes in the core of educational practice seldom penetrate more than a small fraction of US schools and classrooms, and seldom last for very long when they do. By 'the core of educational practice', I mean how teachers understand the nature of knowledge and the student's role in learning, and how these ideas about knowledge and learning are manifested in teaching and classwork. The 'core' also includes structural arrangements of schools, such as the physical layout of classrooms, student grouping practices, teachers' responsibilities for groups of students, and relations among teachers in their work with students, as well as processes for assessing student learning and communicating it to students, teachers, parents, administrators, and other interested parties.

One can think of schools as generally representing a standard set of solutions to these problems of how to manage the core. Most teachers tend to think of knowledge as discrete bits of information about a particular subject

---

This chapter has been edited.

and of student learning as the acquisition of this information through processes of repetition, memorization, and regular testing of recall (e.g., Cohen, 1988). The teacher, who is generally the center of attention in the classroom, initiates most of the talk and orchestrates most of the interaction in the classroom around brief factual questions, if there is any discussion at all.

Hence, the teacher is the main source of information, defined as discrete facts, and this information is what qualifies as knowledge. Often students are grouped by age, and again within age groups, according to their perceived capabilities to acquire information. The latter is generally accomplished either through within-class ability groups or, at higher grade levels, through 'tracks', or clusters of courses for students whom teachers judge to have similar abilities. Individual teachers are typically responsible for one group of students for a fixed period of time. Seldom working in groups to decide what a given group of students should know or how that knowledge should be taught, teachers are typically solo practitioners operating in a structure that feeds them students and expectations about what students should be taught. Students' work is typically assessed by asking them to repeat information that has been conveyed by the teacher in the classroom, usually in the form of worksheets or tests that involve discrete, factual, right-or-wrong answers (Elmore, 1995).

At any given time, there are some schools and classrooms that deliberately violate these core patterns. For example, students may initiate a large share of the classroom talk, either in small groups or in teacher-led discussions, often in the context of some problem they are expected to solve. Teachers may ask broad, open-ended questions designed to elicit what students are thinking and how they are thinking, rather than to assess whether they have acquired discrete bits of information. Students' work might involve oral or written responses to complex, open-ended questions or problems for which they are expected to provide explanations that reflect not only their acquisition of information, but also their judgments about what kinds of information are most important or appropriate. Students may be grouped flexibly according to the teacher's judgment about the most appropriate array of strengths and weaknesses for a particular task or subject matter. Teachers may share responsibility for larger groups of students across different ages and ability levels and may work cooperatively to design classroom activities that challenge students working at different levels. In other words, students' learning may be assessed using a broad array of tasks, problems, mediums of expression, and formats.

In characterizing these divergences from traditional educational practice, I have deliberately avoided using the jargon of contemporary educational reform – 'teaching for understanding', 'whole language', 'heterogeneous grouping', 'team teaching', 'cooperative learning', 'authentic assessment', etc. I have done this because I do not want to confuse the problems associated with the implementation of particular innovations with the more general, systemic problem of what happens to practices, by whatever name, that violate or challenge the basic conventions of the core of schooling. The names of these practices change, and the intellectual traditions associated with particular versions of the practices ebb and flow. But, the fundamental problem remains: Attempts to change the stable patterns of the core of schooling, in the fundamental ways described above, are usually unsuccessful on anything more than a small scale. It is on this problem that I will focus.

Much of what passes for 'change' in US schooling is not really about changing the core, as defined above. Innovations often embody vague intentions of changing the core through modifications that are weakly related, or not related at all, to the core. US secondary schools, for example, are constantly changing the way they arrange the schedule that students are expected to follow – lengthening or shortening class periods, distributing content in different ways across periods and days, increasing and decreasing class size for certain periods of the day, etc. These changes are often justified as a way to provide space in the day for teachers to do a kind of teaching they wouldn't otherwise be able to do, or to develop a different kind of relationship with students around knowledge.

However, the changes are often not explicitly connected to fundamental changes in the way knowledge is constructed, nor to the division of responsibility between teacher and student, the way students and teachers interact with each other around knowledge, or any of a variety of other stable conditions in the core. Hence, changes in scheduling seldom translate into changes in the fundamental conditions of teaching and learning for students and teachers. Schools, then, might be 'changing' all the time – adopting this or that new structure or schedule or textbook series or tracking system – and never change in any fundamental way what teachers and students actually do when they are together in classrooms. I am not interested, except in passing, in changes that are unrelated to the core of schooling, as I have defined it above. My focus is on that narrower class of changes that directly challenge the fundamental relationships among student, teacher, and knowledge.

In some instances, such as the high-performance schools described by Linda Darling-Hammond (in press), a whole school will adopt a dramatically different form of organization, typically by starting from scratch rather than changing an existing school, and that form of organization will connect with teaching practices that are dramatically different from those traditionally associated with the core of schooling. At any given time there may be several such model schools, or exemplars of good practice, but as a proportion of the total number of schools, they are always a small fraction. In other words, it is possible to alter organization and practice in schools dramatically, but it has thus far never been possible to do it on a large scale.

The closer an innovation gets to the core of schooling, the less likely it is that it will influence teaching and learning on a large scale. The corollary of this proposition, of course, is that innovations that are distant from the core will be more readily adopted on a large scale. I will later develop some theoretical propositions about why this might be the case.

The problem of scale is a 'nested' problem. That is, it exists in similar forms at different levels of the system. New practices may spring up in isolated classrooms or in clusters of classrooms within a given school, yet never move to most classrooms within that school. Likewise, whole schools may be created from scratch that embody very different forms of practice, but these schools remain a small proportion of all schools within a given district or state. And finally, some local school systems may be more successful than others at spawning classrooms and schools that embody new practices, but these local systems remain a small fraction of the total number in a state.

The problem of scale is not a problem of the general resistance or failure of schools to change. Most schools are, in fact, constantly changing – adopting new curricula, tests, and grouping practices, changing schedules, creating new mechanisms for participation in decisionmaking, adding or subtracting teaching and administrative roles, and myriad other modifications. Within this vortex of change, however, basic conceptions of knowledge, of the teacher's and the student's role in constructing knowledge, and of the role of classroom- and school-level structures in enabling student learning remain relatively static.

Nor is the problem of scale a failure of research or of systematic knowledge of what to do. At any given time, there is an abundance of ideas about how to change fundamental relationships in the core of schooling, some growing out of research and demonstration projects, some growing directly out of teaching practice. Many of these ideas are empirically tested and many are based on relatively coherent theories of student learning. We might wish that these ideas were closer to the language and thought processes of practitioners, and that they were packaged and delivered better, but there are more ideas circulating about how to change the core processes of schooling than there are schools and classrooms willing to engage them. There are always arguments among researchers and practitioners about which are the most promising ideas and conflicting evidence about their effects, but the supply of ideas is there. The problem, then, lies not in the supply of new ideas, but in the demand for them. That is, the primary problem of scale is understanding the conditions under which people working in schools seek new knowledge and actively use it to change the fundamental processes of schooling.

Why is the problem of scale important to educational reform?

Two central ideas of the present period of US educational reform raise fundamental, recurring problems of US education. One idea is that teaching and learning in US schools and classrooms is, in its most common form, emotionally flat and intellectually undemanding and unengaging; this idea is captured by that famous, controversial line from *A Nation at Risk*: 'a rising tide of mediocrity' (National Commission on Excellence in Education, 1983). This is a perennial critique of US education, dating back to the first systematic surveys of educational practice in the early twentieth century and confirmed by contemporary evidence. One recent survey characterized typical classroom practice this way:

> No matter what the observational perspective, the same picture emerges. The two activities involving the most students were being lectured to and working on written assignments . . . Students were working alone most of the time, whether individually or in groups. That is, the student listened as one member of a class being lectured, or the student worked individually on a seat assignment . . . In effect, then, the modal classroom configurations which we observed looked like this: the teacher explaining or lecturing to the total class or a single student, occasionally asking questions requiring factual answers; the teacher, when not lecturing, observing or monitoring students working individually at their desks; students listening or appearing to listen to the teacher and occasionally responding to the teacher's questions; students working individually at their desks on reading or writing assignments; and all with little emotion, from interpersonal warmth to expressions of hostility. (Goodlad, 1984, p. 230)

Every school can point to its energetic, engaged, and effective teachers; many students can recall at least one teacher who inspired in them an engagement in learning and a love of knowledge. We regularly honor and deify these pedagogical geniuses. But these exceptions prove the rule. For the most part, we regard inspired and demanding teaching as an individual trait, much like hair color or shoe size, rather than as a professional norm. As long as we consider engaging teaching to be an individual trait, rather than a norm that might apply to any teacher, we feel no obligation to ask the broader systemic question of why more evidence of engaging teaching does not exist. The answer to this question is obvious for those who subscribe to the individual trait theory of effective teaching: few teachers are predisposed to teach in interesting ways. Alternatively, other explanations for the prevalence of dull, flat, unengaging teaching might be that we fail to select and reward teachers based on their capacity to teach in engaging ways, or that organizational conditions do not promote and sustain good teaching when it occurs.

The other central idea in the present period of reform is captured by the slogan, 'all students can learn'. What reformers seem to mean by this idea is that 'all' students – or most students – are capable of mastering challenging academic content at high levels of understanding, and the fact that many do not is more a testimonial to how they are taught than to whether they are suited for serious academic work. In other words, the slogan is meant to be a charge to schools to make challenging learning available to a much broader segment of students than they have in the past. The touchstone for this critique is consistent evidence over the last two decades or so that US students do reasonably well on lower level tests of achievement and cognitive skill, but relatively poorly on tests that require complex reasoning, inference, judgment, and transfer of knowledge from one type of problem to another (National Center for Education Statistics, 1993).

It is hard to imagine a solution to this problem of the distribution of learning among students that does not entail a solution to the first problem of increasing the frequency of engaging teaching. Clearly, getting more students to learn at higher levels has to entail some change in both the way students are taught and in the proportion of teachers who are teaching in ways that cause students to master higher level skills and knowledge. It is possible, of course, that some piece of the problem of the distribution of learning can be solved by simply getting more teachers to teach more demanding academic content, even in boring and unengaging ways, to a broader population of students. But, at some level, it seems implausible that large proportions of students presently disengaged from learning academic content at high levels of understanding will suddenly become more engaged if traditional teaching practices in the modal US classroom remain the norm. Some students overcome the deadening effect of unengaging teaching through extraordinary ability, motivation, or family pressure. Other students, however, require extraordinary teaching to achieve extraordinary results. The problem of scale, then, can be seen in the context of the current reform debate as a need to change the core of schooling in ways that result in most students receiving engaging instruction in challenging academic content.

This view of educational reform, which focuses on changing fundamental conditions affecting the relationship of student, teacher, and knowledge, might be criticized as being either too narrow or too broad. My point in focusing the analysis wholly on the core of schooling is not to suggest that teaching and learning can be changed in isolation from an understanding of the contextual factors that influence children's lives. Nor is it to suggest that the object of reform should be to substitute one kind of uniformity of teaching practice for another. Rather, my point is that most educational reforms never reach, much less influence, long-standing patterns of teaching practice, and are therefore largely pointless if their intention is to improve student learning. I am interested in what is required before teaching practice can plausibly be expected to shift from its modal patterns toward more engaging and ambitious practices. These practices might be quite diverse. They might involve creative adaptations and responses to the backgrounds, interests, and preferences of students and their families. And they might be wedded in interesting ways to solutions to the multitude of problems that children face outside of school. But the fundamental problem I am interested in is why, when schools seem to be constantly changing, teaching practice changes so little, and on so small a scale.

The Evidence

The central claims of my argument, then, are that the core of schooling – defined as the standard solutions to the problem of how knowledge is defined, how teachers relate to students around knowledge, how teachers relate to other teachers in the course of their daily work, how students are grouped for purposes of instruction, how content is allocated to time, and how students' work is assessed – changes very little, except in a small proportion of schools and classrooms where the changes do not persist for very long. The changes that do tend to 'stick' in schools are those that are most distant from the core.

The progressive period

To evaluate these claims, one would want to look at examples where reformers had ideas that challenged the core of schooling and where these ideas had time to percolate through the system and influence practice. One such example is the progressive period, perhaps the longest and most intense period of educational reform and ferment in the history of the country, running from roughly the early teens into the 1940s. What is most interesting about the progressive period, as compared with other periods of educational reform, is that its aims included explicit attempts to change pedagogy, coupled with a relatively strong intellectual and practical base. Noted intellectuals – John Dewey, in particular – developed ideas about how schools might be different, and these ideas found their way into classrooms and schools. The progressive period had a wide agenda, but one priority was an explicit attempt to change the core of schooling from a teacher-centered, fact-centered, recitation-based pedagogy to a pedagogy based on an understanding of children's thought processes and their capacities to learn and use ideas in the context of real-life problems.

In a nutshell, the progressive period produced an enormous amount of innovation, much of it in the core conditions of schooling. This innovation occurred in two broad forms. One was the creation of single schools that exemplified progressive pedagogical practices. The other was an attempt to implement progressive pedagogical practices on a large scale in public school systems. In discussing these two trends, I draw upon Lawrence Cremin's *The Transformation of the American School* (1961), which provides a detailed review of progressive education.

The single schools spawned by the progressive movement represented an astonishing range of pedagogical ideas and institutional forms, spread over the better part of four decades. In their seminal review of pedagogical reform in 1915, *Schools of To-Morrow*, John and Evelyn Dewey documented schools ranging from the Francis Parker School in Chicago to Caroline Pratt's Play School in New York, both exemplars of a single founder's vision. While these schools varied enormously in the particulars of their curricula, activities, grade and grouping structures, and teaching practices, they shared a common aim of breaking the lock of teacher-centered instruction and generating high levels of student engagement through student-initiated inquiry and group activities. Furthermore, these schools drew on a common wellspring of social criticism and pre-scription, exemplified in John Dewey's lecture, *The School and Society* (1899). According to Cremin, *The School and Society* focused school reform on shifting the center of gravity in education 'back to the child. His natural impulses to conversation, to inquiry, to construction, and to expression were . . . seen as natural resources . . . of the educative pro-cess' (1961, pp. 118–19). Also included in this vision was the notion that school would be 'recalled from isolation to the center of the struggle for a better life' (p. 119).

This dialectic between intellect and practice continued into the 1920s and 1930s, through the publication of several books: William Heard Kil-patrick's *Foundations of Method* (1925), an elaboration of Dewey's think-ing about the connection between school and society; Harold Rugg and Ann Schumaker's *The Child-Centered School* (1928), another interpretive survey of pedagogical practice like Dewey's *Schools of To-Morrow*; and Kilpatrick's *The Educational Frontier* (1933), a restatement of progressive theory and philosophy written by a committee of the National Society of College Teachers of Education (Cremin, 1961, pp. 216–29). Individual re-formers and major social educational institutions, such as Teachers College and the University of Chicago, designed and developed schools that ex-emplified the key tenets of progressive thinking.

One example illustrates the power of this connection between ideas and institutions. In 1915, Abraham Flexner, the father of modern medical edu-cation, announced his intention to develop a model school that would do for general education what the Johns Hopkins Medical School had done for medical education. He wrote an essay called 'A Modern School' (1917), a blueprint for reform describing a school that embodied major changes in curriculum and teaching. It was designed to serve as a laboratory for the scientific study of educational problems. In 1917, Teachers College, in collaboration with Flexner and the General Board of Education, opened the Lincoln School, which became a model and a gathering place for pro-gressive reformers, a major source of new curriculum materials, and the intellectual birthplace of many reformers over the next two decades. The school survived until 1948, when it was disbanded in a dispute between its parents' association and the Teachers College administration (Cremin, 1961, pp. 280–91).

The second form of innovation in the progressive period, large-scale reforms of public school systems, drew on the same intellectual base as the founding of individual schools. A notable early example was the Gary, Indiana, school district. The Gary superintendent in 1907 was William Wirt, a former student of John Dewey at the University of Chicago. Wirt initiated the 'Gary Plan', which became the leading exemplar of progres-sive practice on a large scale in the early progressive period. The key elements of the Gary Plan were 'vastly extended educational opportunity' in the form of playgrounds, libraries, laboratories, machine shops, and the like; a 'platoon system' of grouping whereby groups of children moved *en masse* between classrooms and common areas, allowing for economies in facilities; a 'community' system of school organization in which skilled tradespeople from the community played a role in teaching students; and a heavily project-focused curriculum (Cremin, 1961, pp. 153–60).

In 1919, Winnetka, Illinois, hired Carleton Washburn of the San Francisco State Normal School as its superintendent. Washburn launched a reform agenda based on the idea of individually paced instruction, where the 'common essentials' in the curriculum were divided into 'parcels,' through which each student advanced, with the guidance of teachers, at his or her own pace. As students mastered each parcel, they were examined and moved on to the next. This individualized work was combined with 'self-expressive' work in which students were encouraged to develop ideas and projects on their own, as well as group projects in which students worked on issues related to the community life of the school. Over the next decade, the Winnetka plan was imitated by as many as 247 other school districts, but with a crucial modification. Most districts found the practice of tailoring the curriculum to individual students far too complex for their tastes, so they organized students into groups to which they applied the idea of differential progress. In this way, a progressive reform focused on individualized learning led to the development of what is now called tracking (Cremin, 1961, pp. 295–8).

A number of cities, including Denver and Washington, DC, undertook massive curriculum reform projects in the late 1920s and early 1930s. These efforts were extraordinarily sophisticated, even by today's relatively rarefied standards. Typically, teachers were enlisted to meet in curriculum revision committees during regular school hours, and outside experts were enlisted to work with teachers in reformulating the curriculum and in developing new teaching practices. In Denver, Superintendent Jesse Newlon convinced his school board to appropriate $35,500 for this process. Denver became a center for teacher-initiated and -developed curriculum, resulting in the development of a monograph series of course syllabi that attained a wide national circulation. The resulting curriculum changes were sustained in Denver over roughly two decades, when they were abandoned in the face of growing opposition to progressive pedagogy (Cremin, 1961, pp. 299–302; Cuban, 1984, pp. 67–83). In Washington, DC, Superintendent Frank Ballou led a pared-down version of the Denver curriculum revision model: Teacher committees chaired by administrators met after school, without the support of outside specialists. Despite these constraints, the process reached large numbers of teachers in both Black and White schools in the city's segregated system (Cuban, 1984, pp. 83–93).

Larry Cuban concluded in *How Teachers Taught: Constancy and Change in American Classrooms, 1890–1980*, his study of large-scale reforms of curriculum and pedagogy in the late-progressive period, that progressive practices, defined as movement away from teacher-centered and toward student-centered pedagogy, 'seldom appeared in more than one-fourth of the classrooms in any district that systematically tried to install these varied elements' (Cuban, 1984, p. 135). Even in settings where teachers made a conscious effort to incorporate progressive practices, the result was more often than not a hybrid of traditional and progressive, in which the major elements of the traditional core of instruction were largely undisturbed:

> The dominant pattern of instruction, allowing for substantial spread of these hybrid progressive practices, remained teacher centered. Elementary and secondary teachers persisted in teaching from the front of the room, deciding what was to be learned, in what manner, and under what conditions. The primary means of grouping for instruction was the entire class. The major daily classroom activities continued with a teacher telling, explaining, and questioning students while the students listened, answered, read, and wrote. Seatwork or supervised study was an extension of these activities. (Cuban, 1984, p. 137)

The fate of the progressive movement has been well documented. As the language of progressivism began to permeate educational talk, if not practice, the movement began to lose its intellectual edge and to drift into a series of empty clichés, the most extreme of which was life adjustment education. Opposition to progressivism, which had been building through the twenties, came to a crescendo in the forties. The movement was increasingly portrayed by a skeptical public and press in terms of its most extreme manifestations – watered-down content, a focus on children's psychological adjustment at the expense of learning, and a preoccupation with self-expression rather than learning. Abraham Flexner, looking back on his experiences as a moderate progressive, observed that 'there is something queer about the genus "educator"; the loftiest are not immune. I think the cause must lie in their isolation from the rough and tumble contacts with all manner of men. They lose their sense of reality' (Cremin, 1961, p. 160).

The particular structure that educational reform took in the progressive period, though, is deeply rooted in American institutions and persists to this day. First, contrary to much received wisdom, intellectuals found ways to express their ideas about how education could be different in the form of real schools with structures and practices that were radically different from existing schools. There was a direct and vital connection between ideas and practice, a connection that persists up to the present, though in a much diluted form. But this connection took the institutional form of single schools, each an isolated island of practice, connected by a loosely defined intellectual agenda that made few demands for conformity, and each a particular, precious, and exotic specimen of a larger genus. So the most vital and direct connections between ideas and practice were deliberately institutionalized as separate, independent entities, incapable of and uninterested in forming replicates of themselves or of pursuing a broader institutional reform agenda. A few exceptions, like the Lincoln School, were deliberately designed to influence educational practice on a larger scale, but the exact means by which that was to happen were quite vague. For the most part, progressive reformers believed that good ideas would travel, of their own volition, into US classrooms and schools.

Second, where public systems did attempt to change pedagogical practice on a large scale, often using techniques that would be considered sophisticated by today's standards, they succeeded in changing practice in only a small fraction of classrooms, and then not necessarily in a sustained way over time. Sometimes, as in the case of Washburn's strategy of individualizing instruction in Winnetka, as the reforms moved from one district to another they became sinister caricatures of the original. The district-level reforms produced impressive tangible products, mostly in the form of new curriculum materials that would circulate within and outside the originating districts. The connection to classroom practice, however, was weak. Larry Cuban likens this kind of reform to a hurricane at sea – 'storm-tossed waves on the ocean surface, turbulent water a fathom down, and calm on the ocean floor' (Cuban, 1984, p. 237).

Third, the very successes of progressive reformers became their biggest liabilities as the inevitable political opposition formed. Rather than persist in Dewey's original agenda of influencing public discourse about the nature of education and its relation to society through open public discussion, debate, and inquiry, the more militant progressives became increasingly like true believers in a particular version of the faith and increasingly isolated from public scrutiny and discourse. In this way, the developers of progressive pedagogy became increasingly isolated from the public mainstream and increasingly vulnerable to attack from traditionalists.

The pattern that emerges from the progressive period, then, is one where the intellectual and practical energies of serious reformers tended to turn inward, toward the creation of exemplary settings – classrooms or schools – that embodied their best ideas of practice, producing an impressive and attractive array of isolated examples of what practice *could* look like. At the same time, those actors with an interest in what would now be called systemic change focused on developing the tangible, visible, and material products of reform – plans, processes, curricula, materials – and focused much less, if at all, on the less tangible problem of what might cause a teacher to teach in new ways, if the materials and support were available to do so. These two forces produced the central dilemma of educational reform: We can produce many examples of how educational practice could look different, but we can produce few, if any, examples of large numbers of teachers engaging in these practices in large-scale institutions designed to deliver education to most children.

Large-scale curriculum development projects

Another, more recent body of evidence on these points comes from large-scale curriculum reforms of the 1950s and 1960s in the United States, which were funded by the National Science Foundation (NSF). In their fundamental structure, these reforms were quite similar to the progressive reforms, although much more tightly focused on content. The central idea of these curriculum reforms was that learning in school should resemble, much more than it usually does, the actual processes by which human beings come to understand their environment, culture, and social settings. That is, if students are studying mathematics, science, or social science, they should actually engage in activities similar to those of serious practitioners of these disciplines and, in the process, discover not only the knowledge of the subject, but also the thought processes and methods of inquiry by which that knowledge is constructed. This view suggested that construction of new curriculum for schools should proceed by bringing the best researchers in the various subjects together with school teachers, and using the expertise of both groups to devise new conceptions of content and new strategies for teaching it, The earliest of these projects was the Physical Sciences Study Committee's (PSSC) high school physics curriculum, begun in 1956. Another of these was the Biological Sciences Curriculum Study (BSCS), begun in 1958. A third was *Man: A Course of Study* (MACOS), an ambitious social science curriculum development project, which began in 1959, but only received its first substantial funding from the Ford Foundation in 1962 and NSF support for teacher training in 1969 (Dow, 1991; Elmore, 1993; Grobman, 1969; Marsh, 1964). These were among the largest and most ambitious of the curriculum reform projects, but by no means the only ones.

From the beginning, these curriculum reformers were clear that they aimed to change the core of US schooling, and their aspirations were not fundamentally different from the early progressives. They envisioned teachers becoming coaches and coinvestigators with students into the basic phenomena of the physical, biological, and social sciences. Students' work was to focus heavily on experimentation, inquiry, and study of original sources. The notion of the textbook as the repository of conventional knowledge was to be discarded, and in its place teachers were to use carefully developed course materials and experimental apparatus that were keyed to the big ideas in the areas under study. The object of study was not the assimilation of facts, but learning the methods and concepts of scientific inquiry by doing science in the same way that practitioners of science would do it.

The curriculum development projects grew out of the initiatives of university professors operating from the belief that they could improve the quality of incoming university students by improving the secondary school curriculum. Hence, university professors tended to dominate the curriculum development process, often to the detriment of relations with the teachers and school administrators who were expected to adopt the curricula once they were developed and tested in sample sites. The projects succeeded to varying degrees in engaging actual teachers in the development process, as opposed to simply having teachers field-test lessons that had already been developed.

Teachers were engaged in one way or another at the developmental stage in all projects, but were not always codevelopers. In PSSC, a few teachers judged to be talented enough to engage the MIT professors involved in the project were part of the development process; the main involvement of teachers came at the field-testing stage, but their feedback proved to be too voluminous to accommodate systematically in the final product (Marsh, 1964). In MACOS, one school in the Boston area was a summer test site, and teachers were engaged in the curriculum project relatively early in the process of development. Later versions of the curriculum were extensively tested and marketed in schools throughout the country (Dow, 1991).

By far the most ambitious and systematic involvement of teachers as co-developers was in BSCS. BSCS was designed to produce three distinct versions of a secondary biology curriculum (biochemical, ecological, and cellular), so that schools and teachers could have a choice of which approach to use. The development process was organized into three distinct teams, each composed of equal numbers of university professors and high school biology teachers. Lessons or units were developed by a pair composed of one professor and one secondary teacher, and each of these units was reviewed and critiqued by another team composed of equal partners. After the curriculum was developed, the teachers who participated in development were drafted to run study groups of teachers using the curriculum units during the school year, and the results of these study groups were fed back into the development process. Interestingly, once the curriculum was developed, NSF abandoned funding for the teacher study groups. NSF's rationale was that the teachers had accomplished their development task, but this cut-off effectively eliminated the teacher study groups, potentially the most powerful device for changing teaching practice (Elmore, 1993; Grobman, 1969).

Evaluations of the NSF-sponsored curriculum development projects generally conclude that their effects were broad but shallow. Hundreds of thousands of teachers and curriculum directors were trained in summer institutes. Tens of thousands of curriculum units were disseminated. Millions of students were exposed to at least some product or by-product of the various projects. In a few schools and school systems, teachers and administrators made concerted efforts to transform curriculum and teaching in accord with the new ideas, but in most instances the results looked like what Cuban (1984) found in his study of progressive teaching practices: A weak, diluted, hybrid form emerged in some settings in which new curricula were shoe-horned into old practices, and, in most secondary classrooms, the curricula had no impact on teaching and learning at all. While the curriculum development projects produced valuable materials that are still a resource to many teachers and shaped people's conceptions of the possibilities of secondary science curriculum, their tangible impact on the core of US schooling has been negligible (Elmore, 1993; Stake & Easely, 1978).

Most academic critics agree that the curriculum development projects embodied a naive, discredited, and badly conceived model of how to influence teaching practice. The model, if there was one, was that 'good' curriculum and teaching practice were self-explanatory and self-implementing. Once teachers and school administrators recognized the clearly superior ideas embodied in the new curricula, they would simply switch from traditional textbooks to the new materials and change long-standing practices in order to improve their teaching and the chances of their students succeeding in school.

What this model overlooked, however, was the complex process by which local curricular decisions get made, the entrenched and institutionalized political and commercial relationships that support existing textbook-driven curricula, the weak incentives operating on teachers to change their practices in their daily work routines, and the extraordinary costs of making large-scale, long-standing changes of a fundamental kind in how knowledge is constructed in classrooms. In the few instances where the advocates for the curriculum development projects appeared to be on the verge of discovering a way to change practice on a large scale – as in the BSCS teacher study groups, for example – they failed to discern the significance of what they were doing because they saw themselves as developers of new ideas about teaching and not as institution-changing actors.

The structural pattern that emerges from the large-scale curriculum development projects is strikingly similar to that of the progressive period. First, the ideas were powerful and engaging, and they found their way into tangible materials and into practice in a few settings. In this sense, the projects were a remarkable achievement in the social organization of knowledge, pulling the country's most sophisticated thinkers into the orbit of public education and putting them to work on the problem of what students should know and be able to do. Second, the curriculum developers proved to be inept and naive in their grasp of the individual and institutional issues of change associated with their reforms. They assumed that a 'good' product would travel into US classrooms on the basis of its merit, without regard to the complex institutional and individual factors that might constrain its ability to do so. Third, their biggest successes were, in a sense, also their biggest failures. Those few teachers who became accomplished teachers of PSSC physics, BSCS biology, or MACOS approaches to social studies only seemed to confirm what most educators think about talent in the classroom. A few have it, but most do not. A few have the extraordinary energy, commitment, and native ability required to change their practice in some fundamental way; most others do not. The existence of exemplars, without some way of capitalizing on their talents, only reinforces the notion that ambitious teaching is an individual trait, not a professional expectation.

[. . .]

The Role of Incentives

Nested within this broad framework of institutional and political issues is a more specific problem of incentives that reforms need to address in order to get at the problem of scale. Institutional structures influence the behavior of individuals in part through incentives. The institution and its political context help set the values and rewards that individuals respond to within their daily work life. But individual values are also important. As David Cohen (1995) cogently argues in his discussion of rewards for teacher performance, incentives mobilize individual values; that is, individual values determine to some degree what the institution can elicit with incentives. For example, if teachers or students do not value student academic performance, do not see the relationship between academic performance and personal objectives, or do not believe it is possible to change student performance, then it is hard to use incentives to motivate them to action that would improve performance.

Thus, individual acts like the practice of teaching in complex institutional settings emanate both from incentives that operate on the individual and the individual's willingness to recognize and respond to these incentives as legitimate. Individual actions are also a product of the knowledge and the competence that the individual possesses. As Michael Fullan has argued, schools routinely undertake reforms for which they have neither the institutional nor the individual competence, and they resolve this problem by trivializing the reforms, changing the language they use, and modifying superficial structures around the practice, but without changing the practice itself (Fullan, 1982; Fullan & Miles, 1992). Individuals are embedded in institutional structures that provide them with incentives to act in certain ways, and they respond to these incentives by testing them against their values and their competence.

One way of thinking about the aforementioned evidence is that it demonstrates a massive failure of schools to harness their institutional incentives to the improvement of practice. I think this failure is rooted not only in the design of the institutions, but also in a deep cultural norm about teaching that I referred to earlier: that successful teaching is an individual trait rather than a set of learned professional competencies acquired over the course of a career.

Both the progressive reformers and the curriculum reforms of the 1950s and 1960s focused on connecting powerful ideas to practice, developing exemplars of good practice and attracting true believers. These efforts largely failed, often in very interesting and instructive ways, to translate their ideas into broad-scale changes in practice. A very large incentive problem is buried in this strategy: Reform strategies of this kind rely on the intrinsic motivation of individuals with particular values and competencies – and a particular orientation toward the outside world – to develop and implement reforms in schools.

[. . .]

Without some fundamental change in the incentive structure under which schools and teachers operate, we will continue more or less indefinitely to repeat the experience of the progressives and the curriculum reformers. Like our predecessors, we will design reforms that appeal to the intrinsic values and competencies of a relatively small proportion of the teaching force. We will gather these teachers together in ways that cut them off from contact and connection with those who find ambitious teaching intimidating and unfeasible. We will demonstrate that powerful ideas can be harnessed to changes in practice in a small fraction of settings, but continue to fail in moving those practices beyond the group of teachers who are intrinsically motivated and competent to engage in them.

Working on the Problem of Scale

What might be done to change this self-reinforcing incentive structure? Probably the first step is to acknowledge that social problems of this complexity are not amenable to quick, comprehensive, rational solutions. Fundamental changes in patterns of incentives occur not by engaging in ambitious, discontinuous reforms, but rather by pushing hard in a few strategic places in the system of relations surrounding the problem, and then carefully observing the results. My recommendations will be of this sort.

Furthermore, it seems important to continue to do what has yielded success in the past and to continue to do it with increasing sophistication. I have argued that the most successful part of the progressive and curriculum reform strategies was the creation of powerful connections between big ideas with large social implications and the micro-world of teaching practice. The progressives succeeded in creating versions of educational reform that both exemplified progressive ideals and embodied concrete changes in the core of schooling. Likewise, the curriculum reformers succeeded in harnessing the talent of the scientific elite to the challenge of secondary school curriculum and teaching.

This connection between the big ideas and the fine grain of practice in the core of schooling is a fundamental precondition for any change in practice. Capacity to make these connections waxes and wanes, and probably depends too heavily on the idiosyncrasies of particular individuals with a particular scientific or ideological ax to grind. One could imagine doing a much better job of institutionalizing the connection between big ideas and teaching practice. Examples might include routine major national curriculum reviews composed of groups with equal numbers of school teachers and university researchers, or a national curriculum renewal agenda that targeted particular parts of teaching and curriculum for renewal on a regular cycle. The more basic point, however, is that preserving the connection between big ideas and teaching practice, embodied in earlier reform strategies, is an essential element in tackling the problem of scale.

With these ideas as context, I offer four main proposals for how to begin to tackle the problem of scale. Each grows out of an earlier line of analysis in this article, and each embodies an argument about how incentives should be realigned to tackle the problem of scale.

1.   Develop strong external normative structures for practice.

The key flaw in earlier attempts at large-scale reform was to rely almost exclusively on the intrinsic commitment of talented and highly motivated teachers to carry the burden of reform. Coupled with strong cultural norms about good teaching being an individual trait, this strategy virtually guarantees that good practice will stay with those who learn and will not travel to those who are less predisposed to learn. One promising approach, then, is to create strong professional and social normative structures for good teaching practice that are external to individual teachers and their immediate working environment, and to provide a basis for evaluating how many teachers are approximating good practice at what level of competence.

I use the concept of external normative structures, rather than a term like standards, because I think these structures should be diverse and need to be constructed on different bases of authority in order to be useful in influencing teaching practice. [. . .]

Why is the existence of external norms important? Because it institutionalizes the idea that professionals are responsible for looking outward at challenging conceptions of practice, in addition to looking inward at their values and competencies. Good teaching becomes a matter for public debate and disagreement, for serious reflection and discourse, for positive and negative feedback about one's own practices. Over time, as this predisposition to look outward becomes more routinized and ingrained, trait theories of teaching competence should diminish. Teachers would begin increasingly to think of themselves as operating in a web of professional relations that influence their daily decisions, rather than as solo practitioners inventing practice out of their personalities, prior experiences, and assessments of their own strengths and weaknesses. Without external normative structures, teachers have no incentive to think of their practice as anything other than a bundle of traits. The existence of strong external norms also has the effect of legitimating the proportion of teachers in any system who draw their ideas about teaching from a professional community, and who compare themselves against a standard external to their school or community. External norms give visibility and status to those who exemplify them.

2.   Develop organizational structures that intensify and focus, rather than dissipate and scatter, intrinsic motivation to engage in challenging practice

The good news about existing reform strategies is that they tend to galvanize commitment among the already motivated by concentrating them in small groups of true believers who reinforce each other. The bad news is that these small groups of self-selected reformers apparently seldom influence their peers. This conclusion suggests that structures should, at a minimum, create diversity among the energetic, already committed reformers and the skeptical and timid. But it also suggests that the unit of work in an organization that wants to change its teaching practice should be small enough so that members can exercise real influence over each others' practice. Certain types of structures are more likely than others to intensify and focus norms of good practice: organizations in which face-to-face relationships dominate impersonal, bureaucratic ones; organizations in which people routinely interact around common problems of practice; and organizations that focus on the results of their work for students, rather than on the working conditions of professionals. These features can be incorporated into organizations, as well as into the composition of their memberships.

[. . .]

3.   Create intentional processes for reproduction of successes

One of the major lessons from past large-scale reforms is their astounding naiveté about how to get their successes to move from one setting to another. The progressives seemed to think that a few good exemplars and a few energetic superintendents pursuing system-wide strategies of reform would ignite a conflagration that would consume all of US education. If any social movement had the possibility of doing that, it was the progressive movement, since it had, at least initially, a high degree of focus, a steady supply of serious intellectual capital, and an infrastructure of committed reformers. But it did not succeed at influencing more than a small fraction of schools and classrooms. The curriculum reformers thought that good curriculum models would create their own demand, an astoundingly naive idea in retrospect, given what we know about the limits within which teachers work, the complex webs of institutional and political relationships that surround curriculum decisions, and the weak incentives for teachers to pay attention to external ideas about teaching practice.

[. . .]

I suggest five theories that might serve as the basis for experimentation with processes designed to get exemplary practices to scale.

Incremental growth

The usual way of thinking about increases in scale in social systems is incremental growth. For example, according to the incremental growth theory, the proportion of teachers teaching in a particular way would increase by some modest constant each year, until the proportion approached 100 percent. This model implies a fixed capacity for training a given number of teachers per year in an organization.

The problems with this model are not difficult to identify. The idea that new practice 'takes' after a teacher has been trained is highly suspect. The notion that a fixed number of teachers could be trained to teach in a given way by circulating them through a training experience seems implausible, although it is probably the way most training programs are designed. Teaching practice is unlikely to change as a result of exposure to training, unless that training also brings with it some kind of external normative structure, a network of social relationships that personalize that structure, and supports interaction around problems of practice. The incremental model, if it is to work, needs a different kind of specification, which I will call the cumulative model.

Cumulative growth

The cumulative growth model suggests that 'getting to scale' is a slower, less linear process than that described by the incremental model. It involves not only creating interventions that expose teachers to new practices, but also monitoring the effects of these interventions on teaching practice. When necessary, processes may be created to compensate for the weaknesses of initial effects. Cumulative growth not only adds an increment of practitioners who are exposed to a new practice each year, but also involves a backlog of practitioners from previous years who may or may not have responded to past training. This problem requires a more complex solution than simply continuing to provide exposure to new practice at a given rate. It might require, for example, the creation of professional networks to support the practice of teachers who are in the process of changing their practice, or connecting the more advanced with the less advanced through some sort of mentoring scheme.

Discontinuous growth

Another possibility is a sharply increasing, or discontinuous, growth model. This could occur through a process like a chain letter, in which an initial group of teachers learned a new kind of practice, and each member of that group worked with another group, and so on: The rate of growth might go, for example from x, to 10x, to 100x, to 1000x, etc.

This discontinuous growth model shares the same problem with the incremental growth model, but on a larger scale. As the number of teachers exposed to new practices increases, so too does the backlog of teachers for whom the initial intervention was inadequate, eventually reaching the point at which this accumulation of teachers overwhelms the system. It also seems likely that the discontinuous growth model would create serious quality control problems. As growth accelerates, it becomes more and more difficult to distinguish between teachers who are accomplished practitioners of new ways of teaching, and those who are accomplished at making it appear as though they have mastered new ways of teaching.

In all the examples of growth models so far, teachers operate in a system of relationships that provides training and support, but not as members of organizations called schools. In addition to these three models that construct training and support around teachers, two additional models treat teachers as practitioners working in schools.

Unbalanced Growth

One of these models is the unbalanced growth model. This extends and modifies the standard model of innovation in education: collecting true believers in a few settings. Whereas the standard model socially isolates true believers from everyone else, virtually guaranteeing that new practices do not spread, versions of the unbalanced growth model correct for these deficiencies. A version of unbalanced growth might involve concentrating a critical mass of high-performing teachers in a few schools, with an explicit charge to develop each other's capacities to teach in new ways. The growth of new practice would be 'unbalanced' initially because some schools would be deliberately constructed to bring like-minded practitioners together to develop their skills. Such schools might be called 'pioneer' schools or 'leading edge' schools to communicate that they are designed to serve as places where new practices are developed, nurtured, and taught to an ever-increasing number of practitioners. Over time, these schools would be deliberately staffed with larger proportions of less accomplished practitioners and teachers not yet introduced to new models of practice. The competencies developed in the high-performing organizations would then socialize new teachers into the norms of good practice.

The main problem with this model is that it goes against the grain of existing personnel practices in most school systems. Teaching assignments are typically made through collectively bargained seniority and/or principal entrepreneurship, rather than on the basis of a systematic interest in using schools as places to socialize teachers to new practice. Younger teachers are typically assigned to schools with the largest proportions of difficult-to-teach children, and spend their careers working their way into more desirable assignments. Principals who understand and have mastered the assignment system often use it to gather teachers with whom they prefer to work. In order for the unbalanced growth model to work, a school system would have to devise some deliberate strategy for placing teachers in settings where they would be most likely to develop new skills. Teachers, likewise, would have to be willing to work in settings where they could learn to develop their practice as part of their professional responsibility.

Cell division, or reproduction

The other model of growth that treats teachers as practitioners working in schools is the cell division, or reproduction, model. This model works from the analogy of reproductive biology. Rather than trying to change teaching practice by influencing the flow of teachers through schools, as in the unbalanced growth model, the cell division model involves systematically increasing the number and proportion of schools characterized by distinctive pedagogical practices.

The cell division model works by first creating a number of settings in which exemplary practitioners are concentrated and allowed to develop new approaches to teaching practice. Then, on a more or less predictable schedule, a number of these practitioners are asked to form another school, using the 'genetic material' of their own knowledge and understanding to recruit a new cadre of teachers whom they educate to a new set of expectations about practice. Over time, several such schools would surface with strong communities of teachers invested in particular approaches to teaching.

[. . .]

These alternative models of growth each embody an explicit practical theory of how to propagate or reproduce practice. They also have a transparent logic that can be understood and adapted by others for use in other settings. More such theories, and more documented examples of how they work in use, should help in understanding how to get to scale with good educational practice.

4. Create structures that promote learning of new practices and incentive systems that support them

Reformers typically make very heroic and unrealistic assumptions about what ordinary human beings can do, and they generalize these assumptions to a wide population of teachers. Cremin (1961) made the following observation about progressive education:

> From the beginning progressivism cast the teacher in an almost impossible role: [she] was to be an artist of consummate skill, properly knowledgeable in [her] field, meticulously trained in the science of pedagogy, and thoroughly imbued with a burning zeal for social improvement. It need hardly be said that here as elsewhere . . . the gap between the real and the ideal was appalling. (p. 168)

Likewise, the curriculum reformers appeared to assume that teachers, given the existence of clearly superior content, would simply use the new curricula and learn what was needed in order to teach differently. Missing from this view is an explicit model of how teachers engage in intentional learning about new ways to teach. According to Fullan and Miles (1992), 'change involves learning and . . . all change involves coming to understand and to be good at something new' (p. 749). While knowledge is not deep on this subject, the following seem plausible: teachers are more likely to learn from direct observation of practice and trial and error in their own classrooms than they are from abstract descriptions of new teaching; changing teaching practice even for committed teachers, takes a long time, and several cycles of trial and error; teachers have to feel that there is some compelling reason for them to practice differently, with the best direct evidence being that students learn better; and teachers need feedback from sources they trust about whether students are actually learning what they are taught.

These conditions accompany the learning of any new, complicated practice. Yet, reform efforts seldom, if ever, incorporate these conditions. Teachers are often tossed headlong into discussion groups to work out the classroom logistics of implementing a new curriculum. They are encouraged to develop model lessons as a group activity and then sent back to their classrooms to implement them as solo practitioners. Teachers are seldom asked to judge if this new curriculum translates well into concrete actions in the classroom, nor are they often asked to participate as codesigners of the ideas in the first place. The feedback teachers receive on the effects of their practice usually comes in the form of generalized test scores that have no relationship to the specific objectives of the new practice. In other words, the conditions under which teachers are asked to engage in new practices bear no relationship whatsoever to the conditions required for learning how to implement complex and new practices with success. Why would anyone want to change their practice under such conditions?

A basic prerequisite for tackling the problem of scale, then, is to insist that reforms that purport to change practice embody an explicit theory about how human beings learn to do things differently. Presently, there are few, if any, well-developed theories that meet this requirement, although I have sketched out a few above. Furthermore, these theories have to make sense at the individual and at the organizational level. That is, if you ask teachers to change the way they deal with students and to relate to their colleagues differently, the incentives that operate at the organizational level have to reinforce and promote those behaviors. Encouragement and support, access to special knowledge, time to focus on the requirements of the new task, time to observe others doing it – all suggest ways in which the environment of incentives in the organization comes to reflect the requirements of learning.

[. . .]

References

Cohen, D. (1988) Teaching practice: plus que ça change . . . In P. Jackson (Ed.) *Contribution to Educational Change: Perspectives on Research and Practice*, Berkeley, CA, McCutcheon.

Cohen, D. (1995) Rewarding teachers for student performance. In S. Fuhrman & J. O'Day (Eds.) *Rewards and Reforms: Creating Educational Incentives that Work*, San Francisco, Jossey-Bass.

Cremin, L. (1961) *The Transformation of the American School*, New York, Knopf.

Cuban, L. (1984) *How Teachers Taught: Constancy and Change in American Classrooms, 1890–1980*, New York, Longman.

Cuban, L. (1990) Reforming again, again, and again, *Educational Researcher*, 19(1), 3–13.

Darling-Hammond, L. (forthcoming) Reward and reform: creating educational incentives that work. In S. Fuhrman & J. O'Day (Eds.) *Restructuring Schools for High Performance*, San Francisco, Jossey-Bass.

Dewey, J. (1899) *The School and Society*, Chicago, University of Chicago Press.

Dewey. J. & Dewey, E. (1915) *Schools of To-Morrow*, New York, E. P. Dutton.

Dow, P. (1991) *Schoolhouse Politics: Lessons from the Sputnick Era*, Cambridge, MA, Harvard University Press.

Elmore, R. (1993) *The Development and Implementation of Large-Scale Curriculum Reforms* (paper prepared for the American Association for the Advancement of Science). Cambridge, MA, Harvard Graduate School for Education, Center for Policy Research in Education.

Elmore, R. (1995) Teaching, learning, and school organization: principles of practice and the regularities of schooling, *Educational Administration Quarterly*, 31, 355–74.

Flexner, A. (1917) A modern school. In *Publications of the General Education Board* (Occasional papers, No. 3), New York, General Education Board.

Fullan, M. (1982) *The Meaning of Education Change*, New York, Teachers College Press.

Fullan, M. & Miles, M. (1992) Getting reform right: what works and what doesn't, *Phi Delta Kappan*, 73, 744–52.

Goodlad, J. (1984) *A Place Called School*, New York, McGraw-Hill.

Grobman, A. (1969) *The Changing Classroom: The Role of the Biological Sciences Curriculum Study*, New York, Doubleday.

Kilpatrick, W. H. (1925) *Foundations of Method: Informal Talks on Teaching by William Heard Kilpatrick*, New York, Macmillan.

Kilpatrick, W. H. (1933) *The Educational Frontier*, New York, Century Company.

Marsh, P. (1964) *The Physical Sciences study committee: a case history of nationwide curriculum development, 1956–1961*. Unpublished doctoral dissertation, Harvard University Graduate School of Education, Cambridge, MA.

National Center for Education Statistics (1993) *NAEP 1992 Mathematics Report Card for the Nation and the States: Data from the National and Trial State Assessments*, Washington, DC, US Department of Education.

National Commission on Excellence in Education (1983) *A Nation at Risk: The Imperative for Educational Reform*, Washington, DC, US Department of Education.

Powell, A., Farrar, E. & Cohen, D. (1985) *The Shopping Mall High School*, Boston, Houghton Mifflin.

Rugg, H. A. & Schumaker, A. (1928) *The Child-Centered School*, Chicago, World Book.

Stake, R. & Easely, J. (1978) Case studies in science education. In *The Case Reports*, Vol. 1 & 2. Washington, DC, US Government Printing Office.

Index